CHRISTENDOM

CHRISTENDOM

THE CHRISTIAN CHURCHES,
THEIR DOCTRINES, CONSTITUTIONAL FORMS
AND WAYS OF WORSHIP

BY

EINAR MOLLAND

Dr. Theol. (Oslo), Hon. D.D. (Durham)
Professor of Ecclesiastical History in the University of Oslo

LONDON
A. R. MOWBRAY & Co. LIMITED

First English Edition published in 1959
Second Impression, with minor revisions, 1961

PRINTED IN GREAT BRITAIN BY
A. R. MOWBRAY & CO. LIMITED IN THE CITY OF OXFORD
0507

ORDINI THEOLOGORUM
UNIVERSITATIS DUNELMENSIS
AUCTOR
AD SUMMUM GRADUM DOCTORIS
PROMOTUS
GRATO ANIMO

D.D.D.

FOREWORD

In July 1953 it was my privilege and pleasure, as Public Orator of the University of Durham, to present Einar Molland to be admitted to the degree of Doctor of Divinity *honoris causa*. It is now my privilege and pleasure to introduce him—if that is necessary—to a wider public. Since 1939 he has been Professor of Ecclesiastical History in the University of Oslo and for some years Dean of the Faculty of Theology. As a patristic scholar he has made a notable contribution to the interpretation of the great Alexandrians and, more recently, he has been working on the difficult problems raised by the Pseudo-Clementine literature. His range, however, is a wide one. He contributed an important article on Apostolic Succession to the first number of the *Journal of Ecclesiastical History*, and he has published in English a vivid picture of *Church Life in Norway, 1800–1950*.

As the present book was on the verge of publication in its original Norwegian form when Professor Molland came to Durham in 1953, he gracefully dedicated it to our Faculty of Theology. Very well received by those who could read Norwegian, it is not surprising that an English version of it was soon called for. It must be admitted that, despite what we in England may justly believe to be our honourable part in the ecumenical movement, we do not possess in our own language any such wide-ranging and up-to-date survey of the Churches of Christendom as Professor Molland has now given us. It is no mere compilation. To the scholarship of a trained historian there is added the practical experience of a man who has been fully engaged both in the life of his own Church (he is a close friend of Bishop Berggrav) and in the work of the ecumenical movement (he is a member of the Faith and Order Commission). He has often been in England and knows the Church of England well; he has studied in Paris in company with Roman Catholic scholars; and we should all benefit by looking at our own and other churches through his Lutheran eyes, a Lutheranism which, I venture to say, is invigorated by the breezes of the North.

As he himself tells us, the production of an English translation
has enabled the author to take account of suggestions made by
reviewers. Further, when the first draft of a version was sent to
some of his friends in this country, it appeared to them that
modifications in the balance of the book would make it more
serviceable to readers here and in the United States of America.
Professor Molland agreed, and so he has altered the scale of
several sections. Certain chapters have also been read afresh by
members of the Churches which they concern. It remains
Professor Molland's own book, of course; but he is the first to
acknowledge how much it owes, in its new form, to the energy
and ecumenical knowledge of my colleague, Canon H. E. W.
Turner.

This is more than a reference book in which we can look up
the occasional fact we need at the moment. It is an attempt at
understanding in which, while there is sometimes criticism,
sympathy predominates; and the concluding chapter calls our
attention to fundamental principles. The Church of Christ is one
in Him. It *is* one, despite the many and painful divisions which
keep us from the fullest and happiest experience of unity and mar
its proper visible expression. That we should earnestly strive to
understand one another, with respect for all that is good in the
particular heritage of each communion and with Christian
charity in offering whatever criticism appears to be necessary, is
one of the principal conditions of that growth in unity for which
we hope and pray and work and of which, by God's grace, so
many evident signs have already been vouchsafed to us in this
generation. *Det Deus incrementum.*

S. L. GREENSLADE

DURHAM, 1959

AUTHOR'S PREFACE

THIS book appeared in Norwegian in 1953. The interest it provoked in the Scandinavian countries and the kind reception with which it was met in many quarters, together with the suggestion of an English reviewer, that it should be translated into English, have induced me to venture to prepare an English translation.

It is extremely difficult to write a book of this kind. My task has been to write with impartiality and fairness about all the Churches and denominations of Christendom and to give an accurate picture of their doctrines, constitutional forms and ways of worship. I am afraid many readers will detect my short-comings when confronted with this ideal of objectivity and accuracy. The statistical figures present special difficulties. They have been drawn from many sources, some of which may certainly be out of date or incorrect. I have tried to check my information as to doctrinal tenets and forms of worship by consulting the original sources.

Two Scandinavian reviewers have criticized the pictures originally given of Roman Catholicism and of Lutheranism as being too static. I have felt they were right and have therefore added new sections on recent developments in both Churches. I wish I had been able to give a similar treatment of all the other Churches which I have described. But here the problem did not arise in the same way, as recent changes have normally been taken into account in these chapters.

I wish to express my gratitude to Messrs. A. R. Mowbray & Co. for their willingness to publish this book and for the kindness and patience they have shown me during the preparation of the English edition. My thanks are due to a considerable number of consultants who have produced valuable notes and criticisms of details in my description of their Churches and who have helped me much. I am especially indebted to three English scholars, Canon S. L. Greenslade, Father H. E. Symonds, C.R., and Canon H. E. W. Turner, who have read the entire manuscript and given me a great number of useful suggestions which have been of the greatest value to me. Canon Turner has been so kind as to correct the rather clumsy English in which the manuscript appeared when it was submitted to him. His work in doing so has amounted to a complete re-writing of the whole book in order to make its style idiomatic. Moreover, he has checked details and suggested the re-phrasing of statements as well as the addition or omission of certain material, with the result that every chapter of the book has been improved through his work. He has also helped me in correcting the proofs and has compiled the index. I want to thank him most heartily for the service he has done to me. He is not, however (any more than the other consultants), to be made responsible for the views expressed in the book, except those which occur in his initialed footnotes.

In the Preface to the Norwegian edition I thanked my wife who had followed the work from its first beginnings and who had helped me at every stage by her encouragement and criticism. She has played the same part in the long process which has led to the publication of an English edition.

The Norwegian version of this book was dedicated to the Faculty of Theology in the University of Durham as a token of my gratitude and high esteem. My indebtedness to the two members of that Faculty whose names are mentioned above and who have helped me so generously makes it still more imperative that I should dedicate the English edition to the Ordo Theologorum Universitatis Dunelmensis.

EINAR MOLLAND

OSLO, 1959

In this second impression a considerable number of minor alterations have been introduced in the text, many of them occasioned by suggestions put forward by my reviewers, and by correspondents whom I want to thank sincerely for having drawn my attention to errors and inaccuracies. The greatest changes occur in the chapters on the Old Catholic Church and on the Moravian Church.

OSLO, 1961

E. M.

TABLE OF CONTENTS

PART I

THE CHURCHES OF CHRISTENDOM

xi

TABLE OF CONTENTS

xiii

TABLE OF CONTENTS

PART II

RELIGIOUS SYSTEMS CONTAINING ELEMENTS DERIVED FROM CHRISTIANITY

CHRISTENDOM

INTRODUCTION

1. The Nature and Method of Comparative Symbolics

SYMBOLICS is the term traditionally applied to the branch of theology which deals with the various Churches of Christendom, their doctrines, constitutions, devotional life and distinctive features studied as a whole. In recent times it has come to be known as Comparative Symbolics or (in German) *Konfessionskunde*.

There is much disagreement on the question whether the subject belongs to historical or systematic theology. A historian would define its purpose as the description of the contemporary Churches and sects of Christendom and as an attempt to understand the historical evolution of their distinctive characters. Thus its aim is neither to offer a critical assessment of the various Churches, nor to justify any particular confession. On the other hand, a systematic theologian would lay the principal stress upon a comparative and critical appraisal, using as his measuring-rod his own doctrinal standpoint and ecclesiastical ideals.

In the present work Comparative Symbolics will be treated as a historical study. This will be in harmony with the evolution of the subject itself, for, while it originated as a branch of Systematic Theology, it has since developed into an independent historical discipline.

Comparative Symbolics took its origin from the controversial theology of the sixteenth century, also called the *theologia polemica*. It was the most important, though not the only form of exchange of ideas between the Churches. The leading figure in Lutheran circles was Martin Chemnitz (1522–86), who wrote an *Examen Concilii Tridentini* in four large volumes (1565–73), in which he reviewed critically all the dogmatic resolutions of the Council of Trent. The principal Roman Catholic controversialist was Roberto Bellarmino (1542–1621), whose three

B   1

folio volumes, entitled *Disputationes de controversiis Christianae fidei* (1586-93), gave a complete survey of all the differences in doctrine between the Roman Catholic and Evangelical Churches. His work provoked more than fifty treatises in reply from his opponents.

The main interest of controversial theology was to stress the differences between the Churches. In the seventeenth century, however, a more irenic method of approach arose in opposition to the general temper of the age. The most important representative of this new tendency was Georg Calixtus (1586-1656), a German Lutheran who had become acquainted with other Churches from the inside in the course of study both in England and France, and who subsequently put forward the view that the three main sections of the Church, the Roman Catholic, the Lutheran and the Reformed, had a common basis of doctrine in the heritage which they had received from the Early Church and which was of greater significance than their theological differences. Calixtus thus introduced a new approach to this field of study; it now became important not only to investigate doctrinal differences, but also to call attention to the features which the Churches had in common.

A further change of direction came with the Age of the Enlightenment. The main interest of theology as a whole shifted from dogmatics to history, the historical study of the Bible and the history of the Church. The existing doctrinal differences between the Churches came to be studied historically and the discipline of Symbolics therefore became comparative and historical. The credit for this change of standpoint must be given to G. J. Planck (1751-1833), Professor of Church History at Gottingen, who published in 1796 a work with the characteristic title *Abriss einer historischen und vergleichenden Darstellung unserer verschiedenen christlichen Hauptparteien* (A short historical and comparative exposition of our principal Christian divisions).

Other developments were destined to take place in this branch of theology. The old name 'Symbolics' denotes the doctrines of the Symbols or Creeds and Articles of Faith (the so-called Symbolic Books). During the periods alike of Orthodoxy and of the Enlightenment it adhered faithfully to the terms of reference implicit in the word, an examination of the official doctrine of the Churches recorded in their confessional documents. A much-needed extension of the subject came in the nineteenth century. The new programme was formulated by Philipp Marheineke (1780–1846), professor at Berlin, who pointed out that an exhaustive description of a Church cannot be provided on the basis of its doctrine alone. The special character of a Church cannot be known apart from its constitution, worship and devotional life. The task of Symbolics henceforth became a study of the Churches from all these aspects and an analysis of the relationship which always exists between doctrine, constitution, worship and religious life.

This formulation of the scope of Symbolics has now become normative, and German scholars who have worked in this field have suggested the wider title Konfessionskunde to describe a study of the various confessions or Christian bodies from all aspects.

The task of Comparative Symbolics is, therefore, to provide as faithful a representation as possible of the various Churches of Christendom, to investigate their statistics and geographical distribution, their doctrines, constitutions, ways of worship and devotional life, and to try to understand their special characteristics from a historical standpoint.

The method of this branch of study follows from its aim. It must be descriptive, historical and comparative. Its ideal is complete objectivity, the understanding of each Church on the basis of what it considers to be the centre of its own life. Its target is to portray Roman Catholicism in such a way that a Roman Catholic would acknowledge that the picture given is just and fair, and to depict the Baptist Church in terms which a Baptist could accept. It must avoid both idealization and caricature.

Comparative Symbolics is not only a subject of study which is important in itself; it is also relevant to contemporary Church life. Every minister and teacher of religion needs to be acquainted with Churches other than his own. The ecumenical conversation which is being carried on between the Churches to-day calls as never before for an adequate knowledge of other Churches no less than of the Church to which we ourselves belong.

2. Distinctions of Type and Arrangement of Material in the Comparative Study of Churches

One of the principal tasks of Comparative Symbolics is to determine and analyse the different types of Christian bodies. This in turn will provide the principles which will determine the order in which individual Churches are treated.

In the earlier stages of the development of the subject it was often the custom to deal with the principal doctrines separately and to give an account of the doctrinal differences between the various Churches under each head. Such a procedure, however, can afford no understanding of the organic unity which each Church represents. An alternative method was first to develop the doctrine of the Church to which the author himself belonged, and to interpret all other doctrinal formulations as divergences from it. But this approach becomes quite unsatisfactory if the subject is conceived as a descriptive or historical study rather than a branch of comparative dogmatics. A division into types cannot therefore be based upon doctrinal principles; it must rest upon a sociological and theological analysis of their structure.

1. It is natural to divide Christendom into two wings which may be called 'Right' and 'Left' respectively. The designation 'Right' covers such characteristics as conservatism and loyalty to Tradition. Churches of this type have retained in their doctrine, constitution and liturgy much of the heritage of the Early and Mediaeval Church. 'Left Wing' Churches, on the other hand, have rejected or lost in one way or another much of this tradition. Thus, for example, a body like the 'Seventh Day Adventists' who have abolished the observance of Sunday in favour of the Sabbath must be placed to the left of the Churches which retain the customary practice. Closer examination reveals many other peculiarities associated with this body which combine to give it a position well to the left of Christendom.

The terms 'Right' and 'Left' can also be applied to differences of type within a single Church corresponding to the descriptions 'High' and 'Low' Church or 'Catholic' and 'Protestant.'

On the basis of this division into types it is possible to arrange the Churches and sects of Christendom in a definite sequence, with few cases of doubt. Thus in its present form Anglicanism occupies a position to the right of Lutheranism, while the Baptist Church stands well to the left of Methodism. There may be some doubt whether the extreme right wing of Christendom is occupied by the Roman Catholic or the Orthodox Churches. Our choice might well fall upon the former, but for practical purposes it seems preferable in the present work to begin with the latter.

A further advantage of this division into types is that (with certain important exceptions) the Churches will be considered in the order in which they emerged, or in which they acquired their characteristic form.

2. According to their sociological structure religious communions fall into two main groups, frequently called Churches and sects. But since the latter term can be used in a derogatory sense, the two contrasted types have also been called 'institutional Churches' and 'Voluntary associations.' In earlier English theology a similar distinction was often drawn between 'multitudinous' and 'gathered' Churches.

Christian communions of the 'Church' type are inclusive by nature and often embrace practically the whole of a nation, or at least as many as possible of its members. Baptism administered in infancy is the criterion of membership. As Noah's Ark contained both clean and unclean animals, these Churches are designed on principle for a mixed membership. Understood in this sociological and non-dogmatic sense a 'Church' always possesses a sacramentally orientated piety, an ordained ministry and more or less liturgical forms of service.

Similarly a religious body of the 'sect' type is by nature exclusive and strives to be a pure community composed of real believers. Membership is on principle a matter of voluntary adhesion, which is often accompanied by Adult Baptism, or some similar rite in which the believer expresses his personal faith. Infant Baptism is either repudiated or divested of positive significance. A communion of this type is always non-sacramental, lacks any ecclesiastical office in the traditional meaning of the term, and its services are generally non-liturgical in character.

This classification agrees admirably with the division of Christendom into right and left wings. Those communions which, according to their sociological structure, must be placed on the right wing prove to be 'Churches,' while those on the left wing fall naturally into 'voluntary associations' or 'sects.' Some intermediate forms, however, undoubtedly exist.

In the present work the term 'sect' will be avoided as far as possible, and all Christian bodies will be called 'Churches.'

3. One further subdivision of a different kind is required for purposes of exposition. It will not affect the order in which the Churches are considered, but must be employed in the analysis of the special character of individual Churches.

A knowledge of the distinctive character of a particular Church involves the study not only of its doctrine, constitution and worship, but also of its ethos. By the word 'ethos' we do not mean ethics or code of living, but rather the characteristic attitude to life associated with a particular confession. There is always some correlation between these four aspects of a Church. Each type of doctrine normally has both a corresponding pattern of worship and a characteristic ethos. An organic relationship exists between all the aspects of the life of a religious communion.

In analysing the distinctive character of a Church it must always be borne in mind that for the communion itself one feature is normally regarded as the heart of its life. The accent falls upon doctrine or church order, or on one of the other elements. Thus for the Lutheran Church doctrine is the dominant factor in the organic synthesis of doctrine, church order, worship and ethos. The unifying bond between the various Lutheran Churches is to be found not in church order, but in doctrine. Worship must always be in conformity with right doctrine, and there is no possibility (as in some other Churches) of a revision of doctrine arising from the development of new forms of worship. In Roman Catholicism the stress is laid upon constitution. The fundamental element in its conception of Christianity is the idea of the visible kingdom of God upon earth represented by the Roman Catholic Church and embodied in its constitution and canon law. The simplest and most pertinent definition of right doctrine is to be found in the phrase 'what the Church teaches.' Thus the true starting-point for an understanding of this type of Christianity is its view of the constitution of the Church. A third type of Church in which the central feature is worship is to be found in Orthodoxy, while some Churches in the English-speaking world belong to yet a fourth category, and cannot be properly understood, or adequately described without reference, in the first place, to their Puritan ethos.

It is not, however, a question of permanent types sharply differentiated from one another. In the course of time a change of emphasis may take place within a particular Church, of which an example may be found within the history of the Anglican Communion. But this classification will prove of value in the analysis of their structures. Earlier studies in this subject restricted themselves far too narrowly to the doctrinal systems of the various Churches, and wrongly regarded differences under this head as of the greatest importance.

In our description of the various Churches we shall have to reproduce statistical figures. This is a subject which is beset with considerable difficulties. Bodies of the 'Church' type will naturally include all who have been baptized in their communions, whereas bodies of the other type will restrict their statistical returns to active adult members. In many cases, the figures given by the Churches themselves are based upon estimate rather than upon exact record, and sometimes there is a considerable difference between the figures provided by the communion itself and those drawn from other sources. Churches are normally eager to reckon converts who come into their faith from other bodies, but statistics do not reveal the number of lapsed members who have not formally left their communion. Again in some parts of the world, such as the United States of America and the Scandinavian countries, the official census includes the ecclesiastical allegiance of the citizen, whereas data of this type are not returned in the official statistics of countries like Great Britain and France.

The difficulties connected with religious statistics may be illustrated by the fact that the number of Roman Catholics in the world to-day is put at 331 million on page 43, in accordance with more cautious estimates, whereas the figure of 464 million is given in the *Annuario Pontificio*. In the *International Year Book and Statesmen's Who's Who* for 1955 Professor Norman Sykes estimates the total Christian population of the world at 639 million including 162 million Protestants. The figures given below are 692 million and 206 million respectively. These examples indicate the uncertainty which attends the study of religious statistics and the restricted value which they possess. Nevertheless, it is impossible to dispense with statistics altogether in a comparative study of the Churches, for it is important to obtain some idea of the comparative strength of the bodies which we are studying.

The following exposition falls into two main parts:

1. The Churches of Christendom.
2. Religious bodies outside Christendom possessing certain elements taken over from Christianity.

In the first section the more important Churches of contemporary Christendom will be described in the order explained above, beginning with the Orthodox Church. The second part inevitably includes some bodies which themselves claim to be Christian, but which cannot properly be considered as belonging to Christendom. The theological problem presented by the disunity of Christendom will be discussed in conclusion and a short survey of the pre-history and history of the Ecumenical Movement is given in an appendix.

PART I

THE CHURCHES OF CHRISTENDOM

CHAPTER I

THE ORTHODOX CHURCH

1. Designation, Distribution and Statistical Data

THE official designation of the Orthodox Church is the Orthodox Eastern Church (ἡ ὀρθόδοξος ἀνατολικὴ ἐκκλησία), embracing a number of Churches, all of which have emerged in the course of history from the Byzantine Imperial Church of later antiquity. To-day the Orthodox Church is composed of several autocephalous Churches; that is to say, Churches responsible for their own administration, though normally in full communion with one another. They possess the same liturgy, doctrine and canon law, and produce a common type of Christian spirituality. The majority of these Churches are national Churches, and are intimately bound up with the national life of their respective countries.

At a rough estimate the total membership of the Orthodox Church and of the other Eastern Churches and sects may be put at approximately 150 million, if a large proportion of the population of Russia may still be included in the figure. Orthodoxy represents the traditional faith and, in varying degrees, the National Churches of Russia, Rumania, Greece and Bulgaria. A considerable part of the Jugoslav people also belong to this Church. Thus it represents the dominant faith of Eastern Europe. There are, in addition, a few million in Asia and emigrant Churches in America and Australia with a membership of approximately one million. Rumania has about fourteen million Orthodox, Jugoslavia seven and a half million, Greece seven and Bulgaria six million.

The oldest and most venerable of the Orthodox Churches are the four ancient Patriarchates of Constantinople, Alexandria, Antioch and Jerusalem. At one time great and powerful Churches, they have now shrunk to inconsiderable size, partly owing to the advance of Islam into the areas which they formerly occupied with the consequent loss of membership to the Christian

11

Faith, and partly because of the achievement of independence on the part of their daughter Churches.

The most important Orthodox Churches are the following:

1. *The Patriarchate of Constantinople*

The Patriarch of Constantinople (at one time the capital city of the Empire) was second only to the Bishop of Rome in status and influence. He still bears the title of 'Ecumenical Patriarch,' and has precedence over the primates of all other Eastern Churches. On his head he wears the Imperial diadem, and on his breast the eagle emblem of the Byzantine Emperor. Since the conquest of Constantinople in 1453 the Patriarchate has been under Turkish rule, and for some centuries the Turks appointed and deposed the Patriarchs at will. At present he is the supreme head of a Church with about 100,000 members. The Orthodox Churches of Finland and Czechoslovakia have placed themselves under his jurisdiction.

2. *The Patriarchate of Alexandria*

Partly owing to the Monophysite schism, and partly to the Arab invasion, the Orthodox Church in Egypt has been reduced to insignificant proportions. The Patriarch now has jurisdiction over some 170,000 members, mainly Greeks.

3. *The Patriarchate of Antioch*

This once extended as far as the Euphrates and in the fourth century comprised two hundred dioceses. After the rise of the Monophysite and Nestorian schisms and the advance of Islam in the fifth and succeeding centuries, the Patriarchate dwindled in importance and almost ceased to exist. To-day it numbers about 250,000 members and the Patriarch lives at Damascus.

4. *The Patriarchate of Jerusalem*

Here there has been an even greater reduction in numbers through similar causes. It now possesses a membership of only 35,000, mostly Arabophones, or Arabic-speaking Palestinians.

5. *The Russian Church*

Russia adopted the Orthodox Faith from Constantinople in the tenth century. In 955 the Russian Grand Duchess Olga was baptized in the imperial city. In 988 her grandson, the Grand

Duke Vladimir, brought with him Greek missionaries, and introduced Christianity by force of arms, meeting with little resistance.

As an offshoot of the Byzantine Church, the Russian Church continued to be dependent upon Constantinople. Originally it was governed, not by a Patriarch, but by a metropolitan resident at Kiev, who was responsible to the Patriarch in Constantinople. In course of time the centre of gravity within Russia itself passed from Kiev to Moscow to which the metropolitical see was transferred in 1328. After the fall of Constantinople in 1453 the Russian Church became virtually independent of the Patriarch.

When the 'second Rome' (Constantinople) fell into the hands of the Turks, the view became current in Russia that Moscow was the 'third Rome' and the Russian Church was described as 'the Holy and Apostolic Church of the third Rome, resplendent in the light of the true faith, shining to the ends of the earth.' In 1589 the metropolitical see of Moscow was raised to the status of a Patriarchate, and the severance from Constantinople was henceforth complete. The Patriarch was to hold the same office and rank as that enjoyed by the heads of the four ancient Patriarchates, and the new claim was embodied in the title of 'Patriarch of all the Russias and the new Rome' which he now assumed.

In Russia, Church and State were united in a manner which was to have momentous consequences for the Church. After a dispute between the Patriarch and Peter the Great, the office was left vacant from 1700, and a new constitution for the Church was introduced in 1721. The Church was now governed by a consistory court called 'the Most Holy Synod' under the presidency of a layman, the Czar's Minister for ecclesiastical affairs. As the clerical members of the Synod were also appointed by the Czar, and as all resolutions required his approval, the result was sheer Caesaropapism.

The most devastating effects of this union of Church and State were felt after the 1917 revolution. The Church was now to suffer from its association with the old régime. At the revolution the Church was separated from the State. In the autumn of 1917 a Council was held, the patriarchal office was reinstated and Tichon elected Patriarch. But a time of trial lay before the

Church. All Church property was nationalized; some buildings were converted into clubs, cinemas and the like, though the majority were still reserved for divine service. The theological colleges were closed, and in the schools courses on Leninism were substituted for religious instruction. Open persecution began in 1918, and several thousand people were martyred. In the course of this persecution the devotion of the Russians to their Church became evident. From 1921 onwards the secular authorities changed their policy, and gave their support to the Communist element within the Church. This party broke away and organized itself as a separate body under the title of the 'Living Church.' As it pronounced Communism to be the teaching of Jesus, it was favoured by the State which placed several cathedrals at its disposal. Although it received recognition from the Ecumenical Patriarchate, it subsequently diminished in importance.

After the comparative failure of this policy, the State once more came into the open against Christianity, with virulent anti-Christian propaganda and the prohibition of religious processions and meetings, as well as of all forms of Christian education. The atheistic movement made great headway, but the Church did not allow itself to be suppressed. An act of 1929 permitted liberty of worship, but forbade religious propaganda and any organized Christian activity apart from worship. These provisions were repeated in the constitution of 1936, but a change took place at the outbreak of war in 1941. Anti-Christian propaganda ceased, and the Church came back into favour. In 1943, by agreement with the State authorities, Sergius was appointed to the Patriarchate, but no change took place in the constitutional separation of Church and State. Permission was given for the creation of an institute of theology, and a number of seminaries were opened for the training of priests.

During the past few decades the Church in Russia has been subjected to many disruptive forces, which have had their repercussions in the emigrant congregations outside Russia. The laity have, however, been less affected by these disruptions than might have been expected. For devout Russians the Orthodox Church is a living entity, and their devotion to their

Church and its worship is one of the finest features in the life of Christendom to-day.

6. The Bulgarian Church

Christianity reached Bulgaria earlier than Russia in the course of the ninth century. Its prince vacillated between Rome and Constantinople, but finally chose the latter, as Rome was not prepared to make the country an independent archbishopric. The famous missionaries, Cyril (826–69) and Methodius (c. 815–885) worked among the Bulgarians, and introduced the Slavonic language into the liturgy. The Archbishop later assumed the title of Patriarch, and the autonomy of the Bulgarian Church was recognized by Constantinople in the tenth century. Since that time the Bulgarian people and their Church have experienced many vicissitudes. The Patriarchate ceased to exist, and has not yet been re-established. The Bulgarian Church, however, remains autocephalous, and drew up its own constitution in 1883.

7. The Serbian Church

The Serbs were converted to Christianity by Greek and Roman missionaries early in the Middle Ages, but there could be no question of any profound attachment to their new faith until the translation of the Orthodox Liturgy into the vernacular in the ninth century. The Serbian Patriarchate, founded in 1351, was later abolished under Turkish rule and only re-established in 1878. Approximately half of the population of modern Jugoslavia belongs to the Orthodox Church.

8. The Rumanian Church

Christianity in a Latin form reached Rumania as early as the third century, but the Byzantine liturgy was introduced at the beginning of the Mediaeval period. The Language of the Church was first Slavonic, then Greek, and finally Rumanian. An independent Rumanian Patriarchate was created in 1925.

9. The Greek Church

The traditions of the Greek Church date back to the Apostolic Age. In the fourth century it belonged to the province of Illyria, which was subject to the Patriarchate of Rome. Under Leo the Isaurian (Emperor, 717–40), the whole province passed under the control of the Patriarchate of Constantinople. The Greek War of Liberation in the nineteenth century resulted not only in national independence but also in the autonomy of the Church. Organized in 1833 as an established Church, it secured a new constitution in 1923 which gave a greater measure of independence from the State.

10. *Other Orthodox Churches*

After the first World War the Orthodox Churches in Finland, Esthonia, Latvia, Lithuania, Poland and Czechoslovakia became autonomous. Finland and Czechoslovakia have, however, more recently given their allegiance to Constantinople.

2. THE CHARACTERISTIC FEATURES OF THE ORTHODOX CHURCH

As its name implies, the Orthodox Church regards itself as the guardian of the true doctrinal tradition of the early Church. This conception is of fundamental importance for the understanding of Orthodoxy. The refusal to allow members of other Churches to partake of the Eucharist is due to the fact that adherence to the Orthodox Faith is regarded as a necessary condition of intercommunion.

Yet this tradition is no sharply defined system. Within Orthodoxy clear-cut doctrinal tenets do not play the same part as in Roman Catholicism or in Lutheranism. There is much wider scope for individual theological interpretation than in the Roman Catholic Church. While the main content of the tradition is embodied in the doctrinal resolutions of the seven Ecumenical Councils, Tradition itself is interpreted as a living stream admitting of wide theological variations.[1]

This whole conception depends upon the Orthodox doctrine of faith which is regarded as a function of the heart acquired through mystical incorporation into religious truth. From this point of view their theologians sometimes describe Orthodoxy as the Church of St. John in contrast to Roman Catholicism as the Church of St. Peter and Protestantism as the Church of St. Paul.

The Orthodox Church also guards its constitution as an

[1] The seven Ecumenical or General Councils are those of Nicaea (325), Constantinople (381), Ephesus (431), Chalcedon (451), Constantinople (553), Constantinople (680) and Nicaea (787).

indispensable part of the Tradition, and sets a correspondingly high value upon Canon Law. The Church is a visible divine community on earth, with fixed offices, forms and body of law. But canon law in Orthodoxy (unlike the Roman Catholic Church) is not officially codified in every detail, since the idea of the Church also includes a spiritual element, which does not admit of such a process. Orthodox theologians often assert that the Church is indefinable, and that this provides the best proof that it is a living body. The Church is the 'fulness' (πλήρωμα) 'of Him that filleth all in all' (*Ephesians* i. 23). It is composed of all who are in Christ. This conception of the Church permits Orthodox theologians to adopt widely different attitudes to other Churches without overstepping the bounds of their tradition.

But the special character of the Orthodox Church is displayed above all in its Liturgy. Orthodox Churches are bound together by a common tradition of worship, and form a community based upon fellowship in worship to a degree attained by none of the Western Churches. Orthodoxy cannot be understood apart from the Liturgy which is regarded as a union of earthly and heavenly worshippers, in which the story of Redemption is dramatically represented. Many of the doctrines which are most significant in practice belong to the central core of Orthodoxy, not because they have ever been defined by an Ecumenical Council, but because they are implicitly contained in the Liturgy of the Church. Examples may be found in the transformation of the bread and wine in the Eucharist, its character as a Sacrifice, the efficacy of prayers for the dead, the veneration of the Blessed Virgin and of the saints. Here the maxim '*Lex orandi, lex credendi*' clearly applies.

3. DOCTRINE

The sources and norms of Orthodox doctrine are Holy Scripture and Tradition. The extent of the Canon of Scripture has never been officially defined. The Orthodox Church took over the Septuagint version of the Old Testament, and therefore accepted the Apocrypha as well as the Hebrew Canon of Scripture. Under the dictatorial church administration of Peter the Great, who wished to follow Protestant opinion on the subject,

the Russian Church temporarily rejected the Apocrypha. The
complete Orthodox Canon of Holy Scripture has, however, since
been restored. In the Orthodox Bible the Apocryphal writings
do not form a separate section, but are inserted at various points
among the other books.

Tradition is conceived as a living stream running through the
whole history of the Church, and not simply as the mechanical
transmission of an immutable doctrinal heritage. It is embodied
in certain doctrinal documents, but is not conterminous with them
in the sense that they alone constitute the doctrine of the Church
or that all their contents are unconditionally binding.

In the strict sense the dogmatic standards are the following:

1. The Niceno-Constantinopolitan Creed,[1] which is frequently
used in the Liturgy, and has been called the very embodiment of
Orthodoxy.

2. The doctrinal definitions of the seven Ecumenical Councils.

Two works written in the seventeenth century as a defence
against Protestant tendencies within the Orthodox Church are
considered as subordinate standards of faith. In 1638 Peter
Mogila (1597–1646), Metropolitan of Kiev, wrote a *Confessio
Orthodoxa* in Latin. It was translated into modern Greek and
accepted by all Orthodox Patriarchs in 1643. Dositheus (1641–
1707), Patriarch of Jerusalem, also wrote an exposition of the
faith, usually known as the *Confessio Dosithei*, which was approved
by a synod at Jerusalem in 1672, and sent to Russia with a letter
from the Greek Patriarchs. At a later date it was sent to the
Anglican archbishops as an expression of the substance of Orthodoxy. More recent Orthodox theology, however, strongly
emphasizes that these documents do not possess the same authority
as the doctrinal definitions of the Ecumenical Councils.

The most important norm of traditional Orthodox doctrine
is, however, undoubtedly the Liturgy.

A typical feature of Orthodox theology is the admixture of
Biblical concepts with the Neoplatonic idea of God. On the one
hand God is True Being ($\tau\grave{o}$ $\breve{o}\nu\tau\omega\varsigma$ $\breve{o}\nu$) and the Supreme Good

---

[1] The Niceno-Constantinopolitan Creed is the technical description of the Nicene
Creed, as used in the Anglican Book of Common Prayer, with the omission of the words
'and the Son' (the so-called *Filioque*) in the clause 'Who proceedeth from the Father and
the Son.' (H.E.W.T.)

(τὸ ἄκρον ἀγαθόν), and on the other hand the Creator, the God of History, and the Father of our Lord Jesus Christ.

The doctrine of the Trinity is the centre of Orthodox theology. As a leading contemporary theologian has put it, it is most important of all mysteries. The Holy Trinity (ἡ παναγία τριάς) is repeatedly invoked and worshipped in the Liturgy, and is the object of speculation alike in the Early Fathers and in recent theology. In discussions of the subject, the Western Church is severely censured for the introduction of the phrase *Filioque* into the Creed which is regarded as an alteration of the Trinitarian doctrine of the Undivided Church.

The Holy Trinity created the visible and invisible worlds (κόσμος αἰσθητός, κόσμος νοερός). The motive force behind Creation was the Love of God Who desired other beings to partake of His mercy and glory.

The spiritual world is composed of angels, of whom there are many orders: angels, archangels, seraphim, cherubim, powers, dominions, and the like. The angelic choir is often mentioned in the Liturgy. They stand before the throne of God in adoration, but they are also conceived as messengers of God, who intercede in Heaven, and serve as the guardian angels of mankind on earth. The fallen angels have become demons.

Man belongs to both worlds, and is described by St. John of Damascus (c. 675–749) as 'the connecting link between visible and invisible nature.' He was created perfect, destined for the contemplation (θεωρία) of God, and endowed with incorruptibility, immortality, and absence of passion (ἀφθαρσία, ἀθανασία, ἀπάθεια). After the Fall, Man lost these supernatural qualities but retained free will and the power to do good, in both cases to a diminished degree. The image of God in which he was created was marred, but not obliterated. In the East there is little emphasis upon original sin. Death and transitoriness (the consequences of sin) have been handed on to all the descendents of Adam, but Orthodoxy does not regard the guilt of sin as transmissible. The Eastern conception of original sin has been relatively little influenced by the controversy between St. Augustine and Pelagius, which did so much to shape the doctrine in the West.

'For our salvation' (διὰ τὴν ἡμετέραν σωτηρίαν, Nicene Creed), the Son of God became man in the fulness of time. He assumed our humanity in all its frailty, transitoriness, and mortality. Through His Resurrection, He restored our original incorruptibility, and deified human nature. In the words of St. Athanasius, 'He became man in order that we might become divine' (αὐτὸς ἐνηνθρώπησεν ἵνα θεοποιηθῶμεν).

The heart of Orthodox Christology is the doctrine of the union of two natures in one person. The history of Orthodoxy provides many examples of devotion to the central theme of the union of God and Man in the single person of Christ, without apparently devoting much attention to the more concrete aspects of the historical personality of Jesus. It is the mystery of Christ upon which faith loves to dwell. Orthodoxy can also, of course, consider Jesus as a personality within history, but always sees in Him the union of God and Man. In popular religion His divine nature completely overshadows His humanity.

Whereas Orthodox Christology is set out to the very last detail, its soteriology, or doctrine of Redemption, is much less fully developed. Two characteristic features should, however, be noted. Salvation is not merely rescue from the guilt of sin, but also from sin as a power, from death and corruption. The idea of salvation as victory over death, or as the deification of humanity, a familiar theme in Greek theology, which occurs as early as St. Irenaeus, is predominant in Orthodox theology to-day. Again, the Redemption wrought by Christ is connected not only with His Crucifixion, but with His whole life. It was through the Incarnation that God and Man became one, and that salvation became possible. The death of Christ is regarded as a propitiatory sacrifice, but the notion of a ransom paid to the Devil is even more characteristic of Greek thought. Orthodoxy, however, thinks of Redemption as not only achieved supremely through the death of Christ, but also through His Resurrection. In no other Church is belief in the Resurrection so much the dominant motive, not only in theology, but also in the Liturgy as well as in popular piety.

The Virgin Mary occupies a prominent place both in theology and in the devotional life. Since the Council of Ephesus (431), she has been called 'Mother of God' (θεοτόκος), and since the second Council of Constantinople (553) the title 'Ever-Virgin' (ἀειπάρθενος) has been included among her attributes. She is a

Virgin 'before birth, during birth, and after birth.' The Liturgy
is full of the praise of Mary, the Mother of God, and her name
occurs almost as frequently as that of our Lord or of the Holy
Trinity. But Orthodoxy has no doctrine of her Immaculate
Conception, a natural omission for a Church in which the idea
of original sin plays so small a part. Some theologians even assert
that she was not free from sin, on the ground that sinlessness is
an attribute which belongs to Christ alone. She is commemorated
on August 15th, the festival of her Assumption into Heaven.
This has been celebrated since the fifth century, and was taken
over from the East into the Western Church.

Unlike the West, the Orthodox Church has no detailed
doctrine of Grace. Western theologians were compelled to
concern themselves with the relationship between the Grace of
God and human free will by the Pelagian controversy in the fifth
century. The Eastern Church was relatively little affected by this
dispute. Pelagianism was condemned at the Council of Ephesus
(431), but in general the Orientals took little interest in the
question. They continued to discuss free will in terms that were
sometimes downright Pelagian, but at the same time expressed
themselves forcibly enough on the subject of the necessity of
Grace. The Eastern standpoint can best be expressed as Synergism.
Man is free to accept or to reject God's offer of mercy. Human
effort (σπουδὴ ἀνθρωπίνη; St. Basil) and God's co-operant Grace
work together for salvation.

The process described in the Western Church as Justification
and Sanctification is called Deification (θεοποίησις) in the Orthodox Church. A doctrine of Justification first emerges in the
seventeenth century documents directed against Lutheran and
Reformed opinion. Man is not justified by faith alone, but by
faith and works (διὰ τῆς πίστεως καὶ τῶν ἔργων). In Russian
theology, however, Grace is often depicted in terms which seem
to imply that works have not the slightest significance for man's
salvation. We are nothing, and are capable of nothing without
the Grace of God.

The deification of man may be compared to the heating of a
piece of iron in fire. As the heat permeates the iron, it becomes
transformed without ceasing to be iron. Similarly man becomes

permeated by the Holy Spirit. The body, saved from transitoriness by the Resurrection, is also included in this process of deification.

Man is saved in and through the Church, which is defined in Orthodox theology as 'a community of people ordained by God and united through the Orthodox faith, divine law, priesthood and sacraments.' But the Church is not identical with the organization of the Orthodox Church on earth. It includes all who are in Christ both in Heaven and on earth. The two elements, often called respectively 'the Church at home' and 'the Church abroad' (ἡ ἐν τῇ παροικίᾳ ἐκκλησία), form a single whole. This feature, prominent alike in Orthodox theology and liturgy, is particularly evident in the veneration of saints.

The Church on earth is divided into two orders, the clergy and the laity, both of whom are necessary for its existence. The headship of the Church belongs to Jesus Christ alone and does not reside in any human being. His representatives in individual churches are the bishops who are 'guardians and pastors,' whose authority derives from Him. It is through the episcopate that Christ fulfils His promise to be with His Church until the end of the world. The bishop is as necessary for the existence of the Church as the sun is for the world. Without bishops the priests are incapable of guarding the flock of Christ. The episcopate is handed down from generation to generation through the Apostolic Succession, which is a mark of the Apostolicity of the Church. But the episcopate alone cannot express the fulness (πλήρωμα) of the Church, for which the lower orders of the clergy and the laity are also necessary.

According to Orthodox doctrine the Church is infallible. This attribute, however, only applies to the Church as a whole, and does not reside in a single bishop or patriarch. It is the unanimous Tradition of the Church that is infallible, and its recipients are the clergy and laity taken together. This conception of the *consensus fidelium* as the final authority, expressed in the term *sobornost*, is particularly characteristic of Russian theology.

This doctrine of Tradition results in a conception of the authority of the Church which differs widely from that current in Roman Catholicism. Some Orthodox theologians dislike the term 'ecclesiastical authority' as too juridical, and maintain that the Church is a stream of life and grace emanating from Christ Himself, rather than a legal institution.

Eschatology is a more prominent feature of Orthodoxy than is commonly the case in Western Christendom; indeed, it possesses a markedly eschatological outlook. Thus the Book of Revelation is favourite Orthodox reading. Some theologians like Berdyaev (1874–1948) accuse the West of a failure to take seriously belief in the return of Christ and the struggle between Christ and Antichrist, a theological defect which reflects itself in the Western attitude to the present world. For some writers like Dostoievsky (1821–81) and Soloviev (1853–1900) these beliefs almost amount to an obsession.

After death a provisional judgement is passed upon the soul, which enters into an intermediate state, to await the return of our Lord and the Final Judgement. The saints are believed to go straight to Heaven, where they enter the presence of the Holy Trinity. They do not, however, attain final beatitude until the entrance into eternal life of all who have attained salvation. According to the statement of the Greeks at the Council of Ferrara-Florence (1439), the saints still await the Kingdom of God and its ineffable blessings. Unlike the Roman Catholic Church, which only invokes them and prays for their intercession, the Orthodox Church includes prayers for the saints in its Liturgy. At the Eucharist the Orthodox Church prays for its spiritual forefathers, the patriarchs, prophets, apostles, evangelists, martyrs and confessors, and especially for the Virgin Mary, as well as for the faithful departed.

With the exception of saints and martyrs, all souls pass after death to Hades (the place of departed spirits). This has two divisions, Paradise or 'Abraham's bosom,' and the Abyss or prison of souls, in which they have a foretaste either of eternal life or of eternal perdition. The intermediate state is thus conceived as a kind of purgatory, although the fully-developed Roman Catholic doctrine on the point is rejected by Orthodoxy. Prayers for the dead, that they may perceive the light of God, and be preserved from the judgement, are considered to be efficacious, and are freely used in the Orthodox Church. The scope of prayer is even extended to those who have died impenitent.

At the Last Judgement, the bodies of all men are raised and united with their souls. The bodies of the saved are transfigured like the body of our Lord on the Mount of Vision, and their souls behold the Holy Trinity. The damned are delivered over to everlasting fire.

A number of Orthodox theologians reject the doctrine of Eternal Punishment. Although the Universalism of Origen (the ἀποκατάστασις πάντων or the Restoration of all things) was condemned at the second Council of Constantinople (553), it has a tendency to reappear in the Orthodox Church. Many fathers and modern theologians cannot reconcile themselves to the notion that the All-Merciful Father and Creator could permit any soul to be damned eternally. It has even been said that the idea of the Restoration is one of the most powerful traditions in Orthodoxy. This belief also seems to be in accordance with Orthodox practice, for the simple believer also intercedes for those who should be condemned to perdition according to the strict teaching of the Church.

4. SACRAMENTS

Sacraments or mysteries may be defined as sacred rites through which the Grace of God is imparted in a hidden way. Orthodox teaching on the subject emphasizes their mysterious character, in contrast to the more rigid definitions of Roman Catholic doctrine.

The number of the Sacraments has not been determined by any Ecumenical Council. St. John of Damascus, the classical exponent of Orthodoxy, recognized two Sacraments only, Baptism (with Confirmation), and the Eucharist. In the mediaeval period a wide variety of sacred rites were considered as Sacraments, but after the Council of Lyons (1274), at which the Orthodox Church renewed its acquaintance with the West, the Western usage of seven Sacraments (Baptism, Confirmation, Penance, the Eucharist, Ordination, Matrimony and Extreme Unction) was normally adopted.

Baptism is the rite of Christian initiation, and effects the regeneration of the recipient. Owing to the numerous rites which accompany it, many of which go back to the early centuries, the baptismal service appears somewhat complicated. The baptism itself is preceded by exorcism, in which the priest breathes thrice on the candidate, and signs him with the sign of the Cross. The Devil is exorcized, partly through direct evocations, 'Satan, the Lord exorcizes thee, get thee hence!,' and partly through prayers that God would drive out the evil spirit. Then follows the renunciation. The candidate turns to the West, thrice exclaims 'I renounce thee' and spits in token of his aversion to the Devil. Turning to the east, he confesses Christ and ejaculates three times 'I surrender myself to Christ.' The Nicene Creed is recited three times. In the case of an infant, one of the godparents makes the profession of faith on behalf of the child. The baptismal water is consecrated by the prayers of the priest who touches it with the flat of his hand, and breathes upon it. After the anointing of the candidate with hallowed oil, the service continues with the baptism proper. This consists of three immersions accompanied by the formula 'The servant of God... is baptized in the name of the Father and of the Son and of the Holy Ghost.' In case of emergency immersion is replaced by sprinkling and the baptismal act may be performed by a deacon or even by a layman.

In earlier times it was customary to re-baptize converts to Orthodoxy from other Churches, on the ground of the supposed invalidity of their previous Baptism. Since the seventeenth century the Russian Church has not practised re-baptism in such cases, and is content to supply whatever elements were lacking in the previous rite. This custom has won considerable support from other Orthodox Churches, although the Greek Church retained the earlier usage until recent times.

Confirmation (βεβαίωσις), also called 'anointing' (χρῖσμα, ἅγιον μύρον) or 'sealing' (σφραγίς), takes place immediately after Baptism. According to the Orthodox Catechism, this anointing represents the conferment of the gifts of the Holy Spirit, to strengthen the candidate for the spiritual life. Those who have been confirmed are full members of the Orthodox Church and are admitted to the other sacraments.

The ointment (μύρον) is prepared according to definite rules from olive oil and a number of other aromatic ingredients. In the Russian Church they number thirty and are said to represent the manifold gifts of the Holy Spirit.

In Orthodoxy the responsibility of the bishop for the sacrament is preserved by the fact that he alone can consecrate the 'chrism' but the sacrament can be administered by any priest. This contrasts with the Roman Catholic practice which still requires the bishop to administer the sacrament personally. The forehead, eyes, nostrils, ears, mouth, chest, hands and feet of the candidate are anointed. Protestants who join the Orthodox Church must be confirmed.

Penance (μετάνοια, more properly translated penitence), or Confession (ἐξομολόγησις) is the rule of the Orthodox Church before the reception of the Eucharist. Confessions are heard in the middle of the nave in the open church. The penitent stands before the priest and makes his confession with bowed head, upon which the priest places his stole. The Orthodox formula of Absolution, like both the Roman Catholic and Anglican forms, combines precatory and declarative elements.

The priest sometimes imposes certain prayers, fasts or pilgrimages as acts of penance. They are, however, never regarded as acts of satisfaction but only as a form of discipline. The system of indulgences has never obtained in the Orthodox Church.

The Eucharist also bears the names of the 'Sacred Rite' (ἱερουργία), 'Sacrifice' (προσφορά, θυσία), 'The Lord's Supper' (κυριακὸν δεῖπνον), or 'Communion' (κοινωνία).

The Eucharistic doctrine of the Orthodox Church represents a form of sacramental realism. Several Greek Fathers maintain that the bread and wine at the Eucharist are not merely a type (τύπος), but become the very Body and Blood of our Lord. Transformation is a favourite description of the change which occurs in the elements as the effect of their consecration. They retain their character after the conclusion of the Liturgy and are therefore reserved and used, for example, for the communion of the sick. They are not, however, exposed on the altar for adoration, as in the Roman Catholic Church. The Eucharist is closely associated with the Incarnation, and the transformation of the sacramental elements has been described as 'a close analogy to the Incarnation, when Christ assumed human flesh and blood.'

A distinctive feature of the Orthodox Liturgy is the Invocation or Epiclesis of the Holy Spirit. After the recital of the Words of Institution in the Great Prayer, God is asked to send His Holy

Spirit and to transform the bread and wine into the Body and Blood of Christ. While in the West from the fourth century onwards the Words of Institution were invested with consecratory powers, the Eastern Church maintained that no change in the elements took place until after the Epiclesis. This principle is often emphasized by contemporary Eastern theologians.

Leavened bread is used in the Orthodox Liturgy in contrast to the Western use of unleavened wafers. This difference of custom became one of the main heads of controversy with the Roman Catholic Church. Because of their use of unleavened bread, Western Churchmen were accused by the Orthodox of being Judaizers and still under the Law.

Unlike Roman Catholicism, the Orthodox Church extends Communion in both kinds to the laity. The Roman Catholic practice is repudiated as an act of disloyalty to our Lord's express command, and as a departure from the common tradition of the Universal Church. An exception to this rule is only made in the case of the smallest children, for in the Orthodox Church the communion of children, and even of infants, is common.

The Eucharist is regarded as a sacrificial rite. It is called a 'bloodless sacrifice' (ἀναίμακτος θυσία) or a 'commemoration (ἀνάμνησις) of the one Sacrifice made by our Saviour.' The sacrificial character of the Eucharist is not, however, emphasized in Orthodoxy in so one-sided a way as in Roman Catholic theology. The Liturgy as a whole is regarded as a recapitulation of the whole economy of salvation (ἀνακεφαλαίωσις τῆς ὅλης οἰκονομίας). Thus the Incarnation and the Resurrection are no less essential to the Eucharist than the Crucifixion. Orthodox theologians also maintain that it is the Risen and Glorified Body of Christ which is present in the sacrament.

Ordination (χειροτονία, χειροθεσία) is the sacrament of initiation into the Christian Ministry. According to Orthodox doctrine there are three major orders of ministry, bishop, priest and deacon. The deacon may only assist in the administration of the Sacraments, the priest has the power to administer them, while to the bishop belongs the authority to transmit this right through Ordination or the laying on of hands.

It was formerly the custom for the clergy of other Churches to be re-ordained on joining the Orthodox Church. Now, however, Roman Catholic and Anglican Orders are sometimes considered valid, though in practice no Anglican priest seems to have been admitted into the Orthodox ministry without being re-ordained.

Deacons and priests are not pledged to celibacy. A marriage contracted before Ordination is permitted to continue, but subsequent marriage is forbidden. Bishops, often drawn from monastic circles, must be celibate. A widower, however, may become a bishop.

Matrimony is considered to be a sacrament on the authority of Ephesians v. 32, where it is described as a mystery (μυστήριον). It is an image of the relationship between Christ and His Church. While the Roman Catholic Church regards marriage as constituted by the contract between the partners, followed by the physical consummation, the Orthodox Church assigns this role to the service in Church.

Unction (εὐχέλαιον) is practised for the aged and infirm, and can be repeated as often as circumstances dictate.

5. Worship

The Orthodox claim that their Church can only be understood through its Liturgy, which brings out the fulness of church life and unites in worship the Church in heaven and on earth.

The Church building consists of three parts. First there is the entrance or vestibule (νάρθηξ), where in early centuries the catechumens and penitents stood during the part of the service which they were allowed to attend. Here the font is placed and here, too, some of the canonical hours are recited. This leads into the nave (ναός), where the congregation stands during the Liturgy. Chairs are only provided for the aged and infirm. The pulpit from which the Gospel is read and the sermon preached stands on a raised dais. The iconostasis, or high carved screen covered with paintings, divides the nave from the chancel (τὸ ἄδυτον, τὸ ἱερόν). This screen does not, however, extend to the roof, so that the congregation is able to hear, although they cannot see, the parts of the service which are performed within it. In the iconostasis there are three doorways, provided with doors or curtains. The central entrance is called the royal door (ἡ βασιλικὴ πύλη), and the others the north and south doors respectively. The screen is adorned with one or more rows of paintings. On the right of the royal door are depicted Christ as high priest and St. John the Baptist, on the left the Virgin Mary and one of the saints to whom the building is dedicated. Over this door is a representation of the Last Supper and above this again the figures of the apostles and prophets.

In the middle of the chancel stands the altar (ἡ ἁγία τράπεζα) covered with an altar cloth, over which a second cloth is laid during the Liturgy. Upon the altar is placed a cross or painted crucifix, the Gospel book and a container for the consecrated bread. To its left stands a table used for the preparations for the Liturgy.

Ikons or sacred pictures play an important part in Orthodox worship. They are consecrated before use, decorated with flowers and honoured by lighted lamps or candles which are placed before them. They are the visible representations of the invisible presence of our Lord, of the Blessed Virgin or of saints and angels.[1] Homage or veneration paid to the ikon is carried to the archetype in heaven, and is really addressed to the one whom it portrays. This explanation of the symbolism has a Neoplatonic ring.

All sculpture is forbidden and only paintings are allowed. The strict Orthodox rules forbid a crucifix, but permit a cross with a painted representation of the body of our Lord. The figures are static and stylized in character. Byzantine ecclesiastical art avoids movement and its devotional ideal is 'apathy' (ἀπάθεια). Liberal use is made of gold and silver.

The Orthodox Liturgy is celebrated in the vernacular, though often in an obsolete form. In Greece the language used is the Greek of the seventh and eighth centuries in modern pronunciation. In Slavonic countries the idiom is that employed by Cyril and Methodius, which is still intelligible to the people. Other liturgical languages in use in the Orthodox Church include Rumanian, Arabic, Esthonian, Latvian, Lithuanian, Finnish and (in the United States) English.

Singing plays an important part in the Liturgy, but is un-

[1] Even the poorest homes possess ikons of our Lord, the Blessed Virgin and some saints.

accompanied as only the human voice may be used in the house of God.

There are two types of divine service, the canonical hours and the Liturgy. The hours are largely confined to the monasteries, but are also recited in the parish churches on the eve of a holy day and at festivals.

The real heart of church life is the Liturgy, which corresponds to the Mass in the Roman Catholic Church. Only one Liturgy can be celebrated at a particular altar on any single day, and, as a church normally has only one altar, this means that in the Orthodox Church the Liturgy has retained congregational character. There is no parallel in Orthodoxy to the Roman Catholic celebration of private masses.

The Liturgy itself is a complex and many-sided rite. Three different forms of the service are in use. During most of the year the service in use is the Liturgy of St. John Chrysostom, which represents the Liturgy of Constantinople in the eighth century. On ten occasions (January 1st, which is kept as St. Basil's Day, the Sundays in Lent, Maundy Thursday, Easter Eve, and the vigils of Christmas Day and the Epiphany), the Liturgy of St. Basil, which presumably dates in substance from the fourth century, is celebrated. The third form is the Liturgy of the Presanctified gifts (λειτουργία τῶν προηγιασμένων) corresponding to the Western *missa praesanctificatorum* or Liturgy of the Pope Gregory the Great, at which the elements employed were consecrated on the previous Sunday. It is therefore not a full celebration of the Eucharist but ends with the Communion of the people. Its use is restricted to Holy Week and to weekdays during Lent.

Before the Liturgy begins, there takes place a preparatory ceremony (called προσκομιδή) with confession of sin and prayers. As each liturgical garment is put on, appropriate prayers are said and ceremonies performed. Then follows the preparation of the sacramental elements. The priest cuts a square portion called 'the Lamb,' which is to be used in the Eucharist, from a large, flat, circular cake. On this piece is stamped the letters IC.XC.NI.KA. in four compartments, which represent the words 'Jesus Christ conquers' ('Ιησοῦς Χριστὸς νικᾷ). The priest then pierces 'the Lamb' with a knife called 'the spear,' with the words 'Sacrificed is the Lamb of God who taketh away the sins of the world, for the life of the world and for its salvation.' While he recites St. John xix. 34, the deacon mixes wine and water in the chalice. The unconsecrated elements are thus mystically identified with the body of the dead Christ. The preparatory prayers conclude with the censing of the church.

The Liturgy proper consists of two parts corresponding to the ancient *missa catechumenorum* and the *missa fidelium*. The transition between the two is marked by the exclamation of the deacon in the middle of the service 'Depart, ye catechumens.' In fact, nobody leaves the church and the ceremony has completely lost its original significance.

The Liturgy of the catechumens opens with adoration, 'Blessed is the Kingdom of the Father, and of the Son, and of the Holy Ghost, now and for ever, world without end,' followed by the Longer Litany (ἡ μεγάλη ἐκτένεια), recited by the deacon.[1] The prayer is continually broken by the congregational response *Kyrie eleison* (Lord have mercy upon us) sung by the choir. It is an extremely beautiful prayer which opens with the petition 'For the peace that is from above and for the salvation of our souls, let us pray to the Lord,' and continuing with intercessions for clergy and people, for the peace of the world and the unity of the Church, for earthly rulers, for the fruits of the earth, for travellers, for the sick and suffering and for those in prison. It is followed by the Anthems, opening with a verse from the Psalms and ending with the Beatitudes from the Sermon on the Mount, sung by the choir.

There follows the peculiar rite known as 'the Little Entrance' (ἡ μικρὰ εἴσοδος), a symbolic representation of the coming of our Lord to earth with the Gospel. The priest takes the book of the Gospels from the altar and hands it to the deacon. Preceded by lights and censers, they pass together through the north door into the nave among the congregation. In the middle of the nave, the deacon raises the book above his head and cries 'Wisdom! Stand upright!' They return to the altar through the royal door, while the choir sings the anthem 'O come, let us worship and bow down to Christ.'

---

[1] The translations of the Liturgy here used are taken from *A Guide to the Liturgy of St. John Chrysostom*, by Leighton Pullan. (H.E.W.T.)

The choir then sings the *Trisagion*, 'Holy God, Holy Mighty, Holy Immortal, have mercy upon us,' which derives its name from the threefold repetition of the word 'holy.' This is followed by the reading of the Epistle or Lesson for the day, to which the choir makes the response 'Alleluia.' Meanwhile the deacon burns incense in a censer, first in the chancel, then in the nave. The deacon takes the book of the Gospels through the royal door and reads the Gospel for the day to the congregation. The choir responds 'Glory to Thee, O Lord, glory to Thee.' The book is then handed to the priest who carries it back to the altar and the doors are closed. Meanwhile the deacon takes up his position before the iconostasis, recites a Litany for all sorts and conditions of men, and finally orders the catechumens to depart.

At this point the Liturgy of the faithful begins. The deacon recites a further Litany, to which the people respond *Kyrie eleison*, while the priest at the altar begins silently the prayers of the faithful in preparation for the oblation. These prayers embody the characteristic Orthodox doctrine of the Eucharistic Sacrifice that our Lord is Himself both priest and victim. This is followed by the Great Entrance (ἡ μεγάλη εἴσοδος) which symbolizes the entry of our Lord into Jerusalem to meet suffering and death. The deacon carries the paten containing the bread and the priest the chalice filled with wine and water. Neither element is as yet consecrated. They pass through the north door while the worshippers bow their heads and make the sign of the Cross. As they return through the royal door, the choir sings the Cherubic Hymn in adoration of Christ.[1] A further Litany is recited by the deacon while the priest reads silently a prayer of oblation. This part of the service is concluded by the recital by priest and people of the Nicene Creed.

The *Anaphora*, or great prayer, opens with the ancient dialogue between priest and people known as the *Sursum Corda*, 'Let us lift up our hearts—We lift them up unto the Lord. Let us give thanks unto the Lord—It is meet and right to worship the Father, the Son and the Holy Ghost, the consubstantial and undivided Trinity.' As the priest continues in a low voice to recall the worship of the heavenly host the choir sings the *Sanctus* (*Isaiah* vi. 3)

[1] A version of this hymn, taken from the Liturgy of St. James, will be found in the *English Hymnal* 318 and *Hymns Ancient and Modern* (1950 edition) 390 and 391. (H.E.W.T.)

and the *Benedictus qui venit* (*St. Mark* xi. 9). The prayer then proceeds to the Words of Institution which are read aloud, though the connecting links supplied by the evangelist are recited in a lower tone. The *Anamnesis*, or commemoration, which opens with the words 'Therefore being mindful of this saving precept,' recalls the Resurrection, the Ascension and the Heavenly Session and looks forward to the Second Coming in glory as well as commemorating the Death and Passion of our Lord. The *Epiclesis* invokes the Holy Spirit 'upon us and upon these gifts set before Thee. And make this bread the precious Body of Thy Christ and that which is in this cup the precious Blood of Thy Christ, changing them by Thy Holy Spirit.' After the consecration of the elements, in the second part of the *Anaphora*, the priest passes to intercession for the Virgin Mary and all the saints, for the departed, for the Church and its hierarchy, for rulers and all mankind, and for all for whom the sacrifice is made. The act of communion is preceded by a prayer for the right reception of the sacrament and the cry 'Holy things to those who are holy.' The priest and the deacon then partake of the sacrament behind the closed doors of the iconostasis. The royal door is opened and they appear before the congregation. The communicants come forward singly, and receive the sacrament standing. The deacon holds the chalice into which the priest drops fragments of consecrated bread. These he takes out with a spoon and administers to the communicants. The vessels are then returned to the altar in what is known as the Last Entrance, which symbolizes the Ascension of our Lord. After a prayer of thanksgiving the service closes with the Benediction.

After the completion of the Liturgy the priest stands outside the iconostasis and distributes the 'blessed bread' (also called the ἀντίδωρον). This is bread prepared for the sacrament but not used in the service itself. The congregation again come forward singly, receive the bread in their hands and consume it at once. It is offered not only to those who have made their communion at the Liturgy, but also to other worshippers, even those who are members of other Churches.

The beauty of the Liturgy, the spirit of worship which pervades it, and the impressive symbolism of the rites themselves convey to the worshipper an idea of the heavenly adoration. On

C

their return to Russia the envoys of the Grand Duke Vladimir in the tenth century reported of Orthodox worship as they had seen it in the Cathedral of St. Sophia at Constantinople that they were not sure whether they were on earth or in heaven.

The Church's Year is composed of a whole series of festivals in honour of our Lord, the Virgin Mary and the saints. The greatest festival is Easter, preceded both by a period of preparation for Lent and by the forty days of strict fasting in Lent itself. The service of Easter night is the climax of the whole year, marked by rejoicing over the Resurrection. On Easter morning itself the general greeting is 'Christ is risen' ($X\rho\iota\sigma\tau\grave{o}\varsigma$ $\mathring{a}\nu\acute{\epsilon}\sigma\tau\eta$) to which is made the reply 'He is risen indeed' ($\mathring{a}\lambda\eta\theta\hat{\omega}\varsigma$ $\mathring{a}\nu\acute{\epsilon}\sigma\tau\eta$).

6. CONSTITUTION

The Orthodox Church possesses the threefold ministry of bishop, priest and deacon. Archbishops and patriarchs receive no further consecration, but merely possess higher rank and greater authority than other bishops. Below the diaconate are certain minor orders such as sub-deacons, door-keepers and singers, but these are of little significance. The monks do not form a separate order, though many of their number are ordained. Much emphasis is laid upon the fact that the laity are no less necessary to the existence of the Church than the clergy. Orthodoxy regards the hierarchical constitution of the Church with its various degrees and orders as a necessary part of its existence.

In theory, and often in practice, the laity take a share in the election of priests and bishops, and even of metropolitans and patriarchs. They also play their part in Church administration. This is partly the result of the close relationship of Church and State, which has been such a prominent feature of the Orthodox world since the Byzantine period.

The supreme authority in the Orthodox Church is the ecumenical council, an assembly of the bishops of all the Orthodox Churches which has the authority to determine all questions of doctrine and canon law. It is a real tragedy for Orthodoxy that it has not for many centuries proved possible to convoke such a council.

7. MONASTICISM

Monasticism originated in the Eastern Church. St. Antony, 'the father of the monks,' lived in Egypt, and it was here that the first monastic communities were established, and from the East again the ideal spread to the West.

Monasticism was brought into close connection with the life of the Church by the great reform carried out by St. Basil towards the close of the fourth century. In place of the earlier predominance of a solitary or hermit existence, he substituted the ideal of life within a community organized in conformity with set rules.

The most important monastic establishment was the monastery built on the Athos peninsula in 963. This has grown into an entire monastic republic. During the past century, however, there has been a decline, and the number of candidates for the monastic life has fallen off considerably. Athos to-day has been called 'a magnificent ruin.'

The Orthodox Church possesses no monastic orders in the Western sense. Each monastery is an independent unit under the jurisdiction of the local bishop. In Orthodox monasticism the life of hermits or recluses still persists side by side with the monastic communities. The cultural standard of the monasteries is usually not high.

Appendix: THE RUSSIAN SECTS

Next to the United States of America, Russia is the country which possesses the largest number of religious sects and in which they play the most significant part in the life of the people. The reasons for this lie deep within the Russian character with its sentimentality, its predilection for the eccentric and its impatience of authority. The sectarians were formerly subjected to considerable persecution, but this only fostered their growth and often gave them a revolutionary character. Many of them remained outwardly members of the State Church, attended its services and received its sacraments, but at the same time held their own meetings in secret. It is therefore difficult to form an exact estimate of the extent of these movements. To-day the number of sectarians in Russia is reckoned at three million, though other authorities put the figure at more than fifteen million.

These communities fall into three main groups, each of which could be still further sub-divided, the Old Believers, the 'Spiritual Christians' and the Evangelical bodies.

1. *The Old Believers*

The origin of the sectarian movement in Russia is to be found in a seventeenth-century schism, which is perhaps the most curious in the whole history of the Church. In the course of centuries a number of errors had crept into the service books of the Russian Church. The Patriarch Nikon (1605–81) ordered a revision in 1666, and introduced some minor changes in the rites of the Church. The name Jesus, which had come to be pronounced 'Issus,' was to be changed to 'Yissus,' and the sign of the Cross made with three fingers instead of two. Superfluous words which had been added to the Creed were to be removed. These reforms aroused violent opposition and in consequence thousands of conservative priests and laymen left the Church. They accused the patriarch of changing the Faith and of betraying Christ like a second Judas. They called themselves the 'Old

Believers' (*starovertsy*), whereupon the State Church retorted with the title 'Schismatics' (*raskolniki*). The secular authorities tried to force them back into the Church, but this only gave them the reputation of being martyrs and the movement took firm hold. Under Peter the Great the dispute entered a new phase. He attempted to introduce Western customs like shaving into Russia, against which a violent popular reaction set in. The Old Believers now declared that a man's beard was part of the Image of God in which he had been created, and continued to wear long beards. Persecution ceased at the end of the eighteenth century, and in 1881 the Old Believers secured recognition from the State as a separate community. In the nineteen-twenties they were said to number nine million.

In course of time the Raskolniki divided into two sections, the priestly (*popovtsy*), and the priestless (*bezpopovtsy*). Only one bishop joined the Old Believers, and he died in prison without having ordained any new priests. The community was therefore compelled to accept the services of priests who had joined them from the State Church.

The more radical wing of the Old Believers, however, refused to recognize ordinations carried out by the Orthodox Church after the introduction of the liturgical reforms, and had therefore to manage without bishops and priests.

Both sections experienced still further divisions, the 'priestless,' in particular, undergoing remarkable developments. They soon abandoned all sacraments, with the exception of baptism, which could be administered by a layman, though confessions were often made to laymen. But according to Orthodox doctrine there could be no valid marriage without a priest. One group, therefore, the so-called Infanticide sect, abolished the institution of marriage and took the lives of all children born within the community. Others carried hostility to the State to the extent of regarding provocation of the authorities as Christian duty and suffered execution in consequence.

2. The 'Spiritual Christians'

This is the collective name given to a group of ecstatic sects. These fanatics reject both Church and State, and their Dualist world-view and vigorous asceticism bear a striking resemblance to the Gnosticism and Manicheeism of Antiquity. They fall into two main groups, the *Chlysts* and the *Skopts*.

The *Chlysts*, or Whippers, were founded in the seventeenth century by a peasant named Danila, who claimed that he was God come down from Heaven. He chose a younger person as Christ and a woman follower as the Mother of God. After their death others were elected in their place, and in the end it was decided that any one who received the Spirit could become a Christ or a Mother of God. The sect spread over the whole of Russia and Siberia. Its members take part in the services of the Orthodox Church and have their children baptized, but in reality they despise the Church and its sacraments. Marriage is repudiated, and complete abstinence from sexual intercourse enjoined. Converts who are already married must separate. The Chlysts abstain from meat, potatoes and onions. At their meetings they hold ecstatic dances and, as their name implies, practise self-flagellation. Convulsions and glossolaly are regarded as signs of the presence of the Holy Spirit. They also reject the doctrine of the Resurrection of the Body.

Still more radical in their self-mortification are the *Skopts*, whose name signifies the 'Castrated.' This remains their most distinctive feature. The title which they give to themselves is, however, 'the White Lambs' or 'the Brethren of Christ.' Their founder was a peasant called Selivanov who castrated himself with a red-hot iron about the year 1770 in supposed obedience to St. Matthew xix. 12. The operation was repeated on his followers. He was arrested, sent to Siberia for nineteen years and then transferred to a lunatic asylum. On his release by the pietistic and tolerant Czar, Alexander I, he spread his teaching in the highest circles of St. Petersburg (now Leningrad), but was again arrested and spent the last twelve years of his life in prison. At the height of his influence he held large crowds of people under his spell. All male members of the sect are castrated, while many of the women have cut off their breasts. The sect may have as many as 100,000 followers.

3. *The Evangelical bodies*

The third group which came into being through Western influence has a different character. German peasants who emigrated to South Russia brought with them their pietistic Lutheranism. From about 1860 a revivalist movement called Stundism (from the German *Stunde*, or hour reserved for Bible reading) sprang from their religious meetings. Baptist propaganda later gained ground and won many followers. Baptist Churches of considerable strength are said to exist in Russia to-day.

CHAPTER II

OTHER ORIENTAL CHURCHES

IN the later centuries of the Patristic period a number of Eastern Churches broke away from the Church of the Byzantine Empire for mixed political and doctrinal reasons. In many cases old national Churches beyond the frontiers of the Empire maintained their independence by adopting solutions of the Christological problem which differed from the Chalcedonian standard accepted by Orthodoxy. Thus the East Syrian Church became Nestorian, while Western Syria, Armenia, Egypt and Abyssinia became Monophysite. In the course of centuries, the doctrinal significance of their differences became less marked, and they are now more akin to Orthodoxy and to each other than their history and traditions would at first sight suggest.

These Churches are autonomous, and their Liturgies also developed independently. Their service-books were originally composed in their respective vernaculars, but to-day this often represents an obsolete, if not an entirely extinct form of the national language.

These Churches can be classified in three ways, by their rites (Armenian, Nestorian, Antiochene or Coptic), by their doctrinal standpoint (Monophysite or Nestorian), or by the language used in the Liturgy (Armenian, Coptic, Ge'ez, Syriac or Arabic).

The Armenian Church, like the nation which it serves, has had a troubled history in Antiquity, during the Middle Ages and in modern times under Turkish rule. It became Monophysite at the close of the fifth century and retained this doctrinal standpoint when it became independent of the Byzantine Church in the middle of the sixth century. The supreme head of the Church bears the title of Catholicos and resides at Etchmiadzin. Its official language is Armenian and its rites are closely allied to those of the Orthodox Church. It now possesses three million members, in Armenia and perhaps another million elsewhere, notably in Russia, India, Palestine and America.

The East Syrian Church, which is Nestorian in doctrine, calls

40

itself the *Messihaye* (Christians or believers in the Messiah), but often receives the name of the 'Assyrian Church.' Its origin is to be found in the ancient Persian Church which broke away from the Patriarchate of Antioch as early as 424 and gave asylum to the followers of Nestorius exiled after the Council of Ephesus (431), later adopting their doctrine. It became most active, sent its missionaries to Palestine, Syria, Egypt and India, and even founded a church in China in the seventh century. The Christian elements in Islam were originally transmitted through this Church.

At the height of its influence in the thirteenth century the Nestorian Church comprised twenty-five archdioceses, over two hundred dioceses and millions of followers. In the later Middle Ages, however, Islam overran its territories and the Mongol overlords spread their religion by force.

The supreme head of the Church, the Catholicos, as well as the bishops, must be celibate. The priests are married and can even remarry if their wives die. They do not use ikons and the interior arrangement of their churches is very simple. Their Liturgy, called the Chaldaean, Persian or Syro-Chaldaean rite, has some interesting features. The Church has perhaps some 70,000 members, mostly in Iraq and Iran.

The West Syrian Jacobite Church is named after its founder, the monk Jacob Baradai (*c.* 500-77). It is Monophysite in doctrine, and flourished in the twelfth century, though it later lost much ground to Islam. To-day it has dwindled to a membership of 100,000. Its supreme head bears the title of Patriarch of Antioch.

The 'Thomas-Christians' in India trace their traditions back to the Apostle, St. Thomas, but their Church, the Malankara Church, is really the outcome of the Nestorian mission. Its subsequent history has been extremely chequered and at some points remains obscure. In 1599, under Portuguese influence, it accepted the authority of the Roman Catholic Church. After the dissolution of the union some sixty years later, most of its members joined the Monophysite Jacobite Church. More recently they have come under the influence of Protestant missions, while retaining their own Church Order and Liturgy.[1] There are about half a million members of this Church.[2]

[1] This wing of the Thomas-Christians is termed the Mar Thoma Church.
[2] For further details about the Uniate section of the Malankara Church see below, pp. 125-6.

The Coptic Church is the ancient Church of Egypt which rejected the Chalcedonian Definition in 451 and thus became an isolated national Church with a Monophysite Christology. Only a handful of Egyptian Christians retained their allegiance to Constantinople. Its numbers have, however, been greatly reduced by persecution and defection to Islam and now amount to no more than one million out of a total population of nineteen million. Its liturgical language, Coptic, is quite unintelligible to the people, though the Scripture lections and some prayers are read in Arabic. During the Church's Year there are as many as thirty-two festivals in honour of the Virgin Mary. Monophysitism is less pronounced than it was and the Copts are correspondingly closer to the faith of the Orthodox Church.

The Ethiopian Church became a national Church in the middle of the fourth century. Three centuries later it became dependent upon the Monophysite Patriarch of Alexandria by whom its supreme head or Abuna was appointed and consecrated for many centuries. Its final independence from Alexandria was only secured in 1946. Of the eight million inhabitants of Ethiopia, approximately five million belong to this Church. Its customs and devotional practices have a Judaistic tinge. Circumcision is practised before Baptism and the Jewish dietary laws are observed. The Ethiopians claim to possess the Ark of the Covenant with the Tables of the Law in their sanctuary at Axum. A festival in commemoration of the Nativity of our Lord is celebrated each month and there are thirty-three festivals in honour of the Virgin Mary. Polygamy is tolerated. The liturgical language is Ge'ez.

CHAPTER III

THE ROMAN CATHOLIC CHURCH

DESIGNATION, DISTRIBUTION AND STATISTICAL DATA

THE official designation of this Church, *ecclesia catholica*, incorporates its claim to be the only true and universal Church. But it also uses the title *ecclesia Romana*. In the dogmatic decrees of the Vatican Council it describes itself as 'the Holy Catholic Apostolic, Roman Church' (*sancta catholica apostolica Romana ecclesia*).

The Roman Catholic Church is the largest and most universal of all the Churches. It is to be found in all countries and every clime. The same Mass is celebrated everywhere in the same hallowed language. At the same time it is Roman; its centre is at Rome, and it has a Roman character. Since the time of Hadrian VI (Pope 1522–23), the Popes have been exclusively Italian, and until after the Second World War the College of Cardinals had an Italian majority.

The total Christian population of the world amounts to about 692 million members, and something like half of these (approximately 331 million) are in communion with the see of Rome, and acknowledge the Pope as their spiritual Head. Of these, approximately 324 million belong to the Roman Catholic Church itself, while the remainder belong to the various Uniate Churches. For purposes of comparison the membership of the Protestant Churches (including the Anglican Communion) may be estimated at 206 million.

A glance at the distribution of the Roman Catholic Church in different parts of the world will reveal how prominently it figures on the Christian scene. Europe, with a population of about 565 million, has approximately 225 million Roman Catholics, roughly the same number as the Orthodox and Protestants taken together. In the whole of North America, out of a population of 170 million, 40 million are Roman Catholics. South America is predominantly Roman Catholic. The missionary Churches in Asia comprise about ten million and those in Africa perhaps a million less.

In Europe the Latin countries are largely Roman Catholic, though there are small Protestant minorities in Italy, Spain and Portugal. Belgium is in a similar position and the greater part of Ireland professes this faith. For France, official religious statistics are not available, but out of a total population of forty-three million, the number of practising Roman Catholics may be put at ten million. Austria and Poland are predominantly Roman Catholic, while in Czechoslovakia three-quarters of the population, and in Hungary two-thirds belong to this Church. In Germany (taken as a whole) the membership of the Roman Catholic Church includes approximately one-third of the population; in Western Germany roughly half the population, and in Eastern Germany about 20 per cent are Roman Catholics. Switzerland is deeply divided in religion and has perhaps 40 per cent Roman Catholics. In Great Britain the Roman Catholic Church has a membership of over three million, and with a vigorous proselytizing movement its numbers may be expected to increase. In Holland, too, it is gaining ground and now includes more than a third of the population; as the Reformed Church itself is divided, it is now the largest single Church in the country. In the Scandinavian countries, however, it plays an insignificant part. Here it has only 30,000 members, of whom 22,000 are in Denmark.

The Roman Catholic Church throughout the world is divided into archdioceses and dioceses. Ten archbishops have the honorary title of Patriarch. At present (1958) there are 1,283 dioceses with a resident bishop, and a further 882 titular bishoprics (*episcopi in partibus infidelium*).

2. THE CHARACTERISTIC FEATURES OF THE ROMAN CATHOLIC CHURCH

Roman Catholicism may also be described as catholic in the sense of 'all-embracing.' In the course of its long history it has absorbed all the religious elements which it has encountered and which proved capable of assimilation—mystery cult, Roman and Germanic Law, Platonic and Aristotelian philosophy, modern evolutionary concepts and much else besides. It belongs to its very essence to be inclusive and syncretistic.

It is not, therefore, without good reason that it has been described as a *complexio oppositorum*. Within it we find belief in authority and philosophical speculation side by side. The Legalism and evangelical freedom, vulgar superstition and the most profound religious philosophy, rationalism and mysticism, asceticism and vigorous cultural activity are combined to an extent without parallel in other Churches. Thomism, which became the official dogmatic system of Roman Catholicism, is a grand endeavour to unite authority with freedom, faith with knowledge, philosophy with Church doctrine, nature with supernature, Scripture with Tradition, dogma with mysticism, Church with State, Christianity with culture. The modernist, George Tyrrell (1861–1909), has described the catholic nature of this Church in the following terms: 'It seems to us that Catholicism is, more than other systems, a religion of the whole man, body, soul and spirit; a religion for every stage of his culture, and not for one only; for every mood of his variability, and not only for the highest; for every sort of man, and not merely for a religious, ethical, intellectual or social aristocracy . . . all of this in virtue of principles and ideals to which it has never been wholly faithful or unfaithful.'

Within this church we find religious elements of all kinds, ritual, sacrament, sacrifice, asceticism, prayer, belief in miracles, hierarchy, monasticism, mysticism and theology. Friedrich Heiler (b. 1892), the historian of religion, claims that the whole history of religion may be studied within this single Church. Here we meet features which belong to primitive religion, legalism, evangelical piety, mystery, ritual, philosophical speculation and mysticism.

Roman Catholicism is an organic combination of all these elements. Its dogma has determined the development of its cultus, but this in its turn has also affected the formulation of its doctrine. There is an organic interplay of order, doctrine and ritual.

In the Introduction attention has already been directed to the importance for the understanding of each Church of the synthesis of these elements. Within the Roman Catholic Church there is little doubt that priority must be assigned to Church Order and Canon Law. The true starting point is the idea of the Church. The Roman Catholic Church claims to be the visible Kingdom

of God upon earth, the mystical Body of Christ. It was established
by Christ Himself, and therefore is of divine origin. Even its
outward form, its hierarchical organization, is part of Divine
Revelation. If the Church of Christ is regarded as a visible,
limited community, it clearly becomes of the utmost importance
for faith and life to be able to define the limits of its membership
and to specify its rightful leaders to whom belongs the power of
making decisions. It must therefore have a divine constitution,
and this in turn will be of decisive importance for its whole
existence.

The importance of Canon Law may be illustrated from many
departments of the Church's life. Together with biblical exegesis
and dogmatic theology it is an essential part of the curriculum
of Roman Catholic theological faculties. Bishops are expected
to show a profound knowledge either of Canon Law or theology.
This law in its present form has been codified in the *Codex Juris
Canonici* of Benedict XV, issued in 1917, whereas since the
Council of Trent there has been no corresponding promulgation
of the doctrine of the Church in the form of Articles of Faith.

Canon Law has left its mark on every part of the life of the
Church. The simplest and most pertinent definition of right
doctrine is the teaching proclaimed by the Church by virtue of
its authority. The dogma of Papal Infallibility defined by the
Vatican Council in 1870 asserts the responsibility of the rightful
holder of the teaching office of the Church for the determination
of what is true doctrine.

The distinctively Roman Catholic doctrine of faith is in harmony with this conception of the authority of the Church. To
believe is to think with assent (*cum assensu cogitare*), to subordinate the intellect to the doctrine of the Church. Hence a
distinction is drawn between two forms of faith, *fides explicita* or
unfolded faith, which is restricted to those who know and accept
the doctrine of the Church in all its details, and *fides implicita*, an
acceptance of the Faith of the Church as it were en bloc with a
knowledge only of its more fundamental articles.

But Roman Catholicism is also a religion which assigns a
central place to worship. The Mass with the miracle of the
Transubstantiation of the elements, its sacrificial character and the
presence of Christ on the altar in the sacrament lies at the heart

of its spiritual life. Adoration, fervour and devotion have found incomparable expression in the Mass, the canonical hours and other forms of worship. Yet at the same time, the whole of divine service is moulded by a fixed ritual and performed according to detailed rubrics. Around it has grown up a complex of rights and duties, the right of a priest to say Mass daily, the duty of a priest to read the canonical hours in the Breviary daily, and of the laity to attend Mass on Sundays and Holy Days.

Again in moral theology the distinction between mortal and venial sins necessarily leads to precise distinctions. Precepts for fasting and abstinence and the whole characteristic system of indulgences must be of a juridical nature.

The cardinal importance of Canon Law also emerges from a consideration of the unifying bond which holds together all Churches recognized by Rome. The whole of Roman Catholic Christendom displays a doctrinal tradition which does not admit of great divergence, and a liturgical life characterized by a high degree of uniformity. But there are, as we shall see, in addition a number of Oriental Uniate Churches, which are in union with the see of Rome because they have submitted to the authority of the Pope and because their Trinitarian and Christological doctrine and sacramental teaching are considered to be orthodox. This bond is not an absolute uniformity of liturgy or doctrine, but is to be found in a recognition of papal authority.

Thus evidence drawn from many fields strongly suggests the primacy of the constitution of the Church as expressed in Canon Law as determinative of the character and ethos of Roman Catholicism.

3. Sources of Doctrine, Canon Law and Ritual

There are three sources of the doctrine of the Church, Scripture, Tradition and the Teaching Office of the Church.

The relation between Scripture and Tradition was laid down by the Council of Trent (1545–63). Both are placed on an equal footing and must be accorded the same pious devotion and veneration (*pari pietatis affectu et reverentia*).

The conception of Tradition current at the time of the Council of Trent was static. Tradition was the sum total of the rites and doctrinal tenets handed down from the Apostles, to whom it had been either orally communicated in substance by our Lord, or revealed by the Holy Spirit. This tradition had been preserved and transmitted within the Roman Catholic Church from generation to generation. It is described as 'the unwritten traditions, which have come down to us, passed down as it were from hand to hand' (*sine scripto traditiones, quae quasi per manus traditae ad nos usque pervenerunt*).

This theory left its mark upon the Roman Catholic interpretation of Church History. The whole content of modern Roman Catholicism, whether in doctrine or ritual, was made as ancient as the sources allowed, and preferably traced back to the Apostles themselves. Where the sources were silent, an explanation was found in the theory of a discipline of secrecy (*disciplina arcani*) in the early Church.

More recently, however, this static conception of Tradition has given place to a more dynamic view. The turning-point in this process is marked by Cardinal Newman's work, *An Essay on the Development of Christian Doctrine* (1845), in which the concept of evolution was introduced into the interpretation of the history of doctrine. It is admitted that the Church has not possessed the same doctrinal tenets or identical rites throughout the centuries. Tradition, considered as a living process, admits of growth and development. True tradition is distinguished from error by certain characteristics such as preservation of type, vitality and adherence to fundamental principles.

Thus in modern Roman Catholicism Tradition is frequently conceived not as the mechanical transmission of a heritage preserved and transmitted from the lips of the Apostles to the present day, but as the organic evolution of potentialities inherent in the Gospel. The precious heritage of the Church has developed gradually in the course of time. This idea was the guiding principle of the Modernist Movement at the beginning of the present century.

The official doctrine of Tradition has avoided the evolutionism with which Modernism was permeated and which in certain aspects was repudiated in the Encyclical of Pius X, *Pascendi dominici gregis* (1907). But the idea of a gradual unfolding of the truth in the course of Church History is fundamental to Roman

Catholicism. New doctrinal decisions such as the bodily assumption of the Blessed Virgin into Heaven are not considered as additions to the faith, but as definitions of beliefs which have always formed part of the Faith of the Church, but which had not previously been stated authoritatively. The use of the verb 'define' (*definire*) in this connection is characteristic.

The living Tradition is represented by the teaching office of the Church (*magisterium*). The decree *De fide* of the Vatican Council of 1870 states that 'by divine and catholic faith all these things are to be believed which are contained in God's Word, written or received through Tradition, and which are set forth by the Church as doctrines to be believed because divinely revealed, whether in a solemn proclamation or in the course of its ordinary and universal teaching office' (*Porro fide divina et catholica ea omnia credenda sunt, quae in verbo Dei scripto vel tradito continentur et ab ecclesia sive solemni judicio sive ordinario et universali magisterio tanquam divinitus revelata credenda proponuntur*). Together with doctrinal resolutions known through solemn proclamation (Conciliar or Papal decrees), mention is here made of doctrines received through the ordinary and universal teaching office of the Church (*magisterium*). One of the German bishops who attended the Vatican Council rightly interpreted the implications of this doctrine: 'Neither the Holy Scriptures nor the Divine Tradition, but the Teaching Church, which unerringly interprets both sources of knowledge, is for us the primary rule of faith.'

This general teaching office of the Church is guaranteed by the Infallibility of the Pope. According to the Vatican Council he is infallible when he speaks *ex cathedra* and makes statements on matters of faith and morals, expressly teaching in virtue of his pastoral office and apostolic authority. In such cases his pronouncements are infallible in themselves and not in virtue of the consent of the Church (*ex sese, non autem ex consensu ecclesiae*). The proclamation of the Mariological dogma in 1950 was the first example of an *ex cathedra* definition since 1870.

Although the resolution of 1870 had retrospective effect, this did not imply that all papal statements of a dogmatic character were infallible. A certain amount of theological discretion is permissible in deciding what statements are *ex cathedra*. In such cases due regard is paid to their motivation, form and content.

The following are the doctrinal norms of the Roman Catholic Church:

1. *Holy Scripture*. According to a decree of the Council of Trent the Apocrypha is included in the Old Testament Canon. The Vulgate is the normative text.

2. The three ecumenical Creeds (the Apostles' Creed, the Nicene Creed and the *Quicunque Vult*, or the 'Athanasian Creed.' All three are used liturgically.

3. *Decreta et canones concilii Tridentini* (1564). The Council of Trent gave its present form to the Roman Catholic Church. The *decreta* contain the positive exposition of its doctrine, the *canones* are concerned with rejected tenets (including several Lutheran doctrines).

4. *Professio fidei Tridentina*. This was a confession of faith drawn up in 1564 after the conclusion of the Council. Subscription was required from clergy, doctors of theology and university teachers. It is also used as a confession for converts. Some short but significant additions were made after the Vatican Council.

The document opens with the Nicene Creed and continues with an acknowledgement of the apostolic and ecclesiastical traditions and of the Scriptures as interpreted by the Church. The confession next passes to an enumeration of the seven sacraments, acceptance of the catholic rites and of the doctrines promulgated by the Council of Trent on the subjects of original sin and justification, the sacrifice of the Mass, purgatory, the invocation of saints, the homage to be paid to sacred pictures and, finally, the primacy of the Pope. It concludes with an acknowledgement of all the decisions of the Council. The resolutions of the Vatican Council with a particular mention of the Infallibility of the Pope were added after 1870.

5. *Catechismus Romanus* (1566). This was the work of a Papal Commission. Since three of its four members were Dominicans, its doctrine of Grace and Salvation approximates in certain important respects to that of the Evangelical Churches. It is a handbook for priests rather than a work for the laity. It comprises four chapters on the Apostles' Creed, the Sacraments, the Commandments and the Lord's Prayer. A number of other

Catechisms are in use, especially diocesan catechisms authorized by the bishop, with considerable similarity in structure and content.

6. *Decreta et canones Concilii Vaticani* (1870). Here the decree on Papal Infallibility is of particular importance for the understanding of the doctrinal norms of the Roman Catholic Church. From this follows the authority of

7. All Papal pronouncements *ex cathedra*.

8. Finally there are the works of the Doctors of the Church, or Fathers who are recognized as standards for Roman Catholic doctrine. From mediaeval times four Latin fathers were honoured with the title *doctor ecclesiae*, St. Ambrose, St. Jerome, St. Augustine and St. Leo the Great. More recently it has become the prerogative of the Pope to specify and to add to the number of doctors of the Church. In 1871 and 1879 respectively, St. Alphonsus Liguori (1696–1787) and St. Thomas Aquinas (1225–1274) were raised to this rank and were thereby recognized as the standard Roman Catholic authorities on ethics and dogmatics.

Although they cannot be strictly described as doctrinal norms, the following items may perhaps be added here as authoritative within the Roman Catholic Church in their respective spheres:

9. The *Codex Juris Canonici*, the official codification of the Canon Law of the Church, published in 1917–18 on the initiative of Benedict XV.

10. The following liturgical books: *Breviarium Romanum* (1568) revised under Pius X (1911) for the canonical hours; *Missale Romanum* (1570) for the Mass, *Rituale Romanum* (1614) revised in 1925, for other rites performed by priests and *Pontificale Romanum* (1596) and *Ceremoniale episcoporum* (1600) for ceremonies restricted to bishops.

4. DOCTRINAL SYSTEM

It is typical of Roman Catholicism that the contrasts between Law and Grace and between Law and Gospel, which are usually regarded as polar opposites in the Evangelical Churches, are not considered to be mutually exclusive. The Gospel is the new Law, the law of Christ, the law of faith (*Romans* iii. 27) and the law of liberty (*St. James* ii. 12). Both the continuity of the Law and the

Gospel in the history of Redemption and their essential harmony are emphasized.

Thus the interpretation of Christianity as a dialectical opposition between the Law and the Gospel, faith and works, is replaced by the conception of two spheres of existence, natural and supernatural, the Realm of Nature and the Kingdom of Grace. These categories are fundamental not only to Roman Catholic doctrine, but also to its way of life, as expressed in literature, for example, in Dante's *Divine Comedy* and in contemporary novels and poetry.

The natural sphere is composed of everything of which man is capable through his own powers and all that he comprehends or desires. The supernatural or the realm of Grace includes whatever is bestowed on mankind from above, faith and all the forces of Grace in the life of the Church or the individual Christian. To the natural order belong human reason, natural law, free-will, the authority of the State and the rule of human law. To the supernatural order, on the other hand, belong faith, Christian Ethics and the Church. Two orders can therefore be established, each consisting of three parts in correspondence to each other, the natural order composed of reason, natural law and human society, and the supernatural order comprising faith, supernatural virtue and the Church.

For Roman Catholicism the harmony between Grace and Nature is no less essential than the distinction between them. There can scarcely be a more characteristic statement than the celebrated dictum of Aquinas: 'Grace does not destroy Nature, but brings it to perfection' (*Gratia non tollit naturam sed perficit*). Through Grace the natural order is raised to a higher plane and thereby attains its true goal. The Creator of the world and the Saviour of mankind are one and the same God Whose Divine Will is consummated in Redemption. In conjunction with Grace man's natural apprehension of God reaches fruition. Natural morality continues on a higher plane in the Kingdom of Grace. In Roman Catholic dogmatics, ethics and sociology frequent mention is made of natural theology, natural morality and natural law as a preparation for Christianity. 'Before the temple of Christian Revelation lies the forecourt of natural theology' (Friedrich Heiler).

Thus it is essential for Roman Catholicism to emphasize the co-operation of the natural will and supernatural grace in the attainment of salvation. Man can truly obey God's laws (*vera legis obedientia*), but cannot attain salvation until he acts in co-operation with the supernatural inspiration (*inspiratio gratiae*).

It will only be necessary to select for consideration here the parts of Roman Catholic doctrine which distinguish it from the teaching of other Churches. A detailed treatment will therefore be confined to two topics, the doctrine of Man and Salvation, and the doctrine of the Sacraments.

Some general comments may, however, be made on the remainder of its doctrinal system. The doctrine of God is largely based upon natural theology. Roman Catholic dogmatics pre-suppose the validity of the philosophical proofs of the existence of God. Atheism is consequently not only a sin, the outcome of unwillingness to submit to God, but also a defect in intellectual apprehension. Since natural theology is taken as a starting-point, dogmatic theology has much to say about God as 'the real being' (*ens realissimum*), or 'the Supreme Good' (*summum bonum*), in addition to the Biblical expressions. So far as the specifically Christian attributes of God are concerned, it can truly be said that God is described as Creator, Law-giver and Father to a greater extent than in Protestantism which tends to pay exclusive attention to the third of these titles.

Apart from the insertion of the Filioque into the Nicene Creed in which it differs from Orthodoxy, the Trinitarian and Christo-logical doctrines of the Roman Catholic Church are common ground with all Churches which are faithful to the dogmatic heritage of the early Church. The doctrine of Predestination (though taught by Aquinas) is not assigned any place of promin-ence, and the role of free-will in the economy of salvation is a characteristic feature of the Roman Catholic system.

5. Doctrine of Man and Salvation

(a) The Doctrine of Man

The natural attributes of man include an immortal soul and free-will, which together constitute the image of God within him.

In his unfallen state (*status integritatis*) man was righteous and holy. Adam was created for fellowship with God and lived in the enjoyment of this experience. In addition to his natural attributes he had also a *donum superadditum*, sanctifying grace.

After the Fall, man lost his original righteousness (*justitia originalis*) and original sin (*peccatum originis*) became his heritage. This consists in *concupiscentia*, or man's sinful desire. The state of his existence after the Fall became a *habitus corruptus*, characterized by a turning away of his will from God (*aversio voluntatis a Deo*). Human nature was not, however, as the Reformers asserted, completely corrupted through the Fall, but only weakened. A shadow has been cast over the intellect, so that it fails to recognize natural and supernatural truth with its original clear perception. The will has no longer the same mastery over our sensual nature as in its former state. Freedom of will is impaired, but continues to exist. 'If any one says that man's free will is lost or extinct after the sin of Adam, let him be anathema' (*Si quis liberum hominis arbitrium post Adae peccatum amissum et exstinctum esse dixerit . . . anathema sit*). This canon of the Council of Trent touches on a fundamental difference between the Roman Catholic and Protestant conceptions of Christianity.

Not all the actions of human beings are sinful. It is possible to do good deeds without grace. But natural man cannot avoid committing mortal sins, because he is born with the tinder of sin (*fomes peccati*) and with an inclination towards sin (*pronitas ad peccandum*). In sinful man good and evil are present side by side. He is not totally corrupt, but neither can he free himself from mortal sin and its consequences, punishment and damnation.

(b) *The objective basis of Salvation*

Salvation is the outcome of the work of Christ, His Incarnation, His life of obedience to the will of God, His Crucifixion and Resurrection. The Grace of God alone was able to save man after the Fall.

This coming was prepared in the Old Testament. Great importance is assigned to the Old Testament, which is regularly read in the Canonical Hours and provides the text for many of the variable parts of the Mass. The fulfilment in Christ of the

Messianic prophecies is a central theme of Roman Catholic theology.

Both in doctrine and devotion the Mother of our Lord has a place which corresponds to her position in Orthodoxy. Her virginity is emphasized. She is 'for ever Virgin' (*Maria semper virgo*). In Roman Catholic exegesis, therefore, the passages relating to the brothers and sisters of Jesus are explained by reference to some lesser relationship such as that of cousin. From 1854 onwards the doctrine of the Immaculate Conception of Mary (*immaculata conceptio*) has been a *dogma declaratum*. It had long been the subject of debate among theologians, asserted by the Scotists but denied by the Thomists. The doctrine asserts that the Virgin Mary was born in a natural manner from human parents, but by a special divine grace was conceived without inheriting original sin. It is also normally taught that she was without actual sin.

In 1950 the Pope proclaimed as a new dogma a tenet which had been widely held and generally accepted since the close of the Patristic period, but which had not previously been accorded the status of a defined dogma.[1] At her death the body of the Virgin was taken up into Heaven. The term 'Assumption' is used in preference to Ascension, which is restricted to our Lord Himself.

Christ's act of salvation began with His Incarnation. He died to restore those who were lost through Adam's fall and to free them from sin and its consequences. His death was a true sacrifice through which He saved us from sin and reconciled us to the Father. No particular theory of the Atonement has been laid down as the official doctrine of the Roman Catholic Church, but the Thomist doctrine of Reconciliation has, on the whole, set the course of theology on the subject. Christ's act is first considered as a vicarious satisfaction (*vicaria satisfactio*). Our Lord has rendered to the Father the obedience which was our due. There is a further *satisfactio superabundans*, through which He acquired merits of which we reap the benefit. Through His suffering and death He also rendered satisfaction to the righteousness of God for the violation of God's Will, of which we have been guilty.

[1] See above, pp. 21, 49.

(c) Justification or the attainment of Salvation

Since the beginning of the Reformation this has been the principal subject of controversy between Evangelical and Roman Catholic theologians.

Here the chief problem lies in defining the extent to which the attainment of Salvation is due to the co-operation of Man. The Orthodox Church has never concerned itself with the problem and scarcely seems aware of its importance. It has, however, been an inevitable question in the theology of Western Christendom since the time of St. Augustine. The Roman Catholic doctrine of Justification is laid down in the *Decretum de justificatione* of the Council of Trent, which was adopted after lengthy discussion. It represents a theological masterpiece in which conflicting tendencies were combined into an integrated whole. The following features are typical of the doctrine in this form.

(i) Justification is the work of God through Jesus Christ; without His grace no one can be justified. In a long chapter devoted to the causes of Justification the various meanings of the word 'cause' are carefully distinguished. The final cause or underlying purpose of Justification is the Glory of God and of Christ and eternal life (*gloria Dei et Christi ac vita aeterna*). Its efficient cause is 'the merciful God Who freely cleanses us' (*misericors Deus qui gratuito abluit*). Its meritorious cause is 'His dearly beloved Son, the only Begotten' (*dilectissimus unigenitus suus*). We are justified 'by divine mercy for Christ's sake' (*divina misericordia propter Christum*). Justification takes place *gratis*, or without anything being paid in return. Nothing rendered by Man before Justification, whether faith or works, can earn this grace.

(ii) Man is expected to play his part. While the very beginning of Justification lies in the prevenient Grace of God (*gratia praeveniens*), man must consent to this bestowal of Grace and co-operate with it. He is not passive towards Grace. A canon directed against the Lutherans anathematizes those who assert that during Salvation man conducts himself like a lifeless creature, and can neither reject if he chooses, nor co-operate with Divine Grace by answering the call of God. Repentance and Faith (belief in the Divine Revelation) form the necessary preparation required for Justification (*praeparatio ad justificationem*). A further anathema is pronounced against those who claim that man's efforts to prepare himself for the reception of Grace (*se disponere ad gratiam*) are sinful.

(iii) The Pauline statement that man is justified *gratia et per fidem* is taken to mean that faith is the beginning of salvation (*humanae salutis initium*) and that we have not earned the grace of Justification. On the other hand the doctrine that we are justified *sola fide* is rejected, for this would imply that nothing more than faith is required of the sinner. Complete union with Christ requires hope and love in addition to faith. As St. James says, faith without works is dead. Thus the faith necessary for salvation is faith informed by love (*fides caritate formata*). A canon directed against the Lutherans rejects the opinion that the faith necessary for Justification is merely confidence (*fiducia*) in the divine mercy which forgives the sinner. According to another canon, again with the Lutherans in mind, the Gospel is not simply a promise of eternal life without the further condition of keeping the Commandments, which can be observed by a justified man who lives by Grace.

(iv) Justification involves a real transformation in Man, and not merely the reception of Christ's Justification, or remission of sins. The Council dissociates itself sharply from the Lutheran doctrines of a purely forensic Justification as well as from the Lutheran watchword *simul justus et peccator*. Grace and love must be infused in the heart if Justification is to be achieved. Justification is also 'a sanctification and renewal of the inner man' (*sanctificatio et renovatio interioris hominis*). In a phrase taken from St. Augustine man becomes just instead of unjust (*ex iniusto fit justus*). We are not only considered righteous, but also justly called righteous, and become so, as we absorb righteousness into ourselves according to the measure which the Holy Spirit imparts to every man and according to his own *dispositio et cooperatio*.

(v) The Tridentine treatment of Justification is characteristically associated with the sacraments. The instrumental cause of Justification is the sacrament of Baptism, which is the laver of regeneration, and where the transition to a state of Grace is effected. Those who are justified may later fall from Grace through infidelity or some other mortal sin, and thus forfeit the grace of Justification. But in the sacrament of Penance, which is necessary for those who wish to be restored to a state of grace, those who have fallen may again be justified, and recover the grace which they have lost. The accompanying canon condemns the doctrine that grace which has been lost can be recovered *sola fide* without recourse to the sacrament of Penance.

(vi) Those who attain Justification experience a growth in righteousness. The justice received through the Grace of God grows as faith acts in conjunction with good works, and as man becomes progressively more righteous. There is an *incrementum justitiae*, or growth in righteousness, which comes about through good works whereby the crown of righteousness mentioned by the Apostle (2 *Timothy* iv. 7–8) can be at length attained. Through good works a further *augmentum gratiae* becomes merited. Although the good works of those who are justified are the result of God's Grace, this does not exclude the merit which attaches to the agent himself.

(vii) The doctrine of assurance of salvation is repudiated. No pious Christian need have any doubts as to the mercy of God, the merits of Christ or the power of the sacraments, but any one who considers his own weakness and unworthiness may be seized by fear. No one can know with full certainty that he has really attained God's Grace or claim with assurance that he is predestined to Salvation. Christians must have fear (*formidare debent*), for they know that they are reborn with a hope of glory, but not yet in glory itself (*in spem gloriae et nondum in gloriam renati sunt*).

Since the Council of Trent there have been a few Papal pronouncements on the subject of Justification. In the seventeenth century the Jansenists stressed the Augustinian doctrines of the incapacity of man to do good, the absolute necessity of Grace and Predestination as the ground of Salvation. Their opponents, he Jesuit theologians, claimed that man had the power to do good and was capable of accepting or rejecting the Grace of God. In their constitutions *Cum occasione* (1653) and *Unigenitus* (1713) two Popes, Innocent X and Clement XI, supported the Jesuits. These resolutions represented a victory for the semi-Pelagian theology of the Jesuits over strict Augustinianism.

There are fundamental divergences between the Roman Catholic and Lutheran doctrines of Justification. The statement of the problem and the doctrinal issues involved are characteristically different. Roman Catholicism is mainly interested in affirming man's share in the attainment of Salvation and his responsibility for his eternal destiny. For Evangelical Lutheran theology the fundamental principle consists in an affirmation of the certainty of salvation which can never rest upon the work of man, but solely on the act of God. The corresponding conceptions of Grace and Faith are also different. For Roman Catholicism Grace is a supernatural gift, a power which does not necessarily exclude any possibility of merit or reward. In religious controversy grace is often compared to medicine, a power imparted to man from without, supporting his own inherent capacity for good. In Lutheran doctrine grace is exclusively God's mercy which forgives sins (*favor Dei*). Lutheran opinion also defines faith as confidence or trust (*fiducia*), and that alone, whereas in Roman Catholicism it is interpreted as faith informed by love (*fides caritate formata*).

6. SACRAMENTS

In the *Catechismus Romanus* a sacrament is defined as a perceptible sign which, according to divine institution, not only illustrates, but also effects Justification and Sanctification. Every sacrament is 'a visible form of an invisible grace.' The necessity for sacraments arises from the fact that, owing to his corporeality, man belongs to the world of sense, and therefore apprehends spiritual phenomena through his own sense experience.

With all sacraments a distinction is drawn between matter and form. The matter is normally the material used, such as water for Baptism and bread and wine for the Eucharist. The form is the formula accompanying the rite; without words there can be no sacrament.

The Roman Catholic Church acknowledges seven sacraments: Baptism, Confirmation, Penance (*sacramentum poenitentiae*), the Eucharist, Extreme Unction, Holy Orders (*sacramentum ordinis*) and Matrimony. The first five are intended for the spiritual health of every Christian, while the last two depend upon special vocation, for the service of the Church and the institution of the Christian family respectively. They are normally mutually exclusive. There is, however, no impediment to the ordination of a widower, and recently in Germany a former Evangelical pastor was ordained to the Roman Catholic priesthood even though his wife was still living. The rule of celibacy is not considered as part of divine law, but only as a rule of order from which dispensation is possible.

No sacrament, not even Baptism, is an absolute condition of Salvation. If there are insuperable physical obstacles to the reception of a sacrament, the will and intention to use it (*votum sacramenti*) takes its place. But the general rule is that the sacraments are necessary for Salvation.

Four conditions must be satisfied for the validity of a sacrament, or the certainty of the operation of divine Grace.

(i) The proper matter. Baptism may only be performed with water. The Eucharist requires bread and wine. The materials to be used are specified in exact terms.

(ii) The proper form.

(iii) The proper person with the right intention. The sacrament requires a *minister sacramenti*. Confirmation and Ordination are reserved for the bishop, but the Eucharist, Absolution and Extreme Unction may also be administered by priests. All these sacraments require a properly ordained minister. It is therefore the Roman Catholic view that the sacraments of most other Churches are invalid, although their efficacy is not denied. There are, however, two sacraments which do not necessarily demand an ordained priest, and which can therefore be accepted by the Roman Catholic Church even in cases where other sacraments of the same Church are regarded as invalid. In common with the greater part of Christendom it is held that a layman can perform a valid Baptism provided that he employs the correct matter and form. It is, however, common practice to require Baptism *sub conditione* in case the original Baptism was defective in either respect. Again, in marriage the two partners themselves confect the sacrament and are its proper ministers to each other provided that they satisfy the necessary conditions.

But it is also required that the proper minister for conferring the sacrament (*persona ministri conferentis sacramentum*) should perform the rite with the intention of doing what the Church does (*cum intentione faciendi quod ecclesia facit*). This does not mean that the validity of the sacrament depends upon the theological or moral qualities of the celebrant, but only that the intention behind his action must be to perform a sacrament. Thus two actors who, as part of a play, satisfied the conditions necessary for a marriage, would not be considered validly married.

This condition for the validity of a sacrament has significance for the attitude of the Roman Catholic Church to the claims of the Anglican and Swedish Churches to possess the Apostolic Succession. It is not now normally denied that the first post-Reformation bishops of these Churches were consecrated by men who had themselves been consecrated bishops in the pre-Reformation Succession, but it is claimed that the changes made in the formulae of Ordination at the time of the Reformation were so considerable as to amount to a change in the intention of the sacrament. Since the Formula no longer included authority to offer sacrifices for the living and the dead, in accordance with the Reformers' rejection of this practice, their ordinations and successions are regarded as invalid according to Roman Catholic doctrine.[1]

[1] Professor Molland gives one form of the Roman Catholic doctrine of Intention together with an example of the cases with which it was designed to deal. Recently, however, some of their theologians have tended to present the argument under somewhat different forms. They refer to a so-called *intentio circa significationem* which links the intention more closely with the form of the rite, to which Professor Molland also directs his attention.

Anglican theologians would make some such reply as the following to Roman Catholic attacks on the validity of their Orders:

1. All the various forms under which the argument from intention has been presented have been shown by different Roman Catholic apologists to be either vulnerable or not to satisfy completely the full conclusions of the Bull of Leo XIII.

2. The precise form of the argument used in the Bull is by no means clear or readily identifiable.

3. In the course of the controversy the scope of the doctrine of Intention has tended to move from an entirely minimal criterion, for which provision must be made, but which it is difficult not to satisfy, to a question which increasingly encroaches upon the argument from the form of the Rite. The danger of a circular argument from Intention to Form and back again becomes correspondingly grave.

4. The intention 'to do what the Church does' is clearly expressed in the Preface to the Anglican Ordinal which governs the whole rite, even if it is not read as part of the service itself. The frequent mention of priesthood (*sacerdotium*) in the Ordinal should be noted.

5. With regard to the Form, the Roman Catholic requirement of the phrase 'to offer sacrifice for the living and the dead' is too narrowly defined as the touchstone of priesthood. It raises acute difficulties with regard to earlier Ordinals even in the Western

62 CHRISTENDOM

The Roman Catholic Church accepts, however, all the sacraments of the Orthodox Churches as valid, but would deny that this constitutes them a part of the true Church.

When these three conditions of validity are satisfied, the sacrament is effective *ex opere operato*, and the transmission of sacramental grace takes place irrespective of the personal qualities of the minister. This formula is intended to safeguard the objectivity of the sacrament, and to exclude the Donatist alternative *ex opere operantis*. The formula does not, however, imply that the sacrament has a magical efficacy, since its effect upon the recipient depends upon a further condition.

(iv) The recipient is required to 'receive worthily' (*digne suscipere*) or, expressed negatively, not to place obstacles in the way of its gracious effect (*obicem ponere*). No subjective qualifications are required for the Baptism of infants, though they are imposed for that of adults and for the sacrament of Penance. For the other sacraments the recipient must be in a state of grace, that is, he should have faith and not have committed any mortal sin for which he has not obtained absolution.

Of the seven sacraments three cannot be repeated, Baptism, Confirmation and Ordination, since they confer a *character indelebilis* upon the recipient; the remainder (including Extreme Unction) may be repeated.

Baptism is the rite of initiation into the Church, and the door of the spiritual life (*vitae spiritualis janua*). The matter of the sacrament is the baptismal water. This is normally consecrated

Church, and ignores other fundamental aspects of priesthood such as the 'power of binding and loosing' which are fully provided in the Ordinal. Similar objections can be raised against the exclusive insistence upon the phrase 'high priesthood' as the touchstone of episcopal consecration.

6. While for some Anglicans the controversy raises grave issues, many (and perhaps most) are completely indifferent to the Roman Catholic assessment of their Orders, since Rome is in any case not the final bar at which their Church is to be judged.

Literature on the Anglican side includes:

The Answer of the Archbishops of England to the Bull *Apostolicae Curae* republished (together with a translation of the Bull) in a brochure 'Anglican Orders,' S.P.C.K., 1954.

C. Gore: *Roman Catholic Claims.*

G. Dix: *The Question of Anglican Orders.*

R. L. Langford James: *The Doctrine of Intention.*

Michael Bruce: Article on 'Intention' in *Theology* for October 1956.

E. L. Mascall: 'Intention and Form in Anglican Orders' in *Church Quarterly Review* for January 1957.

G. F. Lewis: *The Papacy and Anglican Orders.*

(H.E.W.T.)

beforehand in a special rite, but its omission would not render the sacrament invalid. The form is the Baptismal Formula 'I baptize thee in the name of the Father and of the Son and of the Holy Ghost' (*Ego te baptizo in nomine Patris et Filii et Spiritus Sancti*). It is performed by pouring water three times on the head of the candidate (*infusio*), or by sprinkling (*aspersio*). This method of Baptism has been common in the West since the thirteenth century.

Baptism is preceded not only by renunciation (*abrenuntiatio*) and confession of faith in the words of the Apostles' Creed, but also by exorcism or the expulsion of the Devil from the child with the words 'Come out of him, thou unclean spirit, and give place to the Holy Spirit' (*exi ab eo(ea) immunde spiritus et da locum Spiritui Sancto*). The candidate is also anointed with consecrated oil on the forehead, chest and shoulders. The priest breathes on the face of the child symbolizing the Insufflation of the Spirit (*St. John* xx. 22), and moistens its ears with saliva, uttering the word 'Effata' (be opened) used by our Lord in the Gospels (*St. Mark* vii. 34). Each child normally has two god-parents, one of each sex, but one godparent may be sufficient.

While baptism is usually performed by a priest, it can be administered in emergencies by a layman or laywoman, and even by a heretic, or in even more exceptional cases by a heathen, provided that the Trinitarian Formula is used and the intention to perform a Christian Baptism is present. Since the Baptismal Controversy in the middle of the third century the Church of Rome has accepted the validity of baptism performed by heretics, a principle expressly reaffirmed by the Council of Trent. Converts from other Churches who profess the orthodox doctrine of the Trinity and who use the Threefold Baptismal Formula should not therefore be baptized on their entry into the Roman Catholic Church, though in all doubtful cases the practice known as 'conditional baptism' is followed. The Formula then opens 'If thou art not already baptized, I baptize thee.' If, however, the validity of heretical baptism is accepted, it is also maintained that the full efficacy of the rite is only completed by reception into the Roman Catholic Church.

The effect of Baptism is absolution from the guilt of original sin and from any actual sins previously committed. It also secures purification, regeneration and incorporation into the Church.

Confirmation. In the early Church Confirmation consisted in the anointing of the newly-baptized immediately after the administration of the sacrament of Baptism. In the Western Church this act has become an independent rite. Its proper minister is a bishop. The sacramental matter is the oil used for the anointing and its form is found in the words 'I sign thee with the sign of the Cross and confirm thee with the ointment of salvation in the name of the Father and of the Son and of the Holy Spirit' (*Signo te signo crucis et confirmo te chrismate salutis in nomine Patris et Filii et Spiritus Sancti*). Confirmation effects the increase of Grace (*augmentum gratiae*) 'in order that the Christian shall confidently profess the name of Christ' (*ut Christianus audacter Christi confiteatur nomen*). Twelve is the normal age for Confirmation.

The *Eucharist* is the most sacred sacrament (*sacramentum sanctissimum*). It is the very heart of the life of the Church and of the individual Christian. A special place is assigned to this sacrament by the Council of Trent. While the other sacraments must be used to demonstrate their power and efficacy, in the Eucharist the very source of sanctity is present even *ante usum*. Christ is present in the sacrament of the Altar *extra usum*.

According to Roman Catholic catechisms Christ instituted the Blessed Sacrament for a threefold purpose:

1. in order to be present in His Church for ever,
2. that His offering on the Cross might be represented to the Father in the sacrifice of the Mass,
3. to provide nourishment for the souls of His people in the Holy Communion.

The basis of the devotional life associated with the Eucharist is the doctrine of the Real Presence of Christ in the sacramental elements after consecration. By this means the bread and wine are transformed into the Body and Blood of Christ 'truly, really and substantially' (*vere, realiter et substantialiter*). Both His natures, human and divine, are present in the sacrament which can therefore be called *totus Christus*. Accordingly the consecrated elements on the altar are treated as Christ Himself, and the Host, when exposed or carried in procession, is venerated by the faithful who genuflect before it.

The matter of the sacrament is bread and wine. Wafers of unleavened bread are used, but recognition is also extended to the use of leavened bread in the Eastern Churches. As in the early Church and the Eastern Liturgies the wine is mixed with a little water.[1] The form of the Sacrament consists in the Words of Institution of our Lord and the consecration of the bread and wine is effected by the recitation of this formula over the elements by a properly ordained priest (*presbyter regulariter ordinatus*). This sacrament cannot be celebrated either by a deacon or a layman. In popular catechisms and sermons the priest is bluntly described as having 'power to transform bread and wine into the Body and Blood of Christ.'

This act of transformation is technically described as a *transubstantiatio*. Scholastic logic distinguished the accidents, material properties or incidental characteristics of a thing, from its substance or inner unity as an object. Its substance constituted it an individual entity, its accidents clothed it with a recognizable description. As applied to the doctrine of the Eucharist this meant that, while the inner unity of consecrated Bread and Wine became the Body and Blood of our Lord, no change was effected after consecration in the external attributes of Bread and Wine.

The effects of consecration persist after the Mass is over. So long as their outward form remains, the consecrated elements continue to be the Body and Blood of Christ. The whole Christ is present in each particle of the consecrated bread and wine. Thus the layman who is forbidden the chalice does not receive less of Christ's person than the celebrant who receives the sacrament in both kinds.

There is a close connection between Roman Catholic sacramental practice and doctrine. Historically the development of doctrine has been determined by sacramental practice and piety which have given its special character to the devotional life of Roman Catholicism.

[1] This seems to have been the general custom in using wine in early times. The liturgical explanation which arose later to explain the practice is given on pp. 84–5.

D

The act of consecration is the most sacred moment of the Mass. The miracle of the Incarnation is re-enacted, and Christ is present in person. This moment in the service is announced by two chimes of a bell in the chancel when the celebrant recites the Words of Institution over the bread and wine respectively and then elevates the consecrated elements for adoration. After the consecration the priest kneels and adores each of the elements in turn, first the Body of Christ, and then His Blood. The missal uses the strong word *adorare* here, which can only be used of God or of Christ in contrast to the weaker term veneration used of the saints. The decree of the Council of Trent on the Eucharist prescribes that the most holy sacrament shall receive the *cultus latriae* due to the true God. At this point in the service the whole congregation kneels and the worshippers offer their most fervent prayers.

Even after the conclusion of the service, however, Christ is still present through the practice of the Reservation of the Sacrament whereby the consecrated Host is still retained on the Altar. Before the Mass is ended the celebrant must drink all the consecrated wine from the chalice, as well as a little unconsecrated wine which he pours into the chalice, to ensure that all has been consumed. No particle of the Blood of Christ must remain when the Mass is over. Some consecrated Hosts may, however, be reserved. In every Roman Catholic Church there is normally one altar where at least one consecrated host is reserved, and in front of which there hangs a lighted lamp, the symbol of eternity, indicating that the Body of Christ is present in the Reserved Sacrament. Every Roman Catholic who enters the Church salutes the sacrament with a genuflexion towards this altar, and repeats the action whenever he passes in front of it as he moves about the building.

The object of Reservation is partly to provide consecrated hosts for the communion of the sick or for extended communion outside the full service of the Mass on other occasions, and partly for the exposition of the sacrament on the altar for adoration. Thousands of people visit churches every day to say their prayers before the Reserved Sacrament. This practice, which originated in the convents in the later Middle Ages, has since spread to the laity. In modern times the adoration of the host has even taken the form of what is called perpetual adoration in some places. Thus, particularly in some convents, there is a continuous succession of nuns who kneel in adoration before the sacrament by turns for fixed periods day and night.

The consecrated hosts (which include one large host for the purpose of exposition as well as several small ones for extended communion) are normally kept in a *ciborium*, or a chalice with a lid, within a Tabernacle (or sacramental cabinet) which is placed upon the altar.

A favourite form of service is sacramental Benediction. At its climax the priest takes the large host from the *ciborium* and places it on a monstrance or container, preferably of precious metal and of glass or crystal in which it can be exposed. The priest then turns towards the people and blesses them with the monstrance.

The sacrament may also be carried in the monstrance in procession. This is especially the case on the festival of Corpus Christi (French *fête-Dieu*; German *Fronleichnam*), which falls on the Thursday after Trinity Sunday. Next to Maundy Thursday this is the great Eucharistic Festival of the Church's Year. It was introduced in 1264 and both the office and its hymn, *Lauda, Sion, Salvatorem*, were composed by St. Thomas Aquinas. At this festival the devotion of the people is given full scope. The church is decked with all the splendour of luxuriant early summer flowers, and the houses along the route are decorated as well. At various points altars are set up in the open air, similarly adorned with flowers. The climax of the festival is the procession in which the various Roman Catholic societies take part, bearing their processional banners. A large crucifix is attended by choir-boys carrying lighted candles. Hymns of praise are sung and church bells rung. The laity are followed by members of the religious orders and the clergy carrying candles and acolytes with censers and bells. Then follows the bishop or priest under a baldachino, bearing the monstrance in his hands. The crowds on both sides kneel as the host passes by. Prayers are said at each of the improvised altars.

In the Roman Catholic Church the Eucharist is always regarded as a sacrificial rite and the celebrant acts as a sacrificing priest.

This conception of the Eucharist goes far back into history.

In the Didache (early second century), the Eucharist is called a sacrifice (θυσία), and regarded as the fulfilment of the prophecy of Malachi i. 11: 'In every place incense shall be offered unto My Name, and a pure offering.' This exegesis is repeated throughout the history of the Roman Catholic Church, and occurs in the decree of the Council of Trent on the sacrifice of the Mass. As early as the first epistle of St. Clement (in the year 96) the expression 'to present the gifts' is used in reference to the Eucharist.

When the Eucharist is described as a sacrifice in the early Church, reference is often made to the sacramental elements brought by the congregation to church to be offered to God or to the prayers which accompany the rite considered as a sacrifice of praise and thanksgiving rather than to the consecration regarded as a specifically sacrificial act. From the time of Tertullian (c. 200), however, mention is made of a sacrificial rite the intention of which is to reconcile God. In the Church Order of Hippolytus (early third century) the Eucharist is described as a propitiatory sacrifice. The task of the priest is 'to propitiate Thy countenance and to present the sacred gifts of Thy Church' (repropitiari vultum tuum et offerre dona sancta ecclesiae tuae). St. Cyprian (d. 258) develops the theme of sacrifice. The priest sacrifices the Body and Blood of Christ, and may even be said to act on behalf of Christ (vice Christi), and to imitate His action. The Eucharist is an imitation of Christ's sacrifice and 'the suffering of Christ is the sacrifice which we present' (passio est enim Domini sacrificium quod offerimus). Here we are concerned with a mystical-symbolic representation of the sacrificial death of Christ.

St. Gregory the Great (Pope 590–604) gives the full development of the Roman Catholic doctrine of the sacrifice of the Mass. The Eucharist is a real but bloodless repetition of our Lord's sacrifice on Calvary. The sacrifice is an effective means of influencing God, and it can be offered on behalf of those who are not present at the rite, and even for souls in Purgatory.

The doctrine of the Eucharistic sacrifice was laid down in its final form by the Council of Trent. Christ Himself instituted the Eucharist as a sacrifice to ensure that His priesthood should not come to an end when His earthly life was over. In the rite a bloodless sacrifice of Christ is made (incruente immolatur), and the Mass is therefore a propitiatory sacrifice to God for the forgiveness of sins, which may be offered not only for the living, but also for the departed in Purgatory.

The history of the Eucharist in the Roman Catholic Church shows not only that the idea of sacrifice has taken an increasingly prominent place, but also that it has become more and more limited to propitiation. The offertory procession of the congregation to the altar with the bread and wine fell into disuse at the beginning of the Middle Ages and the only surviving trace is a sacrificial prayer read by the priest before the consecration in which he offers the unconsecrated bread and wine to God.[1] The main element in the concept of sacrifice is, however, the action in which the priest sacrifices the Body and Blood of Christ and which is made explicit by the prayers recited over the consecrated elements before the act of Communion. The Canon of the Mass includes the words 'We offer to Thy glorious Majesty from Thy gifts a pure sacrifice, a holy sacrifice, an unblemished sacrifice' (*offerimus praeclarae tuae majestati de tuis donis et datis hostiam puram, hostiam sanctam, hostiam immaculatam*). It is Christ who is sacrificed, yet recent Roman Catholic theology often emphasizes the fact that the Sacrifice of the Mass is not a repetition, but a re-presentation of Calvary.

Early in the Middle Ages the Eucharistic Liturgy evolved in such a way as to become primarily a sacrificial rite performed by the priest at the altar on behalf of the congregation, and its purpose as an act of communion fell into the background. Sacrifice and Communion tended to become separated. The Eucharist was always a sacrifice, but it did not always need to be administered to the people who could perform their obligations by attendance without communicating. This opened the way for the development of private masses, in which the priest performs the sacrificial rite assisted only by a server who makes the congregational responses, a reminder that this was once a service attended by a congregation.

Normally a priest says Mass (but only one Mass) daily. An exception is, however, made on Christmas night when three consecutive Masses are said. The service is normally held in the

---

[1] The restoration of the Offertory procession to something of its former importance is, however, one of the aims of the modern Liturgical Movement. See below, p. 115.

early morning, and fasting or abstinence from food and drink
from the previous midnight is of obligation. Recently, however,
permission has been given to celebrate Mass in the afternoon or
evening with suitable dispensation from the strict rule about
fasting. In churches with more than one priest each celebrates
Mass daily and, from mediaeval times, the larger churches were
equipped with several altars to make possible the practice of
simultaneous celebration. Cathedrals of this period might have
as many as forty-eight altars. In monastery chapels and other
churches served by a number of priests, Mass may be said several
times at the same altar. In such cases one priest follows another
to the altar. A Mass of this type takes about half an hour, and
the priest whispers the words, or even merely moves his lips
though he turns to and from the altar as if a congregation were
present.

According to Roman Catholic teaching the multiplication of
Masses is considered as a means of influencing God. Moreover,
each will have a special intention or purpose. At one altar Mass
may be offered for the recovery of the sick, at another for one
who has died, to shorten his time in Purgatory; at yet a third
for the blessing of a newly married couple.

At most Masses there is no communion of the people. The
congregation does not, as a general rule, communicate at High
Mass on Sundays, but receives the Sacrament at a quiet celebration
early in the morning or even before or after Mass from the
Reserved Sacrament. The contemporary Liturgical Movement
is trying to restore the Communion of the people as the climax
of High Mass. Partly as a result of this movement there is
an increasing tendency towards frequent communion in the
Roman Catholic Church. Daily communion is found not only
among monks and nuns but also among the laity. The practice
was strongly recommended by Pius X in 1905.

The celebrant receives the sacrament in both kinds (*sub utraque*),
partaking both of the consecrated bread and wine, while the laity
and other priests who may be present receive in one kind (*sub
una*), merely receiving the consecrated bread. This custom grew
up in the twelfth and thirteenth centuries. The Council of Constance in 1415 refused the chalice to the laity, and defended its
prohibition on the theological ground that, since the whole

Christ is present in the bread, the laity do not in practice receive less than the priest.

The communicant must receive fasting. Exceptions are, however, made in the case of the sick and of soldiers in the field. Recent changes in the times of service have led to further modifications of this rule. Communicants kneel at the altar rails, and receive the host from the priest's hands directly into their mouths. The words of administration run 'The Body of our Lord Jesus Christ preserve thy soul unto everlasting life' (*Corpus Domini nostri Jesu Christi custodiat animam tuam in vitam aeternam*). A characteristic feature of the Eucharistic Liturgy is the beautiful prayer read by the priest immediately before the act of Communion in the form of a slight variant of the words of the centurion in St. Matthew viii. 8: 'Lord, I am not worthy that Thou shouldest come under my roof, but speak the word only, and my soul shall be healed' (*Domine non sum dignus ut intres sub tectum meum, sed tantum dic verbo et sanabitur anima mea*).

Communion is restricted to members of the Roman Catholic Church. The age of admission is normally seven, and from this time every member of the Church is required to go to confession and to receive the sacrament once a year. First Communion is preceded by a short instruction on the sacrament. This was first prescribed by the fourth Lateran Council in 1215 and the provision has been often repeated. In order to ensure that the communicant is in a state of grace at the sacrament itself, Confession is usually made before partaking of the Eucharist. Saturday afternoon or evening are familiar times for those who are preparing to make their communion on the Sunday. Confirmation is not absolutely necessary for admission to Communion.

The gracious effects of the Sacrament can be best expressed by the word 'communion,' sacramental union with Christ. It achieves the union of the soul with its Lord and Saviour.

Penance. Although in the early centuries the sacrament of Penance was a public act involving the reconciliation of the offender to the whole Church, in practice it is now administered only in the form of private or secret confession (*confessio secreta*).

The form of the sacrament is the formula of Absolution pronounced by the priest over the penitent: 'I absolve thee from thy sins in the Name of the Father and of the Son and of the Holy Spirit, Amen.' (*Ego te absolvo a peccatis tuis in nomine Patris et Filii et Spiritus Sancti.*) The matter, or rather the *quasi materia* (since there is no visible matter in the sacrament), is to be found in the three elements involved in the confession of the penitent, contrition, confession and satisfaction.

The biblical authority for the sacrament is St. John xx. 22–23, which is interpreted as giving authority to the apostles and therefore to their successors. Although the power of absolution resides in the priesthood, only priests who have received episcopal permission for the purpose are authorized to hear confessions. In certain serious cases, the so-called *casus reservati*, absolution is reserved for the highest clerical authority, normally the bishop, but sometimes even Rome itself. A typical feature of the Roman Catholic system can be observed here. Absolution is a judicial act (*actus judicialis*) and, in addition to its more pastoral aspects, confession has an element which brings it within the purview of canon law. According to the *Codex Juris Canonici* the priest who hears a confession is both judge and physician (*judex et medicus*). Confession is framed in, and subject to a number of judicial regulations.

In the early centuries and the first part of the mediaeval period, penances had to be performed before the bishop, or later the priest, declaring the penitent's sins to be forgiven. From the eleventh century onwards, absolution has been pronounced immediately after the confession, and the penance or *satisfactio* is postponed until later. The contemporary sequence, then, is *contritio, confessio, absolutio* and *satisfactio*.

Contrition of heart (*contritio cordis*) is necessary for the remission of sins. This is defined by the Council of Trent as 'sorrow of soul and detestation of the sin committed, together with the resolution not to sin in future' (*animi dolor ac detestatio de peccato commisso cum proposito non peccandi de cetero*). Contrition of heart is deep repentance occasioned by the love of God and sorrow over the breach of His commandments. It is *contritio caritate perfecta*. There is also an imperfect repentance, or *attritio*, arising from the contemplation of the heinousness of the sin and fear of its punishment in Hell. It is recognized as satisfying the requirements of confession provided that it is accompanied by the will to lead a new and a better life.

The next step for the penitent is oral confession (*confessio oris*). This must be made to a priest since by virtue of his office he has authority to confer absolution. All mortal sins of which a penitent is conscious must be included in the confession, after which the priest at his pastoral discretion confers or withholds absolution (remits or retains sins).

All sins can be forgiven, but a distinction is drawn between mortal and venial sins (*peccata mortalia, venialia*). A mortal sin involves the forfeiture of God's grace until it is cancelled by absolution, while venial sins do not exclude the sinner from grace. Although considered intrinsically venial sins are certainly a violation of God's will, they neither imply a revolt against God nor the conscious choice of another object in preference to Him. Mortal sin, on the other hand, involves a turning away from God. Within this category fall fornication and theft, failure to attend Mass without reasonable excuse and sins of thought such as hatred and envy. For mortal sins the sacrament of Penance, or at least desire for the sacrament (*votum sacramenti*), is necessary, but venial sins may be cancelled by many other remedies such as prayer, fasting and good works. It is, of course, only possible to confess those mortal sins which can be recalled by conscientious self-examination, but absolution also extends to sins which cannot be remembered. The point has an important bearing on the question whether assurance of salvation can be given in the Roman Catholic Church. Absolution becomes invalid if the penitent purposely withholds any mortal sins of which he is conscious. As the distinction between mortal and venial sins is very subtle, it is best to confess any sins about which there is any doubt.

Since a priest hearing a confession has to satisfy himself as to the spiritual condition of the penitent, he is entitled to ask for further particulars about the sins which have been committed (circumstances, frequency and the like), though it is a sound principle that such questions should be kept to a minimum. The penitent, however, is forbidden to allude to any sins other than his own. Great demands are made upon a father confessor who must have a deep knowledge of human nature, mingled severity and compassion, and, above all, discretion. A priest is strictly bound to secrecy about anything which he may hear in the confessional. If he betrays his confidence, he is excommunicated and his case judged by the Apostolic See.

After the confession the priest gives the penitent certain penances (*satisfactio*) to perform. In the early Church and at the beginning of the mediaeval period these were very severe: exclusion from the Eucharist for long periods, strict fasts, arduous pilgrimages and the like. The penances which are now imposed are not, however, particularly onerous. They usually consist of short fasts or devotional exercises, such as the recitation of a number of prayers, performed in a spirit of penitence. Even if the penitent fails to carry out his penance, absolution is still valid, but he becomes guilty of a further sin.

In practice the penitent often tests himself beforehand by the use of a so-called penitential mirror, a list of questions which he puts to himself, usually based on the Ten Commandments. Confession normally takes place in Church in a confessional divided into two compartments by a partition. On one side sits the confessor, on the other kneels the penitent. In the partition there is a small opening with a grating. The confessional became part of the furniture of the church after the Middle Ages in order to prevent and to give the lie to rumours concerning improper conduct between the priest and his female penitents. After the examination of conscience the penitent reads a set prayer of confession containing a declaration of his intention to lead a new life. Finally the priest pronounces the formula of absolution.

Devout Roman Catholics make their confession several times a year and even at weekly intervals. The confessional is of great service in helping them to be contrite and conscious of their sins, in the development of their moral and spiritual lives, and as a relief to their consciences.

Extreme Unction (*extrema unctio*) finds scriptural support from St. Mark vi. 13 and St. James v. 14–15, although these passages only speak of physical healing and make no mention of the dying.

The sacramental matter is oil, used for the anointing of the eyes, ears, mouth, hands and feet of the sick. Its form is contained in the words used by the priest during the ceremony 'May God through this anointing and His gracious mercy grant thee remission of whatsoever sins thou hast committed through sight, hearing,' etc. (*Per istam unctionem et suam piissimam misericordiam indulgeat tibi Dominus quidquid per visum, per auditum—deliquisti*). The sacrament is administered to the sick, and especially when death is believed to be imminent. Its effects are the healing of the mind (*mentis sanatio*) and the infusion of faith in the divine mercy (*fiducia divinae misericordiae*). This may be particularly necessary as death approaches, when (according to the decree of the Council of Trent) the Devil does all in his power to disturb our faith.

Holy Order (*sacramentum ordinis*) lies at the heart of the whole sacramental system, for most sacraments can only be administered by a priest. The bishop is the sole minister of ordination and for his consecration the participation of three bishops is required.

According to Roman Catholic doctrine the priesthood was instituted by Christ Himself in and through His institution of the Eucharist as the sacrifice of the New Covenant. The special authority vested in the priest is the power to consecrate the Eucharist, to offer it to God and to distribute it to the people, as well as to remit or retain sins. At the ordination of priests the candidate is handed a chalice and the following formula is pronounced by the bishop: 'Receive the power to offer sacrifice in the Church for the living and the dead in the name of the Father and of the Son and of the Holy Ghost' (*Accipe potestatem offerendi sacrificium in ecclesia pro vivis et mortuis in nomine Patris et Filii et Spiritus Sancti*).[1]

The Council of Trent specified seven different orders of clergy. The four lowest, door-keeper, reader, acolyte, and exorcist (*ostiarius, lector, acolythus, exorcista*), are mere names inherited from the early Church, and even their functions have become obsolete. They are grouped together under the title of 'minor

[1] The ceremony known as the *porrectio instrumentorum* was introduced into the rite of Ordination during the Middle Ages. It was at one time (as by Pope Eugenius IV at the Council of Florence) regarded as necessary for the conferment of valid orders, but in the light of further knowledge of its history, it is not now considered essential for this purpose. (H.E.W.T.)

orders' (*ordines minores*), and are normally conferred en bloc upon theological students. The obligation to celibacy rests upon the three major orders, which comprise the sub-diaconate, the diaconate and the priesthood (*sacerdotium*) which includes both the presbyterate and the episcopate. Elevation to the episcopate involves a new ordination or consecration. The episcopate is the highest degree of order, and archbishops, cardinals and even the Pope himself, although they possess a more extended jurisdiction, receive no further consecration.

The normal minimum canonical ages for the major orders are as follows: 22 for a sub-deacon; 23 for a deacon; 24 for a priest, and 30 for a bishop.

Holy Matrimony (sacramentum matrimonii). The sacrament of marriage consists not in the marriage service itself, which is merely an act of consecration, but in the contract between the partners and in the marital act by which the marriage is consummated. The conjugal life itself is regarded as a visible form of God's invisible grace. Historically the description of marriage as a sacrament arises from the Vulgate rendering of μυστήριον in Ephesians v. 32 by the word *sacramentum*. It is to be noted that the phrase *sacramentum hoc magnum est* in the passage refers to the relationship between man and wife. Conjugal life derives its sacramental character from the idea that it is the earthly image of a heavenly reality, the relation between Christ and His Church.

There can be no higher evaluation of marriage, but side by side with this there is to be found in Roman Catholicism the tendency to depreciate marriage in favour of virginity or celibacy which is often regarded as a higher form of vocation.

Strictly the institution of marriage cannot be derived from our Lord Himself, for it is part of God's plan for His Creation and existed before the coming of Christ. It is, however, through Him that it has been raised to the dignity of a sacrament.

It is not easy to determine the form and matter of this sacrament. The form is not the consecration of the union by a priest, but the mutual consent of the two participants (*mutuus consensus*). Matrimony is established through the pledge of the two partners to be faithful to each other throughout their lives. This promise must be made in the presence of witnesses, usually the priest and at least two or three others. The sacrament is only consummated by the first act of sexual intercourse. Protestant marriages are also recognized as valid, and even as sacraments, although they have not been solemnized in the presence of a Roman Catholic priest. For the validity of such marriages it is, of course, necessary that there should be no canonical impediment.

If both partners are converted to the Roman Catholic faith, they do not require to be remarried, and the adhesion of one of them without the other is not recognized as a ground for the dissolution of the marriage. Roman Catholics are, however, required to make their promises in the presence of a priest, preferably their parish priest, who must satisfy himself that the conditions for a valid marriage in fact exist.

Mixed marriages present a difficult pastoral problem which in some countries has given rise to conflict between Church and State. The ecclesiastical authorities advise against them on the ground that the two partners cannot have intimate fellowship in their religious life and that the religious education of the children is beset with difficulties. In such cases the Roman Catholic Church demands the celebration of the marriage in its own church. This again requires a dispensation, which as a rule is only granted in return for the promise that all the issue of the marriage will be brought up in the Roman Catholic faith.

According to Canon Law there are a number of impediments, which fall into two classes: (1) *impedimenta impedientia*, or circumstances under which the marriage should not take place or should not have taken place, but which, granted the fact of marriage, do not make it invalid. These impediments may be listed as follows:

(a) the previous engagement of one of the partners to a third party,

(b) *religio mixta*, which has been discussed in the previous paragraph,

(c) *vota simplicia*, explained below (see page 102). From all these impediments to marriage a dispensation may be granted.

(2) *impedimenta dirimentia*, or circumstances which render marriage impossible and from which no dispensation can be obtained. These comprise (a) an existing marriage; (b) mental

incapacity (*amentia*) at the time of marriage, (*c*) *votum solemne* (see below, page 102), or ordination, (*d*) consent given under duress (*vis et metus*), (*e*) impotence upon entering marriage, (*f*) certain degrees of kinship, (*g*) complete disparity of faith. Thus a marriage between a Christian and an unbaptized person is invalid.

Roman Catholic teaching lays down that marriage is indissoluble. Unfaithfulness, heresy, neglect, or incompatibility do not constitute grounds for divorce. The most that the Church will allow is separation (*separatio quoad thorum seu quoad cohabitationem*), or the cessation of conjugal life without permission to remarry while the other partner is alive. Divorce, sanctioned in an ordinary court of law, is not accepted by the Church. Recourse, however, is sometimes made to a decree of nullity pronounced by the Papal court called the *Rota Romana*, on the plea of an *impedimentum canonicum*.

The benefits of matrimony are as follows:
(i) children to be brought up in the fear of God;
(ii) the mutual faithfulness of the two partners to each other;
(iii) indissolubility.

In these matters there is a coherent doctrinal tradition ranging from St. Augustine to Pope Pius XI, whose encyclical *Casti connubii* (1930) gave detailed rulings on the problems of marriage, condemning abortion, birth control, divorce and other practices tending towards the frustration of the true ends of marriage.

7. OTHER MEANS OF GRACE

In addition to the sacraments God uses other means to confer His divine grace.

Sacramentals are sacred objects or rites, which do not rank as sacraments but which are vehicles of grace. They are instituted by the Church and not by Christ, and are therefore useful, but not necessary to salvation. They take effect *ex opere operantis*, and not *ex opere operato*. These rites consist partly of exorcisms and partly of benedictions. Both can be used on things as well as on persons. 'I exorcize you rats' (*exorcizo vos pestiferos mures*) is a typical example. Benedictions are legion, the lower orders of consecration, the consecration of kings, the dedication of churches, the consecration of baptismal water and the like. The

Rituale Romanum even contains formulae not only for the blessing of fields and crops, but also of school buildings, and even of telegraph establishments and electrical installations.

The consecrated objects described as sacramentals are holy water, consecrated candles, palm-branches on Palm Sunday, medallions, crosses and pictures.

Prayer plays an extremely important part in Roman Catholic piety, and takes in some respects a form different from that which it bears in Evangelical Churches. A distinction is drawn between oral and mental prayer (*oratio oralis, mentalis*). The latter is silent prayer which has the character of contemplation or meditation. The recitation of the Old Testament Psalms is a customary form of prayer, especially in the Canonical Hours.

A further distinction is drawn between public and private prayer. Public prayer consists both of liturgical prayer said in church and the recitation of the Breviary by the priest. In these regular daily prayers, called the Offices because they are performed as of obligation (*ex officio*), the priest offers the sacrifice of praise (*sacrificium laudis*) on behalf of the whole Church.

Private prayer is often free and spontaneous prayer composed by the worshipper himself. Even during Mass itself prayer of this type is offered up by the congregation. A typical Roman Catholic practice, however, is the use of set or formulated prayers either out of books or from memory. Prayers of this type may be used on many different occasions such as morning or evening, at Mass or before or after Confession. In general, the use of books of prayers is more widespread in the Roman Catholic Church than in the Evangelical Churches. But the two prayers which every one knows by heart either in Latin or in the vernacular are the Lord's Prayer (*Paternoster*) and the Hail Mary (*Ave Maria*). The latter is a combination of the angelic greeting to the Virgin Mary and the salutation of Elisabeth (*St. Luke* i. 28 and 42) with a supplementary prayer of the sixteenth century, 'Hail Mary, full of grace, the Lord is with thee; blessed art thou among women, and blessed is the fruit of thy womb, Jesus. Holy Mary, Mother of God, pray for us sinners now and in the hour of our death, Amen' (*Ave Maria gratia plena, Dominus tecum; benedicta tu in mulieribus, et benedictus fructus ventris tui Jesus. Sancta Maria, Mater Dei, ora pro nobis peccatoribus nunc et in hora mortis nostrae, Amen).*

Kneeling is the customary attitude of prayer and acts of prayer normally open with the invocation 'In the name of the Father and of the Son and of the Holy Ghost.' The element of repetition plays an important part in the Roman Catholic practice of prayer. This may take one of two forms. A number of prayers may be offered in succession or the same prayer repeated a number of times. The second method has been systematized in the use of the rosary.

The rosary was first introduced by the Dominicans but has since spread to other religious orders and to the laity. For the latter its recitation is not of obligation, but it is encouraged by the Church authorities, and is connected particularly with indulgences. The rosary consists of a cord on which a number of small pearls or beads are threaded. It is normally divided into five decades, each composed of ten smaller or Madonna pearls followed by one larger or Paternoster pearl. To the rosary a cross is attached by a short link consisting of three Madonna pearls and one Paternoster pearl. For each Madonna pearl which passes through the hand the Ave Maria is recited, and for each Paternoster pearl, the Lord's Prayer. Its use is accompanied by meditation while the lips are moving and the pearls slide through the hand. At certain times of the year and on certain days of the week the faithful dwell upon the joyful mysteries (the Conception and Birth of our Lord), at other times on the painful mysteries (His Sufferings and Death), at other times again on the glorious mysteries (His Resurrection and Ascension).

The rosary is often recited publicly by the priest and the congregation in the vernacular, the priest reciting the first half of each prayer and the people responding with the second half said together. Individuals also use this form of devotion, as, for example, at the death-bed or by the graveside of their relatives, and even during Mass.

Good works (*opera bona*) can be described as a means of grace since they bring about an increase of grace and of actual righteousness (*augmentum gratiae, incrementum justitiae*). They confer merit on the performer and can even give additional glory in eternity. But in order to be deserving of merit, good works always pre-suppose grace. Although 'natural' good works (*opera naturaliter bona*) can also be done by the unjustified, they do not result in eternal life. On the other hand, the justified believer can achieve salvation through his good works with the help of God's grace. Thus eternal felicity is attained both through the Grace of God and as the reward of good works. In this way the Roman Catholic Church tries to reconcile the divergent statements of the Bible on the subject. The merits of good works are also held to be the merits of Christ working in the soul.

Under the heading of 'good works' are included deeds that are fully consistent with the commandments of God or of the Church. The former are the Ten Commandments (the Old Testament Decalogue) and the whole of Christian Ethics, while the latter consist of the numerous precepts of a ritual nature which are binding upon its members, such as the observance of the festivals of the Church throughout the Christian year, attendance at Mass on Sundays and all feast days, the obligation to go to Confession and to receive Communion at least once a year, the observance of the Lenten Fast and other stipulated fast-days and abstinence from meat on Fridays and other days of abstinence.

A distinction is drawn between fasting and abstinence. On fast-days only one full meal may be eaten daily. According to the *Codex Juris Canonici* meat must not be eaten on days of abstinence, but fish, eggs, milk, butter and cheese are permitted. Fast-days are the forty days of Lent from Ash Wednesday to Easter Eve (Sundays excepted), while every Friday is a day of abstinence. Certain days, especially the Ember Days (Wednesday, Friday and Saturday after the third Sunday in Advent, the first Sunday in Lent, after Whitsunday and the Exaltation of the Cross in the autumn) are days both of fasting and abstinence. All members of the Roman Catholic Church over the age of seven are bound to observe the rule of abstinence, but boys and girls up to the age of twenty-one and old people over sixty are exempted from fasting. Dispensation is also granted to those who lodge with others and who therefore cannot determine their own meals, those engaged in hard manual work and to others according to considerations of time, place and circumstance. In the Middle Ages fasting was a serious burden, but it is not now particularly onerous for the laity. It often leads to peculiar casuistry, but it is not altogether without value in disciplining the spiritual life.

The most important of the commandments is the Love of God and of neighbour. The supreme virtue is therefore love (*caritas*) followed by faith and hope. Since they are related to God and spring from His divine grace, they are called the three 'theological virtues.' To them are added the four 'cardinal virtues,' prudence, justice, temperance and fortitude.

According to Roman Catholic teaching it is possible to do more than merely to obey the commandments, whether of God or of the Church. There are also the evangelical counsels (*consilia evangelica*), through which perfection can be attained. These counsels are the obligations assumed in the monastic life, voluntary poverty, lifelong chastity, self-denial and obedience. But they represent merely an aid to, and not a necessary condition of perfection, and even those who live a normal life and who cannot follow these counsels are not excluded from the possibility of its attainment.

A good action is not merely a matter of keeping the commandments; its intention is also involved in the assessment of its character. In accordance with the intention which lies behind them really good deeds are sacrifices made to God. Thus St. Augustine can say 'Every deed performed with the intention of remaining in holy fellowship with God is a true sacrifice' (*Verum sacrificium est omne opus quod agitur ut sancta societate inhaereamus Deo*).

There are many duties in life which carry with them the opportunity to perform good works. Three in particular, prayer, fasting and almsgiving, are given prominence in the catechisms. Yet, however many good works are performed, they afford no justification for assurance of salvation. Such a conviction is excluded by the guilt which attaches to sin.

Thus Roman Catholicism takes into account the possibility of good works over and above the requirements of duty (*opera supererogatoria*). The saints are men and women who have done more than duty demands and who have therefore earned additional merit. Their *opera supererogationis* constitute a treasury of merit (*thesaurus meritorum*), the existence of which provides the theological basis for the practice of indulgences.

Indulgence (*indulgentia*) is remission of penance. The origin of the practice is to be found in the severity of the penances imposed upon the penitent in the early Church and in the Middle Ages. Since they were punishments inflicted by the Church, they could be modified or remitted for sufficient reason by the same authority as had imposed them. During the Middle Ages the principle became established that these severe penances could be compensated by the payment of fines. Punishments in purgatory were also regarded as being of a temporal and not an eternal character. The idea then grew up that these could be shortened by the Church, and the system of Indulgence was therefore extended even to souls in purgatory. Circumstances became ripe for the scandalous sale of letters of indulgence. This development was finally and completely abolished by the Council of Trent, but the system itself was retained on the ground that the practice was beneficial to Christian people and that Christ had invested the Church with authority to confer indulgences.

The indulgences recognized by post-Tridentine Roman Catholicism are acquired by devotional exercises. Their effect is still defined as the cancellation of punishment awarded by the Church and the sentence to be suffered in purgatory (*poena temporalis pro peccatis actualibus debita*). The regulations of the Church specify certain devotional exercises which carry with them a certain degree of indulgence. The penances imposed in contemporary Roman Catholicism are very light and are therefore not subject to indulgence. It can therefore only relate to punishments in purgatory, and the ground for this remission lies in the fact that the abundance of merit accruing to Christ and the saints is at the disposal of the Church for this purpose.

In many churches a so-called privileged altar may be found with a notice specifying how many days of indulgence can be earned by a given number of repetitions of the Lord's Prayer at the altar. As no penitential sentence is now normally imposed upon penitents here on earth, an indulgence of forty days means the shortening of the time spent in purgatory by a period corresponding to a similar remission of a penitential period on earth. But circumstances certainly tend to encourage the popular error that the prescribed number of prayers shortens the actual sentence in purgatory by a given number of days.

The system of indulgences is still so marked a feature of the Roman Catholic Church that there even exists at Rome a special congregation for its oversight.

8. WORSHIP

Roman Catholic worship makes its appeal to all five senses, especially to the visual sense, not only in pictures of our Lord and of the saints, in Church architecture, processions and liturgical ceremonies, but above all in the consecrated host itself, the Body of Christ, which is elevated for adoration. Communication is also made through the sense of hearing in the sacred words of the Liturgy, the reading of the Scriptures and the sermon as well as through music and singing.[1] But its appeal is also made through the sense of taste through the sacred meal received in communion, to the sense of smell through the burning of incense, and to that of touch through the sprinkling of holy water.

Symbolic actions and gestures abound. On entering and leaving the church, the worshipper sprinkles himself with holy water as a symbolic act of cleansing. In the ceremony known as the *Lavabo*, which takes place before the Offertory prayers in the Mass, the priest washes his hands over a small bowl in token that the one who is to handle the Body and Blood of Christ must himself be clean. During this action he repeats part of Psalm xxv (xxvi): 'I will wash my hands among the innocent; and compass thine altar, O Lord' (*lavabo inter innocentes manus meas; et circumdabo altare tuum, Domine*). This is a typical example of the use of Biblical quotations in the Liturgy as the accompaniment of symbolic action. The use of the censer is also symbolic. According to Revelation v. 8, the burning incense typifies the ascent to God of the prayers of the saints. But it is also regarded as a symbol of divine blessing, and therefore the congregation bow their heads as the censer is swung in their direction.

Two further examples of symbolic action may be given. The significance of the admixture of wine and water in the chalice is expressed in the accompanying prayer. The mystery of this water

---

[1] Church music in the Roman Catholic Church is mainly performed by the choir, and, apart from hymns, the congregation participates in it to a very limited extent.

and wine (*hujus aquae et vini mysterium*) represents the union of the two natures of our Lord. The kiss of peace with which the priests greet each other before the Communion bears its meaning on the surface. There is also an element of symbolism in the different liturgical colours of the vestments, white on the great festivals of our Lord, purple in Advent and Lent, red on festivals of the martyrs and black for Masses for the departed. In Roman Catholicism there is a close connection between the symbolic and the dramatic. In addition to the various symbolic actions performed during the service, the Mass itself is a drama in which the sacrifice of Christ is presented once more without the shedding of blood.

An outstanding part is played by dramatic incident in the ceremonies of Holy Week. On Maundy Thursday Christ's departure from His disciples is typically represented by carrying the host in procession from the tabernacle to one of the chapels of the church or to the sacristy. All altar frontals and other ornaments are removed, the candles extinguished and the stoops containing holy water emptied. Everything must indicate that Christ is no longer present. On the same day the feet of twelve old men seated in the chancel are washed by an abbot or bishop as a representation of the washing of the disciples' feet by our Lord on the last evening as recorded in the Gospel according to St. John. On Good Friday there takes place the Veneration of the Cross. A crucifix is uncovered; the priest elevates it with the words 'Behold the wood of the Cross on which hung the Salvation of the world' (*ecce lignum crucis in quo salus mundi pependit*). He lays it on a platform in the aisle and the people come forward one by one and kiss the crucifix. No less dramatic is the Easter Vigil. The Church is in absolute darkness. The service begins with the entry of a deacon carrying a three-pronged candle which has been lit outside the church door, and with the cry 'The Light of Christ' (*lumen Christi*) the Paschal or Great Candle is lit from this candle, typifying the Gospel of the Resurrection of Christ which sheds light upon the world.

Ritualism and liturgical uniformity are the typical features of Roman Catholic worship. Every word of the Mass, and the Liturgical Hours is prescribed and, in the case of the Mass, every gesture of the priest and each movement at the altar. The aim of

these precise instructions is to ensure that the liturgy is performed
with the maximum correctness and devotion.

All over the world the same divine service is celebrated in the
same language and the same form. All attempts to introduce a
complete celebration of the Mass in the vernacular have been
rejected. Outside the Uniate Churches, the utmost that has been
allowed is that the congregation should recite their part of the
service in the vernacular, while the priest reads his part of the
Mass in Latin. It has long been customary to read the Epistle and
Gospel in the vernacular. This is commonly done by a priest
other than the celebrant or a deacon, at the same time as the
Latin version is read silently by the celebrant at the altar. The
Creed is sometimes recited by the congregation in the vernacular,
but more frequently it is recited in Latin by priest and people
together, or sung in Latin, the sacred archaic language.

These factors give to Roman Catholic worship the character
of a mystery ritual. A contemporary Roman Catholic liturgi-
ologist, Dom Odo Casel, points out that the use of the Latin
language envelops the service in an atmosphere of timeless
eternity. The average churchgoer can usually recite the Lord's
Prayer and the Creed in Latin, but few understand the variable
parts of the Mass in the original language.

This uniformity of rite was not always the rule. At the beginning of the Middle Ages the Western Church had four different
types of liturgy, the Roman, the Ambrosian, the Gallican and
the Mozarabic. During the mediaeval period the Roman Canon
gradually ousted its rivals and became the liturgical norm for the
whole Western Church, while at the same time elements drawn
from other sources found their way into the general structure of
the Roman Mass. Yet each province of the Church had its own
special peculiarities in many details. The complete uniformity of
the liturgy which is strictly observed to-day was first introduced
by the Council of Trent, which laid down that its standard form
should be that of the *Missale Romanum*, except in cases where a
tradition of at least a century could be established. This applied,
for instance, to the archbishopric of Milan and to certain monastic
orders such as the Dominicans, which still retain their own
liturgies. In their present form, however, they do not differ
radically from the Roman rite.

The chief points of difference between the Roman Catholic Mass and the Eastern Orthodox Liturgy are the following. The language used in the Mass is Latin and not a form of the vernacular. The consecration of the elements is effected by the Words of Institution and not by the Epiclesis and the Mass includes a greater number of variable elements than the Liturgy.

The Roman Mass is the product of a very complex history. As it is celebrated to-day it contains elements that are primitive as well as others which have accumulated in the course of its long history—Roman prayers, simple, pregnant and precise; Oriental supplications and hymns like the *Kyrie* and the *Gloria in excelsis*; Gallican prayers, prolix, vague and figurative. The main structure of the Mass never varies. But there are propers which change according to the Sunday, the feast or the fast, such as the Introit, Collect, Epistle, Gradual with Alleluia or Tract (and on five occasions Sequence), Gospel, Offertory and Secret or *Oratio super oblata*, Preface, Communion and Post-Communion.

The Mass opens with the Introit, originally a psalm sung while the ministers of the altar and their procession advanced from the sacristy near the west door of the *basilica*. It consists of a few verses of a psalm or some other text from the Old Testament selected to reveal at once the special character or theme for the day. Thus on the first Sunday in Advent the Introit is taken from Psalm xxiv (xxv): 'To Thee have I lifted up my soul' (*Ad te levavi animam meam*), while on Christmas Day it is drawn from Psalm ii: 'The Lord said to me; Thou art My Son, this day have I begotten thee' (*Dominus dixit ad me; Filius meus es tu, ego hodie genui te*). On Easter Day the Risen Lord Himself speaks in the words of Psalm cxxxviii (cxxxix): 'I arose, and am still with Thee, alleluia; Thou hast laid Thy hand upon me, alleluia; Thy knowledge is become wonderful, alleluia, alleluia' (*Resurrexi, et adhuc tecum sum, alleluia; posuisti super me manum tuam, alleluia; mirabilis facta est scientia tua, alleluia, alleluia*). The Introit is now sung by the choir, while on the steps leading up to the altar the priest quietly recites the preparatory prayers which include a confession of sins.

After the confession of the priest there follows the Ninefold *Kyrie* sung by the choir, and the *Gloria in excelsis* (Glory be to God on high) intoned by the priest and continued by the choir.

The Collect, Epistle and Gospel are variable elements, together
with the Gradual, a short text of Scripture sung by the choir
between the Epistle and Gospel. The *Credo* (the Nicene Creed)
is often sung antiphonally between the choir and the congregation. This concludes the opening part of the service (*missa
catechumenorum*) which passes directly into the Mass of the
faithful (*missa fidelium*). This is introduced by the Offertory,
again a few verses of the Bible sung by the choir, while the priest
prepares the elements and reads a number of offertory prayers
ending with the silent repetition of one of the Secrets, a prayer
of similar intention. The *Sursum corda*, an ancient dialogue
between priest and people, introduces the Preface, a further
variable element of which there are thirteen forms for different
seasons and occasions in the Church's Year. The preface opens
with the common formula: 'It is truly meet and just, right and
availing unto salvation, that at all times and in all places, we give
praise to Thee, O holy Lord, Father Almighty, Everlasting God'
(*Vere dignum et justum est, aequum et salutare, nos tibi semper et
ubique gratias agere, Domine sancte, Pater omnipotens, aeterne Deus*).
At this point is inserted the Proper Preface containing the special
theme appropriate to the season or the day. The Preface then
concludes with the *Sanctus* (Holy, Holy, Holy, Lord God of
Hosts) sung by the choir, in which the Church on earth joins in
the praises of the heavenly host, and the salutation 'Blessed be
He that cometh in the Name of the Lord' (*Benedictus qui venit in
nomine Domini*), here applied to our Lord's sacramental coming
in the Mass.

The Canon proper calls for somewhat closer examination. It
opens with the *Te igitur*, a prayer of oblation for the whole
Church with the following petition *Memento Domine* serving as a
kind of private parenthesis in which are inserted the names of
those for whom the Mass is particularly being offered. With the
Communicantes the Canon proceeds to the commemoration of the
saints, with particular mention of the Virgin Mary, the apostles
and the early Popes. The next paragraph *Hanc igitur oblationem*
virtually recapitulates what has gone before and the *Quam
oblationem* asks God to consecrate the Christian sacrifice. This is
followed by the *Qui pridie*, a recitation with the appropriate

manual acts of the Words of Institution in a low voice by the celebrant, which, according to Roman Catholic teaching, marks the moment of consecration at which the Bread and Wine become the Body and Blood of our Lord. Grammatically this takes the form of a narrative contained in a relative clause. With the *Unde et memores*, recalling the Passion, Resurrection and Ascension of our Lord, the act of offering is finally reached as the celebrant utters the words 'We offer to thy excellent majesty, of thine own gifts bestowed upon us, a pure victim, a holy victim, a spotless victim, the holy Bread of eternal life and the Chalice of everlasting salvation' (*Offerimus praeclarae maiestati tuae de tuis donis et datis hostiam puram, hostiam sanctam, hostiam immaculatam, Panem sanctum vitae aeternae et Calicem salutis perpetuae*). Together with the consecration this forms the heart of the Canon. The remaining clauses plead that the earthly sacrifice may be received and accepted in heaven. After the elevation of the Host, there follow the *Pater noster* (the Lord's Prayer), the *Pax* (the peace of the Lord be always with you) and the *Agnus Dei* (the Lamb of God). The celebrant, and sometimes the people, then make their communion. The Mass ends with a short section including the Dismissal (*Ite, missa est*), the Benediction and the Last Gospel (*St. John* i. 1-14). Ceremonies such as the censing of objects or persons, the *Lavabo* and the kiss of peace make the celebration of the Mass a somewhat complicated procedure.

The Mass is the predominant form of divine service in the Roman Catholic Church. It is celebrated daily at innumerable altars and is the form of service with which the faithful are most familiar. On Sundays they must attend Mass and may also be present at Low Mass on a weekday morning. A Roman Catholic is confirmed at a celebration of the Mass, his marriage is blessed through a Nuptial Mass for the bride and bridegroom, while at his funeral a Mass attended by his next of kin is held for the repose of his soul.

On all these occasions the same Mass is said with the communion of the priest and the same sacrificial character. To this extent Roman Catholic worship is monotonous, but the Mass itself together with its variable elements also has considerable variation of procedure, and even to some extent of structure. Thus a Mass in which the people make their communion has a different devotional emphasis from one in which the priest alone communicates. In Lent the *Gloria in excelsis* is omitted and both the *Gloria* and the Creed at a Requiem Mass for the dead, which takes its name from the Introit: 'Rest eternal grant unto them' (*Requiem aeternam dona eis*). Again a Mass may be celebrated in different ways with varying degrees of ceremonial. The simplest form is Low Mass which the priest reads in a whisper (*missa privata, missa secreta*). A more ceremonial form is the Sung Mass (*missa cantata*) performed by a priest assisted by the choir, while more elaborate still is High Mass or Solemn Mass (*missa solemnis*), at which the celebrant is assisted by a deacon and sub-deacon and choir. Even greater ceremonial attends a Mass celebrated by a bishop, which is called *missa pontificalis*.

The sermon is not a necessary part of the Mass, but, when it occurs, it is placed after the Creed. Otherwise, particularly in Lent, it is held over until the evening service. In parish churches a sermon is frequently preached at High Mass. Sermons in the Roman Catholic Church are usually of a more instructional character than in the Evangelical Churches.

The structure of the Church's Year is complex and elaborate. In addition to the festivals in honour of our Lord which have been retained by the Evangelical Churches (Christmas, Epiphany, Easter, Ascension Day and Whitsunday), the Roman Catholic Church also observes Corpus Christi (the Thursday after Trinity Sunday), the Transfiguration (August 6th) and several other feasts in His honour. The last to be introduced (in 1925) was the Feast of Christ the King which is observed on the last Sunday in October. The two festivals of the Cross, the Invention of the Cross in the spring (May 3rd) and the Exaltation of the Cross in the autumn (September 14th) are ancient in origin.

There are many festivals in honour of the Virgin Mary. Besides the Annunciation commemorating the message of the angel Gabriel (March 25th) may be mentioned her Conception (December 8th), her Nativity (September 8th) and her Assumption into Heaven (August 15th). St. Michael and All Angels are commemorated on September 29th, St. John the Baptist on June 24th and All Saints on November 1st. There is hardly a day in the course of the year to which the commemoration of some saint is not attached.

Saints' days and many other festivals fall on definite days of the calendar year, whereas, of course, Sunday can fall upon any calendar day, and the dates of a number of major festivals depend upon the determination of the date of Easter in any given year. As the great festivals have their Octaves (a second commemoration a week after the festival itself), and some their vigils (a celebration on the previous day such as Christmas and Easter Eve), several feast-days can coincide. In such cases the priest must know which festival takes precedence or how the two festivals can be combined. These situations are governed by fixed rules, the main principle being that festivals in honour of our Lord have precedence over all others. Few festivals are public holidays, or days of obligation for the laity upon which they are bound to attend church.

A form of service with which the laity have little concern, but which takes up no inconsiderable amount of the time of the clergy are the canonical hours. They first came into prominence in the monasteries and the custom later spread to the secular clergy. The Council of Trent laid it down as the duty of all clergy from the order of sub-deacon upwards to read the hours according to the Breviarium Romanum. They are not necessarily to be read at definite times during the day, but the whole of the Divine Office (*divinum officium*) must be completed during its course. The reading of the Breviary takes up more than one hour a day.

The canonical hours are a non-sacramental form of divine service with a common structure. In obedience to Psalm cxix. 164, the monks assemble seven times a day in the monastery chapel at given hours of the day and night to perform the divine office. The seven canonical hours are called Matins (with Lauds), Prime, Terce, Sext, Nones, Evensong and Compline. At each of the canonical hours a set number of Psalms are read or sung antiphonally. The service also includes Versicles and Responses, a short confession of sins followed by a formula of Absolution, the Lord's Prayer and a number of prayers of the Collect type. The Apostles' Creed is also used in some hours together with fixed hymns and readings taken mostly from Scripture but at Matins also from the Homilies of the Fathers and even the legends of saints.

The ceremonial as distinct from the private recitation of offices is confined to monastery chapels, cathedrals and collegiate churches with a large staff of priests. Benedictine monasteries are famous for the dignified and beautiful rendering of the offices, which may take up as much as three or four hours of the entire day. The Dominicans have shorter hours and normally do no more than recite them. Even less time is spent on the offices by the Jesuit Order, whose members do not recite them in choir at all.

9. Purgatory and the Saints

The Roman Catholic doctrine of the future destiny of man is based upon a systematization of various biblical concepts which can only be reconciled with some difficulty. Certain passages in the Bible give the impression that immediately after death man enters either into eternal bliss or eternal punishment, while others equally clearly imply that the final judgement does not take place until the end of time. These two ideas are harmonized in the doctrine of the dual judgement.

Immediately after death every man is subjected to a particular judgement (*judicium particulare*) which determines whether he is to be granted eternal life or condemnation. The damned go at once to Hell which, in Roman Catholic doctrine, consists in separation from God, the loss of the vision of God and condemnation to eternal fire. The question whether this fire is spiritual or apprehensible through the senses is a controverted issue in theological circles. The ordinary layman has a vivid picture of Hell and a materialistic conception of the punishment to be suffered there. The saints are believed to go direct to Heaven, as well as baptized infants who die without having committed any actual sins. But the majority of the souls who will finally attain to eternal life go in the first instance to Purgatory before they can achieve beatitude.

At the end of the world a general judgement (*judicium generale*) will take place when the bodies of the dead are raised up and united to their souls. Both the agony of the damned and the bliss of the saved will thereby be increased.

Biblical support for the doctrine of Purgatory is found in St. Matthew v. 26 and xii. 32, and in 1 Corinthians iii. 12–15. The concept appears as early as Tertullian and Origen, but it is not fully developed until the writings of St. Gregory the Great. In the Middle Ages it came into considerable prominence in connection with indulgences. The short decree of the Council of Trent on the subject merely states that the beneficial doctrine of Purgatory should be followed and propagated, but that in popular teaching the subtle and difficult questions associated with it which do not serve the purpose of edification should be avoided.

The souls in Purgatory will finally attain eternal bliss, but need further cleansing and must therefore first pass through the fire. They cannot themselves gain further merit, but they can be helped by the Church on earth through intercessory prayer, indulgences and the sacrifice of the Mass. The saints in Heaven do not need human intercession, and it is of no avail to pray for those in Hell. Between Heaven and Hell there is, however, this region containing thousands of souls who derive benefit from our prayers. They are allotted a special day in the Church's calendar, All Souls' Day (November 2nd), and are often remembered in private prayer and at Mass. The Canon contains a commemoration of 'those who have gone before us with the sign of faith and sleep in the sleep of peace' (*qui nos praecesserunt cum signo fidei et dormiunt in somno pacis*). In the canonical hours and often in grace before meals the petition 'May the souls of the faithful through the mercy of God rest in peace' (*Fidelium animae per misericordiam Dei requiescant in pace*) is offered for the departed. The great gulf between the living and the dead is bridged by the prayers of the Church both in intercession for the souls in Purgatory and in the invocation of the saints in Heaven. According to Roman Catholic teaching prayer cannot be addressed to the saints. They can only be invoked and their intercession requested. The classic example of the invocation of saints is the Litany of All Saints in which a long list of saints is mentioned and the petition 'Pray for us' (*Ora pro nobis*) added to each name. While liturgical prayer goes no further, in popular worship prayers, usually in the form of short aspirations, are often addressed to the saints. A well-known example is Luther's prayer, 'Help, St. Anne, I promise to become a monk.'

The official veneration of saints consists primarily in the celebration of Mass on their festivals. It is then described as being 'in honour of the saints and in their memory' (*in honorem et memoriam sanctorum*). In such a mass the sacrifice is not offered to the particular saint commemorated, but to God alone to Whom thanks is given for the victories of the saints. A supplementary canon to the decree of the Council of Trent states, however, that one purpose of such a Mass is to obtain the intercession of the saint before the throne of God.

Popular worship goes much further. It includes not only prayers addressed to the saints, but also offerings made to them in the form of candles placed before their images. Thus an element of polytheism, offensive alike to Protestant observers and to enlightened Roman Catholics has invaded Roman Catholicism. The saints have become divine helpers or *Sondergötter* (to use the term employed by the historian of religion, H. Usener). Each class or profession has its own patron saint: St. Joseph for carpenters, St. Luke for painters, St. Crispin for shoemakers and St. Aloysius for students. St. Florian helps to give protection against fire, while to St. Augustine is entrusted the curious task of curing warts. At the close of the Middle Ages the most popular saint was St. Anne. More recently St. Joseph, and next to him St. Anthony of Padua have become the favourite objects of popular veneration, though of late years the Apostle Thaddaeus has tended to outstrip the latter in popular favour.

From the point of view of a historian of religion it is a significant fact that some of the most prominent saints can be split up, as it were, into a multiplicity of local saints. If help is not offered by the Virgin of Einsiedeln, recourse may be had to the Virgin of Lourdes. Even a man of the calibre of Benedict XV (Pope, 1914–22) asked on his death-bed that the Madonna of Pompeii should be invoked on his behalf.

The veneration of the saints goes back far into Christian history. It first attached itself to the memory of the martyrs. Many features can be traced as early as the record of the martyrdom of St. Polycarp in 155. Here the martyrs are said to be examples and models for those who fight the good fight of faith. Their commemoration is a source of joy and thanksgiving to the

Church which will always celebrate the anniversary of their martyrdom. Their earthly remains should be the object of affection. But if the martyrs receive homage and are examples for our imitation, it is Christ alone who is to be worshipped and adored.

In the course of time a further feature was added, the idea of a fellowship in prayer between the saints in Heaven and the Church on earth. While in the East the Church upon earth both prays for the saints and invokes their intercession, the Western Church does not recognize prayers for the saints, but only their petitions on its behalf.

The Roman Catholic Church, then, believes that the saints rule with Christ and offer their intercessions for mankind, and regards their invocation as a good and beneficent religious practice.

There are a great number of saints. In the sixteenth century official figures reckoned over 10,000, of whom the great majority had not received official canonization, but were accounted saints by popular acclaim. Many were purely legendary figures who had no place in history. The first official canonization, or election of a saint by the Pope, took place in 993. The rule that no one should be venerated as a saint without Papal recognition was not laid down until 1170.

The present process of canonization takes the form of two regular hearings on juridical lines with a prosecutor (*advocatus diaboli*) and a defending counsel (*advocatus Dei*), whose duty it is to present the arguments for and against canonization. The decisive criteria are a holy life on earth, and the performance of three miracles either during his lifetime or at his tomb or through his intercession. The first stage is called Beatification, and those whose claims are accepted receive the title Blessed (*beatus*), the second leads to full canonization and carries with it the title of Saint (*sanctus*). Many only achieve the lower status.

Between 1500 and 1903 one hundred and thirteen canonizations and five hundred and forty-seven beatifications are recorded. One of the recent canonizations was that of Joan of Arc (1412–1431), which took place in 1920. Many from all parts of the world (including China and Japan) have attained this status.

10. RELIGIOUS ORDERS AND CONGREGATIONS

The Roman Catholic Church is not content merely to satisfy the spiritual needs of the ordinary believer by instructing him and leading him in the paths of eternal life. It also makes provision in the monastic life for those whose aim is the highest possible fulfilment of their duty towards God.

Monastic life affords the opportunity for the complete realization of the Roman Catholic ideal of piety. By reason of its continual round of worship and its freedom from earthly ties and duties it has been described as the angelic life (*vita angelica*), a reflexion of life in Heaven itself. It is also called the religious life (*vita religiosa*), and the words *religiosus* and *religiosa* in ecclesiastical Latin, like their modern French equivalents, simply mean monk and nun.

The distinction between perfect and imperfect Christians goes far back into history. While for Clement of Alexandria the difference between the ordinary churchgoing Christian and the spiritual élite lay in the degree of comprehension, in later times the accent fell upon the ascetic rather than on the intellectual plane. The Christian élite was now composed of monks who had renounced their family and possessions. The ideal came to be a negative one, the renunciation of all earthly things. With St. Benedict of Nursia (*c.* 480–550) it received positive expression in the concept of the 'service of Christ' (*militia Christi*). The monks are the soldiers of Christ who devote all their time and strength to the good fight of faith. The goal of monasticism both in East and West is also prescribed as the love of God and of neighbour.

In Roman Catholic teaching the monastic life is not itself identical with Christian perfection, but is a means of attaining perfection. It is not certain that the means will lead to the end, and the goal can also be achieved without it by those who still live in the world. The monastic life is a special vocation for the few and not an obligation for the many. In order to qualify for the monastic life it is necessary not only to have a special calling (*vocatio*), but also to show conclusive proof that it is present before final vows are taken.

Unlike the Eastern Churches the Roman Catholic Church has abandoned the ideal of the recluse (the eremitic or hermit life) in favour of a regulated ascetic life in community (the coenobitic life) in monasteries and other religious houses. Thus monasticism is intended to serve the Church and not merely to be the means whereby an ascetic can attain perfection for himself. Particularly in modern Roman Catholicism, the monastic life is connected with the conception of the Church as a living organism in which the duty of praying for the whole Church is specially laid upon the monks. The monastic life carries with it vows of lifelong poverty, celibacy and obedience to superiors (*paupertas, castitas, obedientia*).

The ideal of poverty has its roots in the New Testament and texts like St. Mark x. 21-30 have always played a great part in monastic revivals. The origins of the idea of virginity are, however, more complex. In addition to the teaching of 1 Corinthians vii. 32-40, the tendency of the later patristic period and the Middle Ages to regard Matrimony as a lower type of life has been a patent factor in the evolution of this ideal.

Monastic life consists of prayer and work. There is a harmonious alternation between the *vita contemplativa* and the *vita activa* which is worked out in different ways in the various orders and congregations. The groundwork of Western Monasticism was laid by the Benedictine Order at the opening of the mediaeval period. At a later period, congregations were formed within this Order which developed into independent branches. The mendicant orders, dating from the thirteenth century, were a new departure which broke fresh ground. Typical of modern Roman Catholicism are the Jesuit Order and a number of congregations founded in the sixteenth and seventeenth centuries.

During the past few generations the membership of the religious order has shown a remarkable increase. In the period between 1860 and 1935 the total number of Roman Catholics in Germany rose from sixteen to twenty-four million, while the membership of religious orders increased from 10,000 to 100,000 during the same period. Some of the older orders, however, such as the mediaeval military orders, the Knights Templar and the Hospitallers, have died out.

The religious orders of the Roman Catholic Church can be divided into the following classes:

1. *Regular canons* ('canonici regulares') have little contemporary

E

significance. To this type belong the Augustinian Canons, the Praemonstratensians and some other communities.

This class follows the rule attributed (perhaps rightly) to St. Augustine. It was in any case compiled shortly after his time but was little used until the eleventh century when the movement took firm hold. At this period the priests of the collegiate churches renounced their private possessions and lived a communal life on Augustinian lines. Most of the collegiate churches disappeared during the Reformation and the French Revolution as a result of the secularization of church property. In 1949 the Praemonstratensian Order numbered about 1500. The monks of St. Bernard (now a community of eighty-six members), who have cared for travellers in the Alps since the tenth century, are regular canons.

2. *Regular clergy* ('clerici regulares') are communities consisting entirely or primarily of priests engaged in pastoral work.

The first order of this type, the Theatine, established in Rome in 1524, is now almost completely extinct.

The most important clerical order is *the Jesuit Order*, or Society of Jesus (abbreviation S.J.), established by St. Ignatius Loyola (1491–1556) and approved by the Pope in 1540. The order expanded rapidly in the sixteenth century and played a prominent part at the Council of Trent. Its missionaries were sent to India, China, Japan, South America and later to Canada. After a period of intensive work in the schools and the exercise of strong political and ecclesiastical pressure, it witnessed a considerable decline in prestige in the seventeenth century, was banished from several countries and even dissolved by the Pope in 1773. After its re-establishment in 1814 it again spread rapidly and by 1950 it had some 30,000 members, half of whom were priests, and is now the second largest religious order.

The Society of Jesus is distinguished from the older monastic orders in several ways. Its members are not bound by any rule of enclosure (*stabilitas loci*) and are not obliged to recite the canonical hours in choir. They wear no distinguishing monastic habit and their life is so organized as to permit the fullest measure of active service for the Church in the world.

Particular emphasis is laid upon obedience to superiors. This is called 'cadaveric obedience' after a phrase in their constitution in which it is laid down that a Jesuit shall be as obedient as a corpse (*perinde ac si cadaver esset*). The members of this order are selected with the greatest care and receive a long training in preparation for special tasks according to their particular capabilities. They are divided into four classes: (*a*) Novices. The novitiate lasts for two years after which they take simple vows (*vota simplicia*). Those who are destined for the priesthood then become (*b*) *scholastici* or students. This period lasts between eight and fifteen years and is chiefly devoted to study. Two years are devoted to the study of literature and the classical languages, and three to philosophy. After a period of between three and five years spent in teaching in a school, they study theology for upwards of five years and are admitted to the priesthood at the conclusion of their course. They are then raised to the rank of (*c*) clerical coadjutors, and later have the opportunity of promotion to the grade of (*d*) the *professi quattuor votorum*. In addition to the three normal monastic vows, they take a fourth vow of special obedience to the Pope.

The Jesuits have made a great contribution both to missionary work and to scholarship, not only in philosophy and theology, but also in natural science. In church politics they are ultramontane and contributed largely to the victory of these principles in the nineteenth century.

3. *The monastic orders* ('ordines monastici') in the strict sense of the term are the older type of order, dating from the first half of the Middle Ages. They all possess a more or less strict enclosure (*stabilitas loci*). Their work consists primarily of ascetic exercises, an ordered devotional life as well as of manual work and study. In exact usage the term 'monk' (*monachus*) should be confined to members of these orders.

The most important orders of this type are the Benedictines, the Cistercians and the Carthusians.

The Benedictine Order ('Ordo Sancti Benedicti,' O.S.B.) was established by St. Benedict of Nursia at his monastery of Monte Cassino in 529. During the Middle Ages the order was active in missionary work and the dissemination of culture. About the year 1400 it comprised 15,000 monasteries, but the number was substantially reduced as a result of the Reformation, the French Revolution and its aftermath in the Napoleonic era. In 1815 the order had dwindled to about 400 members residing in thirty monasteries. During the nineteenth and twentieth centuries a renaissance has taken place and in 1957 it had a membership of just over 12,000 in more than two hundred monasteries.

The distinguishing feature of the Benedictine Order is its concentration upon worship. Nowhere is the liturgy celebrated with greater beauty and dignity than in its chapels. The monastery of Solesmes in France is an important centre for church music. The order has also produced many scholars. The French Benedictines of the seventeenth century (the congregation of St. Maur) made a notable contribution to the study of the early Church.

There is a female order under the Benedictine rule with a present membership of about 20,000.

Among other monastic orders in this strict sense of the term is *the Trappist Order*, notable for its extreme asceticism. This is a modern offshoot of the Cistercian Order, and was founded in 1644 when a particularly severe asceticism was introduced in the monastery of La Trappe. It now has sixty monasteries with about 4,000 monks.

The Trappists are pledged to lifelong silence. The monks pray and work, eat and sleep together, but are forbidden to talk to one another. They may only speak to their superiors, and then only by special permission. Where necessary they communicate with each other by means of sign language. The whole community, both priests and lay brothers, do four hours of manual labour each day. Their day begins at 2 a.m. Seven hours are spent in church, seven in sleep and five in study. Trappists are not allowed to eat meat or fish, and can only eat eggs in cases of illness. Milk, butter, oil and cheese are permitted except on days of strict fasting. Every Friday they carry out self-flagellation. The Order makes an appeal to those who feel a strong desire to do penance. The nuns of the Trappist Order number about 1,500.

4. *The Mendicant Orders*, of which the most important are the Franciscans and the Dominicans, date from the thirteenth century. They combine the ideals of poverty and activity in the world, and therefore have no enclosure or *stabilitas loci*.

The Franciscan Order ('Ordo Fratrum Minorum,' O.F.M.) was founded by St. Francis of Assisi (1181–1226) and approved by the Pope in 1223. It has three branches comprising altogether about 44,000 members, the Franciscan Observants or strict Franciscans (brown habit, white rope girdle, bare-legged except for sandals, and beardless), the Capuchins (brown habit with pointed cowl, bearded) and Franciscan Conventuals.

The Franciscans undertake work among the people, and occupy within the Roman Catholic Church a position somewhat similar to that of the Salvation Army among Protestants. The Franciscans and Capuchins are popular preachers and are usually on good terms with the man in the street. The Order has made a great contribution to missionary work and has numbered among its members the eminent theologians, St. Bonaventura (1221–74) and Duns Scotus (d. 1308).

There is also a Franciscan Order of nuns, the Clarisses or Poor Clares (named after St. Clare), numbering to-day about 13,000.

Also included in the Franciscan family are the Tertiaries, or the 'Third Order,' of which mention is first made in 1221. This is composed of men and women who lead a life according to a definite rule of private prayer and public worship, without relinquishing their home ties or secular calling. They recite the Lord's Prayer and the Hail Mary twelve times daily and receive the Blessed Sacrament monthly. To-day the Third Order has three million members.

The Dominican Order ('Ordo Praedicatorum,' O.P.) was founded by St. Dominic (1170–1221) and approved by the Pope in 1216. Its special tasks are preaching, study and the war against heresy. At present it has some 8,000 members. The habit of the order is of white wool with a black cape. It is a clerical order consisting chiefly of priests with the minimum number of lay brothers necessary for the internal economy of the monastery. According to its motto, 'to pass on what has been contemplated to others' (*contemplata aliis tradere*), the Order has the double purpose of contemplation and service for others. It has always pursued scholarship and has produced many outstanding theologians, above all, St. Thomas Aquinas.

The Dominicans also possess an order of nuns with strict

observance numbering about 6,000 and other female congregations comprising 40,000 sisters. Like the Franciscans, they have also established a 'Third Order.'

5. *The Congregations* are a characteristic adaptation of Monasticism to modern conditions. A large number of congregations have been founded since 1500, but the Jesuit Order is the only religious order in the strict sense to be recognized in post-Reformation times. Even since 1800, five hundred new congregations (four hundred of women) are said to have been established. To a greater degree than the orders, the congregations are organized for work among the people and the principle of enclosure plays a corresponding smaller part.

The distinction made in canon law between orders and congregations is a technical matter concerning vows. The members of an order make solemn vows (*vota solemnia*) from which no dispensation is possible, while the members of a congregation take 'simple vows' (*vota simplicia*) from which dispensation may be obtained.

Among the male congregations may be mentioned the *Redemptorists*, established chiefly for home missions by St. Alphonsus Liguori in the eighteenth century, who now number about 7,700. On the other hand, the *Lazarists*, founded by St. Vincent de Paul (1580–1660) in 1625, and now comprising some 5,500 members, devote themselves chiefly to missionary work among the heathen. *The Christian Brothers* ('Frères des écoles chrétiennes'), established at Rheims in 1681 and now numbering 15,000, concern themselves with education.

The female congregations have particularly large memberships. The most important are the *Sisters of Charity*, also founded by St. Vincent de Paul in 1633. They devote themselves to nursing without distinction of class or creed. The dress of the order is grey with a white cowl and large wings. Their present membership is about 45,000. The *English Ladies*, founded by Mary Ward (1585–1645) in 1609, run schools for girls and model themselves on the lines of the Jesuit Order.

The value of the Orders for the Roman Catholic Church can hardly be set too high. They offer a wide range of opportunity for Christian service to men and women who feel the urge to devote themselves entirely to the religious vocation. The

Franciscan and Dominican Third Orders provide valuable contacts with the monastic way of life to those who lead normal working lives. The ideals of the religious orders have also left their mark on the Roman Catholic Church as a whole. The celibacy of the clergy and the reading of the Breviary are direct consequences of the monastic movement.

11. RECENT DEVELOPMENTS

The type of Roman Catholicism so far described in this chapter is that which has been prevalent in most countries during the nineteenth and twentieth centuries, and only brief and incidental reference has been made to features like Modernism and the Liturgical Movement. Most of what has been said needs no modification in the light of recent developments, since it has been concerned with the doctrinal and liturgical basis of the Roman Catholic Church, but in order to complete the picture, some information must be added on recent developments and on the conflicting tendencies within Roman Catholicism at the present time.

(i) In the course of the nineteenth century, the Roman Catholic Church regained much of the spiritual strength, cultural influence and even, to some extent, the political power which it had enjoyed in previous centuries, but which it had lost during the age of the Enlightenment and the French Revolution. When Pius VI died in captivity in 1799, a Protestant observer like Schleiermacher believed that no new pope was likely to be elected and that the Papacy would come to an end; to-day no one would contemplate such a possibility.

The growth of the Roman Catholic Church in strength and influence has continued during the present century. Advances in the mission field and a notable conversion movement in Protestant countries, together with a growing prestige in intellectual and literary circles, have largely offset the losses due to persecution in Mexico and China and the difficult relations with Russia and the states under her influence. The conflict in which this Church has been engaged with the totalitarian régimes has given it a moral authority in the modern world without parallel in the nineteenth century. To its own members and to many outside its communion, Roman Catholicism appears as the strongest spiritual force ranged against the totalitarian political systems and the pagan ideologies of our time.

It is unthinkable that the political power which the Papacy possessed in the Middle Ages or the seventeenth century could ever be restored. In 1870 the Papal State disappeared, and has been replaced by the Vatican City, recognized as an independent state by Italy under the Lateran Agreement as late as 1929. But it is of more than symbolical significance that a number of countries in Europe (such as Great Britain in 1914 and France in 1921) and in other parts of the world have established diplomatic relations with the Apostolic See during the present century. At present (1957) forty-seven countries (including some in which a very small percentage of the population is Roman Catholic) have their embassies or legations at the Vatican. But owing to the strong anti-Roman Catholic feeling in the country, the United States of America have held aloof.

During the pontificate of Pius XI (Pope, 1922–39) important concordats were established with Mussolini's Italy in 1929 and Hitler's Germany in 1933. In Italy the Pope obtained recognition from the State of ecclesiastical marriage as legally valid, clerical exemption from military service, and the introduction of religious teaching supervised by the Church in all State schools. The main points of the German concordat were recognition of the right of the Church to appoint to all clerical offices without interference from the State, guarantees concerning religious instruction of a confessional character for Roman Catholic children in State schools, and certain rights for Roman Catholic youth organizations. In both countries disputes arose over the interpretation of these agreements, chiefly on educational questions. In Germany the concordat was not kept by the State at all points, but it secured for the Roman Catholic Church in the Third Reich a very different position from that accorded to the Evangelical Churches. Both concordats are still in force.

These two concordats with totalitarian powers, together with the notoriously close connection of the Church with the Franco régime in Spain from 1939 onwards, might convey the impression that the Roman Catholic Church has favoured and made possible these dictatorships in the modern world. So far as Spain is concerned this impression is certainly correct, but the Italian and German concordats did not take place at the rise to power of the Fascist and National Socialist movements, but were rather attempts to establish a *modus vivendi* after periods of tension. In fact the Pope actually condemned the National Socialist régime in clear terms in his encyclical *Mit brennender Sorge* (1937) after it had displayed its anti-Christian character on several occasions.

The only political system which has been explicitly condemned as such in our time by the Holy See is Communism, in the encyclical *Divini Redemptoris* of 1937, on account of its hostility to Christianity and its violation of natural law. With the other political systems the Roman Catholic Church has always sought a *modus vivendi*, while wisely avoiding in most countries alliances with particular political parties.

(ii) This Church now enjoys much greater sympathy in non-Roman Catholic countries than was the case half a century ago when it appeared to most Protestant observers as the representative of obscurantism and of obsolete political claims inherited from the Middle Ages. It is significant that the vigorous anticlericalism in France dating from the end of the nineteenth century has almost disappeared from the scene. In many Protestant quarters to-day there is even a tendency to belittle the cultural and religious achievements of the Protestant tradition in favour of Roman Catholicism. The spirit of the age has changed considerably to the advantage of the Roman Catholic Church.

This change is due in no small measure to important Roman Catholic contributions to the intellectual and literary life of our time. In modern philosophy Neo-Thomism is one of the really potent schools with a considerable influence even outside Roman Catholic circles. In literature the names of Paul Claudel (1868–1955), François Mauriac (b. 1885), Sigrid Undset (1882–1949) and Graham Greene (b. 1904) may be mentioned.

Neo-Thomism originated in the middle of the nineteenth century as a philosophical and theological renaissance of mediaeval scholasticism within the Roman Catholic Church. Leo XIII gave it his blessing in his encyclical *Aeterni Patris* of 1879, in which he declared St. Thomas Aquinas to be the supreme authority in philosophy and theology. From that date Thomism

has been taught with a new zeal in seminaries and in both the
philosophical and theological faculties of Roman Catholic
universities.

There are two tendencies within Neo-Thomism which cannot
always be readily reconciled with each other. On the one hand,
this school is concerned with historical studies in mediaeval
scholasticism which is thought to be of real relevance to our
time. It is claimed that the tenets of St. Thomas Aquinas himself
provide the solution of our modern problems. Two outstanding
scholars who have studied mediaeval philosophy and theology
in this spirit are Martin Grabmann (1875–1949) and Étienne
Gilson (b. 1884). But there is also another aspect of Neo-
Thomism which attempts to meet modern problems in the
spirit of St. Thomas with an openness of mind which acknowledges the rights of reason and accepts the spirit and results of
modern science, while at the same time endeavouring to maintain
objective truths in this modern world of relativism and scepticism,
and aiming at a great synthesis comparable to that achieved by
St. Thomas in the thirteenth century. This tendency is best
exemplified by Baron Friedrich von Hügel (1852–1925) and
Jacques Maritain (b. 1882). There is, of course, a tension between
this tendency and the restoration of the mediaeval solutions of
philosophical problems which represents the other main trend
within the Neo-Thomist school.

There are, however, other movements of thought in contemporary Roman Catholicism which far outstrip even the most
liberal Neo-Thomism in broad-mindedness and the courage to
seek new ways of intellectual expression, and which in some
cases even lead to open contradiction of dogmatic Thomism. In
the encyclical *Humani generis* (1950) they are collectively described by Pius XII as 'the new theology.' Especially in French
Roman Catholic theology, a group of brilliant scholars is in
search of new ways of approach to the modern mind and of
adjusting theology to the natural sciences and the results of
Biblical and historical research. This school evidently continues
some of the traditions of the Modernist Movement at the beginning of the century. The originators of the movement are two
Jesuit Fathers, Henri de Lubac and Jean Daniélou, who are
followed by many members of their Order, a surprising fact for

Protestant observers who are generally inclined to associate the
Jesuits with narrow-mindedness and dogmatism. The adherents
of the 'new theology' openly criticize mediaeval scholasticism,
and particularly Thomism, and want to go back to the theology
of the Patristic period. The strong contemporary interest in
Patristic studies in the Roman Catholic Church is often inspired
and accompanied by a high evaluation of Patristic thought as
opposed to mediaeval scholasticism. Biblical studies in this
Church often lead to a similar conclusion. The 'new theology'
criticizes the exclusive adoption of Aristotelianism as the philosophical basis for Roman Catholic theology, and is in search of
an idiom which does greater justice to the concept of history and
which is more 'catholic' or all-embracing than any theology
founded upon the Aristotelian system could ever become. Sometimes the inadequate and symbolical nature of the human knowledge of God is emphasized as against the Thomist belief in the
power of the intellect to grasp metaphysical truths. There is also
in these circles a willingness to listen to Protestant thought and
to enter into a dialogue with it, which is a remarkable feature of
contemporary Roman Catholic theology.

The emergence of views of this kind illustrates the vitality of
Roman Catholic theology despite the very limited liberty
granted to it by the Church. The new tendencies have not,
however, passed unnoticed at Rome, and in 1950 Pius XII
published an encyclical entitled 'On some erroneous opinions
which threaten to undermine the foundations of Catholic doctrine,' opening with the words *Humani generis*. Without mentioning names, it describes persons who turn their backs upon
scholastic theology with the purpose of going back to formulations contained in Holy Scripture and in the early Fathers,
especially the Greek Fathers, people who accept the concepts of
modern philosophical schools and disregard the Church's *magisterium*, who interpret Holy Scripture 'after the manner of men,'
and not as the Church does, who doubt whether human reason
can prove God's existence, and who do not teach the absolute
necessity of belonging to the true visible Church of Christ for
the attainment of salvation and who display a false 'irenism'
aiming at the suppression of differences in doctrinal matters (i.e.
too friendly an attitude towards Protestantism). All these errors

(and others besides) are specified as a warning to dangerous teachers. Thomism and the doctrinal definitions of the Church's *magisterium* are recommended as the exposition of the true theology.

Under the provisions of this encyclical the new theologians are not excommunicated, and no new oath or declaration is required of theological teachers similar to the anti-Modernist oath imposed by Pius X in 1910. But to all liberal circles within the Roman Catholic Church this pronouncement must have been a great disappointment. It should, however, be noted that it contains certain concessions to the 'new theology.' Contacts with modern science and modern philosophy are expressly stated to be of some value. Accommodation to the modern mind is not altogether rejected. Certain aspects of the theory of evolution and some results of Biblical criticism are said to be acceptable. Thomist philosophy may be improved and in the modern errors there may be some elements of truth. Thus the encyclical does not altogether exclude the 'new theology,' but it is clear that its representatives will henceforth have to be extremely cautious. In theological circles a debate has already arisen concerning the interpretation of *Humani generis*.

(iii) Biblical theology plays an important part in contemporary Roman Catholicism. While in practice it is often combined with the 'new theology' it is not identical with it.

In the nineteenth century historical research applied to the Bible and historical (as distant from dogmatic) exegesis were almost a Protestant monopoly. For a long time Roman Catholic contributions in these fields were generally of a dogmatic and apologetic kind. The adoption of Biblical criticism by the Modernist movement towards the end of the century caused a greater stir in Roman Catholicism than in the Evangelical Churches, for the notion of the inerrancy of Holy Scripture maintained in this Church amounted to sheer Fundamentalism. In the encyclical *Providentissimus Deus* of 1893 Leo XIII condemned Higher Criticism and expressly rejected the view that only certain parts of Holy Scripture (passages containing religious and moral truths) were divinely inspired and free from error. The Pope denied the existence of error in the Scriptures, and developed a theory of inspiration which made the Biblical books

THE ROMAN CATHOLIC CHURCH

infallible in every detail. His only concession to Biblical research lay in the admission of the possibility of copyists' errors in the manuscripts. He prescribed that the supreme norm of interpretation should be the doctrine of the Church, and therefore expressly stated that any interpretation which makes the sacred authors disagree with one another or with the Church's teaching must be rejected.

Pius X (Pope 1903–14) continued the fight of his predecessor against Biblical criticism, but at the same time he took important steps to promote Biblical research. In 1904 he instituted a Doctorate in Biblical Science in addition to the already existing Doctorates in Theology and Canon Law, and founded in 1909 the Pontifical Biblical Institute at Rome, a unique centre for Biblical scholarship and teaching on the highest level. He is therefore celebrated to-day as the great promoter of Biblical studies. But it should not be forgotten that he also expressly condemned the application of critical principles to the Bible in 1907 and required all doctors in Sacred Scripture to protest on oath that they submitted to 'the principles and decrees already issued or to be issued in future' (*principia et decreta . . . edita vel edenda*) by the Apostolic See and by the Pontifical Biblical Commission (a body established by Leo XIII in 1902). The 'anti-Modernist Oath' of 1910 contained an express repudiation of Biblical criticism.

In spite of these regulations which to Protestants may appear in the light of restrictions leaving only a minimum of freedom, a true renaissance of Biblical scholarship has taken place within the Roman Catholic Church. In all branches of Biblical scholarship: philology, exegesis, historical research, and even Biblical theology, Roman Catholic scholars occupy leading positions. Biblical scholarship has ceased to be a Protestant monopoly. The chief instruments in this development have been the *École Biblique* founded in 1890 by the French Dominicans in Jerusalem and the Pontifical Biblical Institute.

If the name of a single scholar were to be selected for mention, it should be that of M. J. Lagrange, O.P. (1855–1938).

Within the narrow limits set to exegesis, room has been found for an incredible amount of critical investigation. On many disputed questions where the only permitted solution must seem difficult for a critical scholar to maintain, Roman Catholics will set forth the arguments for and against the traditional opinion with great frankness, leaving the reader to assess the weight of the evidence for himself, while referring to the teaching of the Church.

The outcome of the imposing work of Biblical scholarship within the Roman Catholic Church has been that the decisions of the Pontifical Biblical Commission have become far less rigid during the last few decades. A new attitude can also be perceived in the encyclical *Divino afflante spiritu* published by Pius XII in 1943. Looking back with pride upon the Roman Catholic contribution to Biblical research in this generation, the Pope emphasizes its importance and recommends the study of Holy Scripture in the original languages with the help of textual criticism. The difficulty created by the definition of the Vulgate as the authentic text under a decree of the Council of Trent is overcome by a distinction between the 'juridical authenticity' which the Vulgate still possesses and the 'critical authenticity' belonging to the original texts which must be adduced in order to discover the exact meaning of Holy Scripture. The Pope also recommends that translations into modern languages should be made direct from the Hebrew and Greek texts. He even takes account of the legendary character of many Biblical narratives, while carefully avoiding the actual word. The exegete must be acquainted with Oriental modes of expression which include the frequent use of hyperbole and paradox. The sacred authors accommodated themselves to the contemporary manner of speech. He claims that many Scriptural difficulties have already been solved by the application of this principle. Biblical scholars are described as 'those industrious workers in the Lord's vineyard,' and the other members of the Church are bidden to show them their respect and love and not to be afraid of anything that is new. There are very few texts of which the meaning has been defined by the Church or laid down by a unanimous Patristic tradition. The Pope therefore declares that there is wide scope for the activities of Biblical scholars, provided that they remain in harmony with the teaching of the Church, especially as it concerns the inerrancy of Scripture.

A number of formulations in *Divino afflante spiritu* have been taken over from Leo XIII, but the tone in which Pius XII speaks of 'industrious workers in the Lord's vineyard' differs from the references of his predecessors to contemporary exegetical scholarship. In accordance with this new attitude, the Pontifical Biblical Commission issued a letter in 1948 with the Pope's approval permitting the theory of sources, even of post-Mosaic date, in the Pentateuch and authorizing the view that the first eleven chapters of Genesis contain history told in another way from that employed by classical or modern historians. Two years later, however, the encyclical *Humani generis* contained a warning against those who restrict the inerrancy of Scripture to religious and moral truths, interpreting the Scriptures in a human way, and who venture to measure the teaching of the Church according to their own interpretation of the Bible.

A new attitude to the Bible may also be observed in what is called 'the Biblical Movement' or attempts to disseminate the Bible in modern translations and to promote Bible reading and Bible study among priests and laymen. From the Middle Ages onwards, the Roman Catholic Church, frightened by such experiences as the Waldensian and Wycliffite movements and the Reformation, has been more eager to restrict than to encourage the reading of the Bible by the laity. Thus in 1564 Pius IV declared that more harm than good came from such a practice. He therefore prescribed that the translations of the Bible into the vernacular made by Roman Catholic translators should only be put into the hands of those persons who, in the judgement of their confessors, could read them without danger. In 1757 Benedict XIV permitted the reading of translations authorized by the Apostolic See or accompanied by annotations taken from the Fathers or other approved commentators. Several Popes have issued warnings against the Protestant Bible Societies which arose about the beginning of the nineteenth century. Their activities are even described by Pius VII as 'a pestilence,' while Pius IX recalled that the distribution of translations unauthorized by ecclesiastical authority was 'the ancient device of the heretics.'

From the time of Leo XIII, however, a new spirit can be discerned in Papal utterances on the subject. He was the first Pope to encourage Bible reading by the laity. In 1898 he promised indulgences for Bible reading in a devout spirit, three hundred days for a quarter of an hour's reading of the Gospels and a plenary indulgence for a month's assiduous reading. In the encyclical *Divino afflante spiritu* Pius XII praises those who 'inspired by an apostolic zeal' promote the knowledge and love of the Holy Scriptures among the faithful. He mentions with approval pious societies which issue Roman Catholic translations of the Bible, and exhorts the bishops to promote Bible reading, lectures on Biblical subjects and the reading of periodicals devoted to the Bible.

This change in the tone and content of Papal utterances, partly, no doubt, the outcome of the Biblical Movement, has made its further expansion possible. In many countries, new translations of the Bible into the vernacular have appeared and received wide circulation. Within the last few decades three new translations of the Bible have been produced in France and Belgium, that of Canon Crampon in 1923, the Maredsous Bible (Benedictine) and the Jerusalem Bible (mainly Dominican). The last-named, completed in 1955, is said to be the best from the literary point of view. Three similar translations have recently been published in Germany and Austria, while the English translation of Mgr. R. A. Knox appeared in 1948–49. Societies for the promotion of Bible reading are to be found in French and German-speaking countries, which publish reviews with titles like *Bible et vie chrétienne* and *Bibel und Kirche*. Since its foundation in 1933 the German *Katholisches Bibelwerk* has distributed five million Bibles, New Testaments and Gospels. In other countries the Biblical Movement is much less developed.

(iv) A parallel movement is the Liturgical Movement, whose aim is to go back to the sources and to restore the values which the Church possesses in her Liturgy and to make them a living reality to the ordinary worshipper. The movement originated in Benedictine circles but is not confined to this Order. Other religious orders, in some countries members of the hierarchy, but particularly the parochial clergy, have contributed to the liturgical renaissance.

The origins of the movement are associated with the Abbey of Solesmes and its Abbot Prosper Guéranger (1805–75). His programme was a strict adherence to the Roman rite and a return to its purer forms. Dom Guéranger's work *L'année litur-gique*, in twelve volumes, issued from 1841 onwards, and con-taining the historical and doctrinal explanation of rites and ceremonies, was widely circulated. From Solesmes the move-ment spread to other Benedictine monasteries. Its most important centres have been the monasteries of Beuron (reorganized in 1863) and Maria Laach in Germany, Klosterneuburg in Austria and Maredsous (founded in 1872) and Mont César in Belgium.

In the twentieth century the growth of the Liturgical Move-ment has been one of the most conspicuous features of Roman Catholic Church life. One of its ideals was recommended by Pius X in his advice to worshippers: 'Do not pray in the Mass, but pray the Mass' (do not merely use your own private prayers at Mass, but use the liturgical prayers). The same pope also advocated a return to the purer stages in the history of the Liturgy and of its music. In the last few decades the liturgical renaissance has spread to cathedrals and parish churches, especially in German and French-speaking countries.

One of the aspects of the Liturgical Movement from the start has been the revival of liturgiological studies. A number of scholarly books on the history of the liturgy have appeared in addition to periodicals and year-books for liturgiology. Of the greatest importance has been the publication of the *Dictionnaire d'archéologie chrétienne et de liturgie* in fifteen large volumes (1907–53). Historical studies have been supplemented by dis-cussions of the principles of corporate worship and of the structure of the Christian Liturgy. The choice of subjects for historical research and the spirit in which the history of the Liturgy is studied have to some extent been determined by such theological reflexions. In these circles there is a certain dislike, not only of post-Tridentine developments, but also of late mediaeval forms of worship. The movement goes back to the Early Middle Ages and to the last centuries of Christian Antiquity for the type of liturgical life which it wishes to restore, the eucharistic liturgy celebrated as the common action of the whole congregation. These scholars do not conceal their predilection for the Eastern liturgies and for the early Roman rite and other liturgies of the early mediaeval period. They sometimes trace the decline of liturgical life to the age of Scholasticism and the rise of Gothic art in a somewhat challenging way. Their historical ideals coincide with those of the anti-Thomists.

But the Liturgical Movement is primarily concerned with the contemporary life of the Church. Here its first aim has been to make the Roman Mass in its present form a service of corporate worship. In a number of countries, Missals have been published with the Latin text of all prayers and lessons accompanied by a translation into the vernacular. In Germany a *Messbuch* for the ordinary churchgoer was edited in 1884 by a monk of Beuron, Anselm Schott. In fifty-five years the book went through forty-five editions comprising 1,650,000 copies. One of the principal tasks of the movement has been to teach the people how to follow the Mass and to encourage them to join in the recitation or singing of the Creed and other congregational parts of the service. The Epistle and Gospel are usually read first in Latin and then in the vernacular by the priest, or alternatively, read in Latin in a low voice by the celebrant, and simultaneously aloud in the vernacular by the deacon. The faithful are urged to make their communion at High Mass instead of the extra-liturgical reception of the sacrament which had become customary since the Council of Trent. High Mass with an active participation of the congregation in responses and prayers is an ideal which is realized in many parish churches. In order to make High Mass the very centre of parish life, the most convenient hour is chosen for the service. In recent years notable concessions have been made in this respect by the chief authority in liturgical matters. Thus in 1951 the Pope ordered that the Easter Vigil with its most impressive liturgy should be transferred from what had become its traditional time, early in the morning of Easter Eve, when the ordinary worshipper was unable to attend, to Easter Night. Now it usually begins an hour or two before midnight, a time which makes it possible for the laity to be present. This service has proved a great experience for church people. But still more remarkable is another reform which, unlike the change of time of the Easter Vigil, is a considerable break with the liturgical tradition of the Church from very early in antiquity, though it marks a return to the practice of the Primitive Church. In 1953 the Pope permitted the celebration of the Mass in the evening. He pointed out the fact that in modern society the evening has become the time at which meetings and social events take place, and when people are normally free. The Church should adapt itself to the conditions of modern society. Evening masses with the communion of the laity have become popular.

The representatives of this liturgical renaissance sometimes criticize such 'recent' (mediaeval) practices as the rosary prayers, and in certain cases the custom of private masses which they try to turn into congregational services. In some churches large parts of the Mass are recited in the vernacular; in extreme cases even the Canon. In accordance with the liturgical practice of the Early Church, the celebrant often stands behind the altar, facing the people throughout the service. The High Altar with its reredos is covered by a curtain, and a portable table with a cloth and a crucifix is placed in the chancel, as near to the congregation as possible. Sometimes the Gothic type of crucifix is replaced by the early mediaeval type which depicts Christ reigning from the Cross, which is considered more suitable for the ordinary Mass. A striking feature is the restoration of the offertory procession, in which gifts in kind, such as bread, cheese, butter, fruit and the like, are carried to the altar and distributed after the service among the poor, as in the Early Church.

The official reaction to these developments can be seen from the encyclical *Mediator Dei* published by Pius XII in 1947. In this document certain tenets and practices of the Liturgical Movement are rejected. But the movement itself is not forbidden; on the contrary, the Pope speaks with approval of liturgiological studies and the attempt to promote the understanding of the Liturgy and the participation of the people in its performance. The Pope, however, issues a warning against those who go beyond the limits set by the teaching of the Church. In words directed against the movement he criticizes those who only recognize an 'objective piety' of a liturgical kind to the virtual exclusion of 'subjective or personal piety.' He defends extra-liturgical devotions and prayers, particularly those criticized in these circles such as private prayers during Mass, extra-liturgical reception of the consecrated host, the rosary prayers, the Ignatian spiritual exercises, extra-liturgical adoration of the sacrament exposed on the altar and the use of modern music. He also rejects tenets held by some representatives of the movement, the belief that the New Testament only knows the common priesthood of believers, from which the special priesthood derives its commission, the idea of the 'concelebration' of priests and laity in the Mass, and the doctrine that the climax of the service is to be found in the communion of the people, with the corollary that private masses are of less value. Certain liturgical practices such as the arbitrary introduction of obsolete rites, the use of the vernacular in the Canon of the Mass, the restoration of the primitive form of the altar table, the abolition of black as a liturgical colour, the removal of statues and pictures from the Church and the replacement of the Gothic crucifix are also subjected to censure. The bishops are reminded that the Pope alone is the competent authority for liturgical legislation and the recognition of new rites, and are exhorted to enforce obedience to Papal authority 'if necessary by the application of a salutary severity.'

In this encyclical the Liturgical Movement has received a somewhat restricted recognition. But the Pope is far from insensitive to the need for moderate reform, as is proved by the measures taken since 1947, to which may be added his approval of a new translation of the Psalter for liturgical purposes made from the Hebrew text.

(v) Yet another movement with a similar missionary spirit must be mentioned, the French *prêtres ouvriers*. This is a heroic attempt to establish contact between the Church and the completely secularized proletariat. In 1943, with the approval of the Cardinal Archbishop of Paris, some priests started a work known as the *Mission de Paris*, supplemented by a *Mission de France*, with a special seminary for the training of priests for this task. A number of priests, both secular and regular, decided with the permission of their superiors, to share the conditions of the poorest workers and to live completely in their milieu with the object of winning the proletariat for Christ by being 'workman among workmen, as Christ had been man among men.' They abandoned clerical dress, earned their living by manual work in factories and ports, and shared the interests of the workers. They sometimes concealed the fact that they were priests for a long time, in order to win the confidence of their fellow-workers first. At the height of the movement there were about one hundred *prêtres ouvriers* in the technical sense, besides others who were engaged in missionary work in this milieu without choosing this particular type of life. A number of these priests became engaged in the leadership of the trade unions. In their political views they became socialists, often of a radical kind, and in some cases even communists. They organized demonstrations and strikes, and the management sometimes greatly disliked the presence of such priests among their workpeople. In bourgeois circles, they were subject to suspicion, and frequent denunciations were sent to Rome. The French hierarchy made several attempts to protect the *prêtres ouvriers*, but the Holy See first forbade their numbers to be increased in 1951, and later in 1953 prohibited seminarists from working in factories, pointing out the dangers to their intellectual and moral life involved in such work. This led to the closing of the seminary of the *Mission de France*. In 1953 the three French Cardinal Archbishops were compelled to declare that the activities of the *prêtres ouvriers* could no longer be tolerated in their present form. Priests could only work a limited number of hours (later fixed at three a day) and must leave all secular responsibilities to the laity. The French hierarchy demanded the submission of the *prêtres ouvriers* before March 1st, 1954. Since this date it has been impossible to obtain reliable information about the movement. The French ecclesiastical authorities and the priest workmen themselves seem to have agreed upon a policy of silence. Some sources say that the majority have yielded to the demands of the hierarchy, while others maintain the contrary.

The story of the *prêtres ouvriers* is an instance of the religious vitality of the Roman Catholic Church, comparable to the emergence of the mendicant orders in the thirteenth century; but it also indicates how easily a conflict may arise between the private judgement of such pioneers and the decisions of the ecclesiastical authorities, and how painful the clash between the dictates of private conscience and obedience to ecclesiastical superiors may be to those concerned.

(vi) In some Roman Catholic circles, the attitude adopted towards other Churches and Christian traditions has undergone a profound change in the last generation. In the main this development is confined to Germany, Switzerland, France and

Belgium, where the problems raised by the presence of Protestantism are of long standing, and where the Roman Catholic Church is imbued with a different spirit from that which it displays in Italy or Spain, or even England where a spirit of proselytism is prevalent.

This change of attitude is conspicuous in the tone and spirit in which the Reformers and the Reformation are treated by Roman Catholic historians. The assessment of the personality of Luther and of the motives behind his teaching is especially symptomatic. At the beginning of the century, prominent scholars like Heinrich Denifle, O.P. (*Luther und Luthertum*, 1904) and Hartmann Grisar, S.J. (Luther, 3 vols., 1911; *Martin Luthers Leben und sein Werk*, 1926), displayed an immense amount of erudition in order to discredit the personality of the Reformer. Luther was accused of ignorance, sensuality, drunkenness, and his motives were connected with moral baseness, or a psychopathic explanation was given of his words and deeds. Such explanations still appear in popular tracts and polemical writings, but they have been completely abandoned by scholars and writers on a higher level. Joseph Lortz, who has written the modern standard work on the German Reformation from the Roman Catholic point of view (*Die Reformation in Deutschland*, 2 vols., 1939–40), has done full justice to the religious motives behind the Reformation, and depicts Luther with admiration and rare understanding, while at the same time accusing him of religious 'subjectivism' and one-sidedness. A similar spirit underlies the great work of Adolf Hertz on Roman Catholic presentations of Luther from the Reformation period to the present day (*Das katholische Lutherbild im Banne der Lutherkommentare des Cochläus*, 3 vols., 1943). The small book *Luther in katholischer Sicht* (1947) by the philosopher Johannes Hessen should also be mentioned. A similar change may also be discerned in France in the monumental *Histoire de l'Église* (vol. 15, dealing with the Reformation period, 1950), written in a spirit which would have been unthinkable a generation or two ago. The same may be said of a recent book for the general reader, Daniel-Rops' *L'Église de la Renaissance et de la Réforme* (1955).

The relation of the Roman Catholic Church to other Churches and Christian traditions is one of the crucial points in the lively discussion of ecclesiological problems which is going on in contemporary Roman Catholic theology. Here there is a tension between the insistence on the Roman Catholic Church as the only true visible Church of Christ on the one hand, and the acceptance of the validity of Baptism performed in other Churches, as well as the recognition of the Uniate Churches of the East and, to some extent, of the Orthodox Church on the other. Modern Roman Catholic ecclesiology is marked by a sincere attempt to be faithful to both principles. It is stated that the only possible form of Reunion lies in a return to Rome and submission to the authority of the Pope. But at the same time it is often said that other Churches represent true Christian values and display what are called *vestigia ecclesiae*, traces of the four notes of the Church as One, Holy, Catholic and Apostolic. It is also sometimes suggested that the Roman Catholic Church can learn from other Churches, and might become enriched and more Catholic through union with them and the incorporation of their special inheritance. Notable books written in this spirit are M. J. Congar, O.P., *Chrétiens désunis. Principes d'un oecuménisme catholique* (1937, English translation 'Divided Christendom,' 1939), C. J. Dumont, O.P., *Les voies de l'unité chrétienne* (1954), and Gustave Thils, *Histoire doctrinale du mouvement oecuménique* (1955).

In certain Roman Catholic circles there is a strong interest in ecumenical questions and in personal contacts with representatives of other Churches in a spirit of Christian unity. Christian Unity, and not merely the return to Rome of the 'separated brethren' is a frequent subject of prayer. It is a remarkable fact that the Octave of Prayer for Church Unity (January 18th–25th), which has been observed in many Churches throughout Christendom in the last decades, owes its present form to a Roman Catholic priest, l'abbé Paul Couturier (1881–1953). This Octave originated in 1908 in extreme Anglo-Catholic circles in England and the United States, and originally implied prayers for a reunion of the Churches on the basis of Papal authority. Paul Couturier, a man inspired with a true passion for Christian Unity, saw clearly the difficulties which such prayers created for all non-Roman Catholic Christians who wanted to be faithful to their own Churches. He sought for a

formula which did not hurt confessional loyalties, and found one
in the Roman Missal. With the permission of his Archbishop,
he advocated in 1935 the use of the prayer that 'our Lord would
grant to His Church on earth that peace and unity which were
in His mind and purpose when, on the eve of His Passion, He
prayed that all might be one.' In this spirit, members of all
Churches could join in prayer for the unity of the Church, and
the Octave has been widely observed outside as well as within
the Roman Catholic Church.

Churchmen imbued with the same spirit as the Abbé Couturier
have on several occasions wished to attend the official conferences
of the Ecumenical Movement or unofficial ecumenical gatherings.
Such participation, however, raises difficult problems which have
occasioned the issue of regulations by the Apostolic See. The
attitude of the Roman Catholic Church was given official
expression in the encyclical *Mortalium animos* of Pius XI published
in 1928, in which it is stated that 'the Apostolic See can by no
means take part in these assemblies, nor is it in any way lawful
for Catholics to give such enterprises their encouragement or
support.'

A few Roman Catholics have attended some of the World
Conferences of the Ecumenical Movement as unofficial observers
or as journalists, without becoming official members. More
important are the numerous instances of personal contact and
even of collaboration of different kinds and in varying degrees:
personal friendships between the local priest and pastor, unofficial
conferences, semi-official conversations, publication of articles by
Roman Catholic theologians in non-Catholic reviews and vice
versa. Especially during the war, there were notable cases of
co-operation between Roman Catholic and Protestant Church
leaders, in Germany, in European countries under enemy occupation and in Great Britain, though since the war conditions have
become less easy. It should also be remembered that in some
countries such as Spain and Columbia, instead of collaboration,
we find a legislation which leaves very little liberty to Protestants,
a state of affairs not only tolerated by the hierarchy, but even
exploited by it to deal with the 'Separated brethren.'

The frequent unofficial ecumenical approaches have led to the
formulation of rules by the Apostolic See to regulate Roman

Catholic participation. A *monitum* (warning) *Cum compertum*, issued by the Sacred Office in 1948, reminded members of the Church, both clerical and lay, that participation in mixed gatherings of (Roman) Catholics and 'non-Catholics' (*acatholici*) concerned with matters relating to the Faith, requires special permission from the competent ecclesiastical authorities. For conferences styled 'ecumenical' the consent of the Apostolic See is required and joint worship is expressly forbidden.

On December 20th, 1949, there followed an 'instruction' to all diocesan bishops from the Sacred Office under the title of *Ecclesia catholica* which repeated these rules with certain modifications. In this document considerable sympathy is expressed with the efforts to promote Christian Unity, and the bishops are told to follow the development of the ecumenical movement with constant attention. On the other hand, the dangers attendant upon Roman Catholic participation in ecumenical gatherings are specified: indifferentism in matters of faith and 'irenism.' The competent authority permitting participation in merely local gatherings is stated to be the local bishop who is warned to be most careful only to give such permission to the right person. For conferences on an inter-diocesan, national or international scale, the permission of the Apostolic See is required. It is expressly stated that the prohibition of joint worship does not exclude 'the opening or closing of meetings with a common recitation of the Lord's Prayer or some other prayer approved by the Catholic Church.'

The purpose of these rules is evidently not to prevent all Roman Catholic participation in ecumenical activity, but to keep it under the strict control of the hierarchy. Roman Catholic theologians who are ecumenically minded have emphasized the positive features of *Ecclesia catholica*, and even interpreted it as an exhortation to active participation in ecumenical work.

The trends in contemporary Roman Catholicism which have been passed under review may invite the sympathy of non-Roman Catholic observers and even give rise to hopes of a *rapprochement* between the Roman Catholic and other Churches. To be realistic, however, it should be borne in mind that there are many countries with predominantly Roman Catholic populations which seem to be untouched by such movements. It should also be observed how closely such movements are kept under the control of the Apostolic See and how a number of Papal utterances aim at being a brake upon their development. But the door is never completely shut and there is always some hope of their continuation.

(vii) Besides these trends, there is another of a different character, so different, indeed, that it appears to Protestants as a movement in the opposite direction. The growth of what is called 'Marian piety' and the proclamation of a new 'Mariological dogma' are also features characteristic of modern Roman Catholicism.

On December 8th, 1854, Pius IX proclaimed the dogma of the Immaculate Conception, which was until that date a 'pious opinion' shared by many popes and even contained in their public declarations, but still a theological thesis which could be freely discussed and denied. In 1858 the Virgin appeared in a vision at Lourdes in the South of France to the fourteen-year-old girl, Bernadette Soubirous, and declared 'I am the Immaculate Conception.' Lourdes became a centre for pilgrimages, and a great wave of Marian piety began. Reproductions of the statue of the Virgin of Lourdes were placed in many churches and churchyards all over the world. When the 'Marian Year' (1953–54) was inaugurated by Pius XII, he declared the vision of Bernadette to be the divine confirmation of the dogmatic definition of 1854.

A new centre of Marian piety in our times comparable to Lourdes is Fatima in Portugal. In this place, whose very name was unknown to the world at large until that date, three children, aged ten, nine and seven respectively, had a series of visions in 1917. They claimed to have seen the Virgin on several occasions clad in white and with a rosary in her hand. She told them that the faithful should repent of their sins, do penance and pray the rosary prayers. She desired the world to be dedicated to her immaculate heart and ordered a chapel to be built at Fatima in her honour.

Fatima soon became a popular place of pilgrimage. A crowd of more than 60,000 persons is said to have witnessed the sixth vision on October 13th, 1917, when the Virgin revealed herself in the form of extraordinary meteorological phenomena. On a rainy day the clouds suddenly rolled away, the sun appeared as a revolving ring of fire and the whole scene was lit up in all the colours of the rainbow. This miracle occurred three times at intervals of a few minutes.

At first the ecclesiastical authorities were somewhat reluctant to recognize the visions at Fatima. But official recognition was extended in 1930. A huge basilica has been dedicated to the Madonna of Fatima with a statue which was crowned in 1946 with a golden diadem containing a large number of precious stones. Enormous crowds visited Fatima and the statue of the Virgin has been sent to other countries on what is described as 'pilgrimages.' In 1954 she visited the Archdiocese of Cologne for six weeks. Pius XII has spoken on the radio of the Fatima miracle and of the blessings due to the Madonna of Fatima.

A counterpart in theology to the growth of Marian piety in popular religion was the proclamation in 1950 of the new Mariological dogma, according to which the Virgin was taken up into heavenly glory at her death with body and soul. This tenet has been a widespread pious opinion both in East and West since the beginning of the Middle Ages. In the liturgical year August 15th has been celebrated for centuries as the festival of the Assumption both in the Eastern and Western Churches. Until 1950, however, her bodily assumption into Heaven was not a dogma which had of necessity to be believed. But with the proclamation of the new dogma by the bull *Munificentissimus Deus* on November 1st, 1950, this tenet became a divinely revealed dogma, and those who dared to deny or to doubt it were informed by the Pope that they had fallen away completely from the divine and Catholic Faith.

Before the proclamation of the new dogma the Apostolic See had for several decades received a large number of petitions asking the Pope to 'define' this doctrine. The signatories were members of the hierarchy, the lower clergy, the religious orders and laymen belonging to 'Marian congregations.' In 1946 the Pope prepared the way for the proclamation by issuing an *enquête* to all Roman Catholic bishops asking for their opinion on the desirability of such a definition. It was stated that they voted 'with almost complete unanimity' in its support.

No doubt there are certain quarters within the Roman Catholic Church which have difficulties in accepting the new dogma and which disliked its proclamation in 1950. But few, if any, have left their Church for this reason. It must be remembered that the dogma is not so surprisingly new to them as it appears to Protestant observers, and that obedience to the doctrinal authority of the Church, and especially to the infallible *magisterium* of the Pope, belongs to the essence of Roman Catholicism. But the new dogma has undoubtedly widened the gap between the Roman Catholic and other Churches.

On several occasions Pius XII has favoured the Marian features in popular piety. On December 8th, 1942 he dedicated the whole world to the Immaculate Heart of Mary, in accordance with the desire expressed by the Madonna of Fatima. Portugal alone had received this dedication a few weeks earlier, and it was repeated in 1947 for Canada, in 1949 for England, in 1950 for France and in 1954 for Germany. A cult of the Sacred Heart of Mary in addition to the Sacred Heart of Jesus is a notable feature of the modern Marian piety favoured by the Pope. Towards the end of the Marian Year, Pius XII instituted a new annual Festival of Mary as Queen of Heaven and Earth to be celebrated on May 31st. This is a Marian counterpart to the previously existing feast of Christ the King.

Appendix: THE UNIATE CHURCHES OF THE EAST

In the wider sense of the term, the Roman Catholic Church includes groups of Oriental Christians, who acknowledge the primacy of the Pope, and are therefore united to the see of Rome, but who have also kept many features peculiar to the Eastern Churches. They are called Uniates, and number altogether between seven and eight million.

From the time of the Crusades, efforts have been made by the Roman Catholic Church to win over the Eastern Churches to union with itself. Here and there these efforts have met with success. While in earlier times attempts were made to latinize such groups as much as possible, more recently the policy has been to allow them to keep their own Canon Law and Liturgies. Attempts are even made to ensure that their Oriental rites are kept as free from alien elements as possible. In Rome there are special seminaries for Uniate priests, and one Oriental archbishop has recently been made a cardinal.

Divine service in these Churches is celebrated in the vernacular. Officially they are classified according to their liturgies and are called Uniates of the Byzantine, Chaldaean, Syrian or Coptic rites. The Eucharist is administered in both kinds, and, as a rule, leavened bread is used. They have a married priesthood, but their bishops must be celibate. Their regulations about fasting are much stricter than those of the Western Church. Certain Western usages, such as the Festival of Corpus Christi, are, however, sometimes adopted.

Before the First World War, the largest groups of Uniates, called Ruthenians, were to be found in Poland, West Russia and Rumania. In Poland they numbered three and a half million and represented 11 per cent of the population. In Rumania they total 1,400,000 or 7 per cent of the population.

The oldest Uniate Church, the Maronites of the Lebanon, possesses an interesting history. They differed from other Syrian Christians in their adhesion to Chalcedonian standards of orthodoxy. In 1182, in the time of the Crusades, they became united to Rome and have a present membership of 300,000.

The relations of the Malankara Church in Kerala (India) with the Roman Catholic Church have been chequered. In the sixteenth century, under Portuguese influence, attempts were made by threats and cajolery to reconcile them to the see of Rome. These efforts led to an act of union in 1599, but subsequently the majority regained their ecclesiastical independence. As recently as 1937, a large group joined the Roman Catholic Church, and at the present time about one million of the Thomas Christians are in communion with the see of Rome.

A wing of the East Syrian (Nestorian) Church became a Uniate Church in 1553 when a prominent member of their clergy conformed to Roman Catholic doctrine and was recognized by Rome as 'Patriarch of Mosul.' The present Uniate 'Church of the Chaldaean rite' dates from the re-establishment in 1834 of a 'Patriarchate of Babylon' in communion with Rome. This Church has to-day perhaps 150,000 members, considerably more than the non-uniate East Syrian Church.[1]

[1] See above, p. 40-1.

THE OLD CATHOLICS

On July 18th, 1870, Pius IX proclaimed the new dogma of the Infallibility of the Papacy. There was, however, within the Roman Catholic Church a group which had consistently opposed the doctrine. Although in the course of time all the bishops of this group made their submission, a number of theologians and priests under the leadership of a German professor of Church History, Ignaz von Döllinger (1799–1890), carried their opposition to the point of excommunication, and in 1872 took the step of organizing themselves under the name of the Old Catholic Church.

Even at the Vatican Council itself there had been considerable opposition to the new definition. At a test ballot of 601 members eligible to vote (held on July 13th), there were 91 abstentions, 88 against, and 62 conditionally in favour, against 360 votes in its support. The bishops who opposed the decree left the city in large numbers before the final ballot, and it was ultimately adopted by 533 votes to two.

The Council left a very strained atmosphere within the Roman Catholic Church. After further consideration, all the dissident bishops yielded, and when, a year later, the last of them had affixed his signature to the decree, Döllinger, the leader of the opposition, was excommunicated.

In the same year the opposition adopted the name of the 'Old Catholics.' The selection of this title revealed the programme of the movement. They wished to adhere to Roman Catholicism as it had been understood before 1870, repudiated the new dogma and refused to recognize the excommunication of their supporters.

At a congress held at Cologne in September 1872, the Old Catholics organized their Church which they claimed to be the legitimate continuation of the Catholic Church. Its constitution was, of course, episcopal, the Papacy was rejected and the old dogma and ritual were retained. An indication of later developments can be found in the immediate rejection of certain features peculiar to the Roman Catholic Church, such as the system of indulgences and payment for masses.

The complete absence of Roman Catholic bishops among the dissidents, however, raised an awkward problem for the Old Catholic movement. In 1872 they elected Professor J. H. Reinkens (1821–96) as their first bishop, but were faced with the difficulty of finding bishops within the apostolic succession to consecrate him. In this predicament they enlisted the help of a small Church with a remarkable history, a small separatist Catholic minority in Holland called 'The Roman Catholic Church of the Old Episcopal Clergy.'

After the Reformation the six Roman Catholic sees in Holland survived, although they had a difficult existence during the seventeenth century when the public recitation of Mass was forbidden. There was, however, a regular succession of Archbishops of Utrecht with a hierarchy of priests to serve the needs of the Roman Catholic population. The Jesuits, who were anxious to undertake missionary work in the country, ignored the existence of this hierarchy and further conflicts arose between the Jesuit missionaries and the local clergy on the question of Jansenism. Rome sided with the Jesuits and removed the Archbishop of Utrecht from his office in 1702. He refused to accept his deposition and, on his death, the Cathedral Chapter proceeded to the election of a new archbishop. He received consecration at the hands of a French bishop in 1724 despite the fact that this action was not recognized by the Pope. Rome therefore immediately declared his election to be null and void. As the archbishop refused to resign, a small new Church arose which Rome regarded as schismatic but which still claimed to be part of the Roman Catholic Church. Its own convictions on the matter took the form of sending notification to Rome of every episcopal election and consecration. A reply in the shape of excommunication was as regularly and as promptly received. The custom was maintained for nearly two centuries until in 1910 the Church of Utrecht ceased the practice of sending reports to Rome on the subject of its episcopal elections.

In the first few years after 1872 a large accession of membership to the Old Catholic Church was expected. The State authorities in Prussia, Austria and Switzerland viewed the movement with favour, and there was widespread feeling against the Roman Catholic Church. In Prussia the priests who seceded from the Church of Rome were granted by the State the use of the churches in which they had previously served as parish priests. In Switzerland an Old Catholic theological faculty, which still continues, was founded in 1874 in the University of Berne. But the actual number of secessions was much smaller than had been anticipated.

In 1889 the Old Catholic congregations in Holland, Switzerland and Austria entered upon an act of union at Utrecht and used the occasion to affirm their ecclesiastical principles. They declared their adherence to the Catholic Creeds and the doctrinal resolutions of the ecumenical or general Councils. They rejected the resolutions of the Council of Trent and all the Papal decrees since that date. The doctrine of the sacrifice of the Mass was confined to the idea of a re-presentation of the sacrifice of our Lord and the notion of repetition was excluded. Emphasis was also laid upon reunion between the Churches.

The Old Catholic Church has not grown to any considerable proportions. In Germany and Austria there has been a decrease in membership. But a Church of this type is predisposed by its history to play its part in the Ecumenical Movement. Repeated negotiations with the Eastern Orthodox Church have proved inconclusive, but since 1931 relations of intercommunion have been established with the Church of England without the requirement of complete doctrinal agreement between the two Churches. Old Catholic and Anglican bishops have since taken part in the consecration of bishops of both Churches.

In the course of their short history as an independent Church, the Old Catholics have gradually come to resemble the Evangelical Churches in certain matters of doctrine. Scripture is regarded as the primary rule of faith, though a supplementary role is assigned to Tradition. The criterion of Tradition is acceptance by the whole Church, and it is therefore to be sought in the Undivided Church. The idea of works of supererogation is rejected. The veneration of saints is restricted to a memorial before God of their good works and their acceptance as models

F

for Christians. Belief in the Real Presence of our Lord in the Eucharist is retained without the dogma of Transubstantiation. Mass is celebrated in the vernacular in all Old Catholic churches. The last group to adopt this practice were the Old Catholic congregations in Holland in 1910. Clerical celibacy has been abandoned and once again the Dutch Old Catholics were the last to change their custom in 1923. There are no monastic orders or congregations. Private confession is no longer obligatory. The Roman Catholic doctrine of justifying faith as 'faith informed by love' (*fides caritate formata*) is, however, still retained.

The Union of Utrecht comprises eight National Churches with a total membership of 600,000. In Holland, the Old Catholic Church has 12,000 members, in Germany something like 40,000, in Switzerland 30,000, in Austria 40,000, in Czechoslovakia 5,000, and in Croatia 4,000. The Polish National Catholic Church claims to have 100,000, and its daughter Church in the United States has 370,000 members.

A secession from the Roman Catholic Church of a different character took place in Czechoslovakia in 1920. A group of priests asked for Papal authorization to introduce radical changes: mass in the vernacular and the abolition of the rule prescribing celibacy for the clergy. When their petition was rejected in 1919, they seceded together with a great number of laymen and organized *The Czechoslovak Church* which to-day possesses 950,000 members. In its doctrine on the Trinity and the Incarnation, this Church represents a liberal Protestantism which approaches Unitarianism. Its eucharistic doctrine is spiritualizing. Bishops are elected, but receive no episcopal consecration. Women are ordained as pastors.

CHAPTER V

THE CATHOLIC APOSTOLIC CONGREGATIONS (IRVINGITES)

1. ORIGIN AND HISTORY

THIS religious body which possesses both apocalyptic and catholic features first arose in the period between 1830 and 1850. To-day it is mainly of historical interest. Its structure is so dependent upon apocalyptic expectations that it can hardly last for more than a few generations.

The founder of this Church was the Scottish minister, Edward Irving (1792–1834). In 1822 he was appointed to the Scottish Presbyterian Church in London, where his revivalistic preaching soon attracted widespread attention. The pronounced apocalyptic feeling of the period took hold of him and he joined a group of clergy, ministers and laymen of various denominations who expected the imminent return of Christ. Under the leadership of the banker, Henry Drummond (1786–1860), and at his estate at Albury Park, this group met together to study the fulfilment of prophecy and the revival of the apostolic gifts of grace. In 1830, rumours reached London of the reappearance of speaking with tongues (glossolaly) in Scotland, where a consumptive seamstress had risen from her sick-bed and uttered a prophecy. These phenomena soon broke out in London and prophets of both sexes announced the speedy return of our Lord.

At first Irving tried to keep the services of his own church free from prophecy and glossolaly, but they were soon interrupted by ecstatic phenomena, in which he finally felt bound to acquiesce. Within a short time they became dominated by an ecstatic type of Adventism. Irving's position within the Presbyterian Church naturally became untenable and, as he also held unorthodox views on the Person of our Lord, he was removed from office and even excommunicated in 1832.

This act led to the formation of the Church, but, as he himself possessed no ecstatic powers and could neither prophesy nor speak with tongues, he took a secondary place and the leadership passed to the strong-willed lawyer, John Cardale (1802–77). At a prayer-meeting held in 1833 Drummond prophesied and, turning to Cardale, said: 'Are you not an apostle?'

A new ministry, the apostolate, was therefore created. Irving himself was not of their number, but in 1833, Cardale ordained him 'angel' or bishop of the mother congregation in London. The title 'angel' was drawn from the Letters to the Seven Churches in Revelation i–ii. But by this time Irving was broken by overwork and disappointment. His doctors advised him to take a trip to the South, but one of the prophets invited him to undertake a preaching tour in the North. He decided to accept this invitation and died in Glasgow in the following year.

Cardale now decreed that twelve apostles should be appointed. The twelve were soon designated by the prophets, and on July 14th, 1835, they were ordained by the laying-on of the hands of the seven 'angels' of the seven London parishes. The apostles retired to Albury Park and spent a year in Bible-study in preparation for their missionary work. Each apostle was allotted his 'tribe' or geographical area. Thus, for example, Cardale became apostle for England, and Drummond for Scotland and Switzerland.

In fulfilment of Revelation vii. 4–8 each apostle was to gather twelve thousand 'sealed' servants of God from his tribe and then the end would come.

Before the apostles went out into the world, they issued jointly a pastoral letter, called 'the Apostolic Testimony.' This letter, of which there were Latin, English, French and German editions, filled two hundred pages, and was addressed to the 'patriarchs, archbishops, bishops and other heads of Christ's Church on earth, and other regents ruling over all baptized nations.' The Testimony was presented to the Pope by Drummond and the apostle for Italy. The document declared that the second Coming of Christ was imminent and that he had now appointed twelve apostles.

From the outset the Irvingites had adopted an ecumenical attitude. Now in the Apostolic Testimony they passed the Churches of Christendom under critical review. Thus the Orthodox Church had refused to admit the Procession of the

Holy Spirit from the Father and the Son, and had therefore as a punishment been more oppressed by earthly rulers than any other Church. The Roman Catholic Church was praised as the protector of the orthodox faith, particularly in the Holy Trinity. It had always endeavoured to preserve the unity of the Church in matters of faith and order. But it had also cherished many superstitions and sought after external power, thereby showing that it did not dare to believe in the 'dauntless majesty of truth.' The other churches are grouped together under the general name of 'the Protestants,' and are not highly regarded. They have, it seems, little faith in the Divinity of the Holy Spirit and have nearly lost their faith in the Heavenly Session of our Lord. Protestantism has desired the end, the divine life, but has disregarded the means, the church order laid down by God. Its great error lay in permitting the division of the Church into different bodies. 'The history of Protestantism is not that of one Church, but of many sects; not a history of one faith, one hope, one baptism, but of many kinds of faith, many kinds of hope, and many kinds of baptism.'

At Christmas 1838, twelve hundred and sixty days after the ordination of the apostles (the figure is taken from the Book of Revelation), the prophets were to assemble once more at Albury Park. They then resumed their missionary work, but were compelled to reassemble in 1840, as a crisis had occurred in the Church. Some of the prophets had claimed to possess an authority greater than the apostles. The dispute ended with the recognition of the apostles as the supreme authority in the Church and they were granted the additional right to try the utterances of the prophets. Thus, once again in the history of the Church, the official ministry triumphed over the charismatic gifts of the Spirit.

There follows a period which may be called 'the Romanization of Irvingism.' Sympathy with the Roman Catholic Church is already evident in the 'Apostolic Testimony.' The new developments must be seen against the same background as the rise of the High Church Movement in the Church of England. Much of the doctrine, and even more of the Liturgy of the new movement, was greatly indebted to Roman Catholicism. In 1842 the system of worship was completed by the apostles. As their sources they had taken the Roman Missal, some of the Greek liturgies, and the Anglican Book of Common Prayer, together with some prayers of their own composition. The outcome was a rich and dignified form of service developed to a great extent upon the Roman model. Resplendent vestments were introduced for the Mass as well as such ceremonies as Extreme Unction. After 1850 the consecrated elements were reserved in a tabernacle on the altar after the Roman Catholic fashion. Holy water was introduced in 1868.

The name of 'the Catholic Apostolic Congregations' came into use before 1850 in order to express the non-sectarian character of the movement. The Irvingites did not wish to form a new sect nor did they reject the validity of the sacraments of other churches. 'Even though the apostles are compelled to establish congregations,' wrote the Danish Irvingite, Charles Boehm, 'they distinctly teach that it is not these congregations, but the community of all who have been baptized that constitutes the Church.' Distress at the disunion of Christendom and intercession for all Christians are recurrent themes in their liturgy and writings. In accordance with the recognition of all baptized persons as Christian brethren, they were invited to receive the Holy Communion at Catholic Apostolic altars.

Converts to the Catholic Apostolic congregations were not required to leave the Churches to which they had previously belonged. When the movement spread to Germany, a Roman Catholic priest at Augsburg became interested and joined the new Church, but still carried on his duties as a Roman Catholic priest for ten years before he was excommunicated by his bishop, together with five other priests and four hundred laymen, who had previously been able to reconcile their new loyalty with the old.

The Year of Revolution (1848) made people receptive to apocalyptic preaching. Particularly in Germany, a number of eminent men joined the new Church, among them the well-known theologian, Professor Heinrich Thiersch of Marburg (1817–85), an expert on the early Church, who believed that the realization of his ideals was now imminent.

There were many features of the Catholic Apostolic Church that must have made a great appeal. The movement claimed to be ecumenical and non-sectarian, above parties and even above the divisions between the Churches. It proclaimed the Second Coming of Christ with new conviction. It had a rich devotional life and gave its members liturgical functions to perform. In the tiny Oslo congregation in the 1880's there were as many as twenty priests and twelve deacons, each with definite duties to perform.

The apocalyptic character of the movement inevitably led to a series of crises in the course of its history. Time and again a date for the Second Coming was calculated (in 1835, 1838, 1842, 1845, 1855, 1866 and 1877), all attended by the bitter disappointment of frustrated expectation. It was generally believed that the apostles would survive until our Lord's return. One after another, however, they died. At least, the expected return would take place before the death of the last survivor, but he too died in 1901.

After his death no new ordination could take place, for these could only be carried out by an apostle. Nor, since 1901, has it been possible to perform any 'sealings' or confirmations, for this again was the prerogative of the apostles. All propaganda has now ceased and no new members are admitted with the exception of married partners of different faiths; but in such cases it often happens that it is the Irvingite partner who changes his or her religious allegiance.

2. DOCTRINE, ORDER AND RITUAL

The Catholic doctrines of the Holy Trinity, the Incarnation, Creation and of the Redemptive work of Christ have all been retained by this Church. The Church is regarded as the visible institution through which salvation can be attained, but the Irvingites do not identify the Church with their own communion or refuse to recognize other Christians as members of the Church.

The chief sacraments are Baptism and the Eucharist, but Sealing, Penance and Extreme Unction are also recognized.

Infant Baptism is practised and is believed to effect regeneration and incorporation into the Church.

The Eucharist is both a sacrificial rite and an act of communion. The offering made in the Eucharist, however, is not a propitiatory

sacrifice but the sacrifice of praise and thanksgiving. The doctrine
of the Real Presence is taught and a theological basis for this view
is sought in the doctrine of consubstantiation. In some prayers,
however, the sacramental elements are described as 'symbols of
Thy Son's sufferings, the bread of eternal life and the chalice of
eternal beatitude.'

In accordance with Ephesians iv. 11–13, there are four sacred
offices: (1) apostles; (2) prophets; (3) evangelists; (4) pastors and
teachers. The apostles are restricted to the twelve called by the
Holy Spirit. The prophets shed light on obscure passages in Holy
Scripture and predict future events. The evangelists are itinerant
preachers, and the parochial clergy form the pastors and teachers.
Within this group there are three grades, angel (bishop), elders
(presbyters) and deacons.

The climax of worship is the celebration of the Holy Communion. The whole congregation partakes of this sacrament
every Sunday morning and there are frequent celebrations of the
Holy Communion during the week. The Nicene Creed is recited
at this service, but is replaced by the Athanasian Creed at Christmas, Easter, Whitsunday and on All Saints' Day. The use of
incense was discontinued in 1901 on the ground that it symbolized
the fourfold ministry which now no longer existed.

The Liturgy has preserved the structure of the Roman Catholic
Mass, but it contains an apocalyptic element in the prayer for our
Lord's return. Both prophecy and speaking with tongues sometimes occur, but are rare, mere residual traces of the ecstatic
period in the history of this Church.

3. The Neo-Apostolic Congregations (Neo-Irvingites)

The death of the last surviving apostle created serious problems
for the Church. At a meeting held at Albury Park in 1860, when
six of the apostles had died, the German prophet, Heinrich Geyer,
designated two of the evangelists as apostles. They were only
recognized by the survivors as apostle-coadjutors, charged with
the duty of assisting the apostles in their work, but lacking the
full authority of the office. For the moment Geyer was content,
but in the following year he designated a priest at Königsberg as
an apostle, but for the moment kept this a secret.

In 1862 Geyer was excommunicated by the Catholic Apostolic Church and thereupon formed his own congregation, which later received the name of the Neo-Apostolic Congregation. His followers are also known as Neo-Irvingites, but are not recognized by the original movement.

The new movement allows for the appointment of new apostles to perpetuate the apostolic college after the death of previous members. The Neo-Apostolic Church soon had its own apostolate and spread rapidly, particularly in Germany and thence to the missionary areas. Daughter congregations were formed in North and South America, Java and Australia. To-day the movement is said to have something like 250,000 members, Neo-Irvingism has done away with much of the Catholic character of the original movement, and both in doctrine and ritual has come to bear a closer resemblance to the Reformed Churches. Baptism, Sealing and the Eucharist are considered as sacraments. An unusual feature is the performance of vicarious baptism for the dead (cp. 1 *Corinthians* xv. 29).

CHAPTER VI

THE CHURCH OF ENGLAND AND THE ANGLICAN COMMUNION

1. Distribution and Statistical Data

THE Church of England, as its name implies, is the national Church in England. It is not, however, the Church of the whole English people, for historical developments have led to a greater diversity of Church life in England than in most other European countries. In addition to the Church of England, the Free Churches occupy a prominent place in the national life.

As official statistics in England do not cover church membership, no accurate figures for the membership of the Church of England can be given. Something over half, and perhaps as much as two-thirds, of the total population may be regarded as belonging at least nominally to the Church of England. The rest are divided between the Roman Catholic Church and a large number of Free Churches, while a relatively small minority would disclaim attachment to any Christian community at all. In 1952, 50·2 per cent of the total number of marriages were performed in Anglican churches, 11·8 per cent in Roman Catholic churches, 9·5 per cent in Nonconformist churches, and 27·9 per cent in Registry Offices. In its widest sense the membership of the Church of England is probably about twenty-five million.[1]

But the Church of England is only one among the world-wide fellowship of Churches comprising the Anglican Communion— Churches that have grown up as the result both of colonization and of missionary activity. The Episcopal Church of Scotland and the Church of Ireland, both Churches of the Anglican Communion, have as members only a minority of the population. There is a difference of ethos between the two Churches. In Scotland the High Church or Catholic tradition is accentuated,

[1] The figures given in the *Official Year Book of the Church of England* for 1956 record the number of Easter Communicants as nearly 2,070,000 and of Sunday School scholars as approximately 1,050,000 for the preceding year. These figures are, of course, based on different criteria from those given in the text. (H.E.W.T.)

whereas the Church of Ireland, at least in externals, is markedly Evangelical in tone. This divergence is explained by the fact that in Scotland the Episcopal Church is set against a Reformed or Presbyterian background, while in Ireland the dominant religious factor in the life of the country is the Roman Catholic Church.

In Scotland episcopacy was imposed upon the National Church by James I in 1610 and persisted until the rebellion of 1638, and again after the Restoration in 1661 until the Revolution of 1689. Since that time the Church of Scotland has been Presbyterian in church order and the Episcopal Church of Scotland has become a small Free Church existing side by side with the Presbyterian National Church.

The Church of Ireland was 'established' from the middle of the sixteenth century until its separation from the State in 1869. During the whole period, the great majority of the population was Roman Catholic and the privileged position of the Church of Ireland was therefore much resented. Since 1869 the Church of Ireland has been a small Free Church which has to-day about 150,000 members in the Republic of Eire.

The oldest daughter Church outside Europe is the Protestant Episcopal Church in America. When the American colonies broke away from England in 1776, the Church of England in America became cut off from the mother Church. Since, under English law, the American parishes were within the jurisdiction of the Bishop of London until the American Revolution, they had no bishops of their own. Partly owing to legal difficulties in England and partly to the political circumstances of the time, bishops for America could not be consecrated in England, and new consecrations for America were performed in 1784 by bishops from Scotland. The Protestant Episcopal Church in America has never had a large membership and now comprises some two million members.

From the end of the eighteenth century, the Anglican Communion has undergone great expansion and dioceses have been established all over the British Commonwealth. Branches have also grown up in other parts of the world, particularly in China and Japan. In addition to many independent provinces, a number of dioceses in missionary areas are still under the direct jurisdiction of the Archbishop of Canterbury.

The first Canadian diocese was established in 1787, and within seventy years this precedent was followed in other parts of the Empire (India in 1814, Australia in 1836 and South Africa in 1847). At the outset these daughter churches were considered as 'established' churches, but gradually secured full constitutional independence. In India, for example, the Church received self-government in 1930.

In 1950 the Anglican Communion had no less than 321 Dioceses throughout the world, of which only forty-three are in England itself. The number of bishops is, however, considerably greater than this, both in England and elsewhere, since in addition to Diocesan bishops there are also Suffragan and Assistant bishops. At a rough estimate the number of Church members outside England may be put at twelve million.

With the exception of certain missionary dioceses, the daughter Churches of the Anglican Communion are constitutionally independent of the see of Canterbury. Together, however, they form a single Communion with common traditions of doctrine, liturgy and church order. They are in full communion with the Church of England and with each other and have complete interchangeability of clergy and communicants. The outward expression of this unity is found in the Pan-Anglican episcopal Conferences which have been held at regular intervals (now decennial) at Lambeth Palace in London, and are therefore known as the Lambeth Conferences.

There is no absolute uniformity in the Anglican Communion. All the member Churches have an episcopal church order. The Church of England alone has an official connection with the State, while all other branches of the Anglican Communion have the status of Free Churches. Although some of the Thirty-Nine Articles apply primarily to the Church of England rather than to the altered circumstances of its daughter Churches, the document as a whole is accepted to a greater or lesser degree as a confessional standard in different parts of the Anglican Communion. Each major branch has its own Prayer Book which, while revealing a common pattern of liturgical life, may show considerable variation in detail. Yet such differences are of little ultimate significance, and as against Roman Catholicism and Orthodoxy on the one hand and the Evangelical Churches on the other, it is wholly natural to speak of the Anglican Communion as representing a distinct type of Church.

2. The Characteristic Features of the Anglican Communion

The special character of the Church of England was the outcome of a long historical process which began with Henry VIII's breach with the Papacy, and which cannot be considered complete until the Restoration in 1660.

The date of this breach with Rome can best be put at 1534, when Henry VIII claimed the title of 'Supreme Head of the English Church and Clergy.'[1] The occasion of the severance of relations was the unfortunate affair of the royal divorce. Deeper and more potent forces were, however, at work, including a movement towards the formation of a national Church, a tendency not without parallel on the Continent of Europe but especially marked in England, and towards the criticism and reform of the abuses which had grown up within the mediaeval Church.

These forces contributed greatly towards the course of the English Reformation and their influence is still felt to-day. It remains a national Church. A number of bishops have seats in the House of Lords,[2] and the Church has great influence in the moulding of public opinion. The 'Reform Catholicism' of scholars like Erasmus has also left a permanent mark upon the Church of England. The English Reformation was a moderate reform which adopted a conservative attitude towards the past. In matters of Church Order and Liturgy, it retained as much as possible of its Catholic heritage, and as a result England was less radical in its reformation than countries with a Reformed

---

[1] This title was dropped in 1554 and never subsequently revived. In 1559 Elizabeth I accepted the title of Supreme Governor on the ground that the Supreme Head of the Church is Christ alone. She took the greatest pains to define and limit the constitutional aspects of the new title. These are carefully expounded in Article XXXVII against the background of the doctrine of the 'Godly Prince.'

[2] See below, pp. 167, 169.

(or Calvinist) or even a Lutheran tradition. The Church of England has persistently taken a conservative line coupled, however, with the will to institute reforms when these have been shown to be necessary.

Yet the Reformation in England was not uninfluenced by similar movements on the Continent, whether Lutheran, Calvinist or Zwinglian. Under Edward VI (1547–53) in particular, England became the refuge for persecuted Continental Protestants and its own type of Reformation developed along more Protestant lines. A distinguishing feature of the Reformation in England is that, unlike its continental counterparts, no single dominating personality such as Luther, Calvin or Zwingli left his mark upon the Church. The course of the English Reformation was determined by a number of streams of thought which did not necessarily converge and by certain political events peculiar to England itself. One man, however, Thomas Cranmer (1489–1556), Archbishop of Canterbury, had a lasting influence upon the Church of England. He compiled the first Book of Common Prayer, upon which every subsequent prayer book was based, and thus played a decisive part in shaping the development of the Anglican Communion as a whole.

After the Roman Catholic reaction under Mary (1553–58), the Church of England was re-established on a firm foundation under Elizabeth I (1558–1603), embracing both Catholic and Protestant elements. Under the House of Stuart in the first half of the seventeenth century, the Church came under the dominant influence of the High Church tradition, while extreme Protestantism gained the ascendancy in England under Cromwell. After the Restoration of 1660, the Church of England was again established, and in 1662 the Book of Common Prayer was revised and given the form which it still bears to-day. In view of the important part played by the Prayer Book in the life of the Church of England, this date can be taken as decisive for its subsequent history.

This Church with its complex history has often been called the *via media* or middle way between the two extremes of Roman Catholicism and Protestantism. This term seems to be due to Bishop Joseph Hall (1574–1656) who published a book entitled

Via Media, the Way of Peace in 1622.[1] In the course of the seventeenth century, the formula became the characteristic expression of the self-consciousness of the Church of England. It had previously been considered by many as a member of the Reformed family of Churches. An Anglican delegation had even attended the Synod of Dordrecht (Dort), which marked the climax of Calvinistic orthodoxy, although they expressly reserved their opinion on questions of Church Order. A seventeenth-century Anglican divine, Simon Patrick (1625–1707), contrasts 'the virtuous mediocrity' of his own church with the 'meretricious gaudiness' of the Church of Rome and the 'squalid sluttery' of the 'fanatic conventicles.' The same idea, less pungently expressed, is a familiar theme in Anglican writers of the period. It finds expression in the Preface to the Book of Common Prayer of 1662 (an official document) which opens with the words 'it hath been the wisdom of the Church of *England*, ever since the first compiling of her Publick Liturgy, to keep the mean between the two extremes, of too much stiffness in refusing, and of too much easiness in admitting any variation from it.'

In addition to its consciousness of representing the *via media*, the Anglican Church also regards itself as the legitimate continuation of the early Church. Through its mediaeval accretions, Roman Catholicism has corrupted this heritage, while Protestantism, through the loss or rejection of certain elements, has reduced its true proportions. The Anglican Church, on the other hand, carries on the tradition of the Undivided Church of the first few centuries.

This view of the distinctive character of the Church of England is beautifully expressed in the will of Bishop Thomas Ken (1637–1711): 'I die in the Holy, Catholic and Apostolic Faith, professed by the whole Church before the division of East and West. More particularly I die in the Communion of the Church of England, as it stands distinguished from all Papal and Puritan innovations.'

This principle, however, is not confined to the relations between the Anglican Communion and other Churches. It is also characteristic of its attitude to other questions, such as authority

---

[1] An even earlier use of the term *via media* is to be found in the Preface to Isaac Casaubon's book, *De rebus sacris et ecclesiasticis exercitationes* (1614). (H.E.W.T.)

and freedom. The 'Anglican temper,' with its characteristic avoidance of one-sidedness, has deep roots within the English character itself, which possesses a veritable genius for compromise. This is in sharp contrast both with the French and German temperaments which show a stronger tendency to pursue a line of thought to its logical conclusion. This national characteristic is reflected in Anglican theology which has always been more balanced than, for example, its German counterpart. In matters of faith and theology, Anglicans are always apt to find truth on both sides.

Yet, while officially adopting a middle course, the Church of England has always had within it elements which can be called Catholic and Protestant. It represents a fusion of elements drawn from Lutheranism, Calvinism and Zwinglianism with the old Catholic heritage, in such a way that the synthesis has become neither Lutheranism, Calvinism nor Roman Catholicism, but just Anglicanism.

The Catholic features within the Anglican tradition are its devotion to the faith of the Creeds, its episcopal Church Order and its sacramental life. Especially during the past few generations, much emphasis has been laid upon the episcopate. Throughout the storm and stress of the Reformation period, great care was taken to preserve the continuity of the episcopate through the agency of bishops who had accepted the Reformation Settlement. This continuity of Ordination from the early and mediaeval Church (the Apostolic Succession which constitutes the justification for the cherished claim of the Church of England to be the historic Catholic Church of the country) is of great significance for the Anglican doctrine of the Church at the present time.

The Evangelical element in Anglicanism is to be found principally in its official post-Reformation confessional document, the Thirty-Nine Articles, many of which exhibit Lutheran and Calvinist influences. It has been said that the framework of this Church is Catholic, while its doctrine is Evangelical. One of its own members (William Pitt, the Elder, Lord Chatham (1708–1778)) described the Church of England as possessing a Popish Liturgy, Calvinist Articles of Faith and an Arminian clergy. While many Anglicans to-day would dissent strongly from such a description, it may nevertheless contain a certain element of truth.[1]

In the history of the Church of England there has always been a certain tension between its Catholic and Evangelical poles. Time and again this has resulted in a loss of membership to a greater or a lesser extent, either through the formation of Nonconformist Churches or by individual secessions to the Roman Catholic Church. In this way, from the Reformation times onwards, the extreme Puritans refused to allow themselves to be incorporated within the framework of the Established Church. The most tragic of these schisms was that of the Methodists at the close of the eighteenth century, not only because of the numbers involved, but also because John Wesley himself had not the slightest desire that his movement should become severed from the Church of England. Not least tragic were the factors which contributed to the schism, the absence of understanding on the part of many of the bishops and other clergy of the period, both with regard to the needs of the Church and the aims of his movement, and the failure to provide (largely through political reasons) for an American Episcopate before the outbreak of the War of Independence. Since the rise of the Oxford Movement, individual secessions to the Roman Catholic Church, previously very rare, have become of relatively frequent occurrence.

Thus the Church of England has been repeatedly deprived of many of its most active members with the result that it is now probably only responsible for something over half the English people. It has, however, kept its essential character as both Catholic and Reformed and, despite its losses, possesses considerable vitality. Even taken by itself, this fact seems to show that this ideal has much to commend it.

This story of repeated secessions might give the impression that the Church of England is a rigid institution. The opposite is in fact the case, for, in several respects, it is the most elastic Church in Christendom, holding within itself pronounced contrasts both in worship and doctrine. The doctrinal differences are reflected in the Report of a Commission appointed by the

---

[1] Contrast, for example, the comment in E. J. Bicknell's *A Theological Introduction to the Thirty-nine Articles*, pp. 20–21. (H.E.W.T.)

two Archbishops in 1922 to investigate these divergences within
the Church, published in 1938 under the title *Doctrine in the
Church of England*.[1] The Anglican Church to-day includes, on
the one hand, groups which share the majority of Roman
Catholic doctrines (including the doctrine of the Sacrifice of the
Mass) and who celebrate the Holy Communion according to the
Roman Rite (in the most extreme cases in Latin) and, on the
other hand, groups whose doctrine, worship and devotional ethos
have a good deal in common with the Evangelical Free Churches.
Between these two extremes there are many shades of opinion,
but the great majority of Anglicans seem to represent some sort
of central 'Anglicanism' in which Anglo-Catholic, Evangelical
or Liberal elements may in some cases predominate. A distinctive feature of the Anglican tradition is therefore its
'comprehensiveness.'

Yet the Church of England has not always been so flexible as
it appears to-day. It has always taken up a liberal attitude towards
questions of doctrine, but in earlier centuries it demanded
liturgical uniformity and even took stern measures to enforce it.
Indeed, in Reformation times, its adhesion to fixed liturgical
forms was a principal cause of the Puritan secessions. Neither in
the century of the Reformation, nor after 1662 were variations
in the prescribed use of clerical robes tolerated. Greater flexibility
in this respect was one of the results of the High Church Movement of the nineteenth and twentieth centuries, which led to the
breakdown of liturgical uniformity. The High Church clergy
allowed themselves considerable liberties with the Prayer Book,
at times almost amounting to liturgical chaos, which the Church
authorities proved powerless to prevent.

Thus the capacity of the Church of England for adaptation has
been more sorely tried than that of any other Church in Christendom by reason of the Puritan movements of the century of the
Reformation, the veritable spate of religious movements in the
seventeenth century, the Methodist Revival in the eighteenth,
and the High Church movement in the nineteenth.

[1] The two Reports 'Catholicity' and 'The Fulness of Christ' presented to the Archbishop of Canterbury by representative groups of theologians of the Anglo-Catholic
and Evangelical schools of thought (in 1947 and 1950 respectively) reveal a most encourag-
ing growth together. The two groups met independently of each other and their membership was in each case selected by a leading representative of their own tradition.
(H.E.W.T.)

From Reformation times, the Church of England has embraced three different traditions, to which the names of High Church, Broad Church and Low Church were given during the nineteenth century. The High Church movement has always laid the emphasis upon the Catholic elements within the Anglican tradition. Dating from the seventeenth century with the great names of Lancelot Andrewes (1555-1626) and Archbishop Laud (1573-1645), it received new strength from the Oxford Movement of the eighteen-thirties and has left its mark upon the whole Anglican Communion during the last century. It sets great store by the conception of the priesthood, attaches considerable importance to Tradition and Catholic doctrine, and has succeeded to a great extent in adapting Anglican worship to its own ideals. Thus in many cathedrals and parish churches Holy Communion is now celebrated daily, a practice quite unknown a century ago, when the celebration of the Holy Communion was of much less frequent occurrence.

The Low Church tradition represents the religious attitude of the Evangelical Revival with its emphasis upon the Bible and simplicity of worship in accordance with the Prayer Book. Its roots go back to the earliest period of the English Reformation and it flourished again in the latter part of the eighteenth and the opening of the nineteenth century. Among its leading figures were Charles Simeon (1759-1836), Henry Venn (1725-97) and William Wilberforce (1759-1833).

The Broad Church tradition reflects the liberal and reconciling character of much Anglican theology and has often been associated with a special concern for a close connection between the Church and cultural life. Its ideal is a spacious Church which can embrace the largest number of divergent traditions within the framework of a liberal theology. Members of this tradition particularly represent the humanistic tendencies within Anglican theology and church-life. The limits of this school are not as clearly defined as those of the other two traditions. Many Anglicans would describe themselves as 'liberal Catholics' (High and Broad) or 'liberal Evangelicals' (Low and Broad). In fact, it represents rather an attitude towards divergences within the Church and to contemporary culture rather than a well-defined party within the Church.

If selection were to be made of a particular doctrine as specially characteristic of the Anglican Communion as a whole, it would certainly be the theology of the Incarnation. While other Churches emphasize the Resurrection of Christ or the Atonement, the Anglican Communion regards the Incarnation, the doctrine of the Son of God made man for us men and for our salvation, as the central theme of Christian theology. If the Orthodox Church is 'the Church of Easter,' or the Lutheran 'the Church of Good Friday,' the Anglican Church may be described as 'the Church of Christmas.'

A further characteristic principle of Anglican theology is what some representative Anglican theologians call 'the appeal to sound learning.' Fundamental to sound learning is the harmonious relationship between reason and faith. Its aim can be defined as a rational and realistic theology. Here again we meet the Anglican temper, which differs from that form of Scholasticism which seeks to found all doctrine upon logical proofs as well as from any type of theology which dethrones reason. Terms like 'reasonableness' and 'probability' are typical of this approach to theological thought.

Again, words like 'devotion' and 'adoration' occur more frequently in the religious vocabulary of the Anglican Communion than of the other Churches of the Reformation tradition. Indeed, anyone who has participated for a time in Anglican worship (and not necessarily of the Catholic tradition) will be impressed by its inherent spirit of adoration.

A typical representative of the Church of England, R. W. Church (1815–90), Dean of St. Paul's, sums up the essential character of his Church in four points: (1) Episcopal Church Order; (2) the Book of Common Prayer; (3) the English Bible which came into the hands of the English people through the Reformation, and (4) the Establishment. If the fourth element is confined to the Church of England, the other three form a necessary part of the essential structure of the Anglican Communion.

This analysis of the essential nature of the Anglican Communion is confirmed by a consideration of what it regards as the necessary basis for the Reunion of the Church. Thus, to quote an official statement, the 'Appeal to all Christian people,' issued by the Lambeth Conference of 1920, proposed the following basis for the Reunion of the Church: (1) The Holy Scriptures, as the record of God's revelation of Himself to man, and as being the ultimate standard of faith; and the Creed, commonly called Nicene, as the sufficient statement of the Christian Faith, and either it or the Apostles' Creed as the Baptismal confession of faith. (2) The divinely-instituted sacraments of Baptism and the Holy Communion, as expressing for all the corporate life of the whole fellowship in and with Christ. (3) A Ministry acknowledged by every part of the Church as possessing not only the inward call of the Spirit, but also the commission of Christ and the authority of the whole body. In practice this means for Anglicans the Episcopate in Apostolic Succession.[1]

3. DOCTRINE

What is the relation between doctrine, Church Order, Liturgy and ethos within the Church of England? A partial answer to this question can be found by asking what the Church of England itself regards as its standards for doctrine and life.

At his Ordination (though not as part of the Ordinal itself) every priest of the Church of England must declare his assent to the Thirty-nine Articles and the Book of Common Prayer and declare that the doctrine therein contained is agreeable to the Word of God. This is also clearly stated in the Articles themselves and in the Ordinal which speaks of the Scriptures as containing 'sufficiently all doctrine required of necessity for eternal salvation through faith in Jesus Christ.' The eighth Article mentions the three Creeds of the early Church, Apostles', Nicene and Athanasian, as to be 'thoroughly received and believed; for they may be proved by most certain warrants of Holy Scripture.' Thus in the century of the Reformation, the authority of Creeds, Articles and Prayer Book was binding because their doctrine was thought to be in agreement with Scripture.

It will be of importance to examine further these authorities and their position in the life of the Church.

---

[1] With the subdivision of the first point into two, this represents the Lambeth Quadrilateral of 1888. See below, p. 374. For the previous history of this formula see S. C. Neill and R. Rouse, *A History of the Ecumenical Movement*, pp. 250–51. (H.E.W.T.)

(i) The Bible

According to the Thirty-nine Articles, this comprises the Canonical Books of the Old and New Testaments. Of the Apocrypha it is said that 'the Church doth read them for example of life and instruction of manners; but yet doth it not apply them to establish any doctrine.' On this question the Anglican Church follows the *via media* between the Roman Catholic Church, which places the Apocrypha on the same level as the Canonical Scriptures, and the Reformed Churches which repudiate them.

In Church life Bible-reading plays a prominent part both in private prayer and public worship. One important reason why the knowledge of the Bible is more widespread in England than in other countries is that for centuries Anglican worship has made the people acquainted with it through the lessons. At Mattins and Evensong (Morning and Evening Prayer), two long lessons, one from the Old Testament and the other from the New, are invariably read.

In the course of the nineteenth century it became recognized that the Scriptures must be read in the light of historical research. The inevitable effect of this new approach upon the use of the Bible as a doctrinal authority is clearly recognized in the Report 'Doctrine in the Church of England.'[1]

(ii) *The Three Catholic Creeds* are not only doctrinal authorities, but are used freely in the Prayer Book services. The Apostles' Creed is used as the Baptismal Confession and repeated daily both at Mattins and Evensong. The Nicene Creed is the Eucharistic Creed, and is usually regarded as the unifying bond of Christendom. According to the Prayer Book, the Athanasian Creed is ordered to be said or sung on certain days of the year, but the rubric is seldom honoured in its entirety. In the proposed Prayer Book of 1928, for example, the number of occasions was reduced to three and the omission of the so-called damnatory clauses permitted. In no other Church have worshippers a similar opportunity of hearing all three Catholic Creeds and the ordinary church-goer is conversant at least with both the Apostles' and Nicene Creeds.

[1] The emergence in many quarters of the new Biblical theology suggests the beginning of an answer to this problem and indicates that the Bible still retains its pride of place as a doctrinal authority in the Church of England. (H.E.W.T.)

(iii) *The Thirty-nine Articles* represent the confessional document of the Church of England. Perhaps, however, the term may be misleading, for it is taken from the terminology of the Lutheran Church, and the Church of England has never had any single document of this type corresponding in status and authority to the *Confessio Augustana*. Neither in defining their doctrine in relation to other Churches, nor in affirming their own confessional allegiance within the Church have Anglicans ever relied exclusively upon the Thirty-nine Articles.

In the course of its history the Church of England has grown accustomed to a certain flexibility in the interpretation of this document. As early as the beginning of the seventeenth century, Archbishop Ussher of Armagh (1581–1656) could write: 'We do not suffer any man to reject the Thirty-nine Articles of the Church of England at his pleasure; yet neither do we look upon them as essentials of saving faith, or legacies of Christ and the Apostles—neither do we oblige any man to believe them, but only not to contradict them.' Since 1865, a more general formula of assent to the Articles has been required from candidates for Ordination. Anglican churchmen of the present day often urge that the Articles deal with problems which were acute at the time of the Reformation, but which to a considerable degree have lost their relevance. The living issues of contemporary theology do not come within their scope.[1] It is a significant fact that the Book of Common Prayer has always been considered as a subsidiary authority in addition to the Articles.

The first confessional document of the English Reformation were the Ten Articles of 1536 issued by order of the King. Their standpoint is that of 'Reform Catholicism,' emphasizing the Real Presence in the Eucharist, the invocation of saints and prayers for the dead. Later in the same reign there was published a document known as the Thirteen Articles with a more Lutheran tinge, largely dictated by the political wishes of the King. As nothing came of the proposed Lutheran alliance, the King finally issued in 1539 the Six Articles which laid down the doctrine of

---

[1] See, for example, the careful statement of Archbishop William Temple in the Chairman's Introduction to the Report 'Doctrine in the Church of England,' p. 9. An Interpretation of the Articles differing in some respects from that of Professor Molland may be found in E. J. Bicknell, *Theological Introduction to the Thirty-nine Articles*, pp. 9–27. (H.E.W.T.)

Transubstantiation, Communion in one kind, the celibacy of the clergy and the practice of private masses. A more Protestant line was adopted in the reign of Edward VI, of which the outcome was the Forty-two Articles of 1553 compiled by Cranmer. They display Calvinist influence, together with certain Lutheran traits, particularly with regard to the doctrine of the Eucharist. The Articles of Faith did not receive their final form until 1563 when, as the Thirty-nine Articles, they were approved by the Convocations. In 1571 they were enacted as law by Parliament as a counterstroke to the Papal Bull of the previous year which declared Elizabeth I to be illegitimate, and therefore excluded from the Royal Succession. Thus, since 1571, the Thirty-nine Articles have been the legal Articles of Faith of the Church of England. They are current both in an English and a Latin version which are not completely identical. The English text is bound up with every copy of the Book of Common Prayer. This practice has not, however, been universally followed in the Prayer Books of other branches of the Anglican Communion.

The teaching of the Thirty-nine Articles may be analysed as follows. The Catholic element in them is most pronounced in the first eight Articles which reaffirm the Catholic Faith in the Trinity and the Incarnation and which accepts the Catholic Creeds. There is a strong resemblance in phraseology to the *Confessio Augustana*, but a point of contrast with the Lutheran confessional document, which goes back to the heritage of the Catholic past, is to be found in Article VII 'Of the Old Testament,' which states that 'both in the Old and New Testaments everlasting life is offered to mankind by Christ.'

In their teaching on sin, grace, salvation and free-will, the Articles are Augustinian in tone. In Article XVII, the doctrine of Predestination is expounded in cautious terms. No mention is made of double predestination, but only of predestination to life, a doctrine full of 'comfort to godly persons and such as feel in themselves the working of the Spirit of Christ.' Of Free-will (Article X) it is merely said that 'man cannot turn and prepare himself by his own natural strength and good works to faith' (*se praeparare ad fidem*) and that 'we have no power to do good works, pleasant and acceptable to God, without the grace of God by Christ preventing us.'[1]

There is an obvious Lutheran element in the Articles. Man is justified by Faith alone (*sola fide* Article XI which takes the unusual step of referring to a particular Homily). 'We are accounted righteous before God, only for the merit of our Lord and Saviour Jesus Christ by Faith, and not for our own works or deservings; Wherefore, that we are justified by Faith only is a most wholesome doctrine, and very full of comfort.' The Definition of the Church in Article XIX is also decidedly Lutheran in tone. 'The visible Church of Christ is a congregation of faithful men, in the which the pure Word of God is preached, and the Sacraments be duly ministered according to Christ's ordinance in all those things that of necessity are requisite to the same.'

A markedly Protestant tone is to be found, for example, in Article XXI which states that general councils 'may err, and sometimes have erred, even in things pertaining unto God.' Of a similar nature is the next Article which categorically repudiates 'the Romish doctrine concerning Purgatory, Pardons, Worshipping and Adoration, as well of Images as of Reliques, and also invocation of saints.' Expressed in equally sharp terms is the rejection in Article XXXI of 'the sacrifices of Masses, in the which it was commonly said that the Priest did offer Christ for the quick and the dead, to have remission of pain or guilt,' as 'blasphemous fables and dangerous deceits.'

The teaching of the Articles on the Eucharist (Articles XXVIII and XXIX) is clearly Calvinist in character and differs sharply both from the Roman Catholic and Lutheran doctrines. 'The Body of Christ is given, taken and eaten, in the Supper, only after a heavenly and spiritual manner. And the means whereby the Body of Christ is received and eaten in the Supper is Faith.' 'The wicked, and such as be void of a lively faith' are 'in no wise partakers of Christ.'

Article XXXIV, 'Of the Traditions of the Church' is typical of the Anglican temper. 'It is not necessary that Traditions and Ceremonies be in all places one, or utterly like'; yet it also frowns upon those who 'openly break the traditions and ceremonies of

[1] In this context 'prevent' is used in the now obsolete sense of 'going before' or 'preceding' and the whole phrase is a paraphrase of the technical term 'prevenient,' which emphasizes the continual priority of God's action in the life of grace. (H.E.W.T.)

the Church, which be not repugnant to the Word of God, and be ordained and approved by common authority.' Equally characteristic of the temper of the times in England is the stress upon the Establishment. Thus in Article XXI, 'Of the Authority of General Councils,' it is laid down that 'general councils may not be gathered together without the commandment and will of Princes.' A later Article (XXXVII) (Of the Civil Magistrates) acknowledges the Sovereign as possessing 'the chief government' of the Church, but expressly states that 'we give not to our Princes the ministering either of God's Word or of the Sacraments . . . but that only prerogative, which we see to have been given always to all godly Princes in Holy Scriptures by God Himself.'

Little is said on the subject of Church Order. In Article XXIII it is laid down that no one may preach publicly or minister the Sacraments in the Congregation 'before he be lawfully called, and sent to execute the same' (*legitime vocatus et missus*). The conditions for this lawful exercise of ministry are laid down in a later Article (XXXVI) which decrees that all those who have been consecrated or ordered according to the Ordinal of the reign of Edward VI are 'rightly, orderly, and lawfully consecrated and ordered.' The Articles are, however, silent on the doctrines of apostolic succession or of the historic episcopate which are so central a theme of much modern Anglican theology.

It must be concluded that this confessional document (taken as a whole) defines the Protestant or Evangelical aspects of the Anglican Church.[1] Interesting confirmation of this judgement may be found in the fact that, when proposals were made under the House of Hanover for Intercommunion with the German Lutheran Churches, the objection was raised from the German side that, judging by the Thirty-nine Articles, the Church of England was too much under the influence of Geneva, particularly in its doctrine of the Eucharist.

The Articles have never been an object of affection to High

---

[1] Attempts have sometimes been made both within and outside the Anglican Church to reconcile the Thirty-nine Articles with the decrees of the Council of Trent. See, for example, Franciscus a Sancta Clara (Christopher Davenport) and L. E. du Pin from the Roman Catholic side, and Tract XC (Newman) on the Anglican side. A detailed modern study of the subject may be found in H. E. Symonds, *The Anglican Formularies and the Council of Trent*. They seem, however, to fall some distance short of conviction. (H.E.W.T.)

Churchmen. Repeated but unsuccessful attempts were made in the nineteenth century by their Low Church opponents to curb the progress of the more Catholic elements in the Church by appeals to the Articles. The liturgical and doctrinal controversies of the last century led officially to the relaxation of the Formula of Assent and to a changed view of the Articles as constituting a historical example of the *via media* in practice rather than as a finally authoritative corpus of confessional doctrine. Bishop Charles Gore (1853–1932) even proposed that the Articles should be abolished as a doctrinal authority in the Church of England.

(iv) *The Book of Common Prayer*

As the declaration made at Ordination proves, this undoubtedly ranks as a confessional document. The Prayer Book and the Articles have, in fact, always been co-ordinate authorities. This forms one of the distinguishing marks of the Anglican Communion, in contrast, for example, with Lutheranism, which has never reckoned its liturgy to be an authoritative standard of doctrine.

The history of the Book of Common Prayer reflects the chequered fortunes of the Church of England since the Reformation. Its first edition of 1549 was the result of a revision of the traditional services, made in a conservative spirit with the aid of mediaeval English liturgical books and a Reformed Roman Catholic Breviary. The tenor of the whole book owes much to Cranmer who had a positive genius for liturgical style. The Eucharistic Liturgy emphasizes the Real Presence and contains the commemoration of saints, particularly of the Virgin Mary, the prophets, apostles and martyrs, and prayers for the dead. The Epiclesis or Invocation of the Holy Spirit was somewhat curiously introduced before the Words of Institution.

As early as 1552, this first Prayer Book of Edward VI was replaced by the Second Prayer Book of Edward VI, which represents the Protestant high-water mark of Anglican liturgical history. By this time, under the influence of Evangelical refugees from the Continent, the English Reformation had taken a more radical turn and the spirit of the new book shows a corresponding change. The words 'Mass' and 'Altar' are replaced by 'the Lord's Supper' and 'the Lord's Table,' and the fixed altar replaced by a transportable table. It is still technically contrary to ecclesiastical law in England to have a permanent altar of stone, though this provision has often been ignored despite legal prosecutions and trials during the last few generations. The Liturgy of 1552 reveals a symbolic conception of the Eucharist. The ancient Eucharistic vestments were abolished and a famous note, which has acquired the name of the 'Black Rubric,' explains that the practice of kneeling at the reception of the Holy Communion does not signify 'any adoration of the sacramental bread and wine there bodily received, or unto any Corporal Presence of Christ's natural Flesh and Blood.'

After the restoration of the Roman Catholic Mass under Mary, the Anglican Liturgy was reintroduced under Elizabeth I in 1559. This third edition of the Prayer Book was a compromise between the two earlier versions. The Black Rubric and the prohibition of vestments were omitted, otherwise the substance of the 1552 Rite was retained. Particularly interesting are the Words of Administration at the Holy Communion. They consist of the Formula from the first Prayer Book of Edward VI, which presupposes a doctrine of the Real Presence combined with the formula of 1552 which implies a spiritualizing, or even a symbolic conception of the Eucharist. The result is the long formula prescribed in the present book which, with its character of a compromise, is typical of the Anglican tradition. 'The Body of our Lord Jesus Christ which was given for thee, preserve thy Body and Soul unto everlasting life. Take and eat this in remembrance that Christ died for thee, and feed on Him in thy heart by faith with thanksgiving.'[1]

When the Anglican Church was re-established after Cromwell, the Prayer Book was once more revised in 1662 and remains the official Prayer Book of the Church of England to-day. It did not differ from the Prayer Book of 1559 to any considerable extent. Changes introduced since 1662, which consist chiefly in the introduction of a new lectionary in 1871 (later revised under the authority of Convocation) and permission to shorten certain services, are very slight.

---

[1] While historically this account of the matter is, no doubt, correct, an Anglican who hears (or uses) the full formula to-day has no difficulty in assigning a real theological and liturgical significance to it as it stands. The second half is interpreted as the natural complement of the first. The description of what is received is followed by a statement of the means whereby it is received. (H.E.W.T.)

The High Church movement of the nineteenth century led to a desertion of the Prayer Book at many points at which it appeared out of harmony with their ideals. At first the words were normally left unchanged, but more frequent liturgical movement at the altar, genuflexions, vestments, the use of altar candles, and later of incense and holy water were introduced. Many practices of this kind were not taken into account in the authorized Liturgy, and some were even contrary to its spirit. More extreme High Churchmen altered or replaced the prescribed text and followed other models, frequently the 1549 rite, which is highly valued by Anglo-Catholics, and in extreme cases even the Roman Catholic Mass. Attempts to persuade or coerce such priests to conform to the rubrics and spirit of the Prayer Book have proved unavailing.

The new developments resulted in a great variety of liturgical practice. A Royal Commission in 1906 declared that 'the law of the Church of England on public worship is too narrow for the religious life of the present generation' and pointed to 'the desirability of reform so as to provide for reasonable elasticity.' Above all, the law should be so altered that there would be reasonable prospects of securing obedience. In the same year the Convocations were commissioned to revise the Book of Common Prayer and to submit their proposals to Parliament. For various reasons the work was extended over a long period and the proposals in their final form were not submitted to Parliament until 1928. They included the whole of the Prayer Book of 1662 together with some new liturgical alternatives to the old book. The new material may be described as very moderately Anglo-Catholic in tone. It therefore satisfied neither the Evangelicals nor the extreme Anglo-Catholics, yet secured majority votes both in the Convocations and in the Church Assembly.

When the Proposed Book came before Parliament it was rejected by the House of Commons by a small majority and, on its re-introduction with a slight amendment, it met with a similar fate. Many members of Parliament who did not belong to any branch of the Anglican Communion, and some who on their own admission professed no religion, voted against the measure, though this must be seen in the light of the accepted theory of English Parliamentary government that a Member represents his constituency.

After this defeat the Archbishop of Canterbury, joined by the other bishops, declared that the Church (the bishops, clergy and laity taken together) must assert its inalienable right to formulate its own faith and order its own worship. The book was published under the title 'The Prayer Book as proposed in 1928.' It never became popular in its entirety, but the non-controversial parts of the book quickly passed into general use. The bishops agreed to tolerate divergences from the Prayer Book of 1662 which fell within the limits of the new proposals, but in practice many of them display an even greater tolerance of divergences from the standard of 1662 which still remains the only valid use under English law.

When at Ordination the Book of Common Prayer is mentioned as the liturgical and doctrinal norm to be followed, there is good reason to ask which book the bishop and his candidates have in mind. The promise given at Ordination, however, contains a reservation which is not without significance. The candidate promises to 'use the form in the said book and none other except in so far as may be prescribed by lawful authority.' These last words presumably referred originally to the Crown and Parliament, but have come to cover a somewhat widely conceived *jus liturgicum* inherent in the episcopate and even in some respects in the clergy themselves. The problems which beset the interpretation of this phrase to-day are discussed in the Report on Church and State recently presented to the Convocations.

In the course of the nineteenth century the Prayer Book became recognized by many Anglicans as the superior authority, while the Thirty-nine Articles came to occupy the second place. The Articles are read in the light of the Prayer Book and not vice versa. At the same time the character of the Prayer Book has itself changed. From being a fixed standard of liturgical uniformity, it has become a somewhat variable norm, admitting of wide variations.

The formula that the law of prayer is the law of belief (*lex orandi lex credendi*) represents a fundamental principle of the Anglican Communion in modern times. The liturgical life sets the standard for the doctrine of the Church. During the past few generations the Anglican Church has undergone a far-reaching change of emphasis. To-day the Liturgy is the keystone of the organic harmony of liturgy, doctrine, church order and ethos. In this respect, the Anglican Communon has come to resemble the Orthodox Church, for which it has long possessed a high regard.

4. WORSHIP

Divine worship in the Church of England is founded upon the tradition of the Breviary and the Missal of the Western Church.

At the Reformation the canonical hours were preserved in a simplified form and translated into English. The original seven were reduced to two, Mattins and Evensong (Morning and Evening Prayer) and adapted for congregational worship. Since the Reformation only slight changes have been made. These non-sacramental services are conducted from a reading desk in the chancel and not at the altar. They consist of set prayers, the reading of the Bible, Versicles and Responses (said or sung antiphonally) and the recitation (also said or sung) of the Old Testament Psalter.

Both Mattins and Evensong open with a short Scripture passage (one of the texts prescribed, Ezekiel xviii. 27, is frequently used) read as an introduction by the officiant. This is followed by an Exhortation to worship addressed to the congregation, leading into the General Confession which is recited together by the minister and people. While the congregation remains kneeling, the priest rises from his knees and recites the Absolution which is couched in general or declaratory terms. The Lord's Prayer is then said together, kneeling, followed by a number of Versicles and Responses said or sung antiphonally, beginning with the Versicle 'O Lord, open thou our lips.' This part of the service is invariable. Then follows the Psalmody, introduced at Mattins (though not at Evensong) by the Invitatory or *Venite* (*Ps.* xcv). This is omitted when it falls within the portion of the Psalter prescribed for the day. A special Easter Anthem, composed of texts drawn from the Epistles of St. Paul, is substituted on Easter Day. The Old Testament Psalter, in the version of Coverdale known as the Great Bible (1539), is printed in the

Prayer Book, and divided into thirty portions so that the whole book is used during the course of the month.

After the Psalmody, the First Lesson, a passage from the Old Testament is read, either by one of the clergy or by a layman. The Canticle which separates the Old and New Testament Lessons admits of a number of variations. At Mattins the *Te Deum* ('We praise Thee, O God') is normally used, but, particularly in Lent, the *Benedicite, omnia opera* ('O all ye works of the Lord'), taken from the Apocrypha, is often used as an alternative. At Evensong the *Magnificat* ('My soul doth magnify the Lord') is far more frequently used than its Old Testament alternative. The Second Lesson from the New Testament is followed at Mattins by the *Benedictus* ('Blessed be the Lord God of Israel') or its less common Old Testament equivalent, the *Jubilate* ('O be joyful in the Lord, all ye lands'). At Evensong the *Nunc dimittis* ('Lord, now lettest Thou Thy servant depart in peace') is almost invariable. The Apostles' Creed is then said or sung by both clergy and people, standing and normally facing the altar (turning to the East). After the threefold *Kyrie eleison* ('Lord, have mercy upon us, Christ, have mercy upon us, Lord, have mercy upon us'), said or sung in English, and the Lord's Prayer, a set of Versicles somewhat longer than those in the opening part of the service, said or sung antiphonally, there follow three set prayers, the Collect for the Day, and two other collects which differ as between Mattins and Evensong, but which are invariable at either service. This whole part of the service (known technically as the Office) is followed in the Prayer Book by a number of additional prayers (known as the State Prayers). Recently a wide discretion has been permitted at this part of the service. The service concludes with the Prayer of St. John Chrysostom taken from the Orthodox Liturgy and the Grace (2 *Cor.* xiii. 13).

It is laid down that all the clergy shall read Mattins and Evensong daily, either privately or in church. It is traditional in cathedrals and in some parish churches for the offices to be sung daily, though under modern conditions this is less invariable than it once was. The service (sung with anthem but without either hymns or sermon) takes rather more than half an hour.

In parish churches the congregation usually takes an active part, joining in the General Confession, the Lord's Prayer, the

Responses and the Creed. The Psalter and the Canticles are either read antiphonally between clergy and people or sung together. In cathedrals, however, which have their own traditions of choral singing, the part played by the people is restricted to the said parts of the service and to hymns.

Probably in most parish churches Mattins, supplemented by a sermon and a number of hymns, is the principal mid-morning Sunday service. The classical order of Morning Prayer in the Church of England consisted of Mattins followed by the Litany and the Holy Communion, at which a relatively small number of worshippers might stay behind and make their communion. But the great majority of English parish churches to-day would either provide Mattins, often, though not always, followed by Holy Communion, or in churches with a High Church tradition, a sung celebration of the Holy Communion with Mattins relegated to a somewhat secondary position, and, in some cases, attended by relatively few. In nearly all Anglican churches there is a celebration of the Holy Communion at an earlier hour than the mid-morning service, and Evensong is invariably conducted at some hour in the evening or the late afternoon. Holy Communion is often celebrated during the week in churches with a High Church tradition, though such churches are also notably faithful in the public recitation of Mattins and Evensong. Churchmen of all traditions normally celebrate the Holy Communion on major Saints' Days and frequently on some other day when no saint's day falls during the course of the week.

The order for the celebration of the Holy Communion according to the Prayer Book of 1662 is as follows. The service opens with the Lord's Prayer said by the priest alone (a relic of the longer preparation of the mediaeval service books), and the Collect for Purity. He then turns to the people and recites either the Ten Commandments (a Calvinistic element in the Liturgy) or, more frequently to-day, our Lord's summary of the Law, to which the congregation makes the response 'Lord, have mercy upon us, and incline our hearts to keep this law.' After a Collect for the Sovereign there follows the Collect, Epistle and Gospel for the day which are variable items. The Nicene Creed is then

G

said or sung. At this point provision is made in the rubrics for a sermon.

A further stage in the service corresponding to the old *missa fidelium* opens with the Offertory introduced by the Offertory Sentence read by the Priest from the Altar. The alms of the congregation are then taken, received at the Altar by the celebrant, offered to God and placed on the Altar, where they remain until the conclusion of the service. At this point the bread and wine are prepared in paten and chalice and placed upon the Altar in readiness for their consecration later in the service. They are normally handed to the celebrant by an assistant priest or a lay server, though in some churches they are brought up to the Altar by two layfolk in the Offertory procession. After these preparations the celebrant introduces the prayer of intercession with the words 'Let us pray for the whole state of Christ's Church militant here in earth,' which may be preceded by other biddings at his discretion. In this prayer the alms and oblations are presented to God as the offering of the people and intercession is offered for Christian princes, the clergy and the whole people of God. The Prayer Book next includes three alternative forms of Exhortation of considerable length which are rarely used. The service then passes to the Invitation, 'Ye that do truly and earnestly repent you of your sins,' followed by the Confession, 'Almighty God, Father of our Lord Jesus Christ,' which is recited kneeling, by the whole congregation together with the celebrant. The priest then rises from his knees, faces the people, and pronounces the Absolution, which is couched in a precatory form, followed by the Comfortable Words, a set of four New Testament texts, a feature which has been unchanged since 1549.

After this section devoted to the preparation of the people, the Liturgy proceeds to the Preface introduced by the ancient dialogue of Versicle and Response called the *Sursum corda* ('Lift up your hearts. We lift them up unto the Lord'). Six Proper Prefaces are provided for the major festivals of the Christian Year, usually continued during their Octaves. The Preface leads directly into the *Sanctus* ('Holy, holy, holy, Lord God of Hosts') in which the people join. The *Benedictus* of the Roman Mass, retained in 1549, was omitted in 1552 and not restored in either of the two subsequent editions. The celebrant then kneels and recites the beautiful Prayer of Humble Access ('We do not presume to come to this Thy Table, O merciful Lord, trusting in our own righteousness'). Rising from his knees, he then proceeds to the Prayer of Consecration or, to use its more technical name, the Canon. Its last section is composed of the Words of Institution, introduced in the form of a relative clause as in the Roman Rite, 'Who in the same night that He was betrayed' (corresponding to the *Qui pridie quam pateretur* of the Roman Canon). During these words he consecrates the bread and wine with the appropriate manual acts. This is immediately followed by the Communion, first of the priest and then of the people, with the words of Administration mentioned above. If the consecrated elements are exhausted during the Communion of the people, it is provided that more must be consecrated by the priest with the use of the appropriate Words of Institution and manual acts. Whatever remains unconsumed is replaced on the altar. The service then continues with the Lord's Prayer, followed by one of two alternatives, the Prayer of Thanksgiving (sufficiently described by its name) or the Prayer of Oblation in which petition is made that God may 'accept this our sacrifice of praise and thanksgiving' and the offering of 'ourselves, our souls and bodies, to be a reasonable, holy and lively sacrifice.' Then follows the *Gloria in excelsis* ('Glory be to God on high') in full, transferred, somewhat strangely (considering its previous history) from the beginning of the Rite in 1552. The service concludes with the Benediction ('The peace of God which passeth all understanding').

It is expressly laid down that the celebrant (with the assistance of others if need require) should reverently consume whatever is left of the consecrated elements at the altar immediately after concluding the service. This rubric, together with the provision for the repetition of the Words of Institution and the manual acts at any supplementary consecration, sheds light upon Anglican Eucharistic doctrine. The Eucharistic elements are changed into the Body and Blood of Christ through the recitation of the Words of Institution, and so they remain after the Communion of the people; but, in order to prevent such abuses as Reservation or extraliturgical Devotions, their complete consumption is prescribed.

Such is the service of Holy Communion when it is conducted

according to the Prayer Book of 1662. Nothing is stipulated with regard to hymns, but at celebrations on Sundays they are often interspersed at different parts of the service. The vestments used may be either surplice, hood and scarf, surplice and stole (without hood) or alb and chasuble. The third use is adopted by Anglo-Catholics, but is not by any means confined to priests of this school of thought. The service has a dignified and sober simplicity in comparison with the Roman Catholic Mass. Visitors from Protestant Churches will often form the impression that it is a Catholic form of worship.

Anglo-Catholics are not, however, satisfied with the service as it stands. They often use a preparation after the Roman Catholic model said by priest and people or priest and server, and replace the Ten Commandments (with their Calvinist background in liturgical history) by the Ninefold *Kyrie eleison* either in English or in the original. But more characteristic changes are made in the Canon. Much the most frequent alteration (the so-called Interim Rite) is the restoration of the order of the 1549 Rite, in which the Prayer of Oblation completes the Prayer of Consecration and the oblation therein mentioned is more closely associated with the consecrated elements. Extreme Anglo-Catholics go further, read silently the Roman Canon and even celebrate Mass with the congregation represented only by a server. A few even use parts of the Roman Catholic Mass in Latin. The proposed Prayer Book of 1928 met the requirements of this section only to a very limited extent, and did not go far enough to satisfy the extremists.

The question of Reservation is a most controversial subject. This is normally defended on the principle of extended communion, particularly for the sick. Moderate Anglo-Catholics reserve the sacrament in an aumbry set in the wall of the chancel, while in more extreme churches it is reserved on the Altar itself. A sanctuary lamp is often used to denote the Presence of the Reserved Sacrament. Many High Churchmen, however, do not practice Reservation.[1]

[1] The whole subject of Reservation is discussed with considerable learning in W. K. Lowther Clarke and C. Harris, *Liturgy and Worship*, pp. 541–615. The bearing of the rubric discussed by Professor Molland on the previous page is considered on pp. 589–92 and a different conclusion is reached. The Report of a Conference on the subject attended by representatives of all schools of thought in the Anglican Church at Farnham Castle in 1925 was published by the S.P.C.K. in 1926. (H.E.W.T.)

Anglo-Catholicism in general has a large following, but the number of real extremists is relatively small. It may, therefore, be expected that the Prayer Book of 1662, or some modification in the direction either of the rites of 1549 or 1928, will be found in most churches. In some churches, however, strong Romanizing tendencies prevail. The High Church movement has affected the whole Church to such an extent that the Holy Communion occupies a wholly different place in the life of the Anglican Church from that of a century ago.

5. CHURCH ORDER

The Anglican Communion, unlike the Lutheran, assigns a primary place to questions of Church Order. In the Anglican view it is just as vital for the Church to have a right order as it is to have the right doctrine. This attitude becomes apparent in the ecumenical discussions of the present day in which Anglicans strongly advocate certain principles of Church Order. The watchword 'Faith and Order' is a typically Anglican formulation.

There is, however, a considerable difference between the Roman Catholic and Anglican approaches to the question of right order, corresponding to a wider distinction between the strict and well-defined doctrinal system of the Roman Catholic Church and the broad scope and flexibility of Anglican doctrine. The Anglican Church is an episcopal Church, and must therefore, according to its traditions, regard an episcopal Church Order as a constituent element of the Christian Church. But different points of view exist on the significance of this fact for its relationship to other Churches. Some Anglicans will not recognize a communion as part of the Church if it lacks an episcopal ministry guaranteed by the Apostolic Succession. In their view, the sacraments of such churches must be described as 'invalid.' In its full rigour, this view would not be held by any outside the more extreme wing of the Anglo-Catholic party. Evangelicals, on the other hand, do not consider that differences in church order should necessarily prevent relations of Intercommunion between the Churches. Most Anglicans hold positions intermediate between these two views. They draw a distinction between valid (secure or guaranteed) and efficacious, or speak of the sacraments of non-episcopal Churches as valid but irregular or, more properly, defective. This is the attitude (though not the terminology) officially adopted by the Anglican Communion since the Lambeth Conference of 1920 which wrote as follows: 'It is not that we call in question for a moment the spiritual reality of the ministries of those communions which do not possess the Episcopate. On the contrary, we thankfully acknowledge that these ministries have been manifestly blessed and owned by the Holy Spirit as effective means of grace.' At the same time so much importance is attached to the possession of an episcopal Church Order that the Anglican Church finds it difficult to have Intercommunion with Churches which lack the 'Historic Episcopate' (Churches without the Apostolic Succession). In the Anglican view, the Historic Episcopate is one of the constituent elements of the Church, which must be present in the Reunited Church which it regards as the goal of the ecumenical movement.

The Church of England has not always attached so much importance to its episcopal church order. During the first century of the English Reformation, it considered itself as belonging to the Reformed group of Churches and many of its leaders both advocated and practised Intercommunion with Protestants on the Continent. Differences in Church Order were not, therefore, regarded as any impediment to occasional acts of communion. At the Synod of Dordrecht (Dort), however, one of the Anglican delegation put forward the view that the episcopate was of apostolic and divine origin. Since that time, the necessity of an episcopal church order has continually been put forward by Anglican protagonists against the Nonconformists and has gradually come to be regarded as a condition for Intercommunion. But the doctrine of Apostolic Succession, though not unknown before, received a new emphasis from the time of the Oxford Movement.

The Anglican Communion has the threefold ministry of bishop, priest and deacon, conferred in each case by Ordination. The minimum ages for the three orders are twenty-three for deacons, twenty-four for priests and thirty for bishops. Deacons may conduct Mattins and Evensong (apart from pronouncing the Absolution), read the Epistle and administer the chalice at the

Holy Communion and preach, if licensed to do so by the bishop. Priests have authority to administer the sacraments and to preach. The additional authority to perform ordinations and confirmations belongs to the bishops alone.

The Church of England proper consists of two provinces, Canterbury and York, each with its own archbishops. The Archbishop of York has the title 'Primate of England,' while the Archbishop of Canterbury is called 'Primate of all England' and has precedence over York. There is a total of forty-three Diocesan bishoprics, twenty-nine in the province of Canterbury and fourteen in the province of York. Twenty-six bishops have seats in the House of Lords, some by virtue of their see, but mostly by seniority. In the majority of dioceses the bishop is assisted by one or more suffragan bishops who can perform all the episcopal functions but lack full diocesan responsibilities.

Bishops are appointed by the Crown, which means in practice the Prime Minister (even in cases where he is not himself a member of the Church of England). It is usual for him to consult the Archbishop of Canterbury and other ecclesiastical authorities before the selection is made. The procedure for the election of a Diocesan bishop is that the Crown proposes its nominee to the Cathedral Chapter of the Diocese for their election; but the election is merely a formality. The system naturally has the defect of leaving the way open for political appointments, as was frequently the case in the eighteenth century, but it also provides an opportunity for the representation of minority opinions within the episcopal college, which it might otherwise prove difficult to secure.

In each diocese there are one or more archdeacons who are charged with the duty of conducting visitations on behalf of the bishop, inducting the parochial clergy and acting in certain judicial cases within the diocese. They also supervise the church buildings. Each cathedral has a Dean or Provost who is responsible for the services, assisted by a number of canons. These, together with the Dean, form the Cathedral Chapter. Cathedral canonries are offices without the cure of souls, filled by clergy who have merited such appointments by contributions to theological scholarship or distinguished service of other kinds. Some are able to devote themselves to scholarship, but others are diocesan specialists of various kinds (Parochial Missions, Education and the like), while still other canonries are held by suffragan bishops and archdeacons. The parochial clergy or incumbents (usually called either rectors or vicars) are responsible for the spiritual oversight of their respective parishes which includes the conduct of services, preaching and the pastoral cure of souls.

There are something like 11,500 incumbents in the Church of England, together with about 2,500 assistant clergy. Clergy of the Church of England also occupy a variety of other appointments, in the Universities as academic staff or chaplains, or as chaplains to the Armed Services, hospitals, prisons, ports or to large industrial undertakings. The number of non-parochial clergy is about 1,200.

The training of the clergy of the Church of England follows one of two lines. Those who have secured a University degree (not necessarily in theology) after a course extending over three or four years, attend a theological college or seminary for a further two years. Non-graduates normally spend three years' training at a theological college. Special arrangements which vary somewhat in individual cases are made for older men. Great importance is attached to the practical side of theological training.

The appointment of clergy to benefices lies in many different hands. Some appointments are made by the Crown (950); others are in the gift of the bishops (3,000) or of other ecclesiastical authorities such as Cathedral Chapters or the incumbents of ancient parishes (2,500). Others, again, are in the hands of the Universities or of their constituent colleges (850). Less than half are in the hands of lay patrons (about 5,000). A lay patron who is a Roman Catholic is debarred from exercising the right of patronage within the Church of England.

The Church of England possesses a certain measure of self-government both through its clerical offices, particularly the episcopate, and through other constitutional bodies. From the thirteenth century onwards (apart from an interval between 1717 and 1852, when it stood prorogued and was virtually suppressed), the Church has had a legislative body in the two Convocations of Canterbury and York, which may be described as the Parliament of the Church. Each has an Upper House consisting of the bishops of the province and a Lower House composed of elected representatives of the clergy. Each house conducts its own business separately and resolutions must be approved by both houses. Convocation is empowered to discuss all questions relating to the Church. The laity are not represented in the Convocations.

In 1919, as the result of the Enabling Act, new machinery was set up, both at the National and the Parochial level. Parochial Church Councils replaced the incumbent and the churchwardens as the consultative unit in the parishes. The Council, which meets under the chairmanship of the incumbent, is composed of elected lay representatives. The other new body established under the Act is the Church Assembly, which consists of three houses, the House of Bishops (comprising all the Diocesan bishops), the House of Clergy (identical with the Lower Houses of Convocation) and the House of Laity (with 352 elected members). Resolutions passed by the Church Assembly do not become law until they are approved and passed by Parliament. At the intermediate levels of the Diocese and Rural Deanery there are the Diocesan and Ruridecanal Conferences in both of which elected lay representatives are associated with the clergy.

The Church of England is a State or Established Church. The connection with the State implies that the reigning monarch must be a member of the Church of England, and is crowned by the Archbishop of Canterbury. Prayers are read daily in both Houses of Parliament and, as mentioned above, twenty-six bishops have seats in the House of Lords, though clergy of the Church of England may not, even if elected, take their seats in the House of Commons. The Crown has the right of appointment to all bishoprics and deaneries and a number of other offices on the advice of the Prime Minister.

The Established Church holds no privileged position with regard to Education. Most schools are State or Municipal Schools in which religious instruction of a non-denominational kind is given. Both the Church of England and other Churches are allowed to maintain their own schools in which religious instruction according to their particular confession is given, and these stand on an equal footing in respect of State support.

The rejection of the Proposed Prayer Book of 1928 led to a reconsideration of the problem of the relationship of Church and

State in England. A Commission appointed by the two Archbishops issued a Report in 1935 which indicates that, while
very few churchmen desire the abolition of the Establishment,
many would wish for a greater measure of autonomy for the
Church, particularly in the form of the right to legislate in
matters which directly concern the Church and a greater voice
in the appointment of bishops.

6. RECENT DEVELOPMENTS (H.E.W.T.)

Brief mention must be made of some developments which
have been taking place within the Anglican Communion mainly
during the last decade.

(i) Particularly in England itself there have been marked signs
of a Liturgical Movement derived largely from the recovery of
the Biblical insight into the Church as the Body of Christ and
moulded upon Patristic rather than post-Tridentine Roman
Catholic models. Unlike some earlier trends of this kind, this
seems more likely to unite than to divide the two main traditions
within the Church. Thus some leading Evangelicals have
associated themselves with the movement known as 'Parish and
People.' This places in the forefront of its programme the
recovery of the Holy Communion as the central act of worship
in which the laity play a more prominent part and at which the
attendance of whole families is particularly encouraged. A
'Family Communion' or Sung Eucharist at 9.30 a.m. or some
similar hour, at which communicants are welcomed, a short
sermon preached and a simple congregational setting of the service
used, has become a familiar feature in the life of many parishes.
This has often replaced a more elaborate Sung Eucharist at a later
hour at which it was not expected that many worshippers would
make their communion. At some (though not all) of these
services representatives of the laity carry the wafers, wine and
water which are to be used in the service in procession to the
celebrant at the altar, thereby giving a wider meaning to the
People's Offering than the mere presentation of the alms. Again,
in some parishes a simple Parish Breakfast, provided and served
by the worshippers themselves in the Church Hall, follows the
service. There has been much discussion of the so-called 'West-
ward position' of the celebrant in which (following the example

of the Early Church) he stands behind the altar facing the people. This has been adopted in some Churches, though it hardly bids fair at present to become the universal practice, partly owing to the innate conservatism of the English people and partly for architectural reasons. In 1954 a Liturgical Commission was appointed by the two Archbishops at the request of the Convocations to consider all matters of liturgical concern referred to it by the Archbishops and to report upon them. Its membership is thoroughly representative of all schools of thought in the Church, and in 1957 it had already published a valuable preliminary document entitled *Prayer Book Revision in the Church of England*, which surveys the history of the movements for Prayer Book Revision, the new theological climate in the Church of England, guiding principles for future revision and the place of the Prayer Book both as a bond of unity and a standard of doctrine within the Anglican Communion. There was published almost concurrently a similar report of a Select Committee of the Church of India, Pakistan, Burma and Ceylon, entitled *Principles of Prayer Book Revision*, which seems likely to prove influential in later discussions within the Church of England.

(ii) The revision of the Canon Law of the Church of England which had remained unchanged since 1604 has also been set in hand. Steady progress has already been made, though its completion is likely to take several years. While some sections of the Church of England are hostile to the whole attempt, it seems likely to codify what is normal moderate Anglican practice. A special feature of the procedure adopted is the association of the House of Laity in Church Assembly with the Convocations in the discussion and adoption of the Canons.

(iii) In a sermon entitled 'A Step Forward in Church Relations' preached before the University of Cambridge in November 1946, the Archbishop of Canterbury suggested that the non-episcopal Churches of Great Britain should consider the possibility of 'taking Episcopacy into their system,' or growing together into full communion with the Church of England through the possession of mutually acknowledged ministries and sacraments, while still preserving their existing independence as Churches and their distinctive ways of worship. The ground was prepared by a Joint Report entitled *Church Relations in England*, published in 1950, which surveyed the proposal from both sides without committing any church to the conclusions which it contained. Discussions were held between the Church of England and the Episcopal Church in Scotland on the one hand and the Presbyterian Church of Scotland and the Presbyterian Church in England on the other. A unanimous report was published early in 1957 which breaks some new theological ground. It recommends ample time for consideration before any decision is taken by the participating Churches. Similar negotiations with the Methodist Church have reached the stage of the presentation of an Interim Report. Schemes for organic unity in North India and Ceylon, with notable differences in the method employed to unify the ministry from that adopted in South India, were carefully discussed in preparation for the Lambeth Conference in 1958. The section of the Report of the Conference devoted to the unity of the Church gave considerable encouragement to the proposals which were under review. Cordial relations with other Churches continue, though the need for measures to counter the vigorous proselytizing movement of the Roman Catholic Church has been noted and the provision of an Anglican apologetic literature to meet the current form of the Roman Catholic arguments has already begun.

(iv) Theologians of the Anglican Communion are also taking their full part in the revival of Biblical Theology, which is a marked feature in the life of many Churches at the present time. The attempt to pass beyond the technicalities of Biblical criticism and to open up new ways of presenting the theology of the Bible has obvious importance for the classical Anglican appeal to Scripture. The title of a massive trilogy by Fr. Lionel Thornton, C.R., *Revelation in the Modern World*, expresses the principal motif of this whole movement. Notable contributions in different ways and in various fields have been made by the Rev. Sir Edwyn Hoskyns, the present Archbishop of York (Dr. A. M. Ramsey), Fr. A. G. Hebert, S.S.M., Fr. Thornton and Dr. A. M. Farrer. The typological exegesis adopted by some members of this school would not, however, meet with universal acceptance.

(v) In the field of Church Organization the most notable feature of the past few years has been the grouping into independent provinces of missionary dioceses previously dependent directly upon the Archbishop of Canterbury. Two new provinces, one in West Africa (created in 1955) and one grouped round an Archbishop in Jerusalem (inaugurated in 1957), are the most recent stages in this development. The elevation of members of native races to the episcopate, though not in itself an innovation, has been greatly extended during the past decade.

(vi) By far the most important development within the Anglican Communion considered as a whole lies in the sphere of missionary policy rather than of ecclesiastical organization. The Church of the Province of South Africa found itself compelled to resist the policy of *apartheid* adopted by the Government of the country. Its resolute and consistent witness, as expounded in a work by Fr. Trevor Huddleston, C.R., entitled *Nought For Your Comfort*, has won widespread sympathy and support.

(vii) While the Church of England possesses no organization comparable with the *prêtres ouvriers* in France, significant work is being done to try to bridge the gap between the Church and the worker. Chaplains on the staff of the diocesan bishop, whose main work is to carry out pastoral work and conduct services in factories, are a special feature of several industrial dioceses. The work of the Industrial Mission in the diocese of Sheffield is a particularly notable example. Lunch-hour services on weekdays for city workers have long been held in London, and this has become a regular feature of the Church life of other large cities. In London, again, some of the city parishes with little or no resident population have become virtually Guild Churches with the special purpose of ministering to particular sections of the population at work in the city. An interesting feature of this successful experiment is the appointment of the incumbent for a term of years which marks a departure from the normal 'Parson's Freehold.'

(viii) In the field of culture there have been increasing signs of close and friendly co-operation between the Church and the liberal arts. In literature the work of T. S. Eliot, Dorothy Sayers and C. S. Lewis is of special significance. The plans of two modern cathedrals, Guildford and Coventry (the latter replacing an ancient building virtually destroyed during the war), as well as a number of new parish churches, indicate that the Church of England does not feel itself bound to follow traditional designs.

The erection in Llandaff Cathedral of an aluminium statue of
Christ in glory is further evidence of collaboration between the
Church and contemporary art. Religious drama at various levels,
ranging from the nativity tableaux of many Parish Churches to
modern religious plays, sometimes even performed in works and
factories, represent another significant feature of contemporary
English Church life. The complete cycle of mediaeval mystery
plays has been revived as a regular part of the York Festival.
The traditional alliance between the Church and music is maintained by Choir Festivals, of which the Three Choirs' Festival,
held in consecutive years at Worcester, Gloucester and Hereford,
is the most famous. Religious music, specially composed or
suitable for performance in churches, continues to be written by
many leading composers.

CHAPTER VII

THE CHURCH OF SOUTH INDIA

THE Church of South India emerged in 1947 as the result of a movement for Christian unity in the mission field.

At the beginning of this century there was a considerable number of mutually independent Churches in South India. With the exception of the old Mar Thoma Church,[1] they were the outcome of the missionary activity in the last two centuries of the Roman Catholic Church, the Church of England, and a number of Evangelical Churches, European and American. The differences which separated the mother Churches had been transferred to the mission field and had created barriers between the various daughter Churches which were felt to be in many respects meaningless in the new environment. There was a longing for unity among the non-Roman Catholic Christians in India. On the other hand, there was also a loyalty to the special values safeguarded by the various doctrinal traditions and systems of church order which made it impossible to deal in a superficial way with the difficulties which beset the quest for closer union.

Interdenominational conferences attended by representatives of the various Protestant Churches in India had been held from 1855 onwards, and at these conferences attention was drawn to the fact that there was an approximation between the policies of the different Churches in India. The Congregationalists had found themselves compelled for practical reasons to introduce some forms of centralized Church government, and it was pointed out on one occasion that the local Church Councils introduced by the (Anglican) Church of India, Burma and Ceylon resembled Presbyteries. As early as 1870, an Indian Presbyterian minister suggested a union scheme to include the essential principles of Episcopacy, Presbyterianism and Congregationalism. The way leading to this goal, however, proved to be long.

In 1900, two Reformed Churches in South India united, and in 1903 the Congregationalists formed a union which adopted

[1] See above, pp. 125–6.

both a confession of faith and a constitution. Negotiations towards a fusion of these two Churches began in 1905, and in 1907 a union was achieved. This new Church was called the South India United Church.

Anglicans of various schools in the Church of India, Burma and Ceylon also felt a longing for union. The Evangelicals co-operated with other Protestants in practical matters. To Anglo-Catholics the question of the ministry was, of course, the crucial point. The Bishop of Madras, a determined Tractarian when he was consecrated in 1899, changed his views during his episcopate and from 1910 onwards advocated a union on the basis of the Lambeth Quadrilateral.[1] The Holy Scriptures, the Apostles' and Nicene Creeds, the two Sacraments of Baptism and Holy Communion, and the 'Historic Episcopate,' without the acceptance of any particular theory about the episcopate, was suggested as the possible basis for a united Church.

A joint Committee on Church Union was formed in 1920 with officially appointed members representing the Church of India, Burma and Ceylon, the South India United Church and, from 1925 onwards, also the South Indian Province of the Methodist Church. The Mar Thoma Church decided not to take any official part in the work of the Joint Committee, lest its own reunion with the Jacobite Church should be made more difficult. The Lutherans adopted the same attitude, partly owing to their own internal divisions, but also because their strong allegiance to the Lutheran Confessional documents of the sixteenth century made it difficult for them to envisage a union upon any other basis. Members of these Churches had to content themselves with close observation of the negotiations and prayerful interest in them.

In 1929 the Joint Committee adopted unanimously an elaborate scheme of Union. This scheme was revised several times by the Joint Committee (1932, 1933, 1934, 1936, 1939, 1942) and it was the seventh edition of 1942 which finally formed the basis of the Union in 1947.

For about two decades a discussion of all the theological questions implied in the union scheme took place, not only in India, but also in the European and American Churches, whose daughter

[1] See below, p. 374.

Churches were involved in the negotiations. This discussion coincided with, and was related to, the debate on the Faith and Order problems in the Ecumenical Movement.[1] A remarkable aspect of the Indian negotiations was the place occupied by appeals to the history of the Early Church and to Patristic scholarship, on the Congregationalist side no less than on the Anglican. It was felt that the missionary Church of the first centuries possessed a unique authority in these matters.

The furtherance of plans for union was made possible not only by the growing feeling that a common Christian heritage could be presented more forcibly by a united Church, but also by a mutual admission by representatives of the various Churches that the different Christian traditions represented values which had to be incorporated into a united Church. Congregationalists and Presbyterians, as well as Methodists and Anglicans, all fought for the preservation of principles and institutions which were dear to their own traditions. But in all the negotiating Churches there was also a willingness to consider the values represented by the other traditions.

The Anglican insistence on the Apostles' Creed and the Nicene Creed as the doctrinal basis for a union met with criticism from the South India United Church. It was felt that the great principles of the Reformation had to be expressed in a more satisfactory way than had been done in the 1929 Scheme, where the credal statement was formulated as follows:

The uniting Churches hold the faith which the Church has ever held in Jesus Christ, the Redeemer of mankind; and in accordance with the revelation of God which He made, being Himself God incarnate, they worship one God in Trinity and Trinity in Unity.

They accept the Holy Scriptures of the Old and New Testaments as containing all things necessary to salvation and as the ultimate standard of faith.

They accept the Apostles' Creed and the Creed commonly called the Nicene, as witnessing to and safeguarding that faith, which is continuously confirmed in the spiritual experience of the Church of Christ, and as containing a sufficient statement thereof for a Basis of Union.

The guardians of the Protestant tradition wanted a clearer expression of the principle of *sola Scriptura* and of the Church's duty to reform herself in accordance with the teachings of Holy Scripture. At the same time, Churchmen with a Congregational

[1] See below, pp. 380–4.

background felt a natural reluctance to employ creeds and a desire for some liberty in the interpretation of such inherited formulae. But, on the other hand, subscription to a formula safeguarding the Trinitarian faith was felt even by Congregationalists to be necessary as a bulwark against syncretism in the Indian milieu. Protracted deliberations, in which Continental Churchmen took part, led to a significant re-phrasing of the 1929 statement. The 1939 Scheme offered a wording which was finally adopted by all the constituent Churches in 1947. Here the acceptance of the two Creeds is combined with the Protestant insistence on the authority of the Holy Scriptures, and a reasonable scope of freedom in the interpretation of the Creeds is safeguarded in an appended note. The text runs as follows:

The uniting churches accept the Holy Scriptures of the Old and New Testaments as containing all things necessary to salvation and as the supreme and decisive standard of faith; and acknowledge that the Church must always be ready to correct and reform itself in accordance with the teachings of those Scriptures as the Holy Spirit shall reveal it.

They also accept the Apostles' Creed and the Creed commonly called the Nicene, as witnessing to and safeguarding that faith; and they thankfully acknowledge that same faith to be continuously confirmed by the Holy Spirit in the experience of the Church of Christ.

Thus they believe in God, the Father, the Creator of all things, by whose love we are preserved;

They believe in Jesus Christ, the incarnate Son of God and Redeemer of the world, in whom alone we are saved by grace, being justified from our sins by faith in Him;

They believe in the Holy Spirit, by whom we are sanctified and built up in Christ and in the fellowship of His Body;

And in this faith they worship the Father, Son and Holy Spirit, one God in Trinity and Trinity in Unity.

To this statement is added the following rider:

The uniting Churches accept the fundamental truths embodied in the Creeds named above as providing a sufficient basis of union; but do not intend thereby to demand the assent of individuals to every word and phrase in them, or to exclude reasonable liberty of interpretation, or to assert that those Creeds are a complete expression of the Christian faith.

If the formulation of the common faith of the constituent Churches had been a difficult task which required long deliberations, a theological re-thinking of the problems and a mutual willingness to understand the divergent positions of the Churches involved in the Scheme, this was also the case with the problems of Church Order, which for a long time were definitely those in the foreground in the negotiations in India as well as in the discussions which accompanied them in the European and American Churches.

The two extreme standpoints in these discussions were the Anglican insistence on the 'Historic Episcopate' and the Congregationalist interpretation of the common Priesthood of Believers. As long as Anglicans refused to recognize the validity of the non-episcopal ministries and claimed that clergy which had not received episcopal ordination should be reordained, there was no hope for a union. This position was hardly held by any of the responsible Anglican Churchmen in India who were in favour of a united Church. They shared the more generous attitude which found its expression in the *Appeal to All Christian People* issued by the Lambeth Conference in 1920.[1] Accordingly they tried to find solutions which implied some form of recognition of the non-episcopal ministries. One possibility discussed was mutual supplemental ordination or mutual commissioning, whereby ministers who lacked episcopal ordination would receive a supplementary commission at the hands of bishops, and episcopally ordained clergy (including bishops who had been canonically consecrated) the commission of the non-episcopal Churches through the imposition of hands by representative ministers. This idea was, however, ultimately abandoned because of the strong opposition which it aroused in the South India United Church.

The extreme Congregationalists, on the other hand, demanded the recognition of the Common Priesthood of Believers and considered the admission of the laymen's right to celebrate the Lord's Supper as the touchstone of this doctrine. The opinion of the South India United Church was divided on the matter, the majority being against this emphasis on Lay Celebration. What finally undermined the extremists' position was that staunch Protestants both in India and in England drew attention to the distinction between the priesthood of all believers, which implies that all baptized persons have immediate access to the heavenly throne and present their bodies a living sacrifice, and

[1] See below, pp. 374–5.

the existence of a special ministry, by which men are set apart
for special service in the Church. The idea of the priesthood of
all believers was incorporated into the final Scheme: 'All share in
the heavenly High Priesthood of the risen and ascended Christ,
from which alone the Church derives its character as a royal
priesthood. No individual and no order in the Church can
claim exclusive possession of this heavenly priesthood.' But the
section continues by emphasizing the necessity of a special
ministry. 'But in the Church there has at all times been a
special ministry.' In an additional statement the arguments for
an ordered ministry were stated as follows: 'God is the God of
order; it has been His good pleasure to use the visible Church
and its regularly constituted ministries as the normal means of
the operation of His Spirit.'

The main concern of the Presbyterians was to secure the
recognition of Protestant doctrinal tenets and of Church government by Church Courts. All Union Schemes from 1929 onwards
combined Episcopacy with a Synodical organization of the
Church. The 1929 Scheme proposed the establishment of
parochial councils consisting of presbyters and laymen, diocesan
councils of the same structure, and a synod for the whole Church
presided over by a Moderator. All the bishops would be *ex officio*
members of the Synod. According to this plan the Synod would
be 'the supreme governing and legislative body of the united
Church, and the final authority in all matters pertaining to the
Church.' An additional clause devised a procedure to prevent a
proposition concerning doctrine, Church membership, ministerial functions, or worship, from being carried unless supported
by a majority of the bishops. A House of Bishops would thus
emerge, invested with a right of veto in certain questions. An
amendment of the Scheme in 1932 restricted the right of veto
of the bishops, who might be overruled by a three-quarters
majority in the Synod supported by a majority of two-thirds of
the Diocesan Council, to whom the case should be referred. The
system was characterized by a Congregationalist theologian as
'the historic episcopate in a constitutional form,' and 'a more
balanced type of episcopacy,' which proved acceptable. In the
last revisions of the Scheme a lay majority in the Synod was
secured. The diocesan representation in the Synod was fixed at

the minimum of two presbyters (besides the bishop) and four laymen, and a maximum of six presbyters (besides the bishop) and eight laymen for the larger dioceses.

The last problem to be solved was the question of inter-communion within the united Church during the long period in which it would have a dual ministry, some episcopally-ordained presbyters and some without episcopal ordination. From the very outset of the negotiations it had been understood that acceptance of the historic episcopate involved the principle that all future ordinations should be performed by bishops. After a long interim period all clergy in the united Church would be episcopally ordained. But was it possible in the mean-time for Church members with an Anglican background to receive the Sacrament at the hands of a minister who had not been ordained by a bishop? A clause securing that an ex-Anglican congregation should not be placed in the charge of a non-episcopally-ordained minister caused a vivid discussion.

The ice was broken by a statement published in September 1946 by the five Anglican bishops in South India who declared:

After the inauguration of Union we, as Bishops of the Church of South India, shall be ready ourselves to receive communion at the hands of any Bishop or Presbyter of the United Church. . . . All who have the status of Presbyters in the United Church are capable of performing all the functions assigned to Presbyters in the United Church by the Constitution of that Church in every congregation in the United Church. . . . The suitability of a Presbyter for a particular congregation is another question and will have to be considered in all cases by the appointing authority.

After this declaration the time was ripe for a final vote in the governing bodies of the Churches implied in the negotiations.

In September 1946 the General Assembly of the South India United Church decided by a large majority to enter into organic union with the other Churches. In the North Tamil Church Council, however, there had not been a majority of two-thirds for the union, and the congregations represented on this Council therefore remained outside the United Church until they decided in 1950 to join the Church of South India as a new diocese.

In the (Anglican) Church of India, Burma and Ceylon the question was whether this Church would allow the four South Indian dioceses of this Church to be severed from the other

eleven dioceses and become dioceses in the Church of South
India. Here the Diocesan Councils were practically unanimous
in accepting the Union Scheme. In January 1945 the General
Council of the Church of India, Burma and Ceylon finally
permitted the four South India dioceses to enter into the pro-
jected union.

The Methodists had had less difficulties than the other Churches
with accepting the provisions of the various Schemes. As early
as January 1943 the South India Provincial Synod had decided
by an overwhelming majority to join the union.

On September 27th, 1947, the Inauguration Service for the
Church of South India was held in St. George's Cathedral,
Madras. Fourteen dioceses had been created. Of the fourteen
diocesan bishops who had been elected, six were Indians, eight
British. Seven of the bishops were ex-Anglicans, three ex-
Congregationalists, three ex-Methodists, and one ex-Presbyterian.
The Presiding Bishop was an Indian whose forefathers had been
Christians for centuries.

At the Inauguration Service the five Anglican bishops were
solemnly commissioned by a South India United Church presbyter and a Methodist presbyter 'to exercise the office of a bishop
in all the congregations of all Church Councils of the South
India United Church' and 'to exercise the office of a bishop in
all the congregations of the South India Province of the Methodist Church.' The Presiding Bishop then uttered the solemn
Declaration: 'Dearly beloved brethren . . ., I do hereby declare
that these three Churches, namely . . ., are become one Church
of South India.' The nine bishops-elect were then consecrated. In
the act of the laying on of hands three Anglican bishops and three
presbyters from each of the South India United Church and the
Methodist Church participated.

For an interim period of thirty years from 1947, missionaries
from the Congregationalist, Presbyterian and Methodist
Churches whose daughter Churches have formed the Church
of South India will be accepted as presbyters in this Church if
they have been ordained in the sending Churches. After 1977,
the Church itself will decide whether it will make exceptions
from the rule requiring episcopal ordination. The majority of
missionaries from the non-episcopal Churches who have gone

to South India after 1947 have preferred to receive their ordination in the Church of South India.

Although forms of worship had been discussed on various occasions during the negotiations for Church Union, this question had never been in the foreground. There was a general agreement that the different liturgical traditions should continue, and at the same time it was anticipated that in the united Church these usages would inevitably approximate to each other. Development has been in this direction. Since 1952, a new liturgy based on the old Syrian rite with the incorporation of elements from other liturgical traditions, Eastern and Western, has been in use as an alternative form of worship.

The membership of the Church of South India is more than one million. Negotiations are being continued with other Churches in South India, the Lutheran Church and the Mar Thoma Church, with a view to their participation in the union.

CHAPTER VIII

THE LUTHERAN CHURCH

1. Designation, Distribution, Statistical Data and Organization

THE designation 'Lutheran Church' does not convey Luther's own intentions. He had no wish to found a new Church, and when the break with Rome took place, did not regard the Lutheran parishes as constituting a new Church. The name of 'the Lutherans,' originally invented by his opponents, came, however, to be accepted by his followers, who called themselves *'die Lutherischen,'* especially after 1530.

The Confession of Augsburg (*Confessio Augustana*) and other confessional documents do not speak of 'the Lutheran Church,' but only of 'our Churches' or 'the Church here.' The Formula of Concord uses the expression 'the pure Evangelical Church' or 'our Reformed Church.' The title of 'the Lutheran Church' did not appear before the followers of Calvin began to call themselves 'Reformed' and the Lutherans came to emphasize the points which distinguished them from the Calvinists. For a long time the Lutherans were averse to calling themselves after a man, and preferred the names of 'the Evangelicals' or 'the Evangelical Church.' By the time of the Thirty Years' War the designation 'the Lutheran Church' was generally accepted.

In the nineteenth and twentieth centuries, the words 'Evangelical' and 'Protestant' have been in general use as joint descriptions for both 'Lutheran' and 'Reformed.' They are frequently employed to cover all Churches to the left of the Anglican Communion and sometimes even to include it as well. The term 'Protestant' derives from the protest submitted by the Evangelical Estates to the Diet of Speyer in 1529 against its decisions in matters of religion. The use of the term 'Evangelical' to describe a movement also derives from the Lutheran Reformation. The word 'Protestant' has a more negative and polemical ring about it with the primary connotation of 'anti-Roman' or 'anti-

Catholic.' The positive ideals of these Churches are better described by the word 'Evangelical.'

From its homeland in Electoral Saxony, Lutheranism has spread over a wide area, first in Germany, then to Scandinavia and, to some extent, to South-Eastern Europe, and finally through emigration to America and through missionary work to other parts of the world.

The total Lutheran population of the world may be put at approximately sixty-eight million. They do not, however, all belong to purely Lutheran Churches. Certain Churches are Uniate in which both Lutherans and Reformed are united in a single Church. The Uniate Churches in Germany have a membership of twenty-four million, of which the large majority may be reckoned as Lutherans.

Germany (according to the 1950 statistics) has thirty-seven million Lutherans, the Scandinavian countries (including Finland) nearly eighteen million, the Baltic States two million. In Hungary there are half a million Lutherans, in Austria and Czechoslovakia 400,000, in Poland and Rumania some 200,000 and in Russia a few hundred thousand. In Jugoslavia there is a small Lutheran Church and very small Lutheran minorities in Holland and Switzerland. About a quarter of the million Protestants in France are Lutherans.

The number of Lutherans in Europe can therefore be reckoned as sixty million out of a total Protestant population of 110 million.

The Scandinavian countries stand alone as having an almost exclusively Lutheran population. They are also particularly distinctive of Lutheranism since here alone it has been able to develop on its own lines free from other influence. In Central Europe, on the other hand, Lutheranism has in many cases lost some of its distinctive features, either through approximation to the Reformed type, as in Uniate Churches, or through the abandonment of such elements in the Lutheran tradition as were considered Catholic.

In Central Europe it is mainly (though not exclusively) the German or German-speaking groups which are Lutheran. A number of the small minority Churches of Czechoslovakia, Poland, Russia, Hungary, Rumania and Jugoslavia formerly

used German in their services and many of their members are of
German origin. The large majority of the French Lutherans live
in Alsace, where services are conducted in the German language
in most Churches.

From the time of the Reformation onwards, Germany has
been deeply divided on matters of religion. Before the last war,
five-eighths, or perhaps two-thirds, of the country was Evangelical, while one-third was Roman Catholic. The German
Evangelical Church consists of a number of independent
Landeskirchen with some varying features. After the Second
World War, twenty-seven of these Churches were federated in
the Evangelical Church in Germany (organized in 1945), and
ten of the Lutheran Churches in this Union are federated in the
United Lutheran Church in Germany. The largest (of mixed
Lutheran and Reformed origin) is the Prussian with over twenty
million members. Of purely Lutheran Churches of this type are
the Bavarian (which includes about a quarter of the population),
the Württembergian (two-thirds of the population) and the
Hanoverian (three-quarters of the population). The most distinctively Lutheran in doctrine and tradition is the Bavarian
Church. There are also small Lutheran Free Churches, of which
the most important is the old Lutheran Free Church in Prussia
formed in the eighteen-thirties by zealous Lutherans who refused
to join the Prussian Union.

In the United States there are a number of autonomous
Lutheran Churches, mostly formed of Lutheran immigrants who
carried on the traditions of the Churches of their homeland.
Another cause of division was controversy on matters of doctrine
and organization, which under American conditions was a
fruitful source of separation, as dissident minorities formed
themselves into independent Churches. The history of American
Lutheranism is full of disruptions and reunions. Apart from
small minorities who use German or the Scandinavian languages,
the services of the American Lutheran Churches are conducted
in English.

Numerically, the Lutheran Church is the fourth largest Church
in the United States with a total membership of over six million,
only exceeded by the Roman Catholic, the Baptist and the
Methodist. While the Lutheran Churches in Europe are in many

cases national or established Churches, in America the Lutheran Churches are Free Churches with a synodal constitution and democratic organization. They usually lay considerable stress on the specifically Lutheran doctrines.

Of the Lutheran Churches in the mission field, the following may be mentioned. In China a Church with a membership of about 52,000 was formed by the combination of several Lutheran Churches under the title of 'the Church of Justification by Faith.' In India there are several Lutheran Churches with a total membership of over half a million. The Lutherans in Madagascar number 150,000. The largest Lutheran Church outside the Western world is the Batak Church in Indonesia with 600,000 members.

There are marked differences between the Lutheran Churches, not only in their relationship to the State, but also in their attitude to the Reformed Churches, their forms of worship and their constitution. Among Lutherans a uniform Church Order has never been regarded as a condition of Intercommunion. Some Lutheran Churches, as in Scandinavia, have an episcopal constitution, while others have no bishops. The bond of unity for Lutherans lies in their common faith and doctrine.

2. The Characteristic Features of the Lutheran Church

(i) The Lutheran Church, like the Anglican, represents a *via media* in Christendom. In order, worship, ethos and in many points of doctrine, it occupies a central position with the Orthodox and Roman Catholic Churches to its right, and the Reformed Churches and the Fundamentalist groups to its left.

The concept of the *via media* is not much used by Lutheran theologians but it is of considerable assistance towards understanding the particular character of this type of church. Both the Reformer, Luther, and the Church upon which he left his mark can only be properly understood through an appreciation of the two fronts on which they were engaged at the time of the Reformation, against the Roman Catholic Church on the one hand, and against the left-wing tendencies in the Reformation (described by Luther himself as 'Enthusiasm') on the other. The special character of Lutheranism emerges in contrast both to Rome and to the enthusiasts.

In comparison with Roman Catholicism, Lutheranism marks itself out as a personal religion which regards the conscience of the individual Christian as the final criterion in matters of religion. The scene at Worms (1521), where Luther appeals to his own conscience, has left an indelible impression on the Lutheran mind. 'It is not advisable to act against the dictates of one's own conscience.' These words have often provided the starting-point for the interpretation of the Lutheran Reformation. Seen against the background of Rome, the forcefulness of the utterances of Luther on the freedom of a Christian man is striking, freedom from the Law, freedom from outward Church authority, freedom from allegiance to tradition, and even freedom with regard to the Scriptures. Luther himself took the liberty of making some remarkably unrestrained observations on some of the books of the Bible. This affirmation of Christian freedom is repressed to a large extent in the Lutheran confessional documents, but reappears now and again in the Lutheran Church, for example in the liberal theology which was convinced that it was in agreement with genuinely Lutheran principles on this point.

Against 'Enthusiasm,' on the other hand, Lutheranism stands out as a religion of authority. The representatives of the left wing of the Reformation were deeply disappointed with Luther who had, in their opinion, only taken half measures and refused to push matters to their logical conclusion. Luther appealed to the absolute authority of the Word of God against the reliance of the enthusiasts on 'the Inner Light' or 'the voice of conscience.' When it came to the point, he showed himself to be the follower, not of a free and unbound conscience, but of a conscience bound by God's Word. The Word (*Das Wort*) was the supreme authority in matters of religion. Here the Lutheran Church faithfully followed his teaching and even came to outstrip him in its emphasis upon the authority of Scripture. In opposition both to the enthusiasts and to Zwingli, Luther stressed the objectivity of the sacraments in a manner which would astonish many members of the Lutheran Church to-day. Here the Lutheran confessional documents follow his teaching closely.

Lutheranism can thus be put forward as a *via media* between the Roman Catholic Church and the enthusiasts, but certainly not in the sense of a conciliatory mediation which sees the elements of reason and exaggeration on both sides of a question and therefore prudently takes the middle path between them. That is not the Lutheran temper!

Such a type of mediation is excluded, for Lutheranism boasts of being one-sided on certain important points of doctrine and affirms a clear-cut position particularly with regard to the doctrine of Justification by Faith, which lies at the very heart of its system. On the doctrines of Grace and Redemption, Lutheranism takes no *via media*, but adopts a sharply defined point of view, the one-sidedness of which some theological circles such as the Anglicans find it difficult to appreciate.

(ii) The Lutheran Church is the one which gives to doctrine the most absolute primacy over liturgy, order and ethos. Its point of departure was not the idea of the Church, a new ideal of Church Order, a desire for liturgical reform or any new pattern for Christian living. Its starting point was simply Luther's emphasis upon salvation by faith alone and without works, which was new so far as the Roman Catholic Church was concerned. Everything else followed as the natural consequences of this doctrine. His liturgical reform, for example, followed from his criticism of the doctrinal basis and implications of the Eucharistic Sacrifice and, chronologically, it came several years after the reform of doctrine.

The emphasis which Luther placed upon doctrine and its formulation can be illustrated by the Conference at Marburg which took place between Luther and Zwingli in 1529. They discussed the doctrine of the Eucharist and reached agreement on fourteen points. Differences, however, arose on the fifteenth point. Here it was proposed that they should recognize each other in a spirit of Christian love even though they had failed to reach agreement on the question of the Real Presence of the Body and Blood of Christ in the Eucharist. Luther completely rejected the proposal and broke off negotiations. The atmosphere of the conference was typified in his famous reply: 'Your attitude of mind is different from ours.' This refers not so much to the difference in eucharistic doctrine as to Luther's view that disagreement on such an important matter of doctrine was a cogent reason for a complete breach with Zwingli, whereas his opponent was of the opinion that mutual recognition was still possible under these circumstances.

The priority of doctrine in the synthesis of doctrine, liturgy, order and ethos plainly emerges from the attitude adopted by the Lutheran Church with regard to the unity of the Church. In Article 7 of the Augburg Confession it is stated that 'for the unity of the Church, it is sufficient to agree in the doctrine of the Gospel and in the administration of the sacraments (*consentire de doctrina evangelii et administratione sacramentorum*). And it is not necessary that there should be everywhere the same human traditions or rites and ceremonies instituted by men.' Church customs and liturgical forms are therefore of purely secondary importance, but agreement in doctrine and in the administration of the sacraments in accordance with right doctrine is necessary.

The lengths to which this principle may be carried in Lutheranism can be seen in the supplement of Philipp Melanchthon (1497–1560) to the Schmalkaldic Articles (1536), in which he states that he is willing to recognize the Pope, so long as he is prepared to allow free scope for the Gospel and base his own supremacy on human instead of divine right (*jure humano, divino*).[1]

(iii) What, then, is Lutheran doctrine? The doctrinal system of the Lutheran Church is not so sharply defined or fully detailed as that of the Roman Catholic Church. While on certain central points Lutheran doctrine is expressed in clear-cut and rigid formulations, there is a certain amount of room for divergence in other respects, much greater than in the Roman Catholic Church, but undoubtedly less than in the Anglican Communion.

There are several versions of Lutheranism which fall into three main groups:

(*a*) One form frequently found in Lutheran Churches is Biblicist and possesses a general Protestant tinge.[2] It relies on the Scriptures without emphasizing the distinctively Lutheran tenets

[1] For the Schmaldkaldic Articles see below, pp. 207–8.
[2] The terms 'Biblicism' and 'biblicist' are not common in English theological circles, but are applied here to those movements or bodies which consider the Bible as the sole authority for doctrine, institutions and customs, and which recognize no appeal to tradition. While Biblicism is often found in combination with Fundamentalism, this is by no means always the case. It is rather concerned with a way of using the Bible than with a doctrine of Biblical inspiration. (H.E.W.T.)

and is particularly under the influence of Pietism. This was the prevalent form of Lutheranism in the nineteenth century and is not unusual in the Scandinavian Churches to-day.

(*b*) A second type makes a constant appeal to the person of the Reformer and models itself on his character and opinions. In no other Church in Christendom does the authority of a human being play so important a part as that of Luther in certain Lutheran circles. The Lutheran Church stands apart from most other Churches in naming itself after its organizer. A certain type of Lutheran continually dwells upon Luther himself and quotes statements made by him as authoritative. A sermon is rarely delivered from German pulpits in which his name is not mentioned, and his doctrinal opinions play a similarly authoritative role in much contemporary Lutheran theology.

(*c*) A third category is confessional Lutheranism which makes its appeal not to the person of the Reformer but to official confessional documents. A clear distinction is drawn between Luther's personal opinions and the doctrinal standards officially adopted by the Lutheran Church. This can be found both in the form of current Lutheran churchmanship, and particularly in the rigid confessionalism prevalent in some quarters in the nineteenth and twentieth centuries.

(iv) Especially in nineteenth-century theology it was customary to speak of the two principles of Protestantism in general and of Lutheranism in particular. Its formal principle lies in the adoption of Scripture as the sole authority and its material principle in the doctrine of Justification.

On closer examination, the application of the Scriptural principle in Lutheranism is not altogether simple. The Bible is not the only authority in the life of the Church, for the Lutheran Church also recognizes as authoritative the creeds of the early Church and its own confessional documents. The relationship between these various authorities is a problem which has confronted Lutheranism throughout its history. The seventeenth-century Lutheran theologians solved the problem by asserting that the content of the confessional documents was derived from Scripture. Thus the Bible became the *norma normans*, the confessions, the *norma normata*. While in principle Scripture is the superior authority, in practice the Bible is interpreted in Lutheran confessionalism in the light of the Lutheran articles of faith, without any awareness of the problems involved in this attitude.

A further modification of the Scriptural principle arises from the fact that, according to the Lutheran view, not all the contents of the Bible have the same authority. The principle cannot therefore simply be described as formal since it is bound up with a definite conception of what the substance of Scripture is. Luther himself drew a clear distinction within the Scriptures between what points to Christ (*was Christum treibt*) and other elements which are not equally binding. Thus, on the Lutheran view, the legitimacy of a doctrinal tenet or church custom is not immediately established by reference to a passage in the Bible. It depends rather upon an organic relation to the doctrine of salvation in Christ. In the confessional documents this is described as 'agreement with Christ's Gospel.' Such an attitude towards Scripture is wholly different from that of Fundamentalist sects such as the Adventists.

In Article 7 of the Augsburg Confession (German version) it is laid down that the sacraments are to be administered 'in accordance with God's Word.' This has an entirely different meaning from the insistence of the definitely Biblicist bodies that the administration of the sacraments must be modelled on the Biblical pattern, in such a way that the Eucharist is made as much like the Last Supper as possible (the Sacrament received sitting instead of kneeling and the like), or that adults alone should be baptized, in the belief that adult baptism alone was practised in the primitive Church and represents the only Biblical form of the sacrament. Although in the past generation Lutheran theologians have often agreed with the findings of scholars of other Churches on the customs of early Christianity, they have not on that account either wished to change the Eucharistic ritual or to abolish the practice of Infant Baptism. In this respect they have shown a proper understanding of the Scriptural principle in Lutheranism which does not demand conformity with an isolated text of Scripture, but an inherent conformity with the main Biblical concepts of salvation.

A further distinction must be drawn for a proper understanding of the Lutheran appeal to Scripture. It is a popular misconception that Luther put the Bible into the hands of the laity and left each individual free to interpret it as he wished. Despite occasional statements of Luther to this effect, the Lutheran tradition reflects a different attitude to the Bible. Both Luther and Melanchthon were professors of theology and studied the Bible in the original languages and in the light of the philological and historical knowledge at their disposal. This attitude has been passed down to the Lutheran Church which has always attached great importance to the interpretation of the Bible by competent scholars. From a very early date Bible study in Greek and Hebrew came to occupy a leading position in the training of Lutheran pastors. Purely exegetical study is considered in the Lutheran Church as the indispensable element in theological training.

One result of the emphasis upon competent theological knowledge has been the significant position of the theological faculties in the history of the Lutheran Churches. The position of authority held by the faculties is also partly explained by the fact that until recent times the German national Churches did not possess bishops and that in the Scandinavian Churches they have never been regarded as authorities for doctrine, as, for example, in the Roman Catholic Church. One consequence of this fact is that the Lutheran Church has always been a 'professor-church.'

(v) The material principle of Lutheranism is the doctrine of Justification by Faith alone (*Justificatio sola fide*). This doctrine, which finds its classical exposition in Article 4 of the Augsburg Confession, has been described in the Lutheran tradition as 'the article upon which the Church stands or falls' (*articulus stantis aut cadentis ecclesiae*). In the Augsburg Confession it is laid down that 'man cannot be justified before God through his own powers, merits or works, but is justified without making any contribution in return (*gratis*) for Christ's sake (*propter Christum*) through faith (*per fidem*), when he believes that he is being received into grace, and that his sins are forgiven for the sake of Christ who, through His death, has made satisfaction for our sins. God imputes this faith as righteousness before Him.'

The logical basis of the doctrine of Justification is a pessimistic doctrine of man which speaks of Man's total depravity. Man is

H

incapable of pleasing God. This doctrine has the object of making Salvation absolutely dependent upon God's Grace by exploding any idea of Man's participation in it. Fallen man cannot do anything at all to merit Salvation, or even to prepare himself to receive God's Grace (in Roman Catholic theological idiom *se praeparare ad gratiam*). All activity is ascribed to God, in order that all honour should fall to Him and that salvation should depend solely upon His Grace and therefore be absolutely certain. This assertion of assurance of salvation (*certitudo salutis*) is a typical feature of the Lutheran conception of Justification.

Man attains Salvation by faith (*per fidem*). The Lutheran tradition has always taken care to safeguard this formula against the misinterpretation that faith is a matter of human effort, or Man's contribution to the process of salvation. The Fifth Article of the Augsburg Confession speaks of Faith as instilled by the Holy Spirit when and where it pleases God, in those who hear the Gospel. Justifying Faith is *fiducia*, or confidence in God's Grace. Confidence (*fiducia*) is the distinctively Lutheran conception of faith in contrast to the Roman Catholic notion of Faith as assent (*cum assensu cogitare*). But since inevitably faith must also have a certain intellectual content, the idea of assent is not altogether excluded in Lutheranism.

In the typical Lutheran tradition, Justification is not actually a making righteous, but rather an imputation of righteousness (*imputatio justitiae*). God imputes righteousness to the sinner for Christ's sake, but he still remains a sinner (*simul justus et peccator*). Justification is therefore identical with forgiveness of sins.

For Luther himself, the doctrine of Justification and the assurance of salvation are connected with the doctrine of Predestination, the servitude of the human will and the impossibility of an apprehension of God through natural religion. But these doctrines are not included in the Augsburg Confession and do not form part of official Lutheran doctrine, which is not on these matters bound by the opinions of the Reformer.

Justification is a central theme both in Lutheran preaching and hymnody, but it is usually taught without the use of technical terms. Sermons and hymns speak of the forgiveness of sins with an accentuation peculiar to Lutheranism. The need of sinful Man (*Aus tiefer Not schrei ich zu dir*), God's sole activity (Brorson's

'God will arrange all') and the assurance of salvation ('I am saved and dearly bought') are representative examples from the Lutheran hymn-books.

(vi) If the strength of Lutheranism lies in its affirmation of Justification by God's Grace through Faith, little emphasis is placed upon Sanctification, the growth of the Christian life in its striving after perfection. Lutheran preaching and devotion has always been marked by a fear of appealing to human activity or reliance upon human effort. Thus in Lutheran history there has been an occasional tendency towards Quietism or a piety which rests in God without due regard for the ethical tasks imposed by the Christian life.

The Lutheran ethos is marked by a sharp differentiation between the Law and the Gospel. According to Luther, 'the supreme art in Christendom' is that of distinguishing between the Law and the Gospel and of keeping them apart as two diametrically opposite forms of God's Word. In its insistence upon this contrast, the Lutheran tradition has followed the mind of the Reformer. In this context, the word 'Law' means not only the Ten Commandments or the Old Testament legislation in general, but also any Commandment in the New Testament and any word addressed to man, or interpreted by him in such a way as to make a demand upon him. Thus the Sermon on the Mount is Law and not Gospel. Similarly, the word 'Gospel' covers not merely the tidings of salvation in Christ brought in the New Testament, but also any promise which appears in the Old Testament. The Law demands works, whereas the Gospel is accepted through faith, and the two forms of Revelation are therefore diametrically opposed. This distinction is repeated again and again both by Luther and by the confessional documents.

Both the Law and the Gospel derive from God and are the Word of God. The Gospel brings the tidings of salvation, while the primary function of the Law is to prepare man by making him conscious of his sins and evoking the deep despair which is necessary for the effectiveness of the Gospel. It is not, therefore, in actual fact the expression of God's character at the deepest level as Christ has revealed it. The Law and its effects are 'God's strange work' (*opus alienum*), whereas the Gospel is 'His proper work' (*opus proprium*). They cannot, therefore, be put on an equality.

But the Law has other purposes besides the creation of an awareness of sin. The Formula of Concord also takes into account the so-called first use of the Law, its *usus politicus*. Some ethical principles are required if people are to be able to live together in an ordered community. God's Law is the rule of action for this life in community and, throughout its history, Lutheranism has considered it the duty of those in authority to see that the commandments of God are outwardly observed. The same document also includes a 'third use of the Law for the regenerate' (*tertium usum legis in renatis*). The Law must also be preached to the reborn, as a rule of action for their lives. This represents a safeguard against the tendency to antinomianism which can appear in Lutheran preaching.

(vii) The social ethos of Lutheranism is determined both by its characteristic pessimistic anthropology and by the distinction which it draws between the two realms.

The Lutheran Churches cherish a deep-rooted conviction of the incorrigibility of this world. The Kingdom of God is always conceived as transcendent or as destined to come through God's intervention at the end of time. The conception of a millennium on this earth (*chiliasm*) is emphatically repudiated in Article 17 of the Augsburg Confession as 'a Jewish opinion' (Judaica opinio). According to the usual Lutheran view, it is hopeless to try to apply the laws of God's Kingdom to the world. It is not the concern of the Church to solve the problems of human society; its task is rather to preach the consolation of forgiveness of sin and to prepare believers for eternal life.

This form of Christianity differs radically from that current in the English-speaking world, both in the Anglican and the Free Churches. They represent an active type of Christianity which wishes to reform the world and to apply Christian principles to international and social problems. Their aim is to be found in some approximation at least to the Kingdom of God on earth. At the Ecumenical Conference held in Stockholm in 1925, there emerged a strong contrast between the Anglo-American view of

the Church's task in the world, and the emphasis laid by the
German Lutherans on the gulf which separates this world from
the Kingdom of God.

The distinction drawn in Lutheranism between the two realms
tends in the same direction as its pessimistic view of the world.
The Church (the spiritual realm) must confine itself to its allotted
tasks and govern the soul and the conscience alone. The magis-
trate (the secular realm) rules over the other areas of human
existence and for this realm the Church has no right to legislate.
In Article 28 of the Augsburg Confession it is expressly laid down
that the Church has no authority either to dethrone kings as it
had done in the Middle Ages, or to prescribe laws for earthly
rulers.

One result of this distinction between the two realms is that in
Lutheran countries the Church has regarded it as its duty to hold
itself aloof to a large extent from political life. In their treatment
of this particular subject, Lutheran theologians have emphasized
the autonomy of the State. Certain fields of human activity such
as politics and economics have their own laws with which the
Church has no right to interfere. It is the Church's task to preach
God's Law to those in authority, but not to dictate their decisions.
Magistrates are responsible to God alone and not to the Church
for their actions. Lutheran theologians can even maintain that
politics have nothing whatever to do with Christian ethics. A
contemporary German theologian, Paul Althaus (b. 1888) asserts
that 'No Christian Law, no Christian norm exists for the State.'
A different view, however, is taken of the Scandinavian Churches,
notably exemplified by the struggle of the Norwegian Church
under the German occupation. On this question the Reformed
Church and its daughter Churches in the Anglo-American world
differ greatly from the extreme form of German Lutheranism.

(viii) The Lutheran interpretation of Christianity is decidedly
non-ascetic and is marked by a positive attitude towards the
values of this world. Its pessimistic view of the incorrigibility
of the world is counterbalanced by a strong emphasis upon
'the order of Creation' (Schöpfungsordnung). A high regard for
marriage and home life has been an essential feature of Lutheranism. The seventeenth-century pastors who remarried as soon as

they became widowers and who are depicted on monuments surrounded by their wives and numerous children reflect a typical aspect of classical Lutheranism.

This may further be illustrated by the attitude adopted to the tasks and duties of secular life, as covered by the phrase 'ethics of vocation.' The religious term 'vocation' which had come in the Middle Ages to be restricted to the call to the priesthood and the monastic life, is used by Luther exclusively with reference to secular occupations. Vocation or calling becomes synonymous with work or occupation. For daily duty, when it is performed with loyalty, love and faith, is itself a divine calling. The typical Lutheran view is that man cannot only serve God in his profession (*in vocatione*), but also through his secular profession (*per vocationem*). Just as the deeds of St. Paul, St. Athanasius and St. Augustine, and the wars of David were holy activities and sacrifices to God, so we should think of individual good works in the lowliest occupations. This is a representative statement of Luther, in this respect loyally followed by the Lutheran tradition. This vocational approach to ethics is expressed in Lutheran hymns such as those of the Danish bishop Thomas Kingo (1634–1703).

(ix) Lutheranism also possesses distinctive features in sacramental doctrine and practice. Here it follows a *via media* between Churches to the Right which emphasize sacramental ceremony and the desacramentalized Churches of the Left. The German pastor, Claus Harms (1778–1855) characteristically expressed the middle path taken by his Church when, during the Centenary celebrations of the Reformation in 1817, he wrote that the Roman Catholic Church gives the precedence to the Sacraments, the Reformed Church to the Word, but 'more glorious than both is the Evangelical Lutheran Church. She retains and takes her form from the sacraments as well as from the Word of God' (*Herrlicher als beide ist die evangelisch lutherische Kirche. Sie hält und bildet sich am Sacrament wie am Worte Gottes*).

In Lutheran preaching and hymnody we often find the phrase, 'Word and Sacraments.' In the Augsburg Confession the two elements are mentioned together, as the means whereby the Holy Spirit is imparted (Article 5). They are both necessary for the life of the Church and of the individual, but the same grace is received through both (*idem est effectus verbi et ritus*—the Apology for the Augsburg Confession).

In recent times, the Sacraments have often been given a relatively subordinate place in the Lutheran Churches. The Neo-Protestantism of the nineteenth century, in particular, was a non-sacramental religion. The Church of Denmark is the Lutheran Church in which the place of the sacraments is most securely established, but at the present time there are many indications in the Lutheran Churches as a whole of a revival both in the theology and practice of the sacraments.

In the confessional documents great emphasis is placed upon the sacraments and considerable importance assigned to their objectivity. As against Donatism it is asserted in Article 8 of the Augsburg Confession that a sacrament is efficacious even when it is administered by evil men (*per malos*). It is not made an effective vehicle of Grace by the faith of the recipient, but by the Word of God, the Baptismal Formula with Christ's promise and the Words of Institution at the Eucharist. At the same time it is also emphasized that the sacraments have no efficacy *ex opere operato*, but must be appropriated by faith (Augsburg Confession— Article 13).

The Lutheran Church only recognizes Baptism and the Holy Communion as Sacraments, although Absolution has been occasionally included in their number (Augsburg Confession— Articles 9–13).

The necessity of Infant Baptism is most emphatically affirmed in Article 9 of the Augsburg Confession.

The following Article insists upon Sacramental Realism in the Holy Eucharist (*de coena Domini docent quod corpus et sanguis Christi vere adsint*). The Real Presence is also stressed in the words of administration (in the Norwegian Church these read as follows: 'This is the Body of Christ; this is the Blood of Christ'). In accordance with this 'high' sacramental doctrine, the communicant receives the sacrament kneeling.

In the Church Orders of the Reformation period, and for a long time after the sixteenth century, it was laid down that the celebrant was to ascertain the exact number of communicants before the service so as to avoid the consecration of more bread and wine than was actually required for the Holy Communion.

In recent generations, however, the practice has grown up of communicants presenting themselves without previous notification of their intention to communicate. Accordingly the pastor cannot know their exact number, and in most cases he will consecrate more bread and wine than is actually required. After the service the residual elements are neither consumed nor kept apart from unconsecrated elements, but are retained for fresh consecration at a later service. This attitude towards the eucharistic elements will certainly be found inconsistent by representatives both of the Roman Catholic and Anglican Churches, but is considered by Lutherans to be consistent with their emphasis upon the Real Presence in the elements *in usu*. According to Lutheran doctrine, the elements are not the Body and Blood of our Lord *extra usum*. This distinction was originally introduced in the Formula of Concord in a somewhat different context in order to exclude the Roman Catholic practice of the adoration of the Sacrament.

The philosophical basis for this practice is the Biblical philosophy of Action which has permeated Protestantism in contradistinction to a Christian adaptation of Aristotelianism with its dominant category of Substance. Christ is present in the action of the Eucharist and in the elements when they are received, but His presence is not associated with any change in nature or substance of the elements of such a kind that they remain His Body and Blood apart from their reception by the communicants.

(x) A feature which distinguishes the Lutheran Church from the Reformed Churches is its conservatism with regard to the organization of the Church. Thus the Scandinavian Churches retained the episcopal office throughout the Reformation. The Lutheran Church has kept the ecclesiastical year, even observing such festivals as the Annunciation (March 25th, transferred in recent times to the Fifth Sunday in Lent) and All Saints' Day (now observed on the first Sunday in November). The structure of its liturgy is on the lines of the Roman Catholic Mass, while the Reformed Churches follow different models. The Scandinavian Churches (though not the German) still wear the eucharistic vestments (alb and chasuble). Statues and images of

Biblical characters were preserved in Lutheran Churches, and in Central Europe to-day a Lutheran church can always be distinguished from a Reformed church by the presence of a crucifix inside it.

(xi) Lutheranism is also distinguished from other Churches by its doctrine of the Church. The classical Lutheran definition occurs in Article 7 of the Augsburg Confession in which the Church is described as 'a congregation of the saints in which the Gospel is purely taught and the sacraments rightly administered' (*congregatio sanctorum in qua evangelium pure docetur et recte administrantur sacramenta*). Here the emphasis is characteristically laid upon the functions of the Church. The Church is the place in which the Gospel is purely preached and the sacraments duly administered. It cannot, therefore, be identified with any particular Church organization or a single religious communion. Wherever Christ is preached, the Church is to be found, even within the Roman Catholic communion.

The Lutheran Church is the least insistent of all Churches upon a particular form of Church Order. The Roman Catholic, the Anglican and the reformed Churches (not to mention the Fundamentalist bodies) all regard a definite constitution as the only divinely ordained Church Order. The difficulty is that they cannot agree as to its nature. Lutheranism, on the other hand, displays a considerable degree of indifference on such matters. Yet even on the Lutheran view certain forms are necessary for the day-to-day life of the Church. At all events, the Church must have a ministry. The confessional documents draw a sharp distinction between the universal priesthood of all believers and the ministry. Two different terms (priesthood or *sacerdotium* and ministry or *ministerium*) are used in Lutheran theology for these two functions. All Christians become priests at Baptism and through faith, and all do priestly service to God by prayer and thanksgiving and by presenting themselves as a living sacrifice to God. The ecclesiastical office (*ministerium ecclesiasticum*) is something entirely different from this priestly service. It was created by God for the purpose of preaching the Gospel and administering the sacraments (Augsburg Confession—Article 5). The Church is commanded by God to appoint servants to preach the

Gospel and administer the sacraments. God sanctions this office and is Himself present in it (Apology for the Augsburg Confession). Only those who are 'lawfully called' can 'teach publicly' (Augsburg Confession—Article 14). During the popular revivals of the nineteenth century, however, lay preaching came to be generally accepted by the Church as legitimate.

3. Confessional Documents

The very conception of 'confessional documents,' a limited collection of written documents, embodying the official doctrine of the Church, first arose in Lutheran circles. During the doctrinal controversies which followed Luther's death, the German Lutheran princes made such collections of documents (*corpora doctrinae*) for their own national Churches. In all these collections the Augsburg Confession (*Confessio Augustana*) and the Apology for it were included. After doctrinal controversy had lasted for some decades, the middle party won a preponderant position, desire for a settlement became widespread and some of the leading theologians worked out a comprehensive system, which was intended to represent a consensus of Lutheran opinion. This was called the Formula of Concord (*Formula Concordiae*) and was completed in 1577.

The Formula of Concord refers to the following as normative documents containing a summary of the Church's doctrine under the supreme authority of Holy Scriptures: (i) the three Catholic Creeds, (ii) the Augsburg Confession in the original version of 1530, (iii) the Apology for the Augsburg Confession, (iv) the Schmalkaldic Articles, and (v) Luther's Shorter and Longer Catechisms.

The next step was the elevation of the Formula of Concord itself to the status of a confessional document. The Elector of Saxony and his theologians worked towards this end. In 1580 they were in a position to publish the Book of Concord (Liber *Concordiae*), a collection of confessional documents signed by fifty-one princes, thirty-five cities and nine hundred theologians. It included all the documents mentioned in the preceding paragraph together with the Formula of Concord. The work appeared on June 25th, 1580, the fiftieth anniversary of the publication of the Augsburg Confession. A final collection of the Lutheran 'symbolic books' had therefore taken half a century to complete.

The Book of Concord is a binding doctrinal standard for many German National Churches. In the course of time it has been adopted as authoritative by the Swedish Church, but has never been recognized in Denmark and Norway. In these two countries, only the original version of the Augsburg Confession and Luther's Shorter Catechism are regarded as normative authorities.

(i) The most important of all these confessional documents is the *Augsburg Confession*, which is recognized as the decisive doctrinal authority in all Lutheran Churches throughout the world, and which, since 1530, has always been considered the authentic expression of the Lutheran interpretation of Christianity.

The Augsburg Confession (*Confessio Augustana*) is a declaration submitted to the Diet at Augsburg in 1530 by the Lutheran princes and independent cities. It was compiled during the Diet itself by Melanchthon and bears the stamp of the author's moderation and caution. It also reveals the threatening situation which existed at the time. Luther had been outlawed by the Diet of Worms, and could not therefore be present at Augsburg, but a draft of the document was sent to him and received his full approval.

Not all the Evangelicals present at the Diet could give their assent to the Confession. The representatives of Strasbourg and three other South German towns submitted their own articles as they could not append their signatures to Article 10 on the Eucharist which Melanchthon was unwilling to alter.

The Augsburg Confession is extant in a German and a Latin version, both of which were presented to the Emperor on June 25th, 1530. While the German version was being read aloud, the Lutheran members of the Diet stood to indicate their approval of the document.

The two original manuscripts have been lost but, even while the Diet was in session, six printed editions of the German, and one of the Latin text were published. As these were inaccurate,

Melanchthon himself produced an edition in 1531, which ranks as the official *editio princeps*.

Before the publication of this edition, Melanchthon made some stylistic alterations. He continued this process in later editions and treated the Confession as his own private work rather than as an historic document admitting of no further change. In the edition of 1540 he went so far as to make a radical alteration. Article 10 was redrafted in order to approximate to the Calvinistic conception of the Eucharist. For a time this edition was used side by side with the others, but when the South Germans and the Reformed Church began to quote it as authoritative, it was stigmatized in Lutheran circles as the *Augustana variata* and the use of the *Augustana invariata* enforced.

The Augsburg Confession soon came to be regarded as the authentic expression of Lutheran doctrine. It is referred to in the written Church Orders, such as the Pomeranian Church Order of 1535 and the Danish Ordinance of 1537. Assent to the Confession was incorporated into the doctoral oath of the University of Wittenberg and (from 1535) into the ordination vow of the Church of Saxony.

The Preface to the Augsburg Confession explains how it came to be written and the names of the original signatories are contained in an appendix.

The document itself falls into two main parts. The first is called 'Articles of Faith and Doctrine' and comprises twenty-one articles. The second part (in seven articles) deals with Church abuses which have been abolished (the so-called *abusus mutati* of the Latin version).

The object of the treatise is to show that the Evangelicals are orthodox in doctrine and do not teach every possible kind of heresy, as alleged by their Roman Catholic opponents. It is pointed out in Articles 1-3 that they profess the Apostles' and Nicene Creeds and that they hold the same doctrines of God, of Original Sin and of the Person of Christ as the adherents of the Old Faith. In many articles a number of ancient and modern heresies are expressly repudiated, ranging from the Valentinianism and Arianism of the early Church to those of the contemporary Anabaptist Movement. There is a critical reference to the doctrine of Zwingli without any explicit mention of his name.

Only one Roman Catholic theological formula, the expression *ex opere operato*, is explicitly rejected. Both St. Ambrose and St. Augustine are cited as authorities in support of the Lutheran standpoint. The closing section of the first part states that in the doctrine which has been expounded there is no trace of any divergence from the Scriptures, the Catholic Church, or even from the Roman Church as it appears in the early Fathers. 'We are therefore condemned without just reasons by those who assert that we are to be regarded as heretics.' The dispute turns upon certain abuses (*abusus quidam*) which have been abolished here. In the introduction to the second part the statement is repeated that the Lutheran Churches do not deviate from the Catholic Church on any article of faith, but have merely abolished some abuses of comparatively recent origin. The fidelity of Lutheranism to the heritage of the early Church cannot be asserted more emphatically than in the Augsburg Confession. This claim to essential catholicity in matters of doctrine is justified by the careful distinction drawn by the author between Catholicism and the contemporary Church of Rome. Although in the second part the customs and doctrinal concepts of the Roman Catholic Church are sometimes criticized in strong terms, the catholicity of Lutheranism is emphasized and defended by numerous references to the early Church and the Fathers.

At the same time, the Augsburg Confession contains classical formulations of the interpretation of Christianity taught by the Reformation: the Evangelical doctrine of salvation, its relation to good works, the doctrine of the Church and Sacraments and the new attitude to matrimony and the duties of the secular life.

The sequence of ideas in the document can be summarized as follows. The starting-point is the doctrine of God and of Christ (Articles 1 and 3). But since the doctrine of the work of Christ presupposes the doctrine of sin, an article on Original Sin is inserted between them (Article 2). The first three Articles, therefore, prepare the ground theologically for the doctrine of salvation which is set out in Article 4 on Justification. A natural sequence to the next Article on the Ministry is provided by the fact that the Ministry was instituted to enable mankind to participate in Justification. The emphasis on the doctrine that it is by faith alone, and not by works that we are justified before

God makes necessary a closer definition of the doctrine of good works, which is provided in Article 6, 'On the new obedience.'

A new series of articles opens with Article 7 (the definition of the Church), to which Article 8 (the efficacy of the Sacraments even when administered by evil men) serves as a supplement. Then follows the doctrine of the Sacraments (Articles 9 on Baptism, 10 on the Eucharist, 11–12 on Confession, with further comments on the Sacraments as a whole and their proper use in Article 13). That public preaching and the administration of the Sacraments is restricted to those who hold the ecclesiastical office is laid down in Article 14. The following Articles treat of Church Order (Article 15) and the secular order of human society (Article 16). With Article 17 on Christ's second coming to Judgement, the series of doctrinal subjects is brought to completion.

A third subdivision opens with Article 18. Here certain topics which had become the subject of controversy are resumed for fuller treatment. Articles 18 on the doctrine of freewill and its limitations and 19 on the origin of sin may be considered as supplements to Article 2. Article 20 on Good Works refers back to Article 6 and a final article is added on the adoration of saints.

It is difficult to discover any logical arrangement in the second main section. Here seven abuses are considered in a less orderly sequence: Communion in one kind (Article 22), clerical celibacy (Article 23), the Mass (Article 24), Confession (Article 25), precepts concerning Fasting (Article 26), monastic vows (Article 27) and the abuse of the power of the Church in relation to secular authority (Article 28). On all these points the customs and doctrine of the Roman Catholic Church are repudiated in the light of the Evangelical interpretation of Christianity. This is most evident in the reasons assigned for the rejection of the doctrine of Eucharistic Sacrifice and the practice of private Masses. The Roman Catholic practice 'is in conflict with the Holy Scriptures and violates the glory of Christ's Passion' (Article 24). Monastic vows are declared to be in conflict with the doctrine of Justification when they are considered as a means of earning forgiveness of sins and justification before God (Article 27).

In addition to matters of doctrine and Church custom, the

Augsburg Confession also deals with certain ethical questions. It includes a positive evaluation of matrimony as the ordinance of God (Articles 23 and 27) and of the life and precepts of secular society (Articles 16 and 28). The characteristic Lutheran distinction between the spiritual and secular realms is drawn in Article 28.

(ii) *The Apology* was compiled by Melanchthon during the Diet itself as a reply to the Roman Catholic refutation of the Augsburg Confession, usually known as the *Confutatio Confessionis Augustanae*. It was presented to the Emperor who, however, refused to accept it. After further improvements by Melanchthon, a printed version in Latin was published in 1531 and a German translation appeared in the same year.

The Apology is quite a comprehensive work and bears a different character from the Augsburg Confession. It is not a short declaration, but a theological treatise which substantiates in detail all the points in the Confession which had been subject to attack. It follows the arrangement of the Confession and provides its most authentic commentary. The exposition of the doctrine of Justification by Faith is of particular importance.

(iii) *The Schmalkaldic Articles* derive their name from the defensive alliance formed by the Evangelical princes at Schmalkalden in 1531. The Articles were compiled by Luther in 1536 and were occasioned by the Pope's proposal for an ecumenical council to be held at Mantua in 1537, which came to nothing. The Elector John Frederick of Saxony did not approve the idea of a participation of the Evangelicals in the council, but commissioned Luther to compile the articles of faith from which he would in no circumstances depart.

The document was therefore particularly anti-Roman Catholic in tone. It was signed by the Wittenberg theologians, but Melanchthon attached his signature with the reservation mentioned above.[1] When the Evangelicals met at Schmalkalden in 1537, in Luther's absence owing to illness, the articles were not approved by the assembly of princes, but were signed some days

[1] See above, p. 190.

later by the majority of the theological advisers, who accompanied them. In any case the name 'Schmalkaldic' was soon given to the Articles which became authoritative during the next two decades and were finally included in the Book of Concord.

(iv) *The treatise on the power and primacy of the Pope (tractatus de potestate et primatu Papae)* is a tract written by Melanchthon at Schmalkalden in 1537 and printed in the Book of Concord as a supplement to the Articles. Under the influence of the anti-papal spirit which prevailed at the Conference, Melanchthon wrote in more caustic terms than usual.

(v) Luther's two catechisms, both dating from 1529, are the oldest Lutheran confessional documents. They are neither political documents like the Augsburg Confession, nor defences of the Lutheran position, but were produced in order to teach children and adults the elements of the Christian Faith.

The *Shorter Catechism* appeared in the spring of 1529 in the form of printed placards to be hung on the wall. The first three tables with the Commandments, the Apostles' Creed and the Lord's Prayer came out in January. In March, the placard dealing with Baptism and the Holy Communion appeared. Later, three more tables were issued containing morning and evening prayers, graces and the so-called 'House Tables' (*Haustafeln*), a collection of Biblical texts relating to preachers, magistrates, heads of households, domestic servants and children. In May the Catechism appeared in book form. A revised edition was brought out in 1531 with a new section on Confession placed by Luther between Baptism and Holy Communion. Both the 1529 text in five sections and the 1531 edition with the additional section have been frequently republished in the Lutheran Churches. The later version is included in the Book of Concord. In each section the Biblical passages are accompanied by short explanations.

The *Longer Catechism* appeared in April 1529 and contains a detailed interpretation of the text of the Shorter Catechism intended for the use of heads of households and pastors.

The selection of material was determined by the catechetical tradition of the Middle Ages. The originality of the books consists in the arrangement and interpretation of this material.

The religious instruction of children in mediaeval times included the Lord's Prayer, the Hail Mary, the Apostles' Creed and instruction in Christian Ethics. This often consisted in learning by heart a catalogue of the deadly sins and the Christian virtues, but tended in the later Middle Ages to be connected with the Ten Commandments.

Luther omitted the Hail Mary and the catalogues of virtues and vices and added the Biblical texts containing the words of Institution of Baptism and the Eucharist. He also abandoned the traditional sequence and arranged the material on the basis of the Evangelical interpretation of Christianity. The idea underlying the order adopted in the Catechism is that man should first have the law of God put before him, so that he may thereby recognize himself to be a sinner, and then hear the Faith preached, and finally learn how he is to acquire the power to live a Christian life.

The Shorter Catechism is completely uncontroversial and non-theological in formulation, while the Longer Catechism contains a certain amount of controversy directed against Roman Catholicism and Enthusiasm. In the Shorter Catechism, the term Justification is avoided, but the Lutheran doctrine of salvation is expressed in the very structure of the book as well as in the exposition of the second and third articles of the Apostles' Creed. The relation between religion and morality is elicited in a simple yet ingenious way by the introductions to the explanations of each of the Ten Commandments: 'We should so fear and love God as to. . . .' All the Commandments are contained in the first. The individual and personal tone of the exposition of all the Articles of the Creed is also worthy of note. Belief in the Creator is related to the personal existence of the believer in the exposition of the first article (I believe that God has created me). The phrase 'our Lord' in the Apostles' Creed becomes 'my Lord who has redeemed me from damnation' in the exposition. The effect of both sacraments is characteristically expressed in the exposition as to bring about forgiveness of sins. Sacramental Realism is hinted at in the phrase 'the true Body and Blood of our Lord Jesus Christ,' but is not further insisted upon in this manual for children. The exposition of Baptism lays the main stress on its symbolic aspects.

Certain formulations clearly bear the impress of Luther's

patriarchal view of society which accepted the system of superiors and subordinates, heads of households and domestic servants. If there is an indication of a pessimistic view of the world in the exposition of the seventh petition of the Lord's Prayer, a definitely positive attitude to the good things of life is given prominence in the comment on the fourth petition.

The Shorter Catechism was written for the instruction of children in the Christian Faith at home, but it has also been used in the Lutheran Churches as a school text-book. For centuries it was used as the chief reader in Primary Schools and it was the only text-book for Christian instruction until Pietism and the Enlightenment together led to the production of books on Biblical history as supplements to the Catechism. During the century of the Reformation it was also used as a sermon text. The Lutheran Church Ordinances often refer to the Catechism as a standard for doctrine and preaching, and in the Formula of Concord the two Catechisms are called 'the Layman's Bible' which contains in brief everything treated at length in the Holy Scriptures, and necessary for a Christian man to know for his eternal salvation.

(vi) *The Formula of Concord* is the result of protracted theological discussion, arising out of the internal disputes which arose in Lutheranism after Luther's death. The chief authors were Jacob Andreae (1528–90) and Martin Chemnitz. The book was circulated for approval and signed by three Electors, twenty princes, twenty-four counts, thirty-eight independent cities and something like eight hundred theologians. These signatures represented about two-thirds of the Lutheran world.

The document falls into two main parts, the *Epitome Articulorum* or *Summarischer Begriff der streitigen Artikel*, and the *Solida Declaratio*, each containing twelve articles. While the *Epitome* contains the theses which are considered to be orthodox doctrine, the *Solida Declaratio* gives a detailed exposition of the theses which appear in the *Epitome*. The Articles in each document correspond to each other.

The Formula of Concord repudiates a number of doctrinal tenets which had been put forward in the Lutheran Church without mentioning their authors by name. It is, however, easy to recognize the individual or the group against which it is directed. Article 1 (On Original Sin) relates to Matthias Flacius (1520–75), who had asserted that sin was of the essence of man. Article 2 (On Free Will) is concerned with the Synergists, who claimed that the human will played a part in Conversion. Article 3 (On the Righteousness of Faith) is primarily directed against Andreas Osiander (1498–1552), who taught that Justification was a real transformation of our nature through the infusion of the Love of God. Article 4 (On Good Works) has a double object in view, the opinions of Georg Major (1502–74), who taught that good works were necessary for the attainment of salvation, and of Nikolaus von Amsdorf (1483–1565), who maintained that they were a hindrance to this end. Articles 5 and 6 (On the Law and the Gospel and On the third use of the Law) were concerned with the Antinomians, whose protagonist Johann Agricola (1499–1566) asserted that the Law should not be preached to Christians. Article 7 (On our Lord's Supper) and 8 (On the Person of Christ) are directed against the crypto-Calvinists. Several different errors are envisaged in Article 9 (On Christ's Descent into Hell), which contents itself with a warning against speculations going beyond Luther's own teaching on the subject. Article 10 (On Church Customs) has in mind Melanchthon and his followers who defended the accommodations introduced by the Leipzig Interim on the ground that Roman Catholic customs were things indifferent (*adiaphora*). Article 11 (On Eternal Predestination and God's Election) criticizes the Calvinist doctrine of Predestination. Finally Article 12 (On other heresies and sects) deals with the errors of the Anabaptists, the Schwenkfeldians[1] and the anti-Trinitarians.[2]

The Formula of Concord concluded the Lutheran disputes on doctrinal questions in the Age of the Reformation. It introduced the era of Lutheran orthodoxy and is typical of Lutheran scholasticism.

All these documents were included in the Book of Concord. The three Catholic Creeds were set at the beginning and a

---

[1] Caspar Schwenkfeld (1489–1561) was for some time an active follower of Luther, but became an 'enthusiast' and founded a separatist Church. His followers were persecuted and mostly emigrated to America in 1734, where a small Schwenkfeldian Church still exists.   [2] See below, pp. 331–6.

collection of quotations from the Church Fathers on the relationship between the divine and human natures of Christ, designed to
prove that the specifically Lutheran doctrine on the point was
supported by the early Church, was added as an appendix.

The Book of Concord was published in German in 1580,
followed in 1584 by an official Latin version.

4. DOCTRINE

In this section only a few of the most characteristic features of
Lutheran doctrine will be selected for consideration.

It has already been mentioned that the doctrine of Justification
by Faith lies at the heart of the whole Lutheran system.[1] The
Lutheran Churches have constantly opposed any kind of Synergism.[2] The emphasis is always placed on God's sole activity in
the process of salvation. Faith is not a matter of human effort,
but the gift of God conferred through His Word. The Apology
for the Augsburg Confession states quite simply that Justification
is through the Word (*per verbum*).

The Augsburg Confession teaches that Man has a certain freedom of will in matters which do not concern salvation, but which
form part of human justice or are subject to reason; in short he
possesses an ethical freedom. Before Regeneration, however, the
human will is not capable of preparing itself for Grace (*se praeparare ad gratiam*) or of doing works which are pleasing to God.
Man's 'natural reason' and intellect are blind in spiritual matters
and can understand nothing through their own powers. His 'will
is not only averted from God, but also hostile to God so that it
can only will, desire and rejoice over that which is evil and
opposes God's will.' Such is the teaching of the Formula of
Concord. Human nature was completely corrupted by original
sin and salvation is entirely dependent upon God's Grace.

In its refusal to accept the doctrine of Predestination, the
Lutheran tradition follows another aspect of the teaching of the
Reformer, who discourages attempts to probe into the secret
counsels of God. We are not to dwell upon this inscrutable
mystery, but to keep to His Will as revealed in Scripture in such

[1] See above, pp. 193–5.
[2] Synergism is the term applied to the doctrine that man in some way co-operates in
or contributes to his own salvation. (H.E.W.T.)

passages as 'God will have all men to be saved and to come to the knowledge of the truth' (1 *Timothy* ii. 4). In the Formula of Concord a sharp distinction is drawn between God's fore-knowledge (*praescientia*) and His predestination (*praedestinatio*).

On the doctrine of the Atonement, the Lutheran Church borrows its theological ideas from the mediaeval Church, and in particular follows St. Anselm in preaching an objective Atonement. It makes, however, a slight modification in his doctrine, and regards the sufferings of Christ not as a satisfaction, but as a punishment vicariously undertaken on our behalf. This conception of the Atonement is prominent in Lutheran preaching and in the hymns which are sung in church on Good Friday.

Lutheran Eucharistic theology with its attendant Christology was clearly formulated during the internal disputes on doctrine during the sixteenth century. Here, as the Formula of Concord shows, the Lutherans were most conscious of their differences from the Reformed Church.

One essential element in Lutheranism is its doctrine of the Real Presence of Christ in the Eucharist (Augsburg Confession—Article 10). The Lutheran theologians repudiated any doctrine of the presence of Christ in the Eucharist in a purely spiritual manner. He is present in a bodily way, and the communicant partakes of His Body and Blood through their mouths (*manducatio oralis*). Those who partake of the bread receive the Body of Christ. The Formula of Concord expressly rejects the Reformed conception that the communicants are spiritually united with Christ, but merely partake of bread and wine. The Body and Blood of Christ become united with the bread and wine through a sacramental union (*unio sacramentalis*). It therefore follows that the unworthy partake of the Body and Blood of Christ (*manducatio indignorum*), but for judgement, and not for consolation and life. As the Formula of Concord observes, in this acknowledge-ment of the corporeal Presence (*corporalis praesentia*), the Luther-ans acknowledge themselves to be in agreement with the Greek and Roman Churches.

Yet if the Body and Blood of Christ are truly present, the sacramental elements still remain bread and wine, and the communicants partake of both. The Shorter Catechism simply states that the Eucharist is 'the true Body and Blood of our Lord

Jesus Christ under bread and wine.' In the Formula of Concord this sacramental union is expressed in definite terms. The Body and Blood of Christ are present 'in, with and under' (*in, cum, sub*) the bread and wine.

The Roman Catholic doctrine of Transubstantiation is expressly repudiated and the Formula of Concord regards St. Irenaeus as a precursor of the Lutheran view. 'Like him we teach that the Eucharist consists of two elements, an earthly and a heavenly' (*eucharistiam constare duabus rebus, terrena et caelesti*). Technically this doctrine is known as Consubstantiation.

This Eucharistic doctrine is organically related to Lutheran Christology. This in its turn consists of the Catholic doctrine with a short supplement arising out of discussions on the Eucharist.

According to Catholic doctrine, the human and divine natures of Christ are united in a single person in such a way that they are neither commingled nor transformed, yet are inseparably and indissolubly combined. The peculiar nature of each is nevertheless preserved. It is on the basis of this Christology that Lutheran Eucharistic theology has been developed. To the question whether Christ is present in the Eucharist according to both His natures or only in one, the Formula of Concord replies that in the Eucharist both the divine and human natures of Christ are involved.

Such a view naturally involves the corollary that both natures are omnipresent. Controversy arose on the matter with the Reformed Church, which maintained that, after the Ascension, Christ's human nature was on the right hand of the Father, and that therefore only His divine nature could be present at the Eucharist. Against this objection, the Formula of Concord rejoined that at the Incarnation the two natures became inseparably united. Christ has promised to be present in the Eucharist with His Body and Blood. This involves His human nature which must therefore share the omnipresence which is one of the attributes of the Divine Nature.

The Formula of Concord expressly asserts that there is no confusion of natures (*confusio naturarum*) in the Person of Christ. Each nature retains its own peculiar quality. But wherever Christ's divine nature is, there is the human being, Jesus Christ, just as in His lifetime His divine nature was united to the historical Jesus. The two natures are combined in such a manner that through the mutual communication of the peculiar characteristics of each nature (*communicatio idiomatum*), each shares the attributes of the other. But the Formula adds that this must not be taken to imply any commingling or equalization of the two natures, which would amount to monophysitism. The form of this combination can be illustrated by the images used by the Fathers, the union of body and soul or of iron and fire in red-hot iron. The Son of God died for our sins and the Son of Man was made omnipotent.

In this doctrine of the hypostatic union, Lutheranism has merely adopted, with a supplement of its own, the Catholic doctrine of the Person of Christ. Its conformity with the doctrine of the early Fathers is further illustrated by the *Catalogus Testimoniorum* added to the Formula of Concord.

This doctrine of the Person of Christ has influenced Lutheran devotion and hymnody. The miracle of the Incarnation is emphasized in such passages as 'He for whom the universe is too narrow lies here in His Mother's bosom'; 'The bread and wine, now blessed and consecrated . . . are His Body and His Blood.'

5. WORSHIP

In the evolution of the Lutheran forms of service, the canonical hours did not play any noteworthy part. Some were, indeed, retained at the Reformation but were soon transformed into daily sermons. The Lutheran Sunday service is based upon the Roman Catholic Mass, purged of non-evangelical elements and adapted for the ordinary worshipper. The principal changes were as follows:

(i) The Canon with its sacrificial prayers was omitted. This was the first liturgical reform carried out by Luther. The Lutheran Eucharistic Liturgy gives expression to the doctrine of the Real Presence, but not to the concept of sacrifice.

(ii) Divine service was conducted in the vernacular.

(iii) The sermon became an integral part of the service. The Word, in the sense of the Word that is preached, is a prominent feature of Lutheranism.

(iv) The singing of hymns by the congregation has become an important part of the service. While admittedly hymns may be sung both at the Roman Catholic Mass and the Anglican Holy Communion, in Lutheranism the singing of hymns is quite indispensable.

This was the path taken by Luther himself in his German Mass (*Deutsche Messe*) of 1526. The *Credo* and the *Agnus Dei* were replaced by German hymns so that the whole congregation could sing them together. He also replaced the Latin Introit by a hymn in the vernacular and added a hymn after the Epistle in place of the Gradual.

(v) It is typical of the Lutheran tradition that, while it has an orderly liturgical form of service, it does not demand liturgical uniformity in its constituent Churches.

Liturgical development has taken different courses in the various German and Scandinavian Churches. In Germany, the liturgical heritage of Lutheranism has been greatly reduced.

Where Lutheran worship has developed in the greatest independence of other influences, the following features are to be found. It is a service both of the Word and of the Sacraments. In the Scandinavian Churches loyalty to the Word takes the form of a set series of prescribed texts for the sermon as well as for liturgical reading. The service is simple and dignified and has preserved a number of features such as altars, altar candles, vestments, liturgical movements which have been abolished by Churches lying further to the Left. The Lutheran way of worship can therefore be said to represent a *via media* in Christendom.

6. Recent Developments

The type of Lutheranism described in the preceding pages is the classical Lutheranism of the sixteenth and seventeenth centuries, with some reference to modern developments. In order to avoid too static a presentation of the Lutheran Churches some remarks should be added on historical factors which have modified certain features of Lutheranism.

(i) The great Lutheran Churches of Europe have for centuries been established churches which in the German States and in

Scandinavia enjoyed a real monopoly in the spiritual life of their countries. The principle laid down in the Augsburg Treaty of 1555, *cuius regio, eius religio*, was applied with the utmost strictness.

A change in the policy adopted by the Lutheran States towards other churches may be observed in Prussia as early as in the seventeenth century, when the Reformed Church was tolerated as a body besides the national Lutheran Church, and in the Scandinavian countries in the eighteenth century, when a limited amount of religious freedom was accorded to foreigners who were members of non-Lutheran Churches.

In the course of the nineteenth century legislation was profoundly changed in this respect. An ever-increasing amount of religious liberty was introduced in all Lutheran countries. Other religious communities were granted the rights of public worship protected by law, and of propaganda and proselytism. Citizens were allowed to leave their national Church and join other religious communities or stay outside any Church, without losing their civil rights. These changes were introduced rather late in the Scandinavian countries—in Norway in 1845, in Denmark in 1849, in Sweden through a series of Reform Acts in 1860, 1873 and 1951, in Finland through legislation in 1889 and 1922.

A number of practical problems have arisen in connection with these changes which have been solved by the same means. While children whose parents left the National Church were considered to have changed their ecclesiastical allegiance together with them, definite regulations were needed for children of mixed marriages, and an age limit had to be fixed for permission to leave the National Church. In Norway, persons over fifteen years of age are independent of their parents in this respect, while the age limit is fixed at eighteen in Sweden. Other problems are connected with the contraction of marriage. In the course of the last two generations the ministers of the recognized Free Churches have been granted the right to solemnize marriages with legal validity, even when one of the partners is a member of the National Church (in Norway 1891, in Sweden 1915). Civil marriage has been introduced as an alternative which may be chosen even when both partners are members of the National Church (in Sweden 1915, in Norway 1918). Other problems, again, have arisen in connection with religious instruction in the state schools. Until the introduction of modern legislation concerning dissenters religious instruction was compulsory for all school children and was of a definitely confessional character. When the right to leave the National Church was recognized, some changes were inevitable. Children who were not Church members were exempted from religious instruction. In Sweden, where members of the Free Churches technically continued to be members of the National Church, the problem was solved by a change of the character of religious instruction in the elementary schools in 1919 whereby it was made non-confessional, and from 1951 onwards, teachers who give religious instruction no longer have the obligation to be members of the National Church. Their loyalty to Christian doctrine and to general Protestant principles is considered to be safeguarded by the supervision of the schools through school authorities. In Norway, on the other hand, religious instruction in State Schools must be of a confessional character and can only be entrusted to teachers who are members of the National Church or of a Lutheran Free Church. This regulation, of course, only gives an external guarantee for the spirit in which the instruction is given. In Denmark the same conditions prevail, although the regulations concerning the secondary schools are less rigid.

All these changes are due to the rise of a Free Church movement in countries which until the middle of the nineteenth century were purely Lutheran territories. Up to the present time the Free Churches have not gained a large number of adherents in the Scandinavian countries. The large majority of the populations (in the Scandinavian countries taken as a whole about 97 per cent) have remained members of the National Churches. But in order to understand the situation it should be borne in mind that in Sweden the large majority of dissenters are technically members of the National Church, and that in all these countries the indifferent have remained members of the established churches. In countries where nominal membership of the churches is registered, the dissenters figure more largely among the churchgoing population than may be gathered from official statistics. What has been said here of the Scandinavian Churches applies also to their Lutheran sister Churches in Germany.

The presence of a number of Protestant Free Churches in areas which had formerly been exclusively Lutheran has confronted Lutheranism with new problems. The first reaction was naturally one of self-defence and hostility towards all kinds of non-Lutheran Protestantism. Church members were warned against all non-Lutheran teaching. Here the traditions inherited from the age of Orthodoxy were continued. The doctrinal divergencies which separated the teachings of the Free Churches from Lutheranism were emphasized and exaggerated. In the Scandinavian countries the emergence of Free Church propaganda coincided largely with the period at which the Theological Faculties had been imbued by the new spirit of Lutheran confessionalism,[1] and great popular revivals of a definitely Lutheran character were transforming the spiritual life of these nations. Accordingly, one result of the confrontation with non-Lutheran Protestant traditions has been a strengthening of the Lutheran self-consciousness.

But this was not the only outcome of the new contacts with other varieties of Protestantism. Another effect was that after one or two generations, Church leaders as well as Church people had grown accustomed to the fact that Nonconformity existed in their Lutheran countries, and began to feel they had much in common with the Dissenters in a society marked by an ever-increasing infidelity. There was a common Christian front to be maintained. The feeling has become widespread that the Established Churches and the Protestant dissenting bodies together represent a common Christian heritage.

An indication of this change of attitude adopted towards the non-Lutheran Protestant bodies may be found in the solution of the problem of intercommunion. Here it is necessary to distinguish between German and Scandinavian Lutheranism. The German Lutheran Churches have been confronted with the problem ever since the sixteenth century through the presence of Reformed Churches in Germany, and here the enforced union with the Reformed Church in Prussia and some other States[2] has created a very different atmosphere from that existing in Scandinavia, where admission of non-Lutherans to Holy Communion emerged as a practical question late in the nineteenth century.

[1] See below, pp. 228–9. [2] See below, p. 373.

In Germany the rigid attitude of Lutheran Orthodoxy has
generally been maintained within the purely Lutheran Churches
and no intercommunion with the Reformed Church exists. In
Scandinavia the development has gone in the opposite direction.
Scandinavian Lutherans are as a rule grateful when they are
accepted as communicants in churches abroad with which they
feel they are akin—Churches of the Anglican Communion,[1] the
Reformed Church, and the Methodist Church. And in the last
generation all Scandinavian Churches have practised 'open communion' and received as communicants believers from other
churches, foreigners and fellow-countrymen, who desire to receive the sacrament. In 1952, the Swedish Bishops' Conference
signed an official agreement with the Church of Scotland concerning intercommunion, whereas the Norwegian bishops refused
to enter upon an agreement of this kind, on the ground that the
Church of Norway practises Open Communion and accordingly
ought not to make an agreement in this matter with a single
church.

This attitude implies a considerable change when compared
with the attitude towards intercommunion in the Lutheran
Orthodoxy of the seventeenth century.

(ii) The legislative changes described above were not only
occasioned by the emergence of Nonconformity; they were also
the outcome of a secularization of society.

This process, which is one of the most important aspects of
European Church History in the nineteenth and twentieth
centuries, is often judged by churchmen in a rather one-sided
manner and interpreted as mere apostasy from Christianity. It
ought also, however, to be viewed as a differentiation of society
and an emancipation from ecclesiastical tutelage of fields which,
from a Christian and particularly a Lutheran point of view, have
a just claim on autonomy. An evident example is the liberation
of science and the universities from the Church's supervision.
Nor should it be forgotten that churchmen themselves on
several occasions advocated the abolition of laws which implied

---

[1] The present official position with regard to the admission of members of the
Lutheran Churches to Communion is summarized in the Lambeth Report (1958), on
pages 54–5. (H.E.W.T.)

compulsion in religious matters. Thus they have themselves contributed towards the rise of the secular State. But the main current which has led to this result has been the great increase of religious indifference in modern society. The spirit of the age, as it appeared in the press and in literature, often displayed open hostility towards Christianity.

The outcome of this development was the emergence of the purely secular State whose aim is the temporal welfare of the nation and whose educational policy and legislation (in such subjects as marriage) are not always in accordance with Christian principles.

At the beginning of the twentieth century this secular State appeared in the shape of the Liberal State which tolerated and frequently even favoured the Church but did not feel itself bound by its teaching. At a later stage, most of the Lutheran Churches of Europe were confronted with the secular State in the shape of the Totalitarian State which was quite unwilling to respect Christian principles.

Here is not the place to relate the vicissitudes of the Lutheran Churches of Germany and Scandinavia under the National Socialist régime. Suffice it to say that in the fight against the Totalitarian State certain aspects of the Lutheran doctrine of the two realms were emphasized in a new way. The Church's independence of the State 'in matters spiritual' was stressed in sermons and official declarations with an insistence without counterpart in earlier times when it was taken for granted that the State was a Christian State governed by Christian rulers. There was likewise a new insistence upon the Church's duty to proclaim God's will to the secular state and to criticize its actions. In earlier times, the attitude of Lutheranism towards the State had been marked by complacency and confidence in the Christian State. But when the secular State made its appearance in this challenging form, germs which had been latent in the Lutheran tradition were developed and the Lutheran Churches appeared as staunch advocates of justice and human rights over against the unchristian State.

This change of emphasis in the social ethos of Lutheranism became evident in the fight against Totalitarianism, but may also be observed in the attitude of the Lutheran Churches before as

well as after their encounter with the Hitler régime. As a characteristic presentation of the Lutheran view in the modern setting,
mention may be made of Bishop E. Berggrav's book, *Staten og
Mennesket* (1946, German translation, *Der Staat und der Mensch*,
1950).

(iii) From the Reformation period the Lutheran National
Churches have been Established Churches. In each country the
Prince was the supreme governor of the Church which was
administered through agencies appointed by him; in theory a
distinction was sometimes made between measures taken by the
Prince in his capacity of Ruler of the State and as Governor of
the Church, and the organs of ecclesiastical administration were
granted an independent status in relation to the secular chan-
cellery. From the middle of the seventeenth century all clergy in
Denmark and Norway were appointed by the Sovereign and
ecclesiastical legislation was embodied in royal decrees.

The main features of this system were retained throughout the
nineteenth century. In Germany the Lutheran Churches continued to be Established Churches until the Weimar Constitution
of 1919 declared that Church and State should be separated
throughout Germany. In the Scandinavian countries the Establishment is still in force. All the Scandinavian National Churches
are supported economically by the State and administered by a
Ministry of Ecclesiastical Affairs (in Norway and Sweden a joint
Ministry of Church and Education) on the same footing as the
other governmental ministries. Bishops and clergy (with the
exception of assistant curates) are appointed by the Crown (in
Finland and Iceland the President) and Parliament acts as the
Church's legislative body, irrespective of the fact that its members
have no obligation to be Church members. Only very few churchmen and politicians really want radical changes in this system.

In all these Lutheran Churches, however, a movement towards
the creation of elective bodies representing the Church has been
a conspicuous feature of their history in the nineteenth and
twentieth centuries. Some precedent may be found in the
attempt in earlier times to maintain the independence of ecclesiastical courts and bodies in spiritual matters, but in principle this
represents a new development.

Parish Councils and Synods, diocesan and provincial, were introduced in a number of German states from 1817 onwards. These bodies, however, lacked legislative and judicial authority and were only consultative bodies within the framework of the Establishment. Parish Councils elected by Church members as distinct from Municipal Councils were introduced in Denmark 1903, in Norway 1920, in Sweden 1930, but they can only make decisions in purely local matters. In Sweden there were some important anticipations of the institution in the seventeenth and eighteenth centuries, but the separation of local school boards and parish councils occurred as late as in 1930. A Church Assembly was instituted in Sweden in 1863. Its members are the bishops, a certain number of the clergy chosen from their own number, and representatives of the laity. According to a recent revision of its statutes there will always be a majority of laymen. The Church Assembly may pass resolutions on ecclesiastical questions, and its consent is required before laws passed by Parliament which concern the Church can receive the royal sanction. It thus possesses a right of veto against Parliament. Moreover, its opinion is normally asked before the Crown authorizes new liturgical books. In Finland a similar Church Assembly was instituted in 1869. Its competence is wider than that of the corresponding body in Sweden. Church laws are passed by the Church Assembly after which Parliament can only accept or reject the law in question without alteration. Thus Parliament's competence in these matters has been reduced to the right of veto. Moreover, the Church Assembly is the competent authority for all liturgical legislation, and no consent from any secular authority is required. The Churches of Denmark and Norway do not possess any similar institution.

Through these developments some Presbyterian features have been introduced into Lutheranism: elected bodies representing clergy and laity and vested with some legislative competence. But naturally in Established Churches these bodies can only have a limited authority.

(iv) Another new feature in Lutheran Church life is the emergence of voluntary associations for missions abroad, evangelization, youth work and the like.

In the seventeenth century, the age of classical Lutheran Orthodoxy, there was no room in society for associations with a voluntary membership. The Church was considered to be composed of teachers and hearers, and the social framework for devotional life consisted of the Church and the family.

Religious societies could only arise when a certain disintegration of the structure of society had taken place and the soil was prepared for the rise of an individualistic type of piety. Voluntary associations for religious purposes could only emerge when individuals were no longer content with the possibilities offered by the Church's worship and with family devotional life. They are a recent phenomenon in post-Reformation history (though with important forerunners in another social setting in the mediaeval guilds and Third Orders). The whole movement started within the Church of England a few years before the English Revolution of 1689, and throughout the eighteenth century England was the only country where such voluntary associations really flourished. It was also in England that the Methodist Societies which began as organized religious societies within a national Church developed into a separate Church.

Religious societies within the Lutheran Churches emerged after 1730 in what was technically called the Moravian Societies (*Sozietäten*) whose members assembled for worship in their own meetings, though continuing to be members of their national churches at the same time.[1] Their precursors were the *collegia pietatis* advocated by the Pietist pastor, Philipp Jakob Spener (1635–1705), but these were only groups of men and women assembled around the pastor for devotional gatherings in addition to the ordinary services of the Church. Such features as statutes, membership rolls and a board of directors were still lacking.

The expansion of this movement in Lutheran countries began early in the nineteenth century. The foundation of the British and Foreign Bible Society in 1804 gave the impulse for the formation of similar societies in all the Lutheran countries (Nuremberg 1804, Berlin 1805 and several other German societies in the following years, National Societies in Finland 1812, Denmark 1814, Sweden 1815, Norway 1816).

The new interest in the missionary work in the nineteenth

[1] See below, p. 235.

century led everywhere in the Lutheran Churches to the foundation of societies for missions to the heathen. A few voices
advocated the alternative of Church missions instead of independent societies. This idea, however, was difficult to realize in the
Established Churches, partly because these churches had no organ
for such activities, partly because the people interested in missionary work definitely preferred the other form of organization. It
was the English societies founded shortly before 1800 (the Baptist
Missionary Society 1792, the London Missionary Society 1795,
the Church Missionary Society 1799) which set the model.

The first German missionary societies (Basle 1815, Berlin 1824,
Rhineland 1828) were based on co-operation between Lutherans
and members of the Reformed Churches. On the rise of spirit
of confessionalism after 1817, a growing dissatisfaction with
such joint Lutheran-Reformed enterprises made itself felt and
subsequent societies (Leipzig 1836, Hermannsburg 1849, Neuen-
dettelsau 1885) were markedly Lutheran, although some societies
founded late in the century included a Reformed membership.

The Danish Missionary Society was founded in 1821 as a
society on a national scale and of a definitely Lutheran character.
A few younger societies within the National Church owe their
existence to interest in special mission fields or special methods
of work. In Sweden the foundation of a national society in 1835,
the Swedish Missionary Society, was due to the co-operation of
Moravians, Methodists and Lutherans and retained an interconfessional character for some decades. The growth of Lutheran
confessionalism, however, led to the foundation of a Lutheran
society in 1845, merged in 1855 into the Swedish Missionary
Society which consequently severed its connection with the joint
Lutheran-Reformed Basle Society and became exclusively
Lutheran. In 1874 the Established Church itself started missionary
work and in 1876 took over the activities begun by the Swedish
Missionary Society which was now replaced by the Directory
Board for Missions of the Swedish Church. This development is
unparalleled in the other Lutheran national churches. In Norway
the missionary movement first led to the foundation of a con-
siderable number of local societies (of which the first was founded
in 1826). In 1842 these combined to form the Norwegian
Missionary Society. Although Moravian initiative played some

I

part in the beginnings of the movement, this society has from its outset represented Low Church Lutheranism in a marked form. Interest in special missionary fields not covered by the Norwegian Missionary Society, together with differences of churchmanship (High Church, Liberal, extreme Low Church) has later led to the foundation of a number of separate Lutheran missionary societies, of which the one representing extreme Low Church views has been most powerful.

The Home Missions movement aiming at charitable work and evangelization has given rise to a third type of voluntary association for the support and carrying out of such activities. In Germany some important institutions for charitable work were founded in the first half of the century, but the grand programme of a movement covering the whole of Germany was first formulated in 1848 when a Central Committee for Home Missions was founded. This term included organized evangelistic work and social service as well as the production of Christian literature and the distribution of tracts. A special development within this movement was the emergence of societies for devotional and evangelistic purposes of a definitely Pietistic colour, sometimes called Societies for Home Missions (for instance, in Baden, founded in 1849, in Holstein 1857), or 'Pietist *Gemeinschaften*' (Württemberg 1856). A National Union of such societies was formed in 1888 and possesses a membership of a few hundred thousand.

In Scandinavia the designation Home Missions has been connected in the main with the emergence of societies of this type. A Danish Society for Home Missions was founded in 1853 and received its present character through a reorganization in 1861. The counterpart in Sweden is the National Evangelical Foundation dating from 1856. In Norway the movement gained strength through a Pietist revival which from 1853 onwards won adherents among pastors and laymen in all parts of the country. The first local society was founded in 1853 and a national organization in 1868. Although Finland experienced several great revivals in the nineteenth century, the formation of a National Society for Home Missions did not take place until 1904. All the Scandinavian Home Missions Societies are denominational and represent Low Church Lutheranism and Pietism.

In addition to the societies which have been mentioned a great number of voluntary associations for special purposes grew up in the course of the nineteenth century: Sunday schools, youth organizations (Y.M.C.A., Y.W.C.A., Student Christian Movement), societies for Missions to Seamen (characteristic of the seafaring Scandinavian nations), Christian associations of holders of special occupations, for instance, a Christian Commercial Travellers' Union.

This development has to a large extent changed the character of Lutheran Church life. The voluntary associations have created possibilities for lay activity unknown to previous centuries. The Church is no longer considered to be composed of teachers and hearers. There are many tasks to be performed by laymen.

In the religious societies clergy and laymen co-operate on an equal footing. The Home Missions Societies, in particular, constitute a religious milieu which in some respects resembles the Free Churches, although no separation from the National Church has taken place. Their historical analogy is the Methodist Societies in England before 1784.[1] What keeps them within the Established Churches is their loyalty to Lutheran doctrine and their evaluation of the Establishment as a favourable framework for evangelization. In a few cases the Home Missions movement has given rise to secessions under the influence of Baptist propaganda or through a development which has turned it into a Free Church based on Congregationalist principles.[2] But the main stream has remained faithful to the Lutheran Church and in countries like Norway, where this movement is numerically and spiritually strong, it has given the entire Church life a characteristically Low Church tinge.

(v) In the first years of the nineteenth century Lutheran theology was marked by the spirit of the Enlightenment. Recent research has shown that in the Scandinavian countries a large number of the clergy were imbued with the theology of the Enlightenment until the middle of the century.

Pietism and the Enlightenment together had contributed towards the rise of what has been called Neo-Protestantism. In this type of piety Biblical theology is stressed rather than the

[1] See below, p. 268.　　[2] Svenska Missionsförbundet, see below, p. 284.

specifically Lutheran doctrines, and the Bible is seen through the eyes of the nineteenth century which read into Holy Scripture its own ideas of the human personality, of religious experience and of Christian activity. Neo-Protestantism was marked by an aversion to metaphysics and was here in accordance with Kantian philosophy. Pietism and the spirit of empiricism in modern science contributed together towards the emergence of a theology based on religious experience. The movement arose from the epoch-making re-interpretation of theology by Friedrich Schleiermacher (1768-1834), and in the School of Erlangen (von Hofmann, Thomasius, Frank) religious experience was made the corner-stone of theology. Historical research applied to the Bible made it difficult to identify Biblical doctrine naïvely with the Orthodox Lutheran doctrine. Revivalism and the emphasis on subjective experience led in many quarters to an undervaluation of the Sacraments, and the emergence of Low Church religious societies initiated a similar process with regard to the ministry. Thus Neo-Protestantism has been, and is, a potent force in the history of Lutheranism in the last few generations.

There has, however, also been a movement in the opposite direction. Early in the nineteenth century there was a tendency to turn from the Enlightenment ideas to Biblical theology, which, in its turn, frequently led to a revival of Lutheran confessionalism. This development can be observed in the lives of quite a number of Lutheran theologians in the first half of the century, and in the history of some of the chairs in the Lutheran Theological Faculties where two or three holders in succession represent these standpoints. In Germany as well as in Scandinavia the new confessionalism was already making itself felt when the Reformation jubilee was celebrated in 1817.

A new generation of preachers and theologians went back to the doctrines and ideals of classical Lutheranism. In 1829 a young professor of theology, Karl von Hase (1800-90) advocated a return to the Lutheran dogmatics of the seventeenth century in a book entitled *Hutterus redivivus*, after the champion of Lutheran orthodoxy, Leonard Hutterus (1563-1616).

An influential school in German theology combined Biblical studies in an anti-rationalist spirit with Lutheran Confessionalism. Neo-Lutheranism was the term applied to a High Church movement which emphasized the classical Lutheran doctrines of the Church's authority and of the Sacraments, without Romanizing tendencies (Theodor Kliefoth, 1810–95; Wilhelm Löhe, 1808–72). Loyalty to the Lutheran tradition could also, however, take the form of Low Church Lutheranism. This was the case with the Erlangen school which, in spite of its choice of religious experience as its basis, kept strictly to the Lutheran confessional documents and tried to demonstrate that the ideas implied in the Christian's normal experience were exactly those to be found in these books.

At the end of the nineteenth century there were two wings in German as well as in Scandinavian Lutheranism. Liberal Neo-Protestantism was represented by famous theologians of the stature of Adolf von Harnack (1851–1930) and Ernst Troeltsch (1865–1923) and had influential representatives in almost all Theological Faculties. The results of the natural sciences required a rethinking of Christian doctrine, and Biblical criticism and the study of the history of dogma, no less than the whole spirit of the age, seemed to lead to the tenets of Neo-Protestantism. The other alternative was a Conservative Theology which tried to defend the authority of Holy Scripture and to present the essentials of Lutheran doctrine to the modern mind, with characteristic adaptations. Its ideal was to be 'modern and positive.' Theodor Zahn (1838–1933) and Reinhold Seeberg (1859–1935) were prominent representatives of this school.

For one or two generations the conflict between Liberal and Conservative Theology was the most conspicuous feature of Church life in the Lutheran countries. The two wings had their organizations, clerical and lay, and their periodicals, and the controversial points were debated in passionate discussions. In Norway this conflict became exceptionally acute and led to the foundation in 1908 of a private Theological Faculty of a conservative character which in 1913 was granted by Parliament the right, formerly possessed by the State Faculty alone, to confer the academic degree required for ordination in the Established Church. This recognition by the State of a private institution for the training of the clergy was without precedent in the history of Lutheranism. Similar institutions have emerged in the *Kirchliche Hochschulen* in Germany. The first school of this kind was founded at Bethel near Bielefeld in 1905 and was intended to be a counterweight to the Theological Faculties in the universities where the Church had hardly any influence on the appointment of professors, and where there was no contact with parish life. Two new schools of this character were founded in 1935 by the Confessional Church in order to provide institutions which were independent of the National Socialist State.

After the First World War a change in the spiritual climate was observable in the Lutheran Churches. The optimistic belief in progress which had been a basic element in Liberal Theology, disappeared and gave way to a sceptical attitude to the idea of progress, sometimes even to a sentiment of doom and destruction. The eschatological outlook of the New Testament, which had been neglected by Liberal Theology, or not considered to be of the essence of the Gospel, became not only intelligible, but was felt to be a word addressed to the contemporary situation. A distinction was made between the mythological form of Biblical eschatology and the eschatological outlook itself which Lutheran theologians were inclined to interpret in the categories of existentialism. The emphasis on individualism and the rejection of external authority, which also had been basic to Theological Liberalism, gave way to a new understanding of community and an emphasis on the authority of the Bible and of the Church. Biblical research undermined the distinction between 'the simple Gospel' preached by Jesus and belief in Christ as the two different religions contained in the New Testament. On the other hand, Liberal Theology had won the battle over the application of the methods of historical research to the Bible. The legitimacy and necessity of critical research in this field had been recognized in practically all quarters, and the main results of Biblical research had been generally accepted, even among the laity. The situation had changed radically since the end of the nineteenth century.

One of the factors which had contributed towards the emergence of a new theological situation was what has been called the Luther renaissance. Although research upon the subject of Luther and his teaching had taken place throughout the nineteenth century, a new feature appeared after 1900. Since that date a stream of monographs on various aspects of Luther's theology have illuminated the difference between the Reformer's theological thought and the generally accepted idea of Lutheran theology and have demonstrated the relevance of Luther to the modern theological situation. Pioneers of this new phase were the German scholars Karl Holl (1866–1926), C. Stange (b. 1870), H. Boehmer (1869–1927), E. Hirsch (b. 1888), E. Vogelsang (b. 1904), and outside Germany the Swedish theologians E. Billing (1871–1939), whose book on *Luther's doctrine about the State* (1900) inaugurated the school in Sweden, and N. Söderblom (1866–1931). The Luther renaissance is indebted above all to German and Swedish scholarship, but important contributions have also been made by Danish and Finnish theologians. The interest in Luther's theology does not necessarily lead to a narrow Lutheran Confessionalism, as may be seen from the fact that scholars outside the Lutheran Communion like P. S. Watson and G. Rupp in England, have shared this interest and made important contributions to the subject in the same spirit. The study of Luther may have a significance for the emergence of an ecumenical theology.

When the Lutheran Churches were confronted with the ideology of the Totalitarian State from 1933 onwards, the theological basis of their resistance was the Neo-Orthodoxy whose roots we have tried to analyse. In the fight against Nazism this theology in the German Confessional Church even developed into a Lutheran Confessionalism similar to that of the first half of the nineteenth century.

(vi) In the age of the Enlightenment the liturgical life of the Lutheran Churches was marked by a certain poverty. The services had been abbreviated and features like the Preface had been lost. Further reductions were proposed in the plans for Liturgical reform which were discussed about 1800.

In the nineteenth century a movement for restoration emerged in all Lutheran Churches. The first reform in this direction is to be found in the Prussian Service Book (*Preussische Agende*) of 1816, due to the personal initiative of the King (Friedrich Wilhelm III). His ideal was to go back to Luther's liturgical writings (*Formula missae et communionis*, 1523; *Deutsche Messe*, 1526), but he also introduced some elements taken from the Early Church, the Oriental Liturgies, and the Reformed tradition.

In the various Lutheran Churches in Germany a great number of liturgical manuals, official and private, were issued in the course of the nineteenth century. Their general trend was a return to the Lutheran liturgy of the Reformation period, but with adaptations to suit the taste of the age. The restoration movement reached its climax in the new *German Kirchenagende* of 1954 which is based not exclusively on the Reformation pattern, but includes elements from the common liturgical heritage of the Western Churches.

In the Scandinavian Churches a similar development has taken place. The main difference is that liturgical uniformity has been much greater within these National Churches (with the exception of the Danish Church) than in their sister Churches in Germany. Private liturgical manuals played no role in the parochial life in the nineteenth century. In Sweden, Finland and Norway a series of liturgical reforms have been introduced, aiming at the reintroduction of features which belong to the Lutheran tradition as well as to the common heritage of Western Christendom.

The Swedish Church has been more conservative in liturgical matters than the other Lutheran Churches throughout the eighteenth century and possessed a rich and dignified liturgy. A revision of its Service Book in 1811 was marked by the ideals of the Enlightenment. The Sunday Service was shortened and features like the Gospel reading from the altar and the Preface were omitted. On the other hand, a beautiful Introit which was introduced in 1811 has been retained (in a modified form) in subsequent Service Books as the Introit for ordinary Sundays, an indication that the age of the Enlightenment was not so destitute of liturgical understanding as is frequently assumed. The Gospel reading from the altar was reintroduced in 1860, the Preface in 1894. New Service Books were authorized in 1894, 1917 and 1942. A new feature was a Lectionary reform in 1860, the introduction of two additional series of lessons (Gospels and Epistles) for all Sundays and Feasts. Since that reform, two Gospel texts have been read in the Sunday service, one from the altar, the other from the pulpit as the prescribed text for the sermon.

In Norway, a new liturgy for the Sunday service was authorized in 1887. The new features were a Confession of sins followed by the *Kyrie eleison* (in Greek and Norwegian), sung by the congregation, the *Gloria in excelsis* (in Norwegian), intoned by the pastor and continued by the congregation, the recital of the Apostles' Creed (by the pastor or by the pastor and the congregation), and the Preface. A further step was taken in the present Altar Book of 1920, in which the Intercessions, formerly read by the pastor in the pulpit, were given a more satisfactory place immediately before the Eucharistic liturgy and were interspersed with responses. The experience gained since 1920 has shown that the worshippers join increasingly in the recital of the Creed and in the responses. In 1886, two additional series of lessons were introduced after the Swedish model.

In Finland, the Service Book was revised in 1886, and again in 1913. A peculiar feature in the Finnish liturgy is a formula of absolution pronounced by the priest after the *Kyrie*. Two additional series of lessons were authorized in 1886.

In Denmark, the service book of 1685 has remained in force with very small alterations until the present day. Since 1885 the Danish Church has possessed two series of lessons. A new Eucharistic liturgy in which the *Sursum Corda*, *Sanctus*, *Benedictus* and *Agnus Dei* were restored was authorized in 1912. Owing to the absence of any substantial liturgical revision between 1685 and 1912, local liturgical customs display greater variations than in the other Scandinavian Churches, and in 1949 the Danish bishops issued a 'Directory of Worship' containing such deviations as may be considered to have been sanctioned by tradition. In 1959, a Confession of sins, together with the *Kyrie* and the *Gloria*, was reintroduced into the liturgy.

In many Lutheran Churches a Eucharistic renaissance has taken place during the last generation. The number of communicants has increased considerably. It has become usual for many churchgoers to receive the Sacrament more frequently than was the custom one or two generations ago. In many towns it has become customary to celebrate the Holy Communion every Sunday.

CHAPTER IX

THE MORAVIANS

THE Moravian or Bohemian Brethren was the name given to a wing of the followers of Jan Huss (1369–1415), who organized their own community in 1457 and adopted the name of the *Unitas Fratrum*. The Bible was to be the sole doctrinal standard. Its members were to live under strict church discipline in accordance with 'God's Law.' The Brotherhood repudiated military service, the taking of oaths and occupation with public affairs. Members were initiated by Baptism and converts from the Roman Catholic Church were baptized as well as children born within the community. The Brotherhood had bishops and an episcopally ordained clergy, and could claim to have received the Apostolic Succession through a Waldensian bishop.

At the time of the Reformation the Brethren came into contact with Luther, who attracted their attention through the Leipzig disputation of 1519, and later also with Calvin, without abandoning their traditional character. During this period their attitude towards the cultural life changed and they became an important factor in the life of the Czechoslovak people. The Brotherhood underwent considerable persecution during the Counter-Reformation. Many of the Brethren emigrated and further emigrations took place at the beginning of the eighteenth century.

In 1722 a small group of German-speaking Brethren received permission to settle on the Berthelsdorf estate in Oberlausitz in Saxony and there founded a colony which was given the name of Herrnhut. In the previous year the estate had been purchased by Count Nikolaus von Zinzendorf (1700–1760), an eccentric young pietist who had been brought up at Halle.

For him the ideal society was a 'philadelphian' community which should unite Christians of different traditions without taking them away from the Churches to which they originally belonged. In May 1727, Zinzendorf brought about the settlement of an internal dispute within the community. This was followed

234

by a period of intense devotional activity initiated by a celebration of the Holy Communion on August 13th, 1727, which is usually regarded as the birthday of Herrnhutism.

The Herrnhut colony was to belong to the national Church of Saxony and its members were to go to the church at Berthelsdorf and receive the sacrament at the hands of the local pastor. But it was also to have its own morning and evening services daily within the parish of Berthelsdorf. The community was to be led by a kind of Parish Council, consisting of twelve 'elders,' of whom four were 'superior elders' and one a 'general elder.' They drew lots for these positions and Zinzendorf himself became superintendent. The colony was divided into groups or 'choirs,' according to sex and married or unmarried state, each with its leaders, who were responsible for the discipline and spiritual oversight of their 'choirs.' The unmarried men and women were soon accommodated in different buildings and the children separated according to sex. Trade was conducted on a co-operative basis, and important decisions, such as the selection of partners in marriage, settled by ballot. For the daily services, Zinzendorf prepared a special liturgy, chiefly composed of music and singing. Each day a special watchword (*Losung*) was announced consisting of a text from the Bible or some lines of a hymn. Other special features of Moravian worship were the revival of the love-feasts and feet-washing of the early Church.

At an early stage the Moravians began to found 'societies' outside Saxony. As the name indicates, these were not local churches, but associations of devout Christians who shared Moravian views, but continued to be members of their national Churches. Societies of this type were formed in the Scandinavian countries and in England. From 1731 onwards, missionaries to the heathen were sent out from Herrnhut, and before three years had elapsed they were active in three different areas, the West Indies, Greenland and Georgia.

The ecclesiastical policy of the Moravians was, however, indeterminate. Zinzendorf clung to the 'philadelphian' idea, but at the same time insisted that the colony at Herrnhut should conform to the Lutheran standards of faith. But the Brethren soon displayed little interest in Lutheran orthodoxy and manifested a strong desire for independence.

In 1735, David Nitschmann (1694–1772) was ordained bishop at Berlin by the Reformed court chaplain, Daniel Ernst Jablonski (1660–1741), who held the ancient Moravian episcopal office. It was intended that he should act as a missionary bishop. In 1737, after an unsuccessful attempt to become a Lutheran pastor, Zinzendorf received a similar ordination and an independent episcopal Church of the Brethren came into being. Yet at the same time Zinzendorf continued to hold the conception of a 'congregation of Jesus,' above difference of faith.

In 1736, Zinzendorf was accused of heresy and schism and expelled from Saxony. He settled at Wetterau in Western Germany, in a Reformed part of the country. Here he founded the colony of Herrnhag, which was to be the centre of the religion of the heart within the Reformed Church. But the new colony became a completely independent Church with its own administration of the sacraments, dissociated from the Reformed National Church.

By this time it was clear that the Moravian Brethren had become an independent religious community. Zinzendorf himself disapproved of this development and resigned his office as superintendent in protest during an assembly in London in 1741. With him the 'superior elder' of the Brotherhood also tendered his resignation. It was now proposed that the Saviour Himself should be the 'general elder' of the community, and after recourse to the lot the motion was sustained. Leadership was taken over by a 'general conference' with its seat at Herrnhag.

In 1742, Frederick II, seeing that the Moravians were a hardworking and industrious people, gave them permission to set up colonies in Prussia in order to promote industry. On this occasion, the Brethren were recognized as an episcopal Church, independent of the national Church. The German name of this Church was *Die Brüdergemeine*.

At a conference at Herrnhag in 1745, it was stated that the United Brethren had no doctrine of their own. The community consisted of three 'tropes,' the Lutheran, the Reformed and the Bohemian, each with its own doctrinal standards. When Zinzendorf was granted permission to return from exile, the Brethren in Saxony adopted the Augsburg Confession as their doctrinal standard in 1747, and two years later were recognized by the State as a Lutheran Church on the same footing as the national Church. In the same year they were granted similar recognition in England by Act of Parliament as an episcopal Church under the name of *Unitas Fratrum*, but were more commonly known as Moravians.

In 1741, a period of enthusiasm had begun within the community. The Christocentric and sentimental preaching of Zinzendorf predominated with its one-sided emphasis upon the sufferings and death of Christ (the so-called 'blood theology'). This was often expressed in erotic verbal images. The hymns of the Brethren were sensuous in character and their devotional life became quietist. Repose in Jesus' wounds became a principal theme. Development on these lines continued for a time, but a considerable change took place after 1750 owing to the abandonment of Herrnhag which had been the centre of enthusiasm.

On the death of Zinzendorf in 1760, the leadership of the movement passed to August Gottlieb Spangenberg (1704-92), who had been bishop for the Moravian communities in America. Unlike his predecessor, he had a sober and practical nature. Under his leadership the Brethren held Councils in 1764, 1769 and 1775, and approved a church constitution. The Church was to be Christocratic. Legislative authority was to rest with the synod, composed of elected representatives of the churches. The synod was to elect a directorate of nine members to lead the community until the next synod. Each church was to be governed by a council of elders appointed by the directorate and a parochial council elected by the members of the local church. Although the community claimed to be an episcopal Church, their bishops were excluded from the government of the Church and their authority merely extended to the performance of ordinations. The council of 1775 made pronouncements on matters of doctrine without committing the Church to any confessional document. It was merely stated that the Brethren acknowledged themselves to be in conformity with the Evangelical Church. The central theme of their teaching was the Atonement in Jesus' blood. All unsound deviations in doctrine or ritual were to be abolished.

The doctrine of the Brethren was expounded in Spangenberg's work, *Idea fidei fratrum*, with the sub-title *Uebersichtliche Zusammenstellung brüderischer Glaubenslehre*, published in 1778, and

their Hymn-book (*Gesangbuch der Brüdergemeine*) was compiled
at the same time. Although these books are not confessional
documents in the juridical sense, they reflect the distinctive
doctrinal position of the Brethren.

When the Brethren framed their constitution in 1775, they
consisted of sixteen churches in Germany, two in Holland,
fifteen in England, five in Ireland and eighteen in North America.
In all, there were about 16,000 members. At that time the
Brethren were already at work in a great many missionary areas
where they had won about 10,000 converts to Christianity. In
addition, there was a considerable amount of 'diaspora activity'
or the formation of societies within other Evangelical Churches
without any change of membership.

Towards the year 1800 the Brethren experienced a decline, but
new life was infused into the community as the century advanced.
The constitution was revised several times and some of the
customs peculiar to the Brethren were abandoned. In America,
in 1818, it ceased to be obligatory for partners in marriage to be
chosen by lot, and the same concession was extended to Germany
in the following year. The use of the lot as a means of discovering
the will of Christ was completely discontinued after 1889.

The Brethren now number between fifty and sixty thousand,
in addition to their missionary churches with a total membership
of over 110,000. The Church is divided into four provinces, the
German (including congregations in Switzerland, Denmark and
Holland), with its principal seat at Herrnhut, the British and two
provinces in the United States. Numerically the movement is
strongest in America with a membership of approximately 44,000.

The Church still has no confessional document of its own in
the strict sense of a doctrinal standard prescribed by law as of
binding authority. The volume of the *Corpus Confessionum*
devoted to the Moravians includes the documents regarded as
binding or representative, the Church ordinances, catechisms,
liturgical books and hymn-books in use to-day. The Church
ordinances at present in force were approved by a general synod
at Herrnhut in 1914 with a supplement approved in 1931.
A doctrinal statement was issued by a general synod held in
Bethlehem, Pennsylvania, in 1957.

According to the Church ordinances and the catechisms, the

Scriptures, limited to the canonical books of the Old and New Testaments, are the sole doctrinal authority.

In the Church ordinances of 1914, Atonement through Jesus Christ is described as the core of Christian doctrine. The Brethren hold all the corollaries of this doctrine, the total depravity of man, the love shown by God towards fallen humanity, the two natures of Christ, Justification and Sanctification, the communion of saints and the second coming of our Lord.

The religion of the Brethren is Christocentric, or Jesucentric. God and Christ are identified with each other in a naïf modalism. The decisive factor is the attitude of the heart towards Jesus. Their devotional life is marked by a buoyant happiness and the cure of souls is practised with great zeal.

Divine service is held in a room which the Moravians on the Continent prefer to call a 'hall' (German: *Saal*), not a 'church.' It is very simply furnished without altar, crucifix, pictures, and even normally without a pulpit. It has an atmosphere of brightness and harmony. Around the church is the churchyard (*Gottesacker*, or God's acre), which is divided by two intersecting paths into four compartments, one for each choir. Each grave has a gravestone of uniform size and type, bearing the name of the deceased with the years of his birth and death and his number on the roll of membership.

In congregations where the old customs are preserved, brethren and sisters sit apart in the church, each choir by itself. The pastor stands or sits at a table in front of the rows of benches. Purely liturgical services are often held, consisting of antiphonal singing between the minister and the congregation, reading of the Bible and prayers. On certain days the congregation assembles in church for the 'love feast,' when a simple communal meal is taken and hymns sung. The feast concludes with Holy Communion or Evensong.

Each of the great festivals has its own liturgy. For the service on Christmas Eve, the children assemble as a separate choir and sing hymns, bearing lighted candles in their hands. During Holy Week the story of the Passion is read over and over again interspersed with suitable hymns at frequent intervals. The entombment of Christ is celebrated by a special liturgy on Good Friday evening. A 'love feast' is held on Easter Eve. The congregation

assembles in church before sunrise on Easter morning. The
service opens with the words 'The Lord is risen' addressed by the
minister to the congregation, to which is made the response 'He
is risen indeed.' Then follows the long Easter litany of which the
first part is recited in church, and the rest out in the churchyard
among the graves. The whole congregation goes out into the
churchyard in procession, usually just at sunrise.

Holy Communion was formerly always celebrated in the
evening, but to-day morning Communion is not uncommon.
After some hymns and a prayer for forgiveness of sins, the minis-
ter reads the first part of the Words of Institution over the bread.
Then the deacons distribute the bread to the congregation who
do not partake of it until all have received it into their hands.
Then the minister says 'Eat it; it is the Body of our Lord Jesus
Christ, given unto death for us.' At this point all partake and
then kneel, singing 'let us not lose the consolation of Thy death.
Kyrie eleison.' Then the minister reads the second part of the
Words of Institution over the chalices, two of which are circulated among the Brethren and two among the sisters. Every one
drinks of the chalice and passes it to his neighbour. Finally the
minister reads 1 Corinthians xi. 26 and pronounces the Benediction to the congregation. The community has a threefold
ministry of bishops, priests and deacons.

The Moravians have never been very numerous but they have
played a significant part in the history of the Church. Their
contribution to world evangelism has been out of all proportion
to their numbers and their educational institutions attained great
popularity in the eighteenth century.[1] They exercised considerable influence upon men like John Wesley,[2] and Friedrich
Schleiermacher. Their attempt to rise above differences of faith
exercised a certain influence upon the non-confessional outlook
of later revival movements.

[1] The great educational reformer, Johann Amos Comenius (1592–1671), belonged to
the original *Unitas Fratrum*.

[2] The influence of the Moravians upon John Wesley is the subject of a recent study
by C. W. Towlson, *Moravian and Methodist. Relationships and Influences in the eighteenth
century*. London, 1957. (H.E.W.T.)

CHAPTER X

THE REFORMED CHURCH

1. Designation, Distribution and Statistical Data

THE official name of the Church which emerged from the Reformation of John Calvin (1509-64) is the Reformed Church. In English-speaking countries it is usually described as the Presbyterian Church from its system of Church Order.

During the period of the Reformation the term 'Reformed' embraced both Lutherans and Calvinists, but the restriction of the word to the latter tradition dates from the beginning of the seventeenth century. In the Treaty of Westphalia (1648), for example, the Calvinists are described as *ii qui inter illos reformati vocantur* in contrast to the Lutherans. Within the Reformed Church the term 'Calvinists' is now only applied to the champions of a strict confessional orthodoxy. In Lutheran circles the expression 'Reformed Churches' is often used loosely as a collective description of all the Churches to the left of Lutheranism.

Strictly it would be more accurate to speak of 'the Reformed Churches' rather than of 'the Reformed Church,' since they are independent of each other and have no common confessional document. Nevertheless, the Reformed Churches form a spiritual unity to the same extent as their Lutheran counterparts.

In Switzerland, its mother country, the Reformed Church has a membership of approximately two and a half million, or over half the total population. Here it consists of a series of cantonal Churches which are normally 'national' (in so far as this description can be applied to a country which is so deeply divided on matters of faith). Thus in the canton of Zürich, according to law, every Protestant is regarded as a member of the Reformed cantonal Church unless he expressly contracts out of his membership.

In some cantons there is accordingly a close relationship between Church and State. The State contributes largely towards the salary of the pastors. In matters of property there is no

241

clearly marked distinction between the two, and the constitution
of the Church forms part of the law of the land. But the Church
has full freedom to manage its own internal affairs. In the
majority of cantons, however, the Reformed Church is organized
as a Free Church, which determines its own constitution, appoints
and pays its own pastors and exacts the payment of taxes from
its members.

During the earlier part of the nineteenth century several
Reformed Free Churches came to be set up in the French-
speaking part of Switzerland in addition to the national Churches.
These were the result of a movement known as *le réveil* initiated
by a Scottish lay evangelist, Robert Haldane (1764–1842), who
visited Geneva in 1817.[1] As obstacles were placed in the way of
the new movement by the governing body of the Church, its
adherents broke away. The Free Churches even established
independent theological faculties for the training of their pastors
in greater conformity with the spirit of the movement.

In the Pays de Vaud a Free Church was established in 1846 as
a result of the action of the State authorities against the new
Evangelical movement. Special resentment was caused by the
prohibition of conventicles or unauthorized services, and matters
came to a head when a government order was issued that all
pastors should read a political proclamation from their pulpits.
One hundred and sixty pastors expressed a wish to resign from
their posts and, when they persisted in their action, they were
removed from office and expelled from their parishes. They set
up a Reformed Free Church which is still in existence to-day.
It has never had a large membership (it now numbers 5,000 out
of a total Reformed population of 275,000), but it has exercised
a powerful religious influence and was of great significance for
the cause of religious liberty in Europe. In the course of the
nineteenth century the National Church also became independent
and now enjoys internal self-government.

In 1873 a Free Church was also established in Neuchâtel.
Twenty-two of the forty-two parishes in the canton were

---

[1] This movement can best be described as Evangelical without being pietistic (except
in some cases where it accidentally fell under pietistic influences). The most important
difference lay in a spirit of (typically Calvinist) activism which contrasts strongly with
the marked Quietism so characteristic of pietism. While great stress was at first laid
upon orthodoxy, the movement later felt the impact of liberal tendencies.

represented on the Free Church Council and an independent faculty of theology was established. The National Church later secured a certain measure of independence from the State, and the way was consequently opened for a limited amount of co-operation between the two Churches.

In the canton of Geneva, Church and State were separated in 1907, and here the Reformed Church became a free national Church.

Approximately 600,000 of the million Protestants in France belong to the Reformed Church. The Reformed minority in this country plays a part in the intellectual and economic life of the nation out of all proportion to its numbers. Together with the Roman Catholic and Lutheran Churches and the Jewish Synagogue, the Reformed Church was given an established status under Napoleon in 1802, and received financial support in return for a measure of State control. Since 1905, when Church and State were separated in France, it has been a Free Church.

Throughout the whole of the nineteenth century tension existed between the liberal and conservative wings of the Church which led to the formation of two small Free Churches. The more important of them was the *Union des Églises evangeliques libres de France*, formed in 1849 under the influence of Frédéric Monod (1794–1863) and marked by a spirit of Calvinist Evangelicalism. The rejection of a proposal concerning the Declaration of Faith of the French Reformed Church led to the secession of the orthodox wing from the National Church. This movement still exists as a separate body but has a relatively small membership.

The French Protestants maintain two private theological faculties at Montpellier and Paris in addition to the State faculty at the University of Strasbourg.

In Holland about 40 per cent of the population belong to the Reformed Church which bears the title of *De Nederlandsch Hervormde Kerk*. From 1816 the Church was closely linked with the State, but during the nineteenth century it became independent in most respects. Thus the choice of their pastors is now vested in the local congregations.

As in France, two small Free Reformed Churches have been formed in Holland. The first, called the *Christelijk Gereformeerde*

Kerk, is associated with the work of the pastor, Hendrick de Cock (1801–42), who was suspended in 1834 for holding unauthorized services and for baptizing the children of Evangelical parents from parishes other than his own. The formation of the second Free Church in 1886 had wider repercussions. For some time orthodox circles within the National Church had viewed with displeasure the high degree of doctrinal freedom within the Church. When the State made the theological faculties non-confessional, the pastor and statesman, Abraham Kuyper (1837–1920), founded the Free University of Amsterdam in 1880, a private institution on a strictly Calvinist basis. He embarked shortly afterwards upon a controversy on the subject of repelling unworthy communicants from the Holy Communion, with the result that (with many others) he left the National Church. The seceders formed an Orthodox Calvinist Free Church, which united in 1892 with the older body to form *De Gereformeerde Kerken in Nederland.* It has 650,000 members (or 8 per cent of the population) and maintains two theological faculties.

Germany has some purely Reformed Churches, in Hanover (where it is a minority Church), Hesse, Bremen and the Rhineland, with a total membership of nearly four million.

There are also Reformed Churches in Czechoslovakia, Hungary, Austria, Poland and Rumania. The largest of these Churches is in Hungary with a membership of nearly two million. In Austria a confederation has taken place between the Reformed Church and the Lutherans.

Scotland is the only country in which the large majority of the population belongs to the Reformed Church. Out of a total population of nearly five million the communicant membership of the Church of Scotland stands at the figure of one and a quarter million with adherents numbering about a million more. The total strength of the smaller Presbyterian bodies is perhaps around 170,000.

From the time of the Reformation onwards the Scottish Church has struggled incessantly to secure its spiritual freedom and to preserve its distinctive character. Its ecclesiastical history is typified by a series of conflicts on questions of Church government which were held to involve 'the Crown Rights of Christ

in His Kirk,' or the right and duty of the Church to govern itself
according to what it believed to be the will of God. Thus in
1712, Parliament revived the system of lay patronage or the right
of certain laymen to appoint parish ministers, which had been
abolished in Scotland as recently as 1690. This right of patronage
had been the privilege of certain noblemen whose ancestors in
the remote past had built churches on their estates, and whose
descendants therefore inherited the right of appointment in
accordance with mediaeval Teutonic Law. In practice the
exercise of this right often resulted in the appointment of a
minister whom the parish was reluctant to accept. When in
1732 a proposal that no congregation should be forced to accept
a minister against its will was defeated in the General Assembly,
the minister Ebenezer Erskine (1680–1754) left the Church and
established a Free Church, called by its opponents 'the Seceders.'
In 1752 another Free Church, known as the Relief Church, was
founded for the same reasons and on a similar occasion. In 1847
these two bodies came together to form the United Presbyterian
Church. It is worthy of notice that those who seceded from the
National Church declared their intention of returning to
the National Church as soon as it should achieve full spiritual
autonomy.

In 1843, however, a new and much larger Free Church had
arisen. Nine years earlier the General Assembly of the Church of
Scotland had approved the motion that no minister should be
imposed upon a congregation against its will. This resolution,
which was in conflict with the legislation governing the Establishment, soon led to difficulties with the State authorities. The
Supreme Court ruled that the General Assembly had no authority
to adopt a motion which ran counter to the law of the land. The
reforming party then formulated their claim for the spiritual
autonomy of the Church in a memorial submitted to but rejected
by Parliament in 1842. At the General Assembly of 1843 the
champions of reform registered a protest against the control of
the Church by the State, left the Assembly and constituted
themselves the Free Church of Scotland. Two-fifths of the
ministers of the Established Church resigned their charges, and
the extent of the secession can be further illustrated by the fact
that the entire missionary staff of the Established Church joined

the Free Church. The new Church had to relinquish all church buildings and manses, but within two years five hundred new churches were built with manses and schools and a theological college was founded in Edinburgh.

In 1900 the Free Church of Scotland joined with the older Free Church, the United Presbyterian Church, to form the United Free Church of Scotland. This had the object of becoming an independent national Church, and in size it approached the Established Church. Thus in the year of its foundation it had 490,000 communicant members as compared with the figure of 650,000 for the Established Church. In the meantime, however, the constitution of the Established Church had undergone considerable changes in the direction of spiritual autonomy. An especially important factor was the final abolition of private patronage in 1874. The desire for a reunion between the Established Church and the United Free Church naturally arose. Negotiations were opened in 1909 which reached completion in 1929 when both Churches were reunited to form the Church of Scotland, which remains a national Church with complete self-government. Only inconsiderable remnants of the previous Presbyterian secessions still remain outside the reunited Church. In the negotiations with the State which preceded the act of union in 1929, great care was taken to avoid any statement that Parliament was granting or conferring spiritual autonomy upon the Church. In the settlement Parliament was said to recognize the government and jurisdiction of the Church in things spiritual as being derived from the Divine Head of the Church alone, and in no sense dependent upon the sanction of the civil authorities.

In England and Ireland there are also small Presbyterian Churches. There is a strong Scottish element in the Presbyterian Church of England which enjoys a well-deserved reputation for the high standard of its theological education.

In America there are a number of Presbyterian Churches with varying characteristics. Their common elements are Calvinist doctrine and Presbyterian Church Order. They possess different mother churches, and are therefore separate religious communities. Negotiations for unity have so far not led to the establishment of a united Church. Their total membership amounts to three million.

Reformed Churches are also to be found in other parts of the world, especially in South Africa and Australia.

In 1875 the first steps were taken towards the formation of the Alliance of Reformed Churches throughout the world holding the Presbyterian system, on the basis of the supremacy of Holy Scripture, adherence to the consensus of the Reformed Confessions and a general acknowledgement of Presbyterian principles. Periodical conferences, of which the first met in Edinburgh in 1877, are held in different parts of the world. The World Presbyterian Alliance provides an opportunity for mutual consultation and for the discussion of common problems. Its resolutions do not, however, possess any binding force over its constituent members.

2. The Characteristic Features of the Reformed Church

The Reformed and Lutheran Churches have so many features in common, both in doctrine and worship, that they are naturally often grouped together under the designation of 'Protestant.' But the Reformed Church also has characteristics which are unquestionably its own.

1. It differs from Lutheranism in its attitude to the Bible, and emphasizes the formal authority of Holy Scripture in a wholly different way.

Luther claimed the liberty of assessing the value and authority of each canonical book, taking as his measuring-rod the doctrine of Justification by Faith. He evaluated the contents of Scripture on the basis of a definite conception of its substance. Something of this approach has been passed down to the Lutheran Church. The attitude of Calvin to the Scriptures was, however, wholly different. For him they represented an authority to be obeyed irrespective of any judgement as to what their contents ought to be. This approach has become traditional in the Reformed Church.

In practice this difference of outlook is reflected in the part played by the Old Testament in the life of the two Churches. It has been the source of a certain legalism in the Reformed tradition which manifested itself, for example, in the Puritan habit of Sabbath Observance whereby Sunday was kept as a day of rest and any form of amusement strictly excluded.

This attitude to the Bible can be further illustrated by the form of the Ten Commandments current in its worship. The Roman Catholic form (followed by the Lutheran Church) omits the prohibition of image worship, reckons the prohibition of taking the name of God in vain as the Second Commandment and preserves the form of the Decalogue by a subdivision of the Tenth Commandment. The Reformed Church (followed in this respect by the Church of England) adheres to the Biblical form.

Again, in the Reformed Church, the New Testament is regarded as a binding standard for the constitution of the Church, and questions of Church Order are therefore assigned an importance equal to matters of doctrine. Here again there is a marked difference of perspective from the Lutheran Churches in which such questions assume a very minor significance.

In the Reformed tradition the Old Testament Scriptures are confined to the canonical books, and the Apocrypha is therefore excluded. This definition was first adopted by the Westminster Confession of Faith in 1647 but has come to be accepted by the whole of the Reformed world. It is owing to the influence of this conception of the Biblical Canon that since 1826 the British and Foreign Bible Society has only printed editions of the Bible from which the Apocrypha is excluded.

2. Like the Lutherans, the Reformed Church teaches that Justification can be attained through faith alone, but it does not regard the Law and the Gospel as diametrically opposed. In Reformed theology the significance of the Law and of Christian action has always been expressed in a completely different way from the Lutheran.

In contrast to the Lutheran tendency towards quietism, the Reformed Church has traditionally been activist in character and regards the attempt to christianize society as part of its duty. It is no accident that the impulses towards such movements as Christian Socialism and Temperance came from Reformed and Anglican circles.

The idea of a theocracy still persists in Reformed theology, and its corollary that the Law of God must be applied to all fields of human life, economic, social and political, is a living force in Reformed thought and practice.

3. A further characteristic of the Reformed Church is to be found in the conception of the necessity for a particular form of Church Order and a corresponding sensitiveness to any form of State intervention in such matters. While still maintaining the doctrine of the invisible Church and formally rejecting any identification of the Church *simpliciter* with a visible communion, the Reformed Church nevertheless believes that the true and invisible Church manifests itself in particular visible Churches and that it is their duty to model themselves on the principles laid down in the Word of God. It has already been noted above that in the Reformed view the New Testament contains clear directives on the subject of Church Order which have the same validity as other parts of the Bible.

3. CONFESSIONAL DOCUMENTS

Within the Reformed Churches confessional documents have never played the same part as the 'symbolic books' of Lutheranism. This is due partly to their view of the authority of Scripture, which relegated 'articles of faith' to the position of 'subordinate standards,' and partly to the accidents of history that the Reformed Churches have never possessed a common confessional document.

All the Reformed Churches recognize the three Catholic Creeds of the early Church, though in practice the Nicene and Athanasian Creeds play a very minor part.

The following Reformed confessional documents may be mentioned here. (i) The most important Swiss confessions are the *Consensus Tigurinus* of 1549, which was the outcome of an agreement between Heinrich Bullinger (1504–75), representing the Zwinglian reformation at Zürich, and Calvin and Farel (1489–1565), the representatives of Geneva, and the *Confessio Helvetica posterior*, compiled by Bullinger as a private work, but recognized by the Elector Frederick of the Palatinate and by all the Reformed cantons in Switzerland in 1566 as their official declaration.

The adoption of the *Consensus Tigurinus* represented the triumph of the Calvinist doctrine of the Eucharist over the Zwinglian. In the *Confessio Helvetica posterior* (Article 21), it is stated that the sign and the thing signified are sacramentally joined in the two sacraments.

Older than either of these is the *Confessio Basileensis prior* of 1534 drafted by Johan Oecolampadius (1482–1531) in 1531, revised by Oswald Myconius (1488–1552) in the following year and recognized only by Basle in 1534. In this work the purely Zwinglian doctrine of the Eucharist has already been abandoned. Christ is present in the Holy Communion 'for all who truly believe.' Greater importance, however, was attached to the *Confessio Basileensis posterior*, also called the *Confessio Helvetica prior*, of 1536, which represents articles of faith accepted by all the Reformed cantons.

(ii) In France the Reformed Church formulated its confession of faith at a general synod held at St. Germain in 1559, called the *Confessio Gallicana*. The draft of the document came from Calvin's own hand. It is written in French and is distinguished for its elegance and clarity. During the War of Religion which followed, it was the unifying bond of the Huguenots and is still the confessional document of the French Reformed Church. The doctrine of Predestination is lucidly expounded (Article 12). In the Eucharist the Body and Blood of Christ are said to be received spiritually (*spirituellement*, Article 36).

(iii) Germany also produced a Reformed confessional document in the *Heidelberg Catechism* of 1563.

As a result of his Biblical studies the Elector Frederick III of the Palatinate became convinced that Lutheran eucharistic doctrine was 'papistic.' He therefore adopted the Reformed standpoint and transferred the allegiance of his national Church. He commissioned Zacharias Ursinus (1534–83), a follower of Melanchthon and professor at Heidelberg, and Caspar Olevianus (1536–87), a Calvinist and Court Preacher, to compile a Confession of Faith, and himself took part in the work. The result was in the form of a Catechism, based upon earlier Reformed documents of a similar type. It is a practical and edifying work and its eucharistic theology and Christology are moderate in character. No express mention is made of Predestination. It is conciliatory towards the Lutherans but polemical towards Roman Catholicism.

The Heidelberg Catechism has come into widespread use and is accepted in Switzerland, Hungary and Poland.

(iv) The Netherlands adopted a Reformed Confession of Faith, the *Confessio Belgica*, approved by a synod held at Antwerp in 1566. This represents the last Continental document of this type compiled during the period of the Reformation.

In the seventeenth century it fell to the Dutch Reformed Church to formulate Calvinist Orthodoxy in the *Canons of the Synod of Dordrecht* (Dort).

This document arose out of the doctrinal controversy on the question of Predestination. This was held in its full severity by the majority of the ministers and theologians in Holland. God had arbitrarily elected some persons to salvation and predestined others to damnation without the issue being in any way affected by the faith and works of the elect. The sole reason was the inscrutable will of God. But a less absolute tendency was represented by the Arminian party, named after Jacob Arminius (1560–1609), professor at Leyden. In 1610 they submitted a Remonstrance or petition to the government, requesting protection against oppression by the orthodox wing of the Church.

In their petition the Remonstrants (as they came to be called) put forward five theses: (1) God's predestination to salvation rests upon His foreknowledge that certain people will believe in Christ and persevere in this belief to the end. (2) Christ died for the whole human race and performed atonement for all men, but only believers share in his benefits. (3) No one, however, can believe through his own powers, for faith is due to God's regenerative grace. (This represents a certain concession to their opponents.) (4) The Grace of God is not irresistible, for man can resist the Spirit of God. (5) Investigation should be made into the teaching of Scripture on the possibility of a fall from Grace. It is not certain that Grace cannot be lost.

This dispute, the greatest doctrinal controversy in the history of the Reformed Church, turned upon the relation between the sovereignty of God and the responsibility of Man.

The State authorities summoned a national synod to consider the question. It met at Dordrecht and sat from November 13th, 1618 to May 9th of the following year. The assembly included eighty-four ministers and elders, together with eighteen representatives of the State. Owing to the importance of the question at issue, other Reformed Churches were invited to send representatives, and theologians from Switzerland and Germany, and even five Anglicans attended its meetings. At this period the Church of England was regarded as a Reformed Church. The synod therefore became an ecumenical council for the Reformed world. The Remonstrants occupied the position of the accused, and therefore could not participate as members. At the fifty-seventh session of the Synod they were declared to be heretics, but the sentence was not formulated until the one hundred and thirty-seventh session. On this occasion the Anglicans and some of the German delegates abstained from voting.

After the Council about two hundred Arminian ministers and theologians were dismissed and several were imprisoned, including the eminent jurist, Hugo Grotius (1583-1645). The dismissed pastors and their congregations then formed a Church of their own, the *Remonstrantsche Kerk*, which still exists as a liberal Reformed Church.

During the following centuries, however, the significance of Arminianism grew in the Reformed Churches and other Churches closely akin to them. In England there was a strong Arminian element within the National Church, and Wesley and the type of Methodism which he founded sided unhesitatingly with Arminianism and even made it a principal element in their interpretation of Christianity.

After pronouncing sentence upon the Remonstrants, the synod turned to the much more difficult task of formulating the orthodox doctrine. The resolutions of the Synod of Dordrecht on the subject of Predestination are expressed in ninety-three canons, divided into five chapters corresponding to the five theses of the Arminians: (1) The elect are no better than other people, and their election depends solely upon God's decree (*beneplacitum*) without reference to foreknowledge of their faith (*non ex praevisa fide*). (2) Christ died for the elect alone. (3) and (4) Grace is irresistible. (5) Those who have received irresistible Grace cannot subsequently fall away. This does not imply that the elect are free from sin or cannot commit even grave sins, but that God does not allow them to fall away from the grace of adoption or the state of justification (*gratia adoptionis, status justificationis*).

Believers possess a certainty of perseverance (*perseverantiae certitudo*).

The primary religious concern of the Synod of Dordrecht was to safeguard the majesty of God and to affirm the assurance of salvation. On one related question, the problem whether the Divine decree was supralapsarian or infralapsarian (whether Adam's Fall was or was not willed by God), the Synod omitted to formulate any doctrine.

The canons of the Synod of Dordrecht (*Canones Synodi Dordrechtanae*) were a counterpart to the Lutheran Formula of Concord, but they have played a much less significant part than the corresponding Lutheran documents. Outside Holland, the Articles were formally adopted by the French Reformed Church alone. The other participating Churches were content to receive them for information only.

Subsequent doctrinal developments, especially after the Evangelical Revival in England in the eighteenth century, led to a posthumous victory of Arminianism in the Reformed world. At least quite a number of theologians of the nineteenth and twentieth centuries who would claim to hold moderate views approximate more closely to Arminianism than to the Synod of Dordrecht on the question at issue between them.

(v) Great Britain also played a significant part in the formulation of Reformed doctrine in the *Confessio Scoticana* of 1560, the Westminster Confession of 1646 and the two Westminster Catechisms.

The Reformed Faith was recognized as the national religion by the Scottish Parliament in 1560. A group of Protestant noblemen had requested Parliament to throw off Papal authority and reform the Church. They submitted a Declaration of Faith compiled in four days with John Knox (*c.* 1515–72) as its principal author, which was subsequently approved by Parliament.

The *Confessio Scoticana* is a moderately Calvinist document. Its doctrine of the Eucharist is almost Lutheranizing in tone and the doctrine of Predestination is not formulated in definite terms. A special feature is the emphasis which it lays upon Church discipline and on the theocratic ideal. The first duty of kings, princes and others in authority is to ensure that the purity of religion is preserved. There are three distinguishing features of the True Church: (1) the true preaching of the Word of God (*vera verbi divini praedicatio*), (2) the lawful administration of the sacraments (*legitima sacramentorum administratio*), and (3) the strict observance of ecclesiastical discipline (*ecclesiasticae disciplinae severa observatio*—Article 18).

The *Confessio Scoticana* remained the subordinate standard of the Scottish Church until 1647, when by resolution of the General Assembly it was replaced by the Westminster Confession.

The *Westminster Confession* was compiled in 1646 during the English Civil War and was approved by the Parliament of the time as the doctrinal standard for the Church of England. Later developments led to the restoration of the Thirty-nine Articles, but the Westminster Confession remains the doctrinal norm for Presbyterian Churches in the British Isles and America.

In 1640, Charles I summoned the Long Parliament which remained in being until 1648. It soon came into conflict with the King and set about the reform of the Church. In 1642 (the year in which the Civil War broke out) both the episcopate and the Anglican Prayer Book were abolished. In 1643, Parliament appointed a great commission, which was to decide questions of liturgy and doctrine, and to give a Presbyterian constitution to the Church of England. In reality, however, the reform had the further aim of introducing a uniform doctrine, order and worship throughout the British Isles.

The Commission held its meetings in Westminster Abbey and thus received the name of the Westminster Assembly of Divines. One hundred and fifty members were present at its meetings, of whom one hundred and twenty were theologians and thirty members of Parliament. Of the twenty episcopal members of the Assembly only two attended. The Independents had some ten representatives, but the overwhelming majority were Presbyterians. The Assembly was in existence for nine years but only had a shadowy existence during the last three or four years.

The Westminster Assembly first composed a new liturgy, the Directory for Public Worship, and then a Church ordinance, Form of Presbyterian Church Government. In 1646 a draft version of the Confession of Faith was completed. It was studied by Parliament in detail, and published under the title of 'Articles of Christian Religion approved and passed by both Houses or Parliament after advice had with the Assembly of Divines by authority of Parliament sitting at Westminster.'

In Scotland the Westminster Confession was readily approved, first by the General Assembly in 1647 and later by the Scottish Parliament in 1649. The Royal Assent was, however, withheld until after the English Revolution and granted in 1690.

In England, however, a different fate awaited the Westminster Confession. The Civil War led to chaos in ecclesiastical affairs, but after the Restoration of 1660 the Church of England was reinstated as the Established Church with its episcopate, Liturgy and confessional document, the Thirty-nine Articles.

In addition to the Confession, the Westminster Assembly issued two other doctrinal documents, the Shorter and Longer Catechisms, which are assigned the same degree of authority as the Confession in the Presbyterian Churches of the English-speaking world.

All three documents are remarkable theological works, lucid, precise and dignified in style and moderate in tone on the questions under dispute.

The only confessional documents of the Reformed Church which serve any practical purposes to-day are the Heidelberg Catechism, the *Confessio Helvetica posterior*, the Westminster Confession and the two Westminster Catechisms.

4. DOCTRINE

The dominant motif in the doctrine of the Reformed Church is the affirmation of the sovereign majesty and glory of God. This theme also runs through its preaching and hymnody.

Lutheranism may, with some reason, be described as anthropocentric, for its doctrinal system is centred in Man's salvation. Its key themes are Atonement, Justification and Salvation. Calvinism, on the other hand, can fairly be called theocentric in the sense that its governing principle is to be found in the concept that Man was created to serve the Glory of God. It is no accident that the special emphasis upon theocentricity in contemporary theology should have come through Reformed theologians like Barth and Brunner.

The confessional standards speak repeatedly of the Glory of God which Man is to serve and which is his chief end (*universalis finis*). The Genevan Catechism of 1542 opens with the statement that 'God has created us, and put us in this world in order that He may be glorified in us,' and the first answer of the Shorter Westminster Catechism reads in a similar sense: 'Man's chief end is to glorify God and to enjoy Him for ever.'

The distance which separates God and Man, the Creator and the creature, is emphasized in strong terms. Thus the Westminster Confession states that 'the distance between God and the creature is so great that, although reasonable creatures do owe obedience unto Him as their Creator, yet they could never have any fruition of Him as their blessedness and reward, but by some voluntary condescension on God's part, which He hath been pleased to express by way of covenant.'

The doctrines of Predestination and Election are organically related to the doctrine of Divine Sovereignty. The salvation of the elect serves the Glory of God and is due solely to God's election and not to Man's activity. The notion that the rejection of the damned also serves God's Glory occasionally appears, but on this point the influence of Arminianism has definitely asserted itself in Reformed theology and preaching during the last two centuries.

But the doctrine of election to Grace does not, as its opponents have frequently asserted, lead to the paralysis of human activity. On the contrary, activity is an essential feature of the Reformed tradition. Predestination has the effect of an ethical motive, since those who have been elected by God owe Him allegiance. The Reformed theologian John Dall puts the point as follows: 'Calvin's doctrine of election was not so much a gloomy and pessimistic denial of human freedom as the joyous proclamation that Man lived in an ordered universe, where the Sovereignty of God removed from the region of doubt the salvation of the true believer.'

The other distinctive part of the teaching of the Reformed Church is its doctrine of the sacraments.

It is emphasized that God is not bound by the sacraments, but is sovereign over the outward vehicles of grace. But the sacraments which He has ordained belong to the normal life of the

Church. 'We admit that God may sometimes enlighten people without any outward ministry' (*Confessio Helvetica posterior*), but the forms of preaching and sacraments belong to the normal order instituted by God. The principle that sacraments are effectual only to the elect, which is expressly stated in the *Consensus Tigurinus*, is typical of the Reformed tradition.

The Reformed doctrine of Baptism denies that Regeneration is effected through the sacrament. The practice of Infant Baptism, interpreted as 'the ingrafting of the child into Christ' and its reception into the Church, is nevertheless retained.

In the doctrine of the Eucharist the Reformed Church does not adhere to the purely symbolic conception of Ulrich Zwingli (1484–1531), which limits the sacrament to a commemorative meal and a confession of faith in Christ. Nor does it accept the Lutheran doctrine of the bodily presence of Christ in the sacrament with the corollary of an oral participation (*manducatio oralis*). Reformed theologians steer a middle course between these two standpoints. Christ is present in the sacrament, really but spiritually (*spirituellement-Confessio Gallicana*). It is only believers who partake of Him through reception of the sacrament.

The presence of Christ in the sacrament is expounded as follows in the *Confessio Helvetica posterior* (Article 21). 'We do not therefore conjoin the Lord's Body and Blood with bread and wine in such a way that we call the bread itself Christ's Body (unless the expression be taken in a sacramental meaning), or say that the Body of Christ is bodily hidden in the bread, with the result that it should be adored in the form of bread, or that whosoever perceives the sign, also perceives the thing itself. Christ's Body is in heaven, at the right hand of the Father. Our hearts should therefore be lifted up, and not fixed to the bread, nor should the Lord be adored in the bread. And yet the Lord is not absent from His Church when it celebrates the Supper. The sun is absent from us in heaven, but it is nevertheless present among us in an efficacious manner (*efficaciter*). How much more is the Sun of Righteousness, Christ, in spite of His corporeal absence from us in heaven, present for us, not in a corporeal manner (*non corporaliter quidem*), but in a spiritual way (*sed spiritualiter*), through His life-giving operation (*per vivificam operationem*), as He Himself said, in the Last Supper, that He

K

would be present with us (*St. John* xiv–xvi). Whence it follows that we have not the Supper without Christ, but that we have an unbloody and mystical Supper (*coena incruenta et mystica*), as it has been called universally from olden times.'

In Reformed theology it is often stressed that that Christ's presence in the Supper is a 'dynamic presence' or a 'virtual presence.' What the communicant receives is 'the sacrificial virtue or effects of the death of Christ on the Cross.' The sacraments are also sometimes described as 'efficacious signs' (*signa efficacia*).

5. CONSTITUTION

A further special feature of the Reformed Church is the Presbyterian Church Order.

It is held that there is only one ministry or order, the presbyterate. In the New Testament the *episkopoi* are either identical with the *presbuteroi*, or constitute a special group within them charged with the administration of the Word and Sacraments.

According to the Reformed tradition, which is based upon the teaching of Calvin himself, there are four offices in the Church instituted by our Lord Himself: pastors, teachers, elders and deacons (*pasteurs, docteurs, anciens, diacres*), each with their own field of activity. Preaching, together with the cure of souls and the administration of the sacraments, is the special charge of the minister, and lay preaching is therefore repudiated in principle. The congregation chooses its own minister or, in cases where he is appointed by another authority, at least has the right to refuse to accept him. It is also important to note that ministers are subject to Church discipline. The 'teachers' are all those who give instruction in Christian doctrine, from elementary school teachers to professors of theology. Calvin's elders were town councillors appointed by the civic authorities, after consultation with the ministers, to assist them in the administration of ecclesiastical discipline. They were neither ordained nor appointed for life, but were subject to annual re-election. It was not in Geneva under Calvin, but in areas where the civic authorities were indifferent or hostile that the eldership developed towards its present status in the Reformed Churches. In these areas the elders were elected by the congregation and ordained to their

office for life; and this has now become the general practice in
Reformed Churches. With the minister they form the Consistory
or Session which governs the life and discipline of the Congregation. So highly is the office esteemed that the ministers are
sometimes thought of as a special group within the eldership,
teaching as distinct from ruling elders. The task of the deacon
is to look after the poor, but his functions are now frequently
exercised by the Kirk Session.

Scriptural warrant for the four offices is found in Ephesians iv.
11, Romans xii. 7 and 1 Corinthians xii. 28, with the omission
of offices such as apostles, prophets and evangelists which are
either extraordinary or confined to the primitive period of the
history of the Church.

The constitution of the Reformed Church is synodical, or
composed of a number of councils (in Scotland called Church
courts). The parish council is called the Kirk Session (in France
consistoire), and consists of the ministers and elders of a particular
parish. It has administrative and advisory functions and is especially charged with the supervision of Church discipline. The next
authority is the Presbytery, which consists of the ministers of a
wider district and one elder from each parish. The Presbytery
appoints and, where necessary, dismisses ministers. The Synod is
a body with superior authority for a wider area which roughly
corresponds in extent to a diocese in episcopal churches. The
whole Church is represented in the General Assembly which
meets annually and has legislative and judicial authority within
the general framework of the constitution of the Church and
the law of the land. In this Assembly sit representatives, both
ministerial and lay, of all the Presbyteries. Its president, who
in most Reformed Churches is a minister, is called the Moderator.
In the Kirk Session laymen are always in the majority; in the
Presbytery as well as in the Synod and the General Assembly
the membership is equally distributed between ministers and
laity, while in the Swiss Cantonal Synods laymen outnumber
pastors by two to one.

6. WORSHIP

Simplicity is the keynote of the interior of a Reformed Church.
There are no pictures or crucifixes, though in some churches

(particularly in Scotland) a cross is coming into common use. The Holy Table takes the place of an altar. The pulpit is often placed on the long wall of the church opposite the entrance, and high windows admit a considerable amount of light. The general impression is that the building is primarily designed for the preaching of the Word. The minister conducts the service in a black gown without a surplice or other liturgical vestments. On strict Reformed principles, an organ should not be used in church, and only Psalms or Paraphrases from the Bible in metrical form should be sung. This has, however, long since been abandoned, and both organs and hymns are now universally used.

The form of service provided by Calvin for the Church in Geneva represented a translation of the revision of the Roman Catholic Mass made by Martin Bucer (1491–1551). As, however, it was much shortened and ends where the Eucharistic action of the Mass properly begins, it came to resemble a Ministry of the Word accompanied by prayer. While Calvin himself greatly desired a weekly celebration of the Holy Communion and even urged a monthly Communion in the face of the stiff opposition of the civic authorities, but had to content himself with a quarterly observance of the sacrament, this has become the standard practice of the Reformed Churches, although it falls short of the ideals of Calvin himself.

Within each national Church there is normally liturgical uniformity, though this does not extend to the Reformed world as a whole. The constituent parts of the normal Sunday service in the Continental Reformed Churches are the recitation of the Ten Commandments (in the form mentioned above) and of the Apostles' Creed, long lessons from the Old and New Testaments, prayers sometimes forming part of an Order of Worship, but more often prepared at the discretion of the minister, sermon and hymnody. In some parts of the Reformed world, particularly in Scotland, a liturgical revival has taken place within the present century. The Eucharist is normally received sitting, or in some Churches standing. A silver plate containing cubes of bread and a chalice of wine are passed from hand to hand in deep silence.

Appendix I: THE WALDENSIAN CHURCH

The Waldensian Church (*chiesa Valdese*) may be more properly described as an elder sister than a daughter of the Reformed Church. While it has been strongly influenced by the Reformed tradition, its unique history may justify separate treatment.

Its origin is to be found in the brotherhood of evangelical preachers founded by a layman named Waldo (d. *c.* 1218), which was proscribed by the third Lateran Council of 1179. They called themselves 'the poor' or 'the poor of Lyons' (*pauperes de Lugduno*), but soon received the name of Waldensians. They continued their activity despite ecclesiastical prohibitions and the movement spread from Southern France to Italy, Germany and Spain. Older movements of a similar type were merged into the Waldensian stream but a schism took place between the Waldensians of France and Lombardy.

The Waldensians organized themselves as a separate Church whose principal features were the ideal of poverty and the practice of Bible-reading. The Bible was translated into the vernacular and their preachers were required to learn by heart a considerable number of Biblical passages. The movement rejected the Papacy, a number of Roman Catholic doctrines, such as the idea of Purgatory, and the practice of private masses for the dead. The threefold ministry of bishops, priests and deacons was retained, but the number of sacraments was reduced to three, Baptism, Penance and the Holy Communion.

The mediaeval Waldensians are frequently regarded as fore-runners of the Reformation. This is true in certain respects, particularly in their emphasis upon the authority of the Bible and their criticism of certain Roman Catholic institutions and practices. Their piety was, however, of the mediaeval type. They interpreted Christianity as the law of Christ rather than as the message of the Grace of God to sinful man. Virginity and fasting were emphasized in a typically mediaeval manner and Justification by Faith did not form part of their teaching.

In spite of these important differences the Waldensians naturally felt their kinship with the new movement. The main body was strongly influenced by the Genevan Reformation, especially through their contact with Guillaume Farel, and at a synod held at Cianforan in the Angrogna Valley, in 1532, the Waldensian preachers from the Alpine valleys, Lombardy, Provence and Southern Italy adopted the practices of the Reformed Church. Their congregational organization was modified in greater conformity with the Genevan pattern, and their confession of faith presented to the Duke of Turin in 1560 was modelled on the Gallican Confession of the previous year. From this time onwards the Waldensians must be considered as an independent branch of the Reformed Church.

No other Western Church experienced a similar series of persecutions. These began in the Middle Ages, but continued at the period of the Reformation and throughout the seventeenth century. As a result, the Waldensians were exterminated everywhere except in the Alpine valleys where some thousands, some French-speaking and others Italian-speaking, resisted all military attacks and every other form of inducement to return to the Roman Catholic Church. Their heroic struggles aroused the sympathy and admiration of Protestant Europe. At a critical moment in their history Cromwell made a successful diplomatic intervention on their behalf, and Milton celebrated their courage in verse.

When Napoleon conquered the Alpine valleys in 1798, the Waldensians were granted equal rights with the Roman Catholics, though this concession was withdrawn in 1814 during the period of reaction which followed his fall. After 1848 they enjoyed full religious liberty in Northern Italy. In the new Italy which came into being after 1870 the principle of universal toleration was introduced and the Waldensians were even able to start a mission in Rome.

To-day the Waldensian Church is a purely Italian institution which is found mainly in the Alpine valleys (with the small town of Torre Pellice near the French border as its ancient centre), but also in Lombardy, Rome, and even in Sicily. The intellectual centre of the Waldensian Church is a theological school founded at Torre Pellice in 1855, and moved first to Florence and finally in 1922 to Rome. Through emigration and evangelization among the Italian emigrants it has extended its activities to South

America, where in 1937 it had a membership of about 15,000 as compared with approximately 2,000 in the United States. In Italy itself the Waldensians number about 30,000.

Appendix II: PURITANISM AS THE BACKGROUND OF THE RISE OF NEW RELIGIOUS BODIES

The Reformed interpretation of Christianity has proved a fertile soil for the growth of new religious movements. This is partly due to the special emphasis laid upon the authority of the Bible, which gave rise to watchwords like 'Biblical congregations' and 'Biblical baptism' in the new communities. But the most important factor lay in the version of the Reformed ethos which is to be found in English Puritanism.

Puritanism is not a doctrinal system but a type of piety which arose in England during the sixteenth century. It first appeared in 1559 in the form of a protest against the prescribed vestments and other liturgical customs of the Church of England. Towards the close of the century the question of Church Order came to the fore. Here the Puritans took various paths. Some conformed to episcopacy and the Book of Common Prayer, others favoured Presbyterianism and pressed for reform along these lines, while others desired the formation of churches of true believers, organized as autonomous congregations and became Congregationalists or Baptists. But they all possess certain features in common which constitute the Puritan type of Christianity.

The distinctive character of Puritanism did not consist primarily in a specific form of doctrine. They were Calvinists and emphasized the doctrines of Original Sin and Total Depravity, Justification by Faith and Predestination, but most of these tenets were shared by the Continental Lutherans and Calvinists, combined with a different pattern of life. While it may be true that Puritanism presupposes a Calvinist theology, it nevertheless remains an attitude to life, a style of living.

This religious attitude is decidedly non-sacramental and anti-institutional. The individual Christian stands alone before Almighty God and can lean neither upon the sacraments nor on any institutional church. He is completely dependent upon the Grace of God, but this is not tied to any sacramental rites. Thus, for example, the sacrament of Penance is not used in Puritanism, since the minister has no authority to forgive sins by virtue of his office. The Eucharist loses its character as a means of grace and becomes a solemn pledge taken upon themselves by believers. The strictest Puritans even rejected all burial rites on the ground that in the face of death man should not cling to outward observances.

Puritanism is a religion of the Word. It holds to the Bible only without any Church Tradition or Articles of Faith. One of the earliest Puritan objections to the Anglican Liturgy was concerned with standing for the Gospel but not for any other part of the Bible. Thus the Liturgy appeared to place parts of the Bible on different levels, which the Puritans regarded as an unacceptable principle.

Puritanism is also a religion of the will and of ethical action. Will, disciplined and inspired, and activity are of its essence. Seriousness and fervour, the girded loins and the lighted lamps lie at its very heart. It is distinguished outwardly by discipline and self-control, in short by an ascetic way of life. But Puritan asceticism is very different from its Catholic counterpart. It knows neither the monastery nor vows of celibacy, still less dispensations on the part of the ecclesiastical authorities. The solution of renouncing the world by leaving it is foreign to its nature. The only method which Puritanism can recognize is the renunciation of all worldly pleasures or what the German sociologist, Max Weber (1864–1920), has described as 'asceticism within the world' (innerweltliche Askese).

The movement can best be studied, not in the Articles of Faith of any Church, but in the best known of its devotional works, the *Pilgrim's Progress* of John Bunyan (1628–88). The Christian life follows a path from the City of Destruction to the Celestial City. It passes by abysses and over marshes and through the town where Vanity Fair is held. The way is beset with temptation and danger; the pilgrim must hold the goal in view and keep himself unspotted from the world. The good things of life are a temptation to him and this he experiences in fullest measure. On this journey the pilgrim is alone. Certainly he meets with other lonely travellers, with whom he can share his experiences and who may help him, but the impression is never given that he lives in the fellowship of the Church of Christ or, as the Lutheran hymn-writer, Nikolai Grundtvig (1783-1872), puts it, that it is good to be in the shelter of the Church of our Lord. He is guided by the Scriptures and derives strength from prayer, but there is no help to be found in the sacraments. No strict orthodoxy seems to be demanded of the pilgrim. The dogmatic standpoint of the book is a commonplace type of Protestantism, strongly anti-Catholic, but otherwise with no special features. But resolution, endurance, will, and still more will, are demanded of him.

Puritanism had far-reaching repercussions in history. It was an important factor in the formation of modern democracy whose Christian roots run through English Puritanism. For centuries, Roman Catholicism, Lutheranism and Anglicanism supported authoritarian government and to some extent retarded the development of the people as an effective political force. On the other hand, the English Puritans asserted that all men were equal before God and some extended this principle to the sphere of human politics as well. They actively opposed the Stuarts, and through their church constitution and their training in active responsibility laid some of the most important foundations of modern democracy.

Recent research has also maintained that Puritanism was to a considerable extent the soil from which sprang Capitalism in the economic field. The activity of the Puritans found expression in commercial and industrial enterprise. Their renunciation of the pleasures of the world led to prosperity and the accumulation of wealth. Their emphasis upon the Old Testament led to the view that riches were a sign of God's blessing. Moreover, the Calvinist tradition permitted (not without a certain degree of reluctance) the practice of lending money on interest, a practice which the Roman Catholic and Lutheran Churches long continued to condemn. An important factor in the rise of a capitalist class in England is also to be found in the fact that until 1828 Dissenters were excluded from offices of State and even from University degrees, and were therefore compelled to enter occupations, especially in industry and commerce, for which these qualifications were not required.

Of greater importance in the present connection, however, is the emergence of new Churches through secession. Radical Puritans drew inferences from their interpretation of Christianity in the fields of Church Order and the administration of the Sacraments. Between 1580 and 1590, Congregationalism came into being through the formation of separatist bodies in Norwich and London under the leadership of Robert Browne (1550–1633), John Greenwood (d. 1593) and Henry Barrow (*c.* 1550–93). The history of the Baptist Churches proper dates from the adoption (shortly after 1600) of the practice of adult Baptism by some of the refugee Puritan Separatists in Holland. The Quakers (whose origin can be dated between 1650 and 1660) represent an enthusiastic form of Puritanism which repudiated all ecclesiastical institutions, although the movement also marked a reaction against the gloomy doctrine of Man and the conventional way of life characteristic of the Puritans. It is one of the most important sources of eighteenth-century Methodism which is strongly marked by the typically Puritan spirit of 'asceticism within the world.' Finally, as shaped by the Methodist revival, Puritanism led to a 'holiness movement,' the precursor of twentieth-century Pentecostalism and of the religious sects to which it has given rise.

All these new churches were not the result of doctrinal disagreements. Neither (apart from Congregationalism) were they caused by questions of Church Order. Their motivating force was rather a peculiar interpretation of the Christian way of life, and it is in this light that their distinctive character can best be understood.

In the following chapters, therefore, we shall be concerned with a number of Churches whose distinctive character is determined by their ethos.

CHAPTER XI

THE METHODIST CHURCH

1. ORIGIN AND HISTORY

THE Methodist Church arose as the result of the great revival in England initiated by the work of John Wesley (1703-91) and his collaborators.

Wesley himself was the son of a country Rector in Lincolnshire. He proceeded to Oxford where he became attached to the 'Holy Club,' a group of young men who devoted themselves to serious living with a strict rule of life which included the practice of a weekly communion and extended even to their studies. Their strict rule of life earned for them the nickname of 'Methodists.' He was ordained priest in the Church of England and was admitted to a Fellowship at Lincoln College, Oxford, which he held without interruption from 1726 until his marriage in 1751. In 1735 he undertook a missionary journey to Georgia and met on shipboard a party of Moravians. This was his first contact with a movement which was destined to have a profound influence upon his life. His mission to Georgia must be pronounced on the whole a failure, and Wesley returned to England two years later in great distress of soul. As his *Journal* records, it was in 'a society in Aldersgate St.' (London) that he experienced what he came to recognize as his conversion in 1738, and thenceforward devoted himself to itinerant evangelism, while still remaining a priest in the Church of England. One of his best-known sayings is that he regarded the world as his parish.

Several historical circumstances led to the organization of Methodism into a separate Church, a process which can be said to have been completed by 1784. Three main reasons may be assigned for this separation. Revivals generally have within them the seeds of division and Methodism was no exception to this rule. It received a cool reception from the clergy of the Established Church, who showed as a whole little inclination to co-operate. Special difficulties were encountered in America where Wesley had already started work, and where Methodist settlers had no pastors to guide them. Their plight induced Wesley to take the decisive step of ordaining ministers himself.

From 1739 the followers of John Wesley were organized in societies or associations for the promotion of the spiritual life within the Church of England. Taken as a whole, the United Societies formed a home mission society covering the entire country. Since dissenters could also become members, they showed little inclination to emphasize specifically Anglican tenets. For many of their members these meetings became the natural form of divine service, though they continued to receive the sacraments within the Church of England. The term 'Methodist Church' was never encouraged by John Wesley himself, though it was used as early as 1759 by his collaborators, John Fletcher (1729–85) and Vincent Perronet (1693–1785).

In 1784 the Methodist community was licensed as a person at law. In the Deed of Declaration all Methodist chapels and meeting-houses were held in trust for the benefit of the organization, and its Conference which was to meet annually was designated as the body which could act on its behalf. Its members are here described as 'the people called Methodists.'

Like all Anglicans living abroad, the Methodists in America were under the jurisdiction of the Bishop of London. Before the American colonies secured their independence in 1776, several attempts had been made to establish an episcopate for America, which had failed largely owing to government opposition.[1] There were few Anglican clergy in America, and after the American War of Independence it became impossible to continue the practice of ordaining priests in England for work in America. To meet this emergency Wesley himself held ordinations in 1784. At an earlier stage he had reached the conclusion that there was no essential difference between the episcopate and the presbyterate which he himself held.[2] He now ordained several deacons and priests, together with Dr. Thomas Coke (1747–1814), who was already in priest's orders as 'superintendent of the American Methodists.' On his arrival in America, however, Coke proceeded to call himself 'bishop.'

[1] See above, p. 139, for an account of the eventual consecration of bishops for America.
[2] In 1745, Wesley read Peter, Lord King's work entitled *Enquiry into the Constitution of the Primitive Church* (first published in 1691), which maintained this position. (H.E.W.T.)

At the time of Wesley's death in 1791 the Methodist Societies in England had a total membership of 135,000. Many still regarded themselves as primarily members of the Church of England, but for others attachment to Methodism took precedence over any other denominational loyalty. The problem arose whether services in Methodist chapels should be held at the same time as those in the parish churches, and therefore in possible competition with them, and whether the Methodist Church should conduct its own services of Holy Communion. Resolutions (known as the 'Plan of Pacification') were passed by the Conference of 1795 permitting (though not prescribing) both practices and adding the rider that the Holy Communion was only to be administered by persons authorized by the Conference. From this date the separation of the Methodist Church from the Church of England may be said to be complete.

The history of English Methodism during the nineteenth and twentieth centuries is a record of further revivals and of the development of Church organization, but it is also marked by disruptions and subsequent reunions.

The most important separated churches were the Methodist New Connexion (1797), the Primitive Methodists (1807), founded by a preacher who had been excommunicated for holding 'camp-meetings' after the fashion of American revivalist methods, and the Bible Christians (1815), also caused by irregular preaching activity. Both the Primitive Methodists and the Bible Christians also gave offence by admitting women as itinerant preachers. A larger body, the United Methodist Free Churches (1857), itself the result of a union between two earlier movements, the Wesleyan Methodist Association and the Wesleyan Reformers, differed from the parent Church on a constitutional issue. From 1881 a desire for reunion led to the holding of ecumenical Methodist Conferences at decennial intervals.

In 1907, three Methodist Churches in England combined to form the United Methodist Church, which again in 1932 united with the Wesleyan Methodists and Primitive Methodists to form 'the Methodist Church.' Only small Methodist minorities remain outside this union.

In 1784 the Methodists in America constituted themselves 'the Methodist Episcopal Church,' which underwent rapid expansion both in the Southern States and in the newly settled areas of the West. It was fired with missionary zeal and revivals followed in quick succession.

As a result of these revivals and of a process of co-operation with other Evangelical Churches, the spirit of Methodism has leavened other Protestant denominations in America. Among the ways in which Methodism has made its influence felt have been the active participation of laymen in the work of the Church, a tendency to regard differences of doctrine as of minor importance, revivalist campaigns, the insistence upon sudden conversion and a heightened emphasis upon personal sanctification.

Disputes both on constitutional questions and on the issue of slavery, however, led to disruptions in the life of the Methodist Church in America. A section which desired to give greater influence to the laity broke away in 1830 to form the Methodist Protestant Church, which was non-episcopal.

At roughly the same time the Methodists in the Northern States opposed slavery, while those of the South, in common with Christians of other denominations, tended to regard negro slavery as part of the natural order of society sanctioned by God and therefore as compatible with Christianity. In 1836 the Conference forbade preaching on the subject, though some ministers defied the ban and were dismissed from office. In 1843 they founded the Wesleyan Methodist Church, with lay representation and without an episcopate. The great schism in American Methodism occurred in 1845 on the question of slavery and resulted in a split between the Methodist Episcopal Church and the Methodist Episcopal Church South.

A re-union movement led to a fusion of the three largest Methodist Churches in America (the Methodist Protestant Church, the Methodist Episcopal Church and the Methodist Episcopal Church South) in 1939 under the designation of 'the Methodist Church.'

2. DISTRIBUTION AND STATISTICAL DATA

The Methodist revival reached Ireland and Canada during Wesley's own lifetime. While the Methodist Church in Ireland has never reached considerable proportions, in Canada it has always occupied an important position in the life of the country and in 1925 it was one of the constituents of the United Church of Canada.[1]

The Methodists were the first Church to preach the Gospel in Australia after its colonization at the end of the eighteenth century. In France there was a small Methodist community, which has recently united with the Reformed Church. A somewhat more important part is played by the movement in Italy, largely owing to the small numbers of other Evangelical Churches. Here union with the Waldensians has been under discussion. Methodism reached Germany through a Württemberg preacher who became acquainted with it in England and returned to his homeland in 1830. From America it passed into Scandinavia and consequently took the form of the Episcopal Methodist Church.

It is difficult to determine the total membership of the Methodist Church owing to the distinction between two types of membership. Members in the strict sense and persons possessing only 'preparatory membership.' The former have confirmed their baptismal vows in public before the congregation and declared their adherence to the doctrines and ordinances of the Church, the latter, which includes children born and baptized within the Methodist Church, also covers those who have applied for membership and are taken on probation. In practice account is also taken of yet another group known as 'adherents,' which is described as 'all persons connected with the Church and Sunday School either through relatives or personal adherence.'

The total number of members and adherents can be put at between forty and fifty million. The statistics for 1956, however, only take account of eighteen million 'full members,' but in addition there were nearly eight million Sunday School scholars. There were 54,000 ministers and 82,000 lay preachers, high figures in proportion to the membership of the Church.

According to the returns for 1956 in the United States, the Methodist Church has nearly ten and a half million members and the other Methodist Churches one and a half million.

[1] See below, p. 373.

In England the Methodist Church has 800,000 members, but in Ireland only some 30,000. In Australia there are 700,000 Methodists or 7 per cent of the population.

3. THE CHARACTERISTIC FEATURES OF THE METHODIST CHURCH

In the synthesis of doctrine, worship, constitution and ethos in the Methodist Church, the fourth undoubtedly takes precedence over the other three elements. Its keynote is life in the sense of conscious life in God. The description of the marks of the Church in the Methodist Catechisms, while based, like the Anglican Article, on the Lutheran definition, is expanded by the addition of this theme, which is significantly put first. 'It is to be recognized by the faith and sanctity of the believers, by the preaching of God's Word and by the proper administration of the sacraments in accordance with God's institution.'

The Methodist Church bears traces of being the type of Church produced by pietism. Its origin was not the result of any doctrinal disagreement but of a revival which broke down the old forms, and led Wesley himself, and to a greater extent his successors, to stress certain aspects of Anglican doctrine and to ignore others completely. There is also an element of mysticism, a strong Puritan background, and traces of the influence of Luther and of the Moravians in the Methodist Church.

1. The Anglican heritage of Methodism can be detected in its public worship. On Sunday mornings a few churches use a service which is almost identical with Anglican Morning Prayer, while the Methodist Order of Holy Communion is based upon and very similar to the Order in the Book of Common Prayer.

2. A Puritan element is noticeable in the ethos of Methodism; it is an active form of Christianity which demands the renunciation of all worldliness.

The Methodist Church has devoted itself with particular zeal to the Temperance Movement. Although there is no formal rule to this effect either in English or American Methodism, most Methodists, particularly of the older type, are total abstainers from alcohol. Since the union of the American Methodist Churches (carrying on the practice of one of the Uniting Churches) it is obligatory upon all newly-ordained ministers to abstain from tobacco.

The classical example of this Puritan ethos, noteworthy alike for its practical outlook and keen psychological insight into the practical temptations arising from daily life, may be drawn from the General Rules of the Methodist Societies, dating from the year 1743. 'It is expected of all who continue therein (our Societies) that they should continue to evidence their desire for salvation. First, by doing no harm, by avoiding evil in every kind; especially that which is most generally practised; such is, the taking the name of God in vain; the profaning the day of the Lord . . . drunkenness, buying or selling spirituous liquors, or drinking them, except in cases of extreme necessity; fighting, quarrelling, brawling; brother going to law with brother; returning evil for evil, or railing for railing . . . the buying or selling of uncustomed goods . . . the giving or taking things on usury; uncharitable or unprofitable conversation, particularly speaking evil of magistrates or of ministers . . . doing what we know is not for the glory of God . . . the taking such diversions as cannot be used in the name of the Lord Jesus . . . softness, and needless self-indulgence; laying up treasures upon earth; borrowing without a probability of paying or taking up goods without a probability of paying for them. . . . Secondly, by doing good, by being, in every kind, merciful after their power; as they have opportunity, doing good of every possible sort, and as far as is possible, to all men—to their bodies, by giving food to the hungry, by clothing the naked, by visiting or helping them that are sick, or in prison—to their souls, by instructing, reproving, or exhorting all they have any intercourse with . . . by doing good, especially to them that are of the household of faith, employing them preferably to others, buying one of another . . . by all possible diligence and frugality, that the Gospel be not blamed; by running with patience the race that is set before them, "denying themselves and taking up their cross daily"; submitting to bear the reproach of Christ, to be as the filth and offscouring of the world; and looking that men should say all manner of evil of them falsely for the Lord's sake. . . . Thirdly by attending upon all the ordinances of God. Such are, the public worship of God; the ministry of the word, either read or expounded; the supper of the Lord; family and private prayer; searching the Scriptures and fasting, or abstinence.'

Such, then, is the outward form of the Methodist ethos. Its inner spirit, a desire to flee from the wrath to come and to be saved from sin, and the longing for holiness are to be found in the Methodist hymns.

> Thy nature be my law,
> Thy spotless sanctity,
> And sweetly every moment draw
> My happy soul to Thee.

3. Moravian influence can be traced in the special emphasis upon communal life, the mutual control exercised by the members on each other. One distinctive way in which this communal life is achieved and maintained (although historically it may not be Moravian in origin) is the provision that members are required to meet 'in class' for the building up of the Christian life. Other features in which Moravian influence can certainly be traced are particular forms of worship such as love-feasts and vigils. Yet the Methodist Church is sharply distinguished from Moravianism in its emphasis upon Christian activity and personal sanctification.

4. There is a pronounced Lutheran element in Methodism owing to the effect which the writings of Luther had upon Wesley himself. Wesley not only revived the doctrine of Justification by Faith for his contemporaries, but also made it a crucial point in the Methodist interpretation of Christianity.

Like Luther, Wesley also stressed the doctrine of assurance of salvation. Here, however, there emerges a characteristic difference, for in Methodism the assurance of faith derives from experience, and not from faith alone. Methodism tends to subjectivity, Lutheranism to objectivity. In Wesley's own words, Methodism is an 'experimental religion.'

Methodism also takes a different line from Lutheranism on the doctrine of sanctification. This is the second focus of the teaching of the Methodist Church. Wesley himself continually stated that the purpose of Methodism was the propagation of 'Scriptural Holiness.' The doctrine of entire sanctification was the great heritage of 'the people called Methodists.'

Sanctification is regarded as a stage following conversion. The Christian must experience such a growth in love and holiness that he really comes to love God with all his heart, and love his neighbour as himself. Through his preaching of Christian perfection, Wesley wished to awaken a deep desire for holiness.

A special feature of Methodism is its conviction that Christian perfection can be realized in this world. This does not imply the attainment of absolute impeccability, but only of such a stage of sanctification that no conscious breach of God's commandment in fact takes place. This perfection is not attained by our own powers, but is the work of the Holy Spirit. At every stage the Christian can approach God by faith alone and in virtue of God's forgiving grace.

The Methodist conception of sanctification has often been regarded (and not least by Lutheran controversialists) simply as a doctrine; it is rather primarily an ideal for living or a way of life. The strict Puritan pattern meets and is fused with a mystical fervour and that longing for 'otherworldliness' which features so largely in the religious history of England.

The essence of Methodism can be summarized most briefly in a single phrase: 'Experimental religion' leading to 'Scriptural holiness.'[1]

4. DOCTRINE

The Methodist Church regards the Holy Scriptures (limited to the canonical books) as the sole rule for faith and life.

In addition to the Scriptures there are also certain 'standards of doctrine.' To these belong (in British Methodism) 'the historic Creeds,' and certain normative documents which do not rank with the Scriptures, but which are regarded as containing the doctrine of the Church. These are three documents from the pen of John Wesley himself: (i) The Twenty-five articles of 1784, an abridgement of the Thirty-nine Articles; (ii) Notes on the New Testament (1755); and (iii) Forty-four Sermons, the so-called 'Standard Sermons.' In British Methodism only the last two possess this status.

These documents are not 'articles of faith' in the juridical sense. In the detailed legislation of the Methodist Church in America the Articles of Faith are never defined. The questions put to candidates for the ministry merely refer to 'the doctrines of the

[1] See, for example, P. G. Watson, *Let God be God* (for a study of Sanctification in Luther and Wesley) and R. Newton Flew, *The Christian Idea of Perfection*. (H.E.W.T.)

Methodist Church' without further specification. These 'standards' also differ in literary form from the definitions of General Councils. Precise definitions or systematic regulations can hardly be expected in a Bible commentary and a collection of sermons.

In American Methodism the clause 'He descended into Hell' is omitted from the Apostles' Creed, though it is retained in the Book of Offices of British Methodism with the footnote, 'That is Hades, or the World of Departed Spirits.' This omission may be due to the rejection of the doctrine of Purgatory and the possibility of conversion after death. The Nicene Creed is used in the Communion Service of British Methodism, though in America it is neither used nor explicitly rejected. The Athanasian Creed was removed by Wesley from his revision of the Book of Common Prayer.

In the Twenty-five Articles certain Catholic elements were removed from their Anglican source. Wesley omitted the Articles 'Of the going down of Christ into Hell' and 'Of the three Creeds' (Articles 3 and 8). He also omitted Articles 20 and 21, 'Of the Authority of the Church' and 'Of the Authority of General Councils,' possibly as not being sufficiently Protestant for his purpose. Article 26, 'Of the Unworthiness of the Ministers, which hinders not the effect of the Sacrament,' also disappeared. Article 23, 'Of Ministering in the Congregation,' was also deleted, while in Article 32 the word 'Priest' in the title was replaced by 'Minister' and the phrase 'ministers of Christ' substituted for 'Bishops, priests and deacons.' In Article 27 the statement that 'they that receive Baptism rightly are grafted into the Church' was omitted, and the heading of Article 16, 'Of Sin after Baptism,' was altered to 'Of Sin after Justification.' In line with his opposition to Calvinism, Wesley also removed Article 17, 'Of Predestination and Election.' Articles and phrases relevant to the Anglican Establishment were also omitted.

Thus in Wesley's revised text the Articles become at once less Catholic and less Calvinist. They cover the common doctrinal deposit of Protestantism without definite alignment to one or other of its classical traditions. Their character is simplified and they concentrate upon the doctrine of salvation and its implications (the *loci salutares*). This simplification must certainly be taken into account in assigning reasons for the omission of particular articles.

Methodist theology also concentrates upon these *loci salutares*, the doctrine of salvation and its acquisition. On the question of Predestination, Methodism takes a definitely Arminian line. God's offer of salvation is made to all men and Christ died for all mankind. This doctrine of 'free grace,' the principle that grace is offered by God to all men, preached by Wesley in his sermons and theological treatises, has made its way into the hearts, not only of Methodists, but also of the members of other Evangelical Churches, through the hymns of Charles Wesley (1707-88).[1]

The Methodist doctrine of salvation is therefore characterized by certain tenets; an Arminian doctrine of grace, Justification by faith alone, and entire sanctification.

In sacramental doctrine there is a spiritualizing tendency. Baptism does not effect salvation, but (in words taken directly from the Anglican Article) is 'a sign of regeneration or new birth.' In the Eucharist, Christ is received really, but spiritually. Wesley interpreted 'This is' (*hoc est*) as 'this means' (*hoc significat*). A higher doctrine of the sacraments is, however, contained in the hymns of Charles Wesley.

5. LEGISLATION AND CONSTITUTION

From the outset the Methodist Church has attached great importance to organization and discipline, and has created a detailed system of legislation without parallel among the Evangelical Churches. For British Methodism this is embodied in *The Constitutional Practice and Discipline of the Methodist Church*, while the corresponding document for America is entitled *Doctrines and Discipline of the Methodist Church*.

In British Methodism the supreme and final authority is the Annual Conference at which the whole Church is represented. Among its many responsibilities is the stationing of ministers, who are moved at regular intervals, though in nearly every case this merely ratifies an invitation privately given and received between

---

[1] This doctrine of Free Grace led to a split between John Wesley and a fellow member of the 'Holy Club,' George Whitefield (1714-70), and caused the formation of the Welsh Calvinistic Methodist Church in 1742-43 and later of the Countess of Huntingdon's Connexion. (H.E.W.T.)

circuit and minister. Below the Conference is the District which meets in Synod twice a year under an annually elected ministerial Chairman. These Chairmen of Districts have recently been relieved of any pastoral charge of their own. They are responsible to Conference for the observance within their districts of Methodist order and discipline. It is their duty 'to exercise oversight of the character and fidelity of the Ministers' in their Districts and they possess carefully defined powers of visitation. Within each District there are several Circuits (each under a Superintendent Minister appointed by Conference), the affairs of which are regulated by a Quarterly Meeting. Lastly there is the local Church.

The organization of American Methodism with its daughter Churches in Europe is closely parallel. The supreme authority, administrative, judicial and legislative is held by the General Conference which meets every four years and is composed of ministers and laity in equal proportions, elected by the various Annual Conferences which cover a single country or a single area. Other bodies with less authority are District Conferences and, for the smallest units, 'Local Conferences,' which are virtually councils concerned with a single pastoral charge.

6. WORSHIP

When Wesley revised the Book of Common Prayer for the American Methodists, he shortened the liturgy considerably. Many of the Old Testament Psalms were omitted in whole or in part 'as being highly improper for the mouths of a Christian congregation.' At a later date he made a similar revision for English Methodists.

The present service of Morning Prayer in the Book of Offices authorized for British Methodists only differs from Anglican Mattins in a few trivial points. An alternative Declaration is provided for the Absolution. One Psalm (or more) at the minister's discretion follows the *Venite*. The *Benedicite* is omitted and the Nicene Creed is permitted as an alternative to the Apostles' Creed. The words 'a hymn or a psalm' replace 'the anthem' in the rubric after the third collect. The prayer 'for Clergy and People' is entitled 'for Ministers and People,' and the phrase 'Ministers of Thy Gospel' replaces 'bishops and curates' in the body of the prayer. The Prayer for all conditions of men and the General Thanksgiving are incorporated into the service from the additional prayers provided in the Book of Common Prayer. This order of service, though officially available, is not commonly used.

During the revivalist campaign in America, Wesley's liturgy proved unacceptable. The leaders of the movement became impatient of any kind of formulated prayer, and divine service came to take the form of meetings devoted to preaching and extempore prayer.

The typical form of a Methodist service to-day represents a combination of a certain consistency in the liturgy (a fixed liturgical framework and set prayers) with extempore prayers and Biblical passages either chosen at will or (in British Methodism) from an annual lectionary, if the minister so desires. This more normal use represents a considerable departure from the original Anglican model.

The liturgy for the Holy Communion (which is very generally in use) also shows a close dependence upon the Anglican model. Holy Communion is received kneeling. Unfermented grape juice is used instead of wine. From 1755 a Covenant Service has been used as a preparation service for the Holy Communion on the first Sunday of the year, when it replaces the first part of the normal service. The Methodist Church invites all Christians irrespective of denomination to participate in the Holy Communion.

Methodism has always possessed two traditions, the one non-liturgical and the other which regards fixed forms of prayer as of value.

CHAPTER XII

THE CONGREGATIONAL CHURCHES

1. DESIGNATION, ORIGIN, DISTINCTIVE CHARACTER AND HISTORY

IT is scarcely possible to speak of 'the Congregational Church,' for it is a characteristic of this type of Church that it rejects the conception of an outward organic unity in the Church. In Congregationalist circles, the term 'Church' denotes either the local congregation or the invisible community of all believers. It is, however, possible to speak of the 'Congregational Churches' in the plural. The normal description is 'Congregationalism,' and this has now completely superseded the older designation of Independency and Independents.

The use of the term 'Congregational' to express a specific ecclesiastical ideal began almost simultaneously in England and America between 1640 and 1650, and by the end of the century, 'Congregationalism' and 'Congregationalist' were devised to designate this ideal and those who upheld it. During the Civil War they were described as 'Independents,' a term to which they took exception at first, but which later passed into common usage.

Congregationalism is the radical form of English Puritanism. The movement began with the extreme Puritans who broke away from the Established Church and founded Separatist congregations in 1581. Its pioneers were Robert Browne and Henry Barrow, whose writings contain the classical formulation of one stream of Congregationalist thinking.

Robert Browne renounced the idea of a National Church. 'The Kingdom of God was not to be begun by whole parishes, but rather by the worthiest only, were they never so few.' This quotation sets the ideal of a *gathered* congregation over against that of a *multitudinous* Church. In 1581 he formed his own congregation in Norwich. Its members were initiated into it by means of a covenant. They were to hold regular meetings under the leadership of preachers and teachers appointed by themselves; everything was to proceed in a proper and orderly fashion; each member of the Church was to have the right to make protests and to submit questions for debate.

Browne forsook his own ideals and ultimately took priest's orders in the Church of England, while Barrow was executed for his beliefs in 1593.

While recognizing the importance of the Elizabethan Separatists, many modern British Congregationalists would, however, turn to the writings of John Robinson (c. 1575–1625), the pastor of the Pilgrim Fathers, and John Owen (1616–83), Dean of Christ Church and Vice-Chancellor of the University of Oxford under the Commonwealth, for the principles of their tradition. Especially in the latter's work, *True Nature of a Gospel Church*, there is expounded a higher doctrine of the Church set within the general framework of Congregational principles.

Dogmatically Browne, Barrow and their followers were orthodox Calvinists. The only point on which they differed from Presbyterianism and much contemporary Anglican thinking was in their conception of Church Order.

1. They repudiated in principle the idea of an established Church. The State had no right to prescribe the form of Church government.

2. They regarded the Church as a voluntary association of believers. In the words of Browne: 'The Church planted or gathered is a company of Christians or believers, which, by a willing Covenant made with their God, are under the government of God and Christ, and keep his laws in one holy communion.' Thus the visible Church consists of people who acknowledge themselves to be Christians and who have entered into a mutual covenant.

3. The principle of the common priesthood of all believers is strongly emphasized. Again, in the words of Browne: 'Every one of the Church is made a King, a Priest and a Prophet under Christ, to uphold and further the kingdom of God, and to break and destroy the kingdom of Antichrist and Satan.'

4. Each congregation elects its own 'officers,' pastors, teachers, elders, relievers and widows in Browne's formulation. The first

class are ordained by representatives of the congregation by the imposition of hands and prayer.

5. The individual congregations are judicially and administratively independent, but are to render brotherly assistance to each other. John Owen, however, accepted the necessity of regional synods or 'meetings of divers Churches by their Messengers or Delegates, to consult and determine of such things as are of common concernment unto them all, by virtue of this Communion which is exercised in them,' and even concedes to such synods a real authority, declarative, constitutive and executive 'towards Persons and Churches.'

The Pilgrim Fathers who emigrated to America in 1620 were Congregationalists who sought in the New World to organize the Church and everyday life in accordance with their ideals. During the years which followed, a steady stream of emigrants travelled across the ocean from England and settled in the New England States, where they founded the colonies of Massachusetts, Connecticut and New Haven. These colonists were Puritans, but not Separatists. In America, however, force of circumstances compelled them to organize themselves on a Congregationalist basis. Social life in the New England States took on a Puritan tone and the community became a theocratic democracy. They were first and foremost a theocracy, but their democratic principles sprang from what they believed to be the primitive and apostolic Church Order. But here under new conditions a remarkable change took place; Congregationalism, which had previously rejected the idea of a State Church on principle, now became the Established Religion. Until 1664 only Congregationalists could possess civil rights in Massachusetts. Throughout the New England States the State exacted payment of church taxes, paid the salaries of the ministers and convoked synods. The connection between Church and State was not severed in New Haven until 1818, and continued in Massachusetts until 1833.

The Puritans in America took a particularly keen interest in education. The two leading American Universities, Harvard and Yale, were founded by Congregationalists in 1636 and 1701 respectively.

Until the outbreak of the Civil War, Congregationalism made

little headway in England. Under the Commonwealth the Independents were favoured and the Church of England was remodelled on Congregationalist lines. In 1658 a 'Meeting of Elders and Messengers' was held at the Savoy, London, and produced the classical 'Declaration of the Faith and Order owned and practised in the Congregational Churches in England.' This Savoy Declaration includes a Confession which differs only slightly from the Westminster Confession at points where Congregationalism diverged from Presbyterianism.

After 1660 the Congregationalists were faced with hard times, but in 1689 they were granted religious Toleration in common with other Evangelical Dissenters. But by this time much of their former zeal had disappeared, and they led a somewhat lifeless existence until they shared in the spiritual awakening associated with the Methodist Revival.

The London Missionary Society, founded in 1795, was intended to be inter-denominational, but in practice it has been closely linked with Congregationalism. In 1833 the British Congregationalists combined to form the Congregational Union of England and Wales.

The history of Congregationalism in England during the past century has been the story of many tendencies and some definite movements. The friendly acceptance of Biblical criticism contributed to a period of theological liberalism which issued in the 'New Theology' of R. J. Campbell (b. 1867), which had a short vogue. The foundations for a revival of confessional orthodoxy were laid by R. W. Dale (1829–95) and P. T. Forsyth (1848–1921), the latter a theologian (like the Anglican F. D. Maurice) whose full significance is only now being realized. Their work has been succeeded by many others and may even represent a majority movement at present time. This represents a recovery of principles already contained within their own tradition, but it has undoubtedly been stimulated by participation in the ecumenical movement and, recently, by the impact of Biblical and Reformed theology. The democratic principles implicit in the Congregationalist Church Order also led during the century to widespread public service and political activity, as well as to a recognition of the importance of the 'social gospel.' Such openness to new movements is not only a general characteristic of

British Christianity as a whole, but is particularly favoured by the distinctive character of the Congregational Churches. Relations with the Church of England were embittered in the earlier part of the period through the Disestablishment and Education controversies, but have progressively improved during the last half century through the ecumenical movement and other contacts.

In America a similar period of decline set in during the first half of the eighteenth century until the great revival of 1740–42 under the leadership of the Calvinistic Methodist, George Whitefield, and the Congregationalist, Jonathan Edwards (1703–1758). The latter also founded New Jersey College, an important theological school, which was markedly Calvinist in its doctrine of Predestination and Election.

From the beginning of the nineteenth century, Congregationalism began to spread westwards with the new colonists, and to-day three-quarters of the Congregational Churches are outside New England. In 1871 a 'National Council of the Congregational Churches of the United States' was established. It holds triennial meetings but has neither legislative nor judicial authority over the individual churches. A doctrinal declaration issued in 1811 left room for Arminianism.

Since 1891 an International Council has also been in existence, which again has merely consultative functions without administrative or judicial authority.

2. STATISTICAL DATA, CONSTITUTION, DOCTRINE AND WORSHIP

Congregational Churches (in the strict sense of the term) only exist in the English-speaking world. In the Scandinavian countries, however, the *Svenska Missionsförbundet* (founded in 1878) and similar bodies in Norway and Denmark share the same ecclesiastical ideals. In 1949 the Congregationalist Churches in Great Britain had 400,000 members, exclusive of Sunday School scholars and other adherents. In the United States it is estimated that there are over a million members in the more restricted sense. There are also Congregationalists in Australia and South Africa as well as some important missionary churches. Altogether the number of adult members may be reckoned as two and a half million and the total number of adherents as something like ten million.

The Congregationalists have kept faithfully to the forms of their constitution. Each Church is entirely self-governing on democratic principles, with elections and equal franchise. Admission to church membership is determined by the vote of the congregation, after such a profession of faith on the part of the candidate as serves to satisfy the local Church that he is an avowed Christian, and an acceptance by him of the conditions of the Church's covenant. The Declaration of 1833 affirms the scriptural right of every Church to maintain perfect independence in the government and administration of its particular affairs. A characteristic expression of the corporate life of the particular Church is the Church meeting, which has even been described by a modern Congregationalist, Daniel Jenkins, as 'a secondary mark of catholicity.'[1]

Each Church chooses its own minister, decides whether it will make use of any creed, and arranges its worship without being bound by any liturgical standards. The Churches give each other financial support and act in consultation with each other. It has, however, been emphasized that each Church is autonomous and that none can rule another. Yet in line with the development of denominational organization and co-operation with other Churches, whether in the Free Church Federal Council or the ecumenical movement, emphasis has come to be laid upon the complementary truth that the independence which they cherish is not independence of association, but freedom from authoritative control.

On their principles the Congregationalists cannot acknowledge any creed or confessional document as of binding authority. On the rare occasions when they have expressed their doctrinal principles, they have been careful to point out that this is only a presentation of what is commonly believed in their churches, and not a doctrinal law binding either upon churches or individuals. Their doctrinal statements are testimonies rather than articles of

[1] The powers of the 'Church Meeting' are in principle plenipotentiary. It appoints the minister, though, once chosen, he is normally accorded 'the rights of the pulpit' over the conduct of public worship, and elects the deacons and other Church officers as well as delegates to Synods. It also assumes full responsibility for the day-to-day organization of the life of the Church. The right of admission to and exclusion from membership is most carefully reserved for the Church Meeting. (H.E.W.T.)

faith. The Congregationalist objection to Creeds as tests of
membership is well put by John Owen: 'Such a use causeth them
to degenerate from the name and nature of Confessions, and
turneth them into Exactions and Impositions of Faith.'

Yet this doctrinal freedom, which is in principle unlimited,
could be described by P. T. Forsyth as a 'founded freedom.' In
the words of a contemporary Congregationalist, Dr. Nathaniel
Micklem, it represents 'an unqualified freedom to express and
expound the Christian Faith in whatever terms seem best to us;
it is not a freedom to alter and deny the faith. Our liberty is
limited by our loyalty.' There has always been a considerable
degree of unity among Congregationalists. When the Congregational Union was founded in 1833, it was stated, not without
a certain element of justifiable pride, that there was a much
greater degree of unity both in doctrine and practice in their
churches than in any Church which demanded assent to credal
statements.

There exists a remarkably consistent doctrinal tradition within
Congregationalism. It is, however, far from being absolutely
rigid. The Pilgrim Fathers, for example, were fundamentalist in
their view of the Bible, whereas the doctrinal standpoint of
modern Congregationalism has been largely moulded by the
conclusions of Biblical criticism.

There are, however, certain main trends which have remained
unchanged during the whole history of Congregationalism. It
represents an extreme, or, as Congregationalists themselves would
prefer to maintain, a consistent form of Protestantism. The Holy
Catholic Church is conceived first and foremost as a spiritual and
invisible community. Yet many Congregationalists would assert
that this is manifested in particular local churches. Membership
of the local church is based upon voluntary adhesion and the
insistence upon personal profession of faith and (particularly in
earlier times) upon Church discipline arose from a genuine
attempt to make the limits of the local church as far as possible
co-terminous with a local embodiment of the invisible community. Other permanent characteristics of the Congregationalist policy are, as we have seen, the repudiation of all doctrinal
bonds and the maintenance of the democratic principle in Church
government, which is regarded as a direct inference from the

primitive pattern of Church Order and the character of the Church as the People of God.

The minister in Congregational Churches is closely related to the local Church. This was sometimes emphasized in a practice which has now completely passed out of use, the ordination afresh of a minister upon his entry into a new charge. John Owen went so far as to question the propriety of ordaining ministers to work *in partibus infidelium* in cases where as yet there was no local Church within which his ministry could be exercised. Yet so far as the nature of the ministerial office is concerned, Congregationalists have not at their best lacked a high sense of its dignity. In modern times it has been described as 'a gift of God to His Church, exercising its functions only within the Church, but deriving its power from God Himself.' The minister has always been regarded as necessary for the well-being of the Church, and, while admitting the principle that where two or three are gathered together in His Name, there the Church was in essence, John Owen maintained that they only had the right to organize a Church when their numbers were increased 'so that they are sufficient to observe and perform all Church Duties in the way and manner prescribed for their performance.' To the minister is entrusted the performance of the Ordinances of the Church, though without excluding in principle the possibility (for example) of a lay celebration of the Holy Communion. Ordination is in practice invariably performed by laying on of hands with prayer.

Of the Savoy Declaration's list of 'Pastors, Teachers, Elders and Deacons,' only pastors and deacons survive. No mention of Elders as a separate office is contained in the Declaration of 1833 and Congregational Churches are uniformly governed by a minister and a board of deacons. No really clear conception of the office of a deacon seems to have emerged, but some at least of the duties of an elder were discharged under this head. The deacons, for example, helped the minister in the administration of the Lord's Supper.

The character of the Sacraments as Ordinances or Seals of the Church is firmly maintained. They are acts not of the Ministry but of the Church. Traditionally, and at its best in modern

times, the Congregationalist doctrine of the Sacraments approximates to the Calvinist tradition, though there have certainly not
been lacking tendencies and periods in which a Zwinglian
interpretation has been dominant. While the doctrine of Baptismal Regeneration is not part of the Congregationalist tradition,
the Savoy Declaration did not doubt the efficacy of Baptism as
an Ordinance conferring grace. The same Declaration acknowledges a presence of the Body and Blood of Christ at the Lord's
Supper 'not corporally, or carnally present in, with or under the
Bread and Wine; yet as really but spiritually present to the Faith
of Believers in that Ordinance as the Elements themselves are to
their outward senses.' In more recent times the Presence of
Christ has been described as that of a Host with His guests rather
than as specially connected with the elements themselves. A
notable insistence in recent years has been upon the unity of the
ministries of Word and Sacraments.

In its ordering of Divine Worship, Congregationalism is
typically Puritan. The Church buildings, originally called
'meeting-houses,' are furnished round a pulpit and a communion
table (which is not called an altar). The order of worship is not
that of a prescribed liturgy. The earliest Congregationalists sang
Biblical psalms, but hymn-singing became common in the
eighteenth century when the two greatest Congregationalist
hymn-writers lived, Isaac Watts (1674–1748) and Philip Dodd-
ridge (1702–51). The normal sequence of Congregationalist
worship to-day is as follows: Hymn and Prayer; Scripture-
readings to which a response is made either by hymns or by
chanted psalms or canticles, prayer, usually extempore, sermon,
hymn and benediction. The Lord's Supper is observed monthly
and the communicants usually sit throughout the service. The
invitation to communion is to 'all who love our Lord Jesus
Christ to whatever part of His Church they may belong.'

CHAPTER XIII

THE BAPTIST CHURCHES

1. Origin and History

THE Baptists themselves are proud to reckon the Anabaptists of the Reformation period as their forerunners. They claim that, so far from being a sect of recent origin, they are one of the Churches which came into being through the Reformation.

But they also trace their ancestry even further into the past. They are convinced that their baptismal practice and their doctrines alike of the Church and the Sacraments are based upon the principles of the New Testament. They maintain that the Primitive Church exclusively practised Adult Baptism, that its membership was based upon voluntary adhesion and that its structure was Congregationalist. Shortly after the Apostolic Age a period of decline set in. The purity of the Church was lost owing to the introduction of the practice of Infant Baptism and the institution of the hierarchy. Its history during the Patristic and Mediaeval periods is a long record of decay. The Waldensians of the Middle Ages are sometimes reckoned as the forerunners of the Baptist Movement. They held a similar doctrine of the Church, without, however, instituting any reform in the practice of Baptism.

The first enthusiasts of the Reformation period to pass beyond the criticism of the practice of Infant Baptism and to carry out re-baptism were a group of priests and laymen at Zürich who declared in 1523 that believers should break away from the Church and form a 'pure community.' Thus, for the first time in the ecclesiastical history of Europe, was formulated the social ideal of the sect.[1] Communities of this type claim to be wholly independent of the State. Infant Baptism was held to be unscriptural, and even Satanic in origin. The first re-baptism, carried out in 1525, was immediately followed by an outbreak of persecutions. At Easter of that year the priest, Balthasar Hubmaier, of Waldshut (1485–1528) had himself re-baptized by

[1] See above, page 5.

one of the Zürich Anabaptists and proceeded to baptize his entire congregation. Hubmaier wrote some treatises in defence of the Baptist position, but was imprisoned in 1527 and executed at Vienna in the following year.

These enthusiasts were called Anabaptists (or Re-baptizers) by their opponents, but they repudiated the title on the ground that, since Infant Baptism was null and void, there could be no question of repeating the sacrament.

The Anabaptist movement soon spread in Switzerland and Germany, where it underwent persecution at the hands of the authorities, both Roman Catholic and Lutheran. It flourished between 1525 and 1535, but sustained a severe blow through the disaster at Münster. This moral and military debacle involved the downfall in the social and political fields of the radical wing of the Baptist movement, which had also aimed at the establishment of a theocracy, if necessary by force of arms. The movement continued in Holland under new forms, upon which Menno Simons (1496–1561) left his mark. The Dutch Baptists were groups of peaceful and devout men and women who sought to affirm their principles by suffering and martyrdom; they were in fact pacifists. In Holland they became known as Mennonites (after their founder), or de Doopsgezinden.

The English Baptist movement began shortly after 1600 among the refugee Puritan Separatists in Holland. Under Mennonite influence the Congregationalist minister, John Smyth (1554–1612) of Amsterdam became convinced of the unscriptural character of Infant Baptism which in his book, The Character of the Beast (1609), he identified with the 'mark of the beast' of the Book of Revelation. In 1609 he baptized himself and his congregation. Later he entertained doubts as to its validity and the whole process was repeated in a Mennonite congregation in Amsterdam. The ceremony took the form of affusion, not of total immersion.

On his death, Thomas Helwys (1550–1616) became the leader of the movement. He soon returned to England with his flock and by the time of his death there were four Baptist congregations in London.

The outward form of Baptism soon became a burning question. In 1641, Edward Barber (d. 1674) maintained that Total Immersion was the only legitimate form of Baptism. Many of the English Baptists subscribed to this view, and in 1643 sent one of their teachers to Rhijnsburg in Holland to receive Baptism after the proper form. Here there was a congregation of former Mennonites which had adopted this practice. On his return to England, Baptism by Immersion was carried out on all members of the English Baptist Churches in London. Total Immersion was pronounced necessary for a valid baptism, and this has been the official position of the movement ever since.

Division, however, soon arose among the Baptists over one of the most controversial doctrinal questions of the period. On the doctrine of Grace John Smyth and the first Baptists had been Arminian in their theology, but those who adopted the practice of Total Immersion were Calvinists. Those who accepted the doctrine of Universal or Free Grace were called General Baptists, while those who adhered to the doctrine of Election became known as Particular Baptists.

The latter movement spread more widely and came to have the greater significance. Their Declaration of Faith was published in 1644, followed by a similar document issued in 1677, after the Restoration, which was later approved by the Federation of American Baptists at Philadelphia in 1724. In 1660 the General Baptists had produced a separate Declaration of Faith. While to-day the controversy has ceased to have any significance, the two wings of the movement were not reconciled to each other until the nineteenth century. The General Baptists maintained a connexional system of their own in England, though they lost some of their importance in the eighteenth century when many of their churches lapsed into Unitarianism.

One of the leading figures of the Baptist Movement was John Bunyan. He was himself re-baptized as an adult, but caused three of his children to be baptized in infancy. He does not, therefore, seem to have regarded the question of Baptism as the decisive issue, although he clearly adopted the Baptist view of the Church as the assembly of believers who have separated themselves from the world and entered into a voluntary association.

The eighteenth century was a period of general decline, but

the Baptist Churches shared in the general revival of church life which resulted from the Methodist Movement.

The great missionary expansion of the Church during the nineteenth century had its origin among the Baptists. In 1792, William Carey (1761–1834) awakened English Christians to their responsibilities towards the non-Christian world and the Baptist Missionary Society was founded in the same year.

The most notable Baptist preacher in England during the nineteenth century was Charles Haddon Spurgeon (1834–92). To accommodate the large congregations which gathered to hear him, 'Spurgeon's Tabernacle,' an assembly hall capable of holding 6,000 people, was built in London. In 1887 the so-called 'Down Grade Controversy' broke out as a result of a series of articles in Spurgeon's own periodical, *The Sword and Trowel*, directed against the liberal theology which had made some headway in Baptist circles. Spurgeon himself entered the lists and urged the Baptist Union to adopt a Declaration of Faith in the basic truths of Evangelical Christianity. Baptists, however, have always been reluctant to commit their conscience to binding articles of faith, and his proposal was rejected. Spurgeon thereupon left the Union, and his followers did not resume their connection until 1939.

The history of the Baptist Movement in America began in 1636 when the Puritan emigrant, Roger Williams (1603–83), founded the colony of Providence in Rhode Island. The members of this colony were to enjoy the same political and civil rights irrespective of their religious views. This was a revolutionary innovation in the seventeenth century. Three years later Williams founded a congregation of General Baptists.

During the nineteenth century the Baptist Movement underwent a remarkable expansion, especially among the new immigrants and the negro population.

In Europe the movement spread to Germany through the agency of Johann Gerhard Oncken (1800–84). He had spent some years in Scotland and England, and later became the agent of an undenominational religious tract society. In 1834 he was baptized in the River Elbe by an American Baptist who happened to be staying at Hamburg. He became a zealous missionary for the Baptist cause on the Continent, and through his converts the movement entered Scandinavia from Germany.

2. Distribution and Statistical Data

The total number of full members of the Baptist Churches throughout the world has been estimated at approximately twenty-one million. With the inclusion of Sunday School scholars, the children of Baptist parents and adherents in a wider sense, the number would be at least three times as large. In the British Isles the Baptists number 327,000. The European country with the largest Baptist population is probably Russia, where the Evangelical revival assumed a Baptist form and vigorous missionary work was carried on at the close of the nineteenth century. In Sweden the Baptist Church is the largest Nonconformist body in the country, with a full membership of about 60,000 or a total of 180,000 including adherents of all kinds. In Europe as a whole there may be as many as 1,200,000 Baptists altogether.

The great majority of Baptists (probably four-fifths of the total number) are Particular or, as they are called in America, Regular Baptists.

Mention may be made of a number of minority groups.

(i) Free Will Baptists is the term applied in America to General Baptists. They form a small minority with an inclusive membership of about 400,000. They practise 'Open Communion,' and admit Christians of all denominations to the Holy Communion.

(ii) Tunkers, or German Baptists, are a small group descended from German immigrants. They are pacifists and oppose any form of theological training, though they have recently set up schools for their young people.

(iii) The Anti-Mission Baptists reject missionary work on the ground that, since God has chosen those who are to be saved, all missionary activity must be vain. They describe themselves as Primitive, or Old Style Baptists, and emerged as a separate group after the foundation of the Baptist Missionary Society in 1813. They number at present about 70,000 members.

(iv) The Seventh-Day Baptists have been led by their study of the Bible to observe Saturday as their day of rest. The sect was first formed in England in 1665 and almost simultaneously in America. It has a membership of a few thousands.

Since 1905 most of these groups have been associated in the
World Baptist Alliance which has held several world congresses.
The Alliance imposes no confessional obligations upon its members, and exercises no administrative or judicial control either over
smaller associations or individual Baptist churches.

3. DISTINCTIVE CHARACTER, DOCTRINE, CONSTITUTION AND WORSHIP

The most striking characteristic of the Baptist churches is
naturally to be found in their baptismal doctrine and practice,
which are considered more fully below.

1. Their doctrine of the Church approximates closely to the
Congregationalist ideal. The local church is regarded as a
gathered company of believers, which is itself a manifestation of
the one Church of God on earth and in heaven. Thus the Baptist
Confession of 1677 maintains that 'churches are gathered according to His mind declared in His Word,' and their members
'willingly consent to walk together according to the appointment
of Christ.' The organized Church must therefore consist of
avowed believers who have joined it of their own free will. The
ideal is a pure community safeguarded by the right of excommunication, which was originally commended by John
Smyth, the Baptist pioneer. While such discipline was at certain
periods strictly observed, the 'withdrawal of the hand of Christian
fellowship' has in England at least virtually fallen into disuse.

2. The principle of religious liberty is originally related to this
doctrine of the Church as a community based upon voluntary
adhesion. This right Baptists have always claimed for themselves and been willing to extend to others. Their repudiation
of Infant Baptism is partly based on the ground that it interferes
with the freedom of the child who should be allowed to make the
choice voluntarily upon reaching years of discretion.

In harmony with this concept of religious liberty, the Baptists
have always asserted that the State should not concern itself with
religion. While the State is a necessary and divinely instituted
instrument for the purposes of public order and social welfare,
the absolute separation of Church and State has always been

drawn as a necessary inference from the doctrine of 'the Crown Rights of the Redeemer in his Church':

> Let Caesar's dues be paid
> To Caesar and his throne;
> But consciences and souls
> To be the Lord's alone.

3. Their interpretation of Christianity is opposed to sacramental mediation in the strict sense, and may more positively be described as 'spiritualizing.' The primary principle is the communion of the soul with God, which is of an inward and spiritual nature and is not brought about by any sacraments, ministry or divine organization. Thus the ministry, though set apart with prayer and very generally with the laying on of hands, is regarded as functional rather than organic to the existence of the Church. While the Gospel Ordinances are reverently observed, they are not normally regarded as constitutive of this communion with God. Certain Confessions of Faith exist, of which the English Confession of 1669 differs only slightly from the Westminster Confession, but they are regarded as confessions rather than as articles of faith, and are therefore not considered as authoritative or treated as tests of membership.

4. The Baptist churches are organized on democratic lines. Ministers have, in theory, no greater rights than members of their congregations. When a candidate applies for membership, his case is examined by two worthy men or women appointed by the local congregation for the purpose. If he is recommended by the minister and this committee, he makes his own personal profession of faith before the congregation, which then gives its consent to his admission. Cessation of membership is handled in a somewhat similar way. The Church Meeting plays an important part in the life of the Baptist churches.

Yet despite their strong insistence upon the autonomy of the democratically organized local church, the Baptists formed associations of local churches as early as the eighteenth century, both in England and America, and there has been a considerable amount of co-operation, both below and at the national level. The Baptists in England have formed their own denominational organization and, as noted above, the Baptist World Alliance has been in existence since the beginning of the century. Baptist churches are members of the (national) Free Church Federal Council of Great Britain, and some, though not all, are linked with the World Council of Churches. Yet, while in some respects local independence in its extreme form has tended to be modified, nothing in this development has been allowed to conflict with the basic position of the local church.

5. The Baptists observe certain ecclesiastical ordinances to which they assign great importance. They are necessary for the life of the Church, though not strictly for salvation. The opinion has even been voiced by eminent Baptists, and may possibly be more widely held, that even Baptism itself may not be necessary for salvation, which depends in the last resort upon faith alone.

There are two sacraments or ordinances (to use the characteristic Baptist word), Baptism and the Holy Communion. They do not, however, effect any bestowal of Grace. To the question, 'Does Baptism effect any change in the person baptized?' a representative English Catechism returns the answer: 'No bodily act can in itself effect any spiritual change.'

Baptism presupposes faith and is primarily considered as a symbol of allegiance and an expression of faith. It would, however, be unjust to overlook the fact that Baptists also speak of Baptism as a sign of God's Grace. It does not, however, of itself, effect regeneration, which occurs in and through conversion. Baptism is essentially a confession on the part of the person who has been converted and an affirmation of rebirth on the part of God. It is 'the outward sign of a previous spiritual change.' Great importance is attached to the form of Baptism by Total Immersion as the only adequate symbol of death and resurrection with Christ (*Romans* vi).

In its doctrine of the Holy Communion the Baptist tradition is Calvinist in outlook. Christ is really but spiritually present. In the course of time the symbolic aspect of the sacrament has come to be so strongly emphasized that N. J. Nordström (b. 1880), a Swedish Baptist who is an authority on the Baptist Churches, has said that the majority of English and Scandinavian Baptists hold a Zwinglian view.[1]

[1] With this may be compared the opinion of Dr. E. A. Payne, General Secretary of the Baptist Union of Great Britain and Ireland. 'From the beginnings of Baptist witness in the seventeenth century, there have been many Baptists who have been staunch Calvinists in their interpretation of the Supper, but there have been many others who have favoured Zwinglian views. It is doubtful if either one or the other can claim to be the dominant tradition' (*The Fellowship of Believers*, p. 32). (H.E.W.T.)

6. There is no altar in the building (sometimes called 'the Tabernacle') in which Baptist services are held. The service is conducted from the pulpit and consists of hymns, extempore prayers, the reading of lessons and preaching.

Baptism is carried out in the presence of the congregation. The baptizer and the candidate, often dressed in white, both descend into the water. Sometimes a baptismal interrogation takes place. A typical question might be 'Do you believe that Jesus Christ is the Son of God, and have you accepted Him as your personal Saviour?' The Baptismal Formula is Trinitarian. Some Baptists require the baptizer to be ordained, while others extend the right to perform Baptism to any baptized Christian.

The Holy Communion is received sitting. Membership of Baptist Churches is normally confined to those who have received Believers' Baptism, but some churches, while composed in the main of baptized believers, also admit to membership avowed Christians who are otherwise baptized. Similar differences exist with regard to participation in the Holy Communion. 'Closed Communion' churches invite only those who are baptized on profession of faith, whereas 'Open Communion' churches welcome 'all who love the Lord Jesus Christ in sincerity.'

CHAPTER XIV

THE DISCIPLES OF CHRIST

THE Disciples of Christ, also known as the Churches of Christ, the Christian Church, or as Campbellites after the name of their founders, are a movement which arose in America in the earlier part of the nineteenth century.

They were founded by two Irish Presbyterians, Thomas Campbell (1763–1854) and his son, Alexander (1788–1866), who emigrated to America in 1807. The latter received his theological training in Ireland and Scotland. His father served at first as a Presbyterian minister and viewed with grave concern the disunion which existed among the scattered groups of his own Church and came to look further afield to the wider disunity of Christendom. He was soon led to publish his *Declaration and Address* in which he urged Christians of different denominations to lay aside their divisions and to unite under the banner of the pure and original form of Christianity. This he found in the practice of Adult Baptism, the Bible as the sole authority and faith in our Lord apart from any articles of belief. His desire for the organic unity of Christendom was so much in advance of his time that his position within the Presbyterian Church became increasingly difficult. The first independent congregation was established in 1811. For a time in America these congregations were associated with the Baptist Churches, but broke away in 1833 owing to suspicion on both sides. Since that time the movement has considered itself as an independent Church characterized by Baptist principles and a Congregationalist Church Order.

The Disciples have undergone the usual vicissitudes which befell other similar Churches during the nineteenth century, but have acclimatized themselves to the new attitudes to the Bible which emerged during the period.

They have been reluctant to speak of themselves as a Church, and have preferred to describe themselves as a movement. Their selection of New Testament terms to describe their churches is due, not to a claim to be 'The Church,' but to their desire not to add to the number of existing denominations. Paradoxically and much against their will, this is, however, what they have become. They differ from other closely related Churches in their strong belief in the organic unity of the Church, and have been from the outset ardent members of the ecumenical movement.

In addition to ministers they recognize elders and deacons. The Holy Communion is celebrated weekly. While their membership has until recently been confined to those who have received Believers' Baptism, they practise Open Communion.

A characteristic distinction is drawn between faith and opinion, which in principle leaves room for wide divergence of views.

The Disciples are chiefly found in America but also have a significant following in Great Britain and Australia. Missionary work is undertaken in various parts of the world. Their numbers in 1947 were just under two million.

CHAPTER XV

THE PENTECOSTALISTS

1. Origin and History

THE Pentecostal Movement is an ecstatic revivalist movement which, in the first few decades of the twentieth century, led to the formation of separatist congregations. It gave particular attention to startling phenomena like speaking with tongues and faith-healing and, as its name implies, sees in such experiences a revival of the gifts of the Holy Spirit at the first Pentecost.

The origin and background of the Pentecostal revival was the longing for fresh spiritual inspiration common to Churches and Christian groups in England and America at the turn of the century, which found expression in prayers for a revival. A typical example is a prayer card circulated by the hundred thousand: 'Will you make this the subject of daily prayers until you receive an answer? Lord, send us a revival and let it begin with me. In the name of Jesus. Amen. Promises: St. Matthew xxi. 22; Zechariah x. 1. Result: Joel iii. 1–2; Acts iv. 31.'

Revival soon followed. The American evangelist, R. A. Torrey, brought about thousands of conversions in Australia. A favourite subject of his addresses was the Baptism of the Spirit. The Welsh revival of 1904–05 was of special significance and took on an ecstatic form. A group of people who met every night for three weeks in corporate prayer suddenly had unusual experiences. They all began to praise God in glowing terms, shed tears and experienced rapturous feelings. The miner, Evan Roberts, who had himself enjoyed an ecstatic experience, preached with remarkable effect. Hundreds of people rose with one accord and professed conversion. The result of this revival has been estimated at a hundred thousand conversions. His preaching aimed at rousing feelings to a climax and starting a tremendous penitential crisis in the hearers. Social life was transformed by the revival. Stolen articles were restored to their owners, debts repaid and public-houses closed. It is said that the pit ponies no longer recognized their drivers' words of command.

The revival in Wales attracted attention all over the world and greatly stimulated missionary activity. Among those who travelled to Wales to acquaint himself with the revival was the American Baptist preacher, Joseph Smale, who received his spiritual baptism and returned home convinced that a new Pentecost was imminent for the people of God all over the world.

In America the ground was prepared for a large-scale revival. Cases of spiritual baptism accompanied by speaking with tongues occurred among the pupils of a Bible-school at Topeka in Kansas as early as 1901. No rapid progress, however, took place until the intervention of the negro preacher, W. J. Seymour. He possessed highly-developed ecstatic powers which he was able to induce in others.

Seymour transferred his activity to Los Angeles where he worked with Joseph Smale. At a prayer-meeting held on April 9th, 1906, an eight-year-old negro boy began to speak with tongues. This is often regarded as the birthday of the Pentecostalist Movement.

The revival now spread over the whole of North America. People poured into Los Angeles from all parts of the United States and Canada in order to experience the gifts of the Holy Spirit. Sensational articles in the local press greatly helped to stimulate interest. The first baptism in the Spirit which took place in Chicago occurred in 1906, and within two years the Pentecostalists had a dozen assembly halls in the city. Though all churches withheld official recognition, the movement made rapid headway, particularly in Baptist and Methodist circles.

The Pentecostalist Movement soon founded its own newspaper, *The Apostolic Faith*. It was issued free of charge, and accepted neither advertisements nor subscriptions. It was financed solely by voluntary contributions. The doctrine of the movement was identical with the subjects of Methodist revival preaching with a strong emphasis upon conversion and entire sanctification. The doctrine of spiritual baptism was added as a characteristic rider. The way of salvation included three stages, conversion, cleansing and baptism by the Spirit. 'He was saved, sanctified and baptized with the Holy Spirit' is a typical description of the whole process.

Special attention was directed to speaking with tongues and miraculous cures. A rich store of tradition, not all equally trustworthy, gathered round these two phenomena. The meaningless words uttered by ecstatics were interpreted by the leaders of the movement, and regarded by believers, as foreign languages. It is said that Chinese was spoken without any previous knowledge of the language, and that Jews were converted through hearing illiterates recite whole chapters of the Bible in their own language.

The revival appealed to preachers who felt themselves to be spiritually barren. Some of them were repelled, but after much prayer and long struggles, others came to have ecstatic experiences, and became effective means of spreading the movement within their own denominations.

It was through a preacher of this type that the movement came to Europe. Thomas Ball Barratt (1862–1940) was a Methodist minister who experienced spiritual baptism during a visit to the United States in 1906. He brought the movement to Norway, whence it spread to the other Scandinavian countries, England and Germany. For some years after his return to Norway, Barratt continued his work in the Methodist Church, but after disputes with other members of his Church, he was forced to resign. He was rebaptized in a Baptist Church, but finally, in 1916, he organized his followers into a separate congregation. The movement spread all over the country, and to-day the Pentecostalist Church is the most powerful of the Norwegian free churches with a membership of 30,000 or 1 per cent of the total population.

In Sweden the ground was prepared partly by Baptist preaching and partly by various revivals with a strongly eschatological tinge, which occurred at the close of the last century. The movement itself originated in visits from a Swedish-American Baptist who had experienced spiritual baptism at Los Angeles and from Barratt who held meetings in Stockholm in 1907. They were described as 'singularly noisy meetings,' and were accompanied by spiritual baptism, convulsions, speaking with tongues and similar phenomena. A special Pentecostalist congregation, originally recognized by the Baptist Church, was founded in 1910, but became an independent community three years later. Its leader since its foundation, Lewi Pethrus (b. 1884), is an impressive personality with unusual gifts, both as a speaker and an organizer. In 1951 there were about six hundred Pentecostalist congregations in Sweden with a total membership of about 90,000.

Through the influence of Barratt the movement made its way to Denmark in 1907 but never came to occupy the same importance as in Norway or Sweden. The first congregation was founded in 1919 by a notable convert, the actress, Anna Larssen Bjoerner (1875–1955), and her husband, but the movement was hindered by several internal dissensions and now numbers little more than 5,000 members. Since its arrival in Finland in 1911 it has won about 35,000 followers.

In England an Anglican clergyman in the diocese of Durham, Alexander Boddy (d. 1930), worked to bring about a Pentecostalist revival without relinquishing his ministry within the Church of England. Barratt was also active in England in 1907–8. Many were influenced by the movement, but relatively few left their own churches to become members of the Pentecostalist congregations. In Germany, Pastor Jonathan Paul (1853–1930) worked in pietistic circles. When the movement was banned in 1936 it had a membership of about two thousand. In France the number of Pentecostalists approaches 3,000, and there are said to be many adherents in Russia.

World Conferences of Pentecostalists have been held at Stockholm in 1939, Zürich in 1947, Paris in 1949 and London in 1952.

2. DOCTRINE, ORGANIZATION AND DEVOTIONAL LIFE

The distinctive character of the movement has been described by a Norwegian Pentecostalist in the following terms: 'On the question of Justification by Faith they are Lutherans, on Baptism, Baptists, on Sanctification, early Methodists, in their work of winning souls Salvationists, but with regard to baptism by the Holy Spirit they are Pentecostalists, as they believe and preach that it is possible to be baptized in, or filled by the Holy Spirit as on the day of Pentecost.' To make his description complete, it should be added that their organization is Congregationalist.

The sole doctrinal authority is the Bible interpreted from a Fundamentalist standpoint. Expressions such as 'Biblical Baptism' and 'The Biblical congregational system' form effective catchwords. The Bible is considered as a code of laws which are applicable to all conditions of life.

Pentecostalist congregations are independent of each other, and each sends out and maintains its own missionaries. They are under the leadership of elected ministers, assisted by 'elders,' and strict discipline is observed.

Their devotional life is permeated by an anti-liturgical spirit. In theory everything should be free and unrestrained; but in practice a definite sequence of hymns, lessons and addresses is observed. Strong appeal is made to the emotions, and hymns with emotional refrains are in common use. The favourite themes of their preaching are Atonement through the blood of Jesus, conversion, spiritual baptism and the second coming. Occasionally speaking with tongues or other similar phenomena take place, but their meetings have become quieter since the movement acquired a certain inner stability.

The ethos of the Pentecostalist Movement is rigidly Puritan with modesty, self-sacrifice and abstinence from all worldly pleasure as dominant characteristics.

CHAPTER XVI

THE SALVATION ARMY

1. ORIGIN AND HISTORY

THE Salvation Army itself claims to be neither a church nor a sect. 'It has never been my intention,' said its founder, 'to create a new sect. . . . Nothing lies farther from me than to aggravate dissension between followers of Christ. . . . We are not a church, we are an army, an army of salvation. That is our speciality. The world needs salvation.' The leaders of the Army have always tried to shield it from doctrinal disputes. Its aim is to be undenominational, in the words of a Danish Church historian (M. Neiiendam), 'neither priest, nor Levite, but a Good Samaritan, who bends down to raise and tend the fallen.' Thus the Army does not require its members to leave their churches when they become Salvationists.

In reality, however, the Salvation Army is a new religious body with a character of its own which it guards jealously. Those who join it seek all their spiritual satisfaction and live their devotional life within its ranks.

The independence of the Salvation Army as a religious body can be illustrated by the career of William Booth (1829-1912). When he founded the Salvation Army in 1865, he had already left the church in which he had grown up and was active in fields outside the scope of the existing denominations. About 1880 an unsuccessful attempt was made to incorporate the work of the Army within the Church of England. In 1882 the priest, Wilson Carlile (1847-1942), founded the Church Army, which adapted the methods of the Salvation Army to an Anglican setting. In Denmark, too, the Salvation Army has a counterpart within the Church in the Church Crusaders established in 1912. Although neither movement plays a part at all comparable to that of the Salvation Army, their foundation affords clear evidence that the Army was felt to be a separate body outside the National Church.

William Booth was the son of a business man who spent the
first half of his life in scraping together a modest fortune, and the
second half in misspending it. He died when William was
fourteen, leaving his family in abject poverty. His mother, Mary
Moss, to whom her son was justly devoted, was of Jewish descent.
Her cast of features, like those of her son, were markedly Jewish.
In him the Jewish people once more produced a prophet.

Shortly before his father's death, William Booth was apprenticed to a pawnbroker, and naturally in this capacity saw much
of the seamy side of life. At the age of fifteen he was converted
under Methodist influence. He attended Methodist class-
meetings and was examined as to his relation to God. It was at
this time that he remembered a sin which he had committed.
He had acquired a silver pencil-case from some companions by
dishonourable means. Day and night the memory of this act
tortured his soul. It had been easy enough to restore it to its
owner. Only after public confession of his sin was the burden
lifted and the way to God stood open. 'I felt that I could willingly
and happily have travelled to the ends of the earth for Christ and
suffer anything in order to help other people.' He never forgot
the change which came over his life from that moment.

He began to preach in the streets of Nottingham. At the age
of seventeen he was accepted as a Methodist local preacher. He
moved to London, where he again took work with a pawnbroker, working long hours to gain a livelihood and spending
his scanty leisure in preaching. He came to know the abject
poverty of London at close quarters. So far from being discouraged, he was strengthened in his determination to spread the
Gospel of Christ by every available means. In 1851 a member
of the Methodist Church made him a grant of a pound a week
to enable him to devote his whole time to preaching. He then
met his future wife, Catherine Mumford (1829-90), and co-
operated with her. She was one of the most remarkable Christian
women of any age and, like her husband, owed her spiritual life
to Methodism. It is said that she had read the Bible eight times
by the time she was twelve years old. She had one passion—to
win souls; as she wrote to her husband: 'It is impossible to live a
holy life without winning souls.' Their marriage in 1855 realized
to the full their hopes of a happy union. She was at her husband's

side in all his work, and in many fields she played the more important part. She was more cultivated, and had a more sensitive approach to pastoral work. When he was self-willed and despotic, she would sometimes remind him 'the Pope can claim infallibility only because he is a bachelor.'

Booth led one evangelistic campaign after another. He was sent to a school for Methodist preachers, belonging to the strictly Calvinistic wing of the Church. On learning the doctrine of the election by God of a limited number of souls for salvation, he left at once. 'I would rather die of hunger than preach such a doctrine.'

His success as a revivalist preacher raised the question in the minds of some Methodists whether he was not a new Wesley. But a breach with Methodism soon came. The Methodist Church demanded strict discipline of its preachers, but Booth was not the type of man to find it easy to submit to discipline. He was born to lead, not to obey. At the Methodist Annual Conference in 1861, he tried to arrange matters so as to be able to carry out independent evangelistic work without being bound to any particular district. The Conference tried to bind him to a compromise. He was on the point of yielding, when Catherine from the visitors' gallery shouted 'Never.' He left the Conference Hall, and the two set out together on a new chapter of their intensely active lives. During the next few years they held revival meetings all over the country.

In 1865, William and Catherine Booth started work in the slums of London. They first used the name 'East London Revival Society,' but changed the name to the Salvation Army in 1878. It was an army to carry the witness to the blood of Jesus and the fire of the Holy Spirit to all parts of the world. Since 1879 the organ of the movement has been called the *War Cry*. The idea of a *militia Christi* pervaded every aspect of the movement. Booth introduced uniform, military flags and martial music. He received a cool reception from ecclesiastical quarters, molestation from the mob and derision from the public. Nothing, however, could daunt his zeal for the salvation of souls. In the army, of which he was the general, he ruled like a despot. He was an evangelist like St. Francis and a dictator like Napoleon.

Booth was a genius in organization and had unusual talent in

financial matters. His enterprise was built up on coppers from
the poor and munificent gifts from princes and moneyed men.
In 1890 he appealed for £100,000 for his work and received
more than he had asked for.

The Army claimed all his time, strength and affection. He had
no home life. It is said that his house was like a railway station,
with some one always going and coming. Six children grew up
in that environment, and even held prayer-meetings with their
dolls. When three of his children whom he had brought up to
be Salvation Army officers broke with the movement and went
their own ways, Booth exclaimed: 'I have no children outside
the ranks of the Salvation Army.'

Booth made many journeys into all parts of the world. He was
also active in the literary field. When Stanley had written
Darkest Africa, he published *In Darkest England and the Way Out*
in collaboration with a journalist (W. T. Stead), of which two
hundred thousand copies were sold in the course of a few weeks.

Between 1880 and 1890 the Salvation Army underwent rapid
expansion, and William Booth became one of the most celebrated
men in England. Work began in America in 1880. In the
following year Booth sent his daughter Catherine, later known
as *la Maréchale*, at the age of twenty-two to France to pioneer the
work there. The Army began work in India in 1882, in Ceylon,
New Zealand and South Africa in the following year, in Italy
and the West Indies in 1887, in Belgium in 1889 and in Argentine
in the next year. Japan was 'invaded' in 1895, and in 1913 the
Army got a foothold in Russia.

So long as William Booth lived, the leadership of the movement remained in his hands as general. At an early date he had
designated his son, Bramwell Booth (1856–1929), as his successor.
He was an excellent administrator, but lacked his father's gifts as
a preacher. Owing to his high-handed conduct, dissension arose
between the general and the Supreme Council. He was declared
unfit to hold office and forced to resign in 1929. It was feared
that the post would become hereditary to the Booth family. The
general is now elected by the Supreme Council and since 1929
the position has only once been held by a relative of the founder,
Evangeline Booth (General, 1934–9).

At the time of Booth's death, the Salvation Army was at work in fifty-eight countries, and had 16,000 officers. In 1949 it was preaching the Gospel in 102 languages, and had 32,000 officers, over 100,000 local officers and 140,000 musicians and singers.

2. ORGANIZATION, DOCTRINE AND DEVOTIONAL LIFE

The Salvation Army is organized on military lines with military titles, ranks and distinctions. It demands strict discipline, obedience and sacrifice from its members. The principle that all its members are set to work gives it a strength which is all its own. The newly-converted are immediately charged with the duty of witnessing to those around them. Men and women are on a completely equal footing; they have 'the same right to all ranks, responsibility, duties and all forms of authority.'

The Army has different sections for each age-group. The infants of Salvationists are enrolled in a 'baby's brigade.' For older age groups there are Sunday Schools, children's societies and youth leagues. Some families have been Salvationists for generations.

New-comers to the Army are first put on probation and then accepted as recruits. On final acceptance, they must sign the sixteen Articles of War, which are both a promise of obedience and Articles of Faith. The Bible is the inspired and sole authority, and belief is enjoined in the Trinity, in Jesus Christ as true God and true Man, in the Fall, in Atonement through the death of Christ, in the necessity for salvation, repentance, faith and new birth, in entire sanctification, in the immortality of the soul and the resurrection of the body, and in the two alternatives of eternal life and eternal damnation. The promise covers renunciation of worldly amusements, alcohol and tobacco, and the obligation to lead a clean life, to be truthful and to obey the Army.

Privates and non-commissioned ranks are unpaid. They continue in their ordinary work and devote their spare time to the Army. Full-time officers must first attend cadet-school. Examinations are taken in such subjects as the conduct of meetings (with special marks for the choice of songs and the selection of a suitable key), Salvationist addresses, prayers and appeals for collections. Officers must not marry without the consent of their superiors, and this is only given when it can be assumed that the choice of a partner will benefit the work of the Army. If this regulation is disobeyed, the offender is degraded to the rank of a private.

The highest position of authority is held by the general. Since an amendment to the constitution made in 1929 and approved by Parliament in 1931, the general is elected by the Supreme Council of the Army, a body of fifty-five members, and is subject to age-limit.

Worship in the Salvation Army takes the form of meetings for revival and sanctification. At all meetings much time is devoted to music and singing as well as to testimonies. Catchy melodies with refrains are sung. William Booth was delighted when a revival song could be set to a music-hall tune. This was to deprive the devil of a weapon and to turn it against himself. Preaching is concerned with a limited number of themes, atonement, conversion, surrender (a military metaphor) and sanctification.

The sacraments are a matter of indifference. Until 1882, Booth used both Baptism and the Holy Communion. Since that time, however, the Army has ceased to observe either sacrament. Baptism is regarded as superfluous since rebirth takes place not at Baptism but at conversion. The command to baptize in St. Matthew xxviii. 19 is held to apply only to Baptism by the Holy Spirit. Salvationists are free to have themselves and their children baptized and to receive Holy Communion in other Churches, but are forbidden to conduct propaganda within the Army on behalf of either sacrament.

On the other hand, the Salvation Army has almost made the public confession of sins into a sacrament. In every Citadel there is a penitent form to which penitents advance, kneel, and make their confessions aloud. The penitent form, which is also called the mercy seat', is a real means of grace.

CHAPTER XVII

THE PLYMOUTH BRETHREN (DARBYITES)

SHORTLY after 1820, groups of devout people with pietistic views were formed in Dublin, and subsequently elsewhere (particularly in Plymouth). The movement began with a desire for simplicity and purity of worship as well as for unity and brotherhood, and was deeply influenced by the apocalyptic spirit of the age. They assembled for private religious meetings, and even for the administration of the Holy Communion. One of their original members, Edward Cronin, urged that true Christians ought to be welcomed at the Holy Communion 'wherever His Table is spread.' At first they had no thought of leaving the Established Church, but were led to this step as their movement grew and developed. In 1828 they were joined by John Nelson Darby (1800–82), who had been trained as a barrister and had later been ordained as a clergyman of the Church of Ireland. His intellectual powers were said to be high and his devotion unquestionably sincere. Especially on the Continent the movement came to bear his name.

Darby was seized with the apocalyptic fervour of the period, and sought to bring together believers of all denominations to await the return of our Lord. As a result of his preaching, the groups in Dublin, Plymouth and elsewhere formed a sect of their own. The name which they chose for themselves was 'the Brethren.' Darby himself published numerous works on apocalyptic and general Biblical subjects, and made missionary journeys to Switzerland, Germany and America as well as within the British Isles.

The movement spread, but was hindered by internal controversy, partly on questions of doctrine and partly on principles of organization. These have left a permanent mark on the history of the movement in the division between Open and Exclusive Brethren. The former are willing to have fellowship with other Christians outside their movement provided that they do not hold doctrines which the Brethren believe to be evil or erroneous, whereas the latter lay down far more exacting conditions.

The Bible, interpreted on fundamentalist principles, is the sole rule of faith. They reject all the existing Churches and recognize no ecclesiastical offices. In theory any believer is entitled to preach or to break bread, though in practice this absolute liberty is not fully observed. Following the Pauline precept, women are not allowed to speak in church. Their communities are voluntary associations of true believers for the purpose of prayer and the Breaking of Bread. Baptism is either not observed or restricted to adults after profession of faith. The Holy Communion, known as the Breaking of Bread, is observed weekly and administered by one of their number. The communicants remain seated throughout the service. The use of the words of Institution is not considered necessary.[1] Their services are extremely simple and consist of extempore prayer, Bible-reading and preaching. Much emphasis is laid upon the Second Coming of our Lord as well as upon the fundamental Evangelical experience of conversion. Their ethos is strictly Puritan and their members are exhorted to 'live separate.'

The Brethren do not reveal the size of their membership on the ground that statistics are unscriptural (2 *Samuel* xxiv). Their membership is perhaps 15,000 in Europe and 25,000 in America.

[1] An interesting account of a visit to a Communion Service held by the (Closed) Brethren is given in an article by the Rev. R. C. Walls in *Theology*, vol. lx (1957). (H.E.W.T.)

CHAPTER XVIII

THE NEW CHURCH, THE CHURCH OF THE NEW JERUSALEM (SWEDENBORGIANS)

THE Swedenborgian Church owes its existence to the literary activity of the Swedish philosopher and scientist, Emanuel Swedenborg (1688–1772).

This remarkable man was the son of a bishop in the Swedish Church, Jesper Swedberg. He had been brought up in the deistic philosophy and had studied mathematics and natural science not only in Sweden, but also in England, France, Holland and Italy. He was a prolific writer on a large number of subjects: engineering, botany, astronomy, anatomy and crystallography. His writings in all these fields bear the unmistakable stamp of genius. He held high office in the service of the King of Sweden and, after being ennobled in 1719 under the name of Swedenborg, played an important part in the Swedish House of Lords for a number of years, and wrote able memoranda on social and economic subjects.

To an increasing extent religious problems came to occupy his mind. During a stay in London in 1745 he had a vision. He saw God in human form and heard the words: 'I am God, the Lord, the Creator and Redeemer. I have chosen thee to interpret the internal and spiritual meaning of the Holy Scriptures, and I shall dictate to thee what thou shalt write.' On the same occasion he was also granted a vision of Heaven and Hell. The reality of the spiritual world was indisputable, and henceforward he devoted the remainder of his life to theosophical speculations on the spiritual world and the relation between spirit and matter.

After his vision in 1745, Swedenborg returned to Stockholm to free himself from his secular duties and settled again in London in 1747. Here he spent most of the rest of his life, and wrote a large number of treatises in Latin dealing with theological, or rather theosophical subjects. His chief interests were the nature of the deity and the structure of the spiritual world. Much of his work takes the form of Biblical exegesis according to a distinctive system.

In 1757 he had a vision in which he saw the Day of Judgement in the spiritual world and the foundation of a 'new church.' This event he considered to be the fulfilment of the Biblical prophecies concerning the Second Coming of our Lord. This became the corner-stone of his system in books with the characteristic titles: *De Caelo et Inferno* (1757), *De nova Hierosolyma et ejus doctrina caelesti* (1758) and *Apocalypsis Revelata* (1766). His main work in this field is the *Arcana caelestia* in eight volumes (1749–58), but perhaps the best summary of his teaching is given in his last work, *Vera Christiana Religio* (1771).

Swedenborg is the Protestant counterpart to Blaise Pascal (1623–62), a scientific genius who abandoned all his scientific activity at the height of his worldly career in order to devote himself to the problems of religion. But, unlike Pascal, Swedenborg had a predilection for unorthodox solutions.

Swedenborg rejected the orthodox doctrine of the Trinity. He could not accept the idea of three Persons in one God. The main defect which he found in this doctrine was that it precluded the worship of Christ as Almighty and as Father. The Council of Nicaea perverted the faith, and ever since the Church has been in a fallen condition, until the revelation vouchsafed to Swedenborg in 1757. His own solution of the Trinitarian problem strongly recalls Sabellianism. The Father and the Son are a single Person revealed in different ways. This can be illustrated by the oracle received by Swedenborg in 1757 quoted above, with its identification of the Creator and the Redeemer. Accordingly a new meaning had to be assigned to concepts like mediation, expiation, propitiation and atonement, which came to signify God's removal of human sin rather than any action of Christ on behalf of mankind. His criticism of other Churches and their theological leaders is significant. Luther and Melanchthon are brought under censure for their doctrine of Justification by Faith on the ground that charity is thereby excluded, Calvinism is rejected because of its doctrine of Predestination and Roman Catholicism for what Swedenborg calls the adoration of the Pope and its concealment of the truths of Holy Scripture from men. The Bible is regarded as the source of the doctrines of the

New Church. Certain books of the Bible are, however, treated
as lacking full authority, such as Job and the Song of Songs in
the Old Testament. In the New Testament only the Gospels and
the Book of Revelation are fully inspired books. The criterion
for this judgement is the presence or absence of the internal sense
of Holy Scripture. This sense, which others may regard as a form
of allegorism, Swedenborg believed to be based upon a 'science
of correspondences,' which interprets every phenomenon in the
material world as the counterpart of a particular spiritual reality.
Here the doctrine of Swedenborg recalls certain aspects of Neoplatonism.

Swedenborg frequently speaks of 'the New Church,' but he
never tried to organize any new church on earth. This step was
taken after his death by some of his followers in England, who
established a congregation of their own in London in 1788.
From England the movement spread to America. Although
there are small congregations in most parts of the world, and
missionary work is undertaken in South and West Africa, these
are the only two countries in which the New Church has any
significant following. Its membership in England is just under
5,000 and in America nearly 6,000.

The New Church has a short Confession of Faith which
embodies its distinctive doctrine of the Trinity. Swedenborg's
writings are held in high esteem, and are considered to be the
necessary key to the hidden meaning of the Scriptures. In England
the New Church possesses an authorized liturgy, and in a few
churches a revised form of Anglican Common Prayer is in use.
There is also a Book of Worship in use in America. Two sacraments, Baptism and the Holy Communion, are recognized. The
form of the Ministry differs between England and America. In
England it consists of three grades, Ordaining Ministers, Ministers
and Ordained Leaders, whereas in America only two grades are
recognized, General Pastors and Pastors.

CHAPTER XIX

THE ADVENTISTS

ADVENTISM is the name given to an apocalyptic revival movement which arose in America between 1830 and 1840, and to the bodies which sprang from it. Its historical background is to be found in the eschatological expectations common in pietistic circles both in Europe and America after the Napoleonic era. In accordance with the teaching of the Pietistic theologian J. G. Bengel (1687–1752) 'the pacific ones of the country' in Württemberg expected the return of our Lord in 1836. In England these expectations found expression in the movements associated with the names of Irving and Darby, and Adventism is to be regarded as their American counterpart.

The founder of the movement was William Miller (1782–1849), a new England farmer with a great thirst for knowledge but no formal education. He read all the literature upon which he could lay his hands, and in consequence became a sceptic and a deist. At the age of thirty-four he was converted under Baptist influence and became a member of the community of Regular Baptists. He made an intensive study of the Bible, particularly of the books of Daniel and Revelation, and became convinced of the imminence of our Lord's Return. This would be followed by the first Resurrection (confined to believers) and the establishment of the Millennium or the Kingdom of God on earth. At its close the second or general Resurrection and the Judgement would take place. Starting from Biblical passages like 2 Peter iii. 8–10, and Daniel viii. 14 and ix. 24–7, he estimated that the Return of our Lord would take place about the year 1843, and published his conclusion from the year 1831 onwards. He gave lectures on the subject in Baptist, Congregationalist and Methodist churches, and in 1834 was approved as a preacher in the Baptist Church.

Many conversions resulted from Miller's preaching. It was his original desire that every one should remain in their existing churches until the coming of our Lord, when the barriers between the various denominations would disappear.

As the appointed year approached, the movement grew. From

1840 it had its own magazine, *The Signs of the Times*, published in Boston, and later known as the *Advent Herald*. Other periodicals were called the *Midnight Cry* and the *Trumpet of Alarm*.

Pressed by his followers for a more exact date, Miller calculated that the Advent would take place between March 21st, 1843, and the corresponding date in the following year, changed to April 18th, 1844, after some discussion with his followers. During that winter many people lived in a ferment of expectation. They sold or gave away their possessions and on the second of the two dates a great crowd was waiting to receive our Lord. But the day passed without the fulfilment of their hopes. One of Miller's followers, however, came forward with a revision of his calculations. The revised date was October 22nd, 1844. The message captured people's imaginations, and Miller accepted the correction. Farmers who joined the movement left their crops unharvested. Despite the witticisms of their opponents, the Adventists conducted a vigorous revivalist campaign. But once more they were doomed to disappointment. One of them wrote: 'That day came and passed, and the darkness of another night closed in upon the world. But with that darkness came a pang of disappointment to the advent believers that can find a parallel only in the sorrow of the disciples after the crucifixion of their Lord. The passing of the time was a bitter disappointment. True believers had given up all for Christ, and had shared His presence as never before. The love of Jesus filled every soul, and with inexpressible desire they prayed, "Come, Lord Jesus, and come quickly," but He did not come.'

Another account compared the pain which they suffered to that of the disciples on Easter Eve. Miller himself admitted in an 'Apology and Defence' in 1845 that he had made a mistake in attempting to calculate the day of Christ's return and declared that in future he would refrain from such attempts.

After the crisis of 1844 several of the Adventists were expelled from their churches, and Miller himself was excommunicated by the Baptist Church. They were therefore compelled to set up their own organization.

In Church polity they were Congregationalist, in their Baptismal practice Baptist, in their doctrine extremely Protestant, with a strong predilection for apocalyptic speculation. Most of them abandoned the attempt to calculate precise dates, and contented themselves with declaring that the Advent was imminent.

Divisions, however, soon arose on various eschatological questions such as the immortality of the soul and the fate of the impenitent after death. Several Adventists' groups were formed; the Evangelical Adventists, the Advent Christian Church, the Churches of God in Jesus Christ. Their numbers are not large and their activity is restricted to America.

The largest group which emerged from this movement was the Seventh-day Adventists. Among the pioneers were James White (1821–81), J. N. Andrews (1829–83), Joseph Bates (1792–1872), J. N. Loughborough (1832–1924), Uriah Smith (1832–1903) and Ellen Gould Harmon (1827–1915), who became the wife of James White. Through contact with the Seventh-day Baptists, a preacher by the name of Frederick Wheeler (1811–1910) became convinced that according to the Decalogue the seventh day of the week should be observed as Sabbath. Later he was joined by Joseph Bates who issued a tract in 1846 about the Sabbath under the title 'The Seventh Day Sabbath, A Perpetual Sign.'

Extensive Bible study convinced the pioneers that the prophetic time mentioned in Daniel viii. 11–14 did not refer to Christ's advent to the earth. They came to the conclusion that the sanctuary mentioned in the text is the Heavenly Sanctuary (*Hebrews* viii. 1–2) where (according to Hebrews ix. 23) Jesus is 'purifying' the sanctuary in the latter part of His priestly ministry. They accepted William Miller's calculation of October 22nd, 1844, as the date indicated in the prophecy, but interpreted it as the time of Christ's entrance into the Heavenly Sanctuary, not as the day of His return to earth.

In 1861, small groups began to unite, but it was not until May 20th–23rd, 1863, that the denomination of the Seventh-day Adventists was organized with a membership of 3,500. Their headquarters are at Battle Creek, Michigan.

The Seventh-day Adventists accept the Bible as the inspired revelation of God to man and the sole rule of faith and practice. The Creeds are not, however, accepted. Their theology embraces the doctrine of Justification by Faith apart from the works of the law and salvation by grace alone. They believe in progressive sanctification by the indwelling Holy Spirit, and hold the doctrine of the Trinity, the Divinity and eternal pre-existence of Christ, His Virgin Birth, vicarious atoning death on the Cross, bodily Resurrection and Ascension, His ministry before the Father, and His Second Coming to this earth.

This return they believe to be imminent. At His Advent the resurrection of the righteous will take place, and they will rule with Christ for a thousand years. After the Millennium the wicked will be punished according to their works (*Revelation* xx. 12). A special feature of Adventist doctrine is the belief that the human soul is not intrinsically immortal. Immortality is granted through Christ alone and bestowed upon believers. The unjust do not have eternal life in themselves and therefore cannot live for ever, but will be blotted out in the second death after receiving their punishment. Believers will live with Christ for ever on a renewed earth.

One of the distinctive teachings of the Seventh-day Adventists is the belief that the Spirit of Prophecy (1 *Corinthians* xiv. 1) was manifested in the person and writings of Ellen White. But they maintain that her writings in no way supersede or add to the canon of Scripture which they consider complete and closed. Acceptance of her writings is not even a test of fellowship. Ellen White always and only called herself 'a messenger.' Commissioned to convey messages of comfort, guidance and reproof, she considered it her mission to draw men back to the Bible as the sole rule of faith and practice. One of her books, *Steps to Christ*, has been printed in seventy-eight languages and five million copies have been sold.

Another distinctive feature is the keeping of the Sabbath. The reasons alleged for this practice are that the Sabbath was instituted at the Creation (*Genesis* ii. 1–3), that it is enjoined in the Decalogue and that it was observed by Christ and His disciples. The Seventh-day Adventists hold their devotional meetings on Saturday and try to avoid all work on that day, but allow necessary occupation and charitable work on the Sabbath.

A health programme forms an important part of their work. In most countries in which they conduct evangelism, they also establish sanatoria, hospitals and clinics, and publish health magazines. In Denmark they established the Skodsborg Sanatorium in 1897, one of the largest of its kind in Scandinavia. Seventh-day Adventists abstain from tobacco and alcohol and most of them do not drink coffee or tea. They do not eat pork blood and strangled animals. These dietary principles, derived from the Old Testament, are also regarded as health measures. Under climatic conditions where there is an abundance of fruit, grain and vegetables, they regard a vegetarian diet as the ideal.

Adventist worship is very simple and consists of Sabbath School and services. In the Sabbath School the congregation is divided into classes, each under a teacher. The subject may be any Biblical theme or a verse by verse study of books of the Bible. The service which follows the Sabbath School consists of the singing of hymns, extempore prayers and a sermon. The two sacraments of Baptism (restricted to adults) and Holy Communion are observed. Before the Holy Communion the congregation wash one another's feet, two by two, the men in one hall, the women in another.

The community is kept together by a strong organization. The General Conference Committee comprises representatives from the thirteen regions into which the world is divided. These are subdivided into seventy unions, and these again into 330 conferences. By the end of 1957, the denomination had one million adult members and was at work in 185 countries.

The most important source of income is the tithe, a system based primarily on the words of Jesus in St. Matthew xxiii. 23. The payment of tithe is not, however, a test of church fellowship. It is possible to be a member of the community without paying the tithe, but in practice it is paid by all faithful members. After receiving instruction, new members are adopted into the churches by vote and are baptized. Re-baptism is not, however, required of those who have already received adult baptism.

The Bible is interpreted uncritically. Special attention is devoted to the Books of Daniel and Revelation with particular reference to the chronological indications which they are supposed to contain. Certain features, such as Millenarianism, the observance of the Sabbath and dietary laws, and the exaction of tithes, recall early Judaistic Christianity.

CHAPTER XX

THE SOCIETY OF FRIENDS (QUAKERS)

I. Origin and History

THE Quakers arose during the Commonwealth of Cromwell (1653–58) at a time of great spiritual ferment. Extreme Puritanism was in the ascendent. The attempt made by the Westminster Assembly to form a Presbyterian National Church had broken down and Independency, sometimes combined with Baptist principles, was making headway. There were, however, other groups which could not rest content with any of these options. Enthusiasts appeared with communist ideals which they based upon the Bible. Their aim was to abolish all social distinctions and any form of ministry, and to establish the Kingdom of God by force of arms. These 'Levellers' were suppressed by Cromwell, who imprisoned their leaders. One group attempted a rising against the Restoration in 1660, but were put down by the troops of Charles II in the following year. This marked the end of revolutionary enthusiasm in England. There were, however, other and more peaceful enthusiasts who could find no satisfaction in any of the recognized forms of Christianity. They were called the Seekers and expected that a new prophet would be sent by the Holy Spirit. It is from their midst that the Quakers took their origin.

George Fox (1624–91) was the son of a weaver in the village of Drayton in Leicestershire. Both his parents were pious folk and his father was noted for his integrity. The son was apprenticed to a shoemaker in Nottingham. He had inherited his father's character, but had a strong tendency to day-dreaming and melancholy. In 1643 he underwent a spiritual crisis. At a market in Nottingham he met a cousin and another friend who invited him to drink a glass of beer with them. Both men were avowed Puritans, and George wished to talk with them about God. But the conversation took a very different turn, and the party became a drinking bout. When they decided that the bill should be paid by the one who stopped drinking first, George got up, put the money on the table and left. That night he never went to bed, but paced up and down the room, and repeatedly threw himself on his knees in prayer. He was disgusted at the contrast between the outward pretensions of Puritanism and the inner spirit which he had seen in his friends. The decision which he then took is recorded in his *Journal*: 'At the command of God on the ninth day of the seventh month 1643 I left my relatives and broke off all familiarity of fellowship with young and old.'

Fox then adopted the life of a wanderer. Restless and plagued by doubts and temptations, he went from place to place. Those whom he met failed to understand him and often treated him with scorn. He sought help from several clergy and ministers without finding peace. He often stayed in lonely places and was the object of wonder as he sat under a tree with his Bible while others went to church. 'I was a man of sorrows when the Lord first began to occupy Himself with me.'

In 1646 the clouds began to lift. 'When all my hopes in them [the clergy and devout laity] and in all men were gone, so that I had nothing outwardly to help me, nor could tell what to do, then, oh then, I heard a voice which said: "There is one, even Christ Jesus, that can speak to thy condition," and when I heard it, my heart did leap for joy.' Henceforward he uses the language of the mystics to describe his experiences. 'I was so enveloped in God's love that I could do nothing but wonder at the greatness of God's love.' He claims to have become aware of three truths: (1) True believers are those who have passed into life through being born of God; (2) An education at Oxford or Cambridge is not sufficient to make men servants of Christ (directed against the invariable contemporary training for the ministry of the Church of England); (3) God does not dwell in any outward temple made by men's hands. He developed an aversion to church buildings which he described not as churches but as steeple-houses.

From 1647 he travelled about preaching the Gospel of 'the Inner Light' which was of greater worth than Jewish ceremonies or heathen fables, or of the immediate communion of the soul with God, and of Christian perfection which arises from victory over sin and death, obtained by pure hearts. Naturally this preaching gave rise to many disputes, for it amounted to a direct attack on all the organized churches, on the sacraments, on the Puritan doctrines of the authority of the Scriptures and the nature of man. 'Some were convinced and were confirmed (i.e. in this faith), and stood fast in the truth. But the professors (the Puritans or those who claimed to profess the truth) became angry and spoke of sin and imperfection, and could not tolerate hearing some one speak about perfection and a holy and sinless life.' His appearance and manners were such as to arouse attention. He had long hair, wore a habit made of leather, addressed every one as 'Thou,' refused to take off his hat to any one or to take an oath, and called upon his followers to refuse military service.

His activities led to several imprisonments. The first occasion was in 1649 for interrupting a service and shouting to the minister who had spoken of the Scriptures as the source and standard of all doctrine, 'Not the Scriptures, but the Spirit.' The first term of imprisonment was light, but he later served sentences of up to three years.

But Fox also won followers. They called themselves the Friends, which later became the official name of the society, or 'the Children of Light.' Of the origin of the name 'Quaker,' two alternative explanations have been given. It may be derived from spasms of quaking which occurred at their meetings or from an incident at Fox's trial before Judge Bennett, during which the judge was exhorted to 'quake' or tremble before God, but replied that he was no 'Quaker.'

Despite persecution and derision the movement spread rapidly between 1650 and 1660. It first got a firm foothold in the North of England, but soon spread to other parts of the country, closely followed by persecution and imprisonment. One Friend, John Whitehead (1630–96), always took a nightcap with him when he attended a meeting in case he should be arrested.

In 1654 the movement was introduced into London by two women, and then reached Ireland, North America and Holland. At a meeting held in 1660 mention is made of the work of Friends in America, Germany, France, Italy, Norway, Turkey and Jerusalem. Their missionaries were full of fervour and even wrote letters to the Pope. George Fox himself wrote to the Bey of Algiers and the Emperor of China, while Mary Fisher (*c.* 1623–1697) had an interview with the Sultan. The spread of the movement in England may be judged by the fact that after the Restoration there were 4,200 Quakers in prison and that over thirteen thousand arrests took place between 1661 and 1687.

Until his death the leadership of the movement was in the hands of Fox himself, but notable converts were not wanting. Outstanding among them were the eccentric James Naylor (*c.* 1617–60), the noble William Penn (1644–1718) and Robert Barclay (1648–90), the only Quaker theologian of importance during the period. Naylor became the leader of the congregation in London, but brought the movement into disrepute by allowing himself to be greeted as 'the Prince of Peace' and 'the Everlasting King.' In 1656, as he rode into Bristol, his friends and admirers cast their clothes on the ground before him and cried 'Blessed be he that cometh in the name of the Lord. Hosanna in the Highest.' He was convicted of blasphemy, whipped, imprisoned and branded on the forehead with the letter 'B' (for blasphemy). He later acknowledged his transgression and repented. William Penn was the son of an admiral. He had a strongly mystical side to his nature and joined the Friends in 1667, working as a preacher and author. He was imprisoned for attacking the doctrines of the Church, but out of compliment to his father he was granted a large territory in America to which he gave the name of Pennsylvania. The capital which he founded himself was called Philadelphia and the colony was governed on Quaker principles. Robert Barclay wrote his *Theologiae vere Christianae apologia* in 1676, which represents a Quaker system of dogmatics.

The Friends soon found it necessary to accept a minimum amount of organization. The first General Meeting 'about the business of the Church both in this nation and beyond the seas' was held in 1660 and has met annually since 1672. From 1666 George Fox devoted much thought to the further organization of his Society and Quarterly Meetings for a particular county and Monthly Meetings for smaller units began to be held. A notable feature was the establishment in 1671 of a quarterly 'Meeting for Sufferings,' which was originally necessitated by the persecution of Quakers, but which is now devoted to the cause of humanity as a whole. In course of time the local meeting became known as a Particular or Preparative Meeting. While the Society of Friends has never recognized the need for an ordained ministry, from early times 'faithful Friends and Brethren concerned in the public labours of the Gospel and the general service of the Church of Christ' were given the name of Ministers and were summoned to General Meetings of their own until their functions were taken over by the regular General Meeting in 1905. Responsibility for Particular Meetings is vested in elders (general spiritual supervision) and overseers (pastoral care) elected by the Society from its own members for a period of three years.

After the death of the founder there was a period of decline. Missionary zeal cooled, and during the Age of the Enlightenment the spirit of mysticism tended to be replaced by that of rationalism. The identification, or at least the approximation of 'the Inner Light' to reason would not be a difficult step to take.

The Quakers have an honoured name in all humanitarian causes. They had a considerable share in the abolition of slavery and in prison reform. In the latter connection the name of Elizabeth Fry (1780-1845) must be mentioned.

In the twentieth century the Society of Friends has experienced something of a renaissance, and its members have distinguished themselves in social and educational work. As a recognition of their work in two World Wars they were awarded the Nobel Peace Prize for 1947. The Quaker Settlement at Woodbrooke near Birmingham, established in 1902, is an important religious centre. Several American universities have been founded by wealthy Friends.

The total number of the Society of Friends may be put at approximately 165,000, of whom 110,000 are in America and 20,000 in England and Wales.

2. THE DISTINCTIVE CHARACTER OF THE SOCIETY OF FRIENDS

The official designation of this community is 'the Society of Friends,' but they often use the term 'Quaker' of themselves.

They occupy a position on the extreme Left Wing of Christendom. They are a Church without Articles of Faith, sacraments or ministry, and their organization is as simple as any religious body can have. Despite, or more precisely just because of these features, the Society represents a characteristic type of Christianity.

An official collection has been made of representative statements made by leading Friends covering the whole period of their history and of pronouncements made by the Society itself on various occasions. This was published in London between 1921 and 1931 and is divided into three volumes: (i) Christian Life, Faith and Thought in the Society of Friends, (ii) Christian Practice, and (iii) Church Government. It does not, of course, represent either a legally binding confessional document, or a compendium of doctrine, but is a collection of extracts which the Society itself regards as typical of the Quaker tradition.

The religion of the Quakers is a form of mysticism, not, indeed, of the ecstatic primitive type sought after by the Pentecostalists, but a form of Quietism in which primacy is given to the Inner Light within the human soul. This light (for which St. John i. 9 is the palmary passage) is, or should be, found in the soul of every human being. According to the statement published by the Society of Friends in England in 1920, defining its attitude to the ecumenical movement, 'The Light is potentially present in every one but is only experienced by those who are turned towards the Light and are obedient to it.' The context makes it clear that this is identical with 'having direct contact with the Spirit of Christ.' In early Quaker literature mention is also made of the seed as the basic principle, which is defined as 'a part of the divine nature, capable of growth which is brought into the heart of man.'

No external authority is recognized by the Society of Friends as final in itself. The Bible is read, sometimes at meetings, but more often at home, but it is emphasized that the ultimate court of appeal is not so much the Bible as the Inner Light. Thus it is sometimes asserted that the refusal of military service is not based upon any isolated Biblical text, but upon the respect for human life enjoined by the teaching of Jesus and confirmed by the Inner Light.

It is from this principle that the special features of the Quaker conception of doctrine, Church organization and worship can be deduced. In their statement the English Friends recalled that their seventeenth-century predecessors had often declared that on the whole they agreed with the orthodox teaching of other Churches concerning the Holy Trinity, the divinity and humanity of our Lord, sin and salvation, redemption through Jesus Christ, His Resurrection and the Inspiration of the Scriptures. They could not, however, commit themselves to any formulated articles of faith, partly because the truth can never be established for all time, and partly because a confession of faith is without value unless it is experienced and its contents find expression in human conduct. The Society of Friends persists in this attitude, and they are therefore in their own opinion 'orthodox' and 'evangelical' despite their refusal to subscribe to Articles of Faith. While some Quakers have undoubtedly held unorthodox views, a fact to which the Society does not attach any great importance, many Friends do not differ substantially in their views of the Person and Work of Christ and in their doctrine of salvation from other Evangelical Christians.[1]

Membership is on a voluntary basis. Yet children of Quaker parents are reckoned as members (admission by right of birth) without any further distinction being drawn between 'members' and 'adherents' as in the Methodist Church. Except in such cases membership is by personal application after approval by the Society and ceases on resignation. Certain regulations exist governing Dissociation 'if over a period of years a member has ceased to avail himself of his opportunities of attending Meetings for Worship or of otherwise sharing in the fellowship of the Society . . . and if it is clear that there is no probability of his interest in the concerns of the Society being renewed,' and Disownment 'if a member falls into some grave fault and contrary to the private counsel of Friends he persists therein.' They are not, however, closely defined and discipline, though one of the duties of the overseers and a responsibility of the Monthly Meeting, normally takes care of itself. The presidency of the local congregation or preparative meeting is in the hands of elders and overseers elected for a term of years.

Divine Service takes the form of silent meeting in dependence upon the Light, and the congregation may keep silence for an

---

[1] An American Friend at the Lund Conference stated the attitude of the Society to Creeds as follows: 'Friends are concerned to witness against Creeds where these are held to be sufficient.' (H.E.W.T.)

hour or more.[1] Some kneel in prayer, others sit and meditate. One or more may be moved to stand and say a few words, often merely to recall a passage of Scripture or a certain idea. The atmosphere of such a meeting is well described by the American Quaker, J. G. Whittier (1807–92).

> In calm and cool and silence, once again
> I find my old accustomed place among
> My brethren, where, perchance, no human tongue
> Shall utter words; where never hymn is sung
> Nor deep-toned organ blown, nor censer swung;
> Nor dim light falling through the pictured pane;
> There, syllabled by silence, let me hear
> The still, small voice which reached the prophet's ear
> Read in my heart a still diviner law
> Than Israel's leader on his tables saw.

Neither Baptism nor the Holy Communion are celebrated by the Quakers. The doctrine that outward ceremonies can effect the bestowal of grace is irreconcilable with their mystical approach. The official statement of the English Friends published in 1920 explains that they believe in the inner experiences symbolized by these ceremonies. It is often stated that, since the whole of life is sacramental, separate ceremonies must not be performed as sacraments. Every meal is a Eucharist at which our Lord is invisibly present.

Absolute integrity, simplicity, gentleness, and eagerness to help those in need are essential elements in the Quaker character. These moral qualities derive their significance from the fact that they are cultivated by and realized in men and women who (in the words of an English Friend) 'try to settle every question as it arises, not in passion or prejudice, not chiefly in the light of reason, but preferably through the Light shining in the soul.'

The Quakers are recognized as a Christian community by the World Council of Churches. If the tree is to be known by its fruits, then the Society of Friends is a Christian Church, despite the absence of sacraments, and the relatively subordinate part played by the Word.

---

[1] Compare Fox's famous instruction to the Society: 'Friends everywhere, keep your meetings waiting upon the Light.' (H.E.W.T.)

PART II

RELIGIOUS SYSTEMS CONTAINING
ELEMENTS DERIVED FROM
CHRISTIANITY

CHAPTER I

UNITARIANISM

THE Unitarians are a religious body which repudiates the doctrine of the Trinity as incompatible with a pure monotheism and a scientific view of Christianity.

This line of thought was anticipated in the Early Church by Jewish Christianity and by Monarchianism. Though Arianism is often included under this head, it nevertheless regarded the Son as in some sense within the Godhead and found its own way of interpreting the Divinity of Christ. Some modern Unitarians (though by no means all) are, in fact, virtually Arians, unwilling to reduce the person of Christ to a mere human being or religious genius, but reluctant to attribute to him a divine nature identical with that of the Father.

Modern Unitarianism began in the Reformation period and since that time has run like a tiny stream through Church History. The movement sprang from radical elements on the left wing of the Reformation. Some intellectuals of this type wished to extend criticism of the traditional teaching of the Church to the doctrines of the Trinity and the Incarnation which they regarded as inconsistent both with the New Testament and the dictates of reason. Such Anti-Trinitarianism was rejected both by the Roman Catholic Church and the Churches of the Reformation. Luther, Calvin and Zwingli all opposed it vigorously and considered it subversive of the very foundation of the Christian Faith.

The book of Miguel Serveto, or Michael Servetus (1511-53), *De Trinitatis Erroribus* (1531), caused a veritable sensation. He accepted the Divinity of Christ, but explained it on Sabellian lines. Christ and the Holy Spirit are merely representative forms of the one Divinity, the Father. After overcoming many difficulties he published his second book, *Christianismi Restitutio*, in 1553, in which he demanded a new and more radical Reformation to purge away all the errors of history and dogma which were still retained. He repudiated Infant Baptism and, in general,

331

showed a tendency towards Pantheism. During his stay at Geneva in 1553, Calvin ordered his arrest on the charge of blasphemy, and he was burned together with his books.

In Italy a group of anti-Trinitarians emerged just before 1560. Among them was the lawyer, Lelio Sozzini (1525–62), who led an erratic existence for some years, and took part in theological discussions both with Calvin at Geneva and Melanchthon at Wittenberg. His views are developed in a manuscript which was later published by his nephew, Fausto Sozzini.

The first church to be founded on an anti-Trinitarian basis arose in Poland, a country which was composed of a veritable patchwork of faiths, Roman Catholic, Lutheran, Reformed and Hussite. In 1556 the nobility were given the right to hold divine service in private, and this meant in practice religious freedom for any minority. Polish humanists displayed an interest in the new movement and anti-Trinitarians from other countries sought refuge in Poland. In 1565 they formed their own church characterized by a Unitarian theology, the practice of adult baptism and a symbolical interpretation of the Eucharist. God is one, Christ the Son of God was a created being, and the Holy Spirit was not God, but the gift of God. There was widespread disagreement on points of Christology such as the Virgin Birth. Unsuccessful attempts were made to establish contact with the Lutherans and Calvinists in Poland.

Another anti-Trinitarian centre was Transylvania. Here they enjoyed complete freedom for their propaganda, and were able to take advantage of the discord which existed between Lutherans and Calvinists. In 1568 they constituted themselves as a separate church, and were promised religious freedom by the Diet. They soon had more than four hundred congregations. Their leader was Franz Davidis (1510–79) who died in prison. His rejection of all forms of worship paid to Christ gave a radical turn to the movement.

Fausto Sozzini, or Faustus Socinus (1539–1604), succeeded in reconciling all the elements in the movement into a single church, and provided it with a body of theology. Most of his life was spent in exile. His two main books, *De statu primi hominis* and *De Jesu Christo Servatore*, written at Basle, criticized the doctrines of original sin and the Atonement. His strength lay in his criticism of orthodoxy, but his attempts to reconcile his own conclusions with the Bible were artificial. His interpretation of the Prologue to the Fourth Gospel is as follows. 'In the beginning of the Gospel (when John the Baptist appeared) was the Word or Christ, in the world, as yet unknown to men, but known to God. He was not ὁ θεός (God without qualification) but θεός (held in esteem and endowed with divine power).' In verse 14 'made flesh' is equated with 'was flesh.'

In Transylvania, Sozzini championed the moderate anti-Trinitarianism which regarded the worship of Christ as legitimate. In Poland he came into conflict with a section of the movement through his refusal to be rebaptized. He finally overcame all opposition, and became the organizer of the movement and its acknowledged leader and theologian. Within the movement he is still regarded as their most eminent figure, and the title 'Socinian,' often given to the body by its opponents, derives from his name.

Sozzini also reorganized the community on a synodical basis. In 1605, the year after his death, the Socinians published their confessional document, the Rakow Catechism, first in Polish and later in German and Latin. Its standpoint is stated on the title-page: 'A Catechism for those who maintain that there is no other God but the Father of Jesus Christ, and that Jesus, the human being, born of the Virgin, is the only-begotten Son of God.' The Atonement, original sin, predestination and infant baptism are rejected, and the Eucharist is reduced to a commemorative meal.

The centre of Anti-Trinitarianism in Poland was the town of Rakow, where they founded a famous school in 1602. But the Jesuits soon began an intensive campaign. The school was closed in 1638 and the movement itself proscribed in 1658. Its members were forced to leave the country; some found their way to Transylvania and others sought refuge in Holland.

The movement spread to England in the seventeenth century. The Latin edition of the Rakow Catechism was dedicated to James I, who ordered the book to be burnt by the public executioner, and set on foot the persecution of Anti-Trinitarians. The wide limits of toleration allowed by Cromwell did not extend as far as those who denied the doctrine of the Trinity. The anti-Trinitarian author, John Biddle (1615-62) was repeatedly convicted and imprisoned, and appealed to Cromwell in vain. The sect was even excluded from the toleration extended to all dissenters after the Revolution of 1689.

Considerable headway was made in the eighteenth century in which the movement was in harmony with the prevailing spirit of the age. But it was itself affected by the Enlightenment. Early anti-Trinitarians had accepted the unconditional authority of the Bible as a matter of course, and merely aimed at the restoration of the original form of Christianity. The main stress now came to be laid on natural religion, and Jesus was regarded as the sublime figure who had taught a pure form of monotheism. Theologians of this school began to adopt a deistic philosophy and to develop views based upon a radical criticism of the Bible.

It is to this stage of the movement that the name Unitarianism properly belongs as a description of the positive religious interests of the community. It originated with an Anglican clergyman, Theophilus Lindsey (1723-1808), who founded a congregation known as 'the Unitarian Church' in London in 1774, after the rejection by Parliament of his proposal for the abolition of subscription to the Creeds and the Thirty-nine Articles. An important figure in the history of the movement was Joseph Priestley (1733-1804), who was a Unitarian minister, first in England and later in America. But its outstanding representative in the nineteenth century was the philosopher, James Martineau (1805-1900), whose elegantly written books contain a Christianized form of natural religion with the Fatherhood of God, the brotherhood of man and the immortality of the soul as its leading themes. The official journal of the movement (whose contributors need not, however, be Unitarians) is the *Hibbert Journal*.

The Unitarian Church in England received recognition from the State in 1813, and was reorganized in 1928 under the name of the General Assembly of Unitarian and Free Christian Churches with a membership of about 50,000.

In America, Unitarian propaganda was faced with fewer difficulties than in Europe. By the beginning of the nineteenth century considerable progress had been made. It stood for a liberal, optimistic and undogmatic form of Christianity which made a great appeal in a society in which controversy was raging over the different faiths and doctrinal discussion had often assumed unattractive forms. A critical reaction set in after the vigorous outbreaks of revivalism. As a humanistic movement which claimed to preserve the essential elements of Christianity while remaining free from dogma, Unitarianism made an immediate appeal, and was even regarded as the Church of the intellectuals.

In 1805 the Unitarians secured control of the University of Harvard, traditionally a Congregationalist stronghold, which soon became one of the leading universities in America. The great spokesman of the movement was William Channing (1780–1842). He was a Congregationalist minister who attracted widespread attention by an ordination charge in 1819 on the unchristian nature of the doctrine of the Trinity. Together with his congregation he joined the Unitarians. He regarded Jesus as the realization of the ideals of mankind, accepted His Resurrection, but rejected His Divinity. Channing also affirmed the nobility of man and therefore denied the Atonement. God was a mild and affectionate Father and Jesus the shining example who would raise mankind to His own sublime level.

A more radical thinker, Theodore Parker (1810–60), virtually reduced Unitarianism to a form of natural religion without any connection with history and detached from the authority of the Bible. In his theology he stressed the immanence of God. Another significant figure was Ralph Waldo Emerson (1803–82), who was virtually a Pantheist.

A federation of the American congregations was formed in 1825. Between 1860 and 1870 a conflict broke out between the right and left wings of the movement. The former wanted a Declaration of Faith in which Christ was described as the Lord and the Son of God. The situation was eased in 1894 when a national conference approved a declaration to the effect that 'We accept the religion of Jesus, and believe in accordance with his doctrine that practical religion can be summed up in the love of God and the love of man.'

In America the Unitarian movement has a membership of between 60,000 and 70,000.

Unitarianism has never had a large membership in any country. On a percentage basis it is strongest in Rumania with 73,000 members descended from the anti-Trinitarians of Transylvania. There are 12,000 Unitarians in Hungary.

In the contemporary world Unitarianism has had an extremely small following. The alternatives have become either no Christianity at all or Christianity in a pronounced dogmatic form. A compromise like Unitarianism which represents a faded undogmatic form of Christianity no longer possesses any significant appeal.

CHAPTER II

CHRISTIAN SCIENCE

THE name of this movement is somewhat misleading since, although it claims to be an interpretation of Christianity, it has hardly anything to do with Science, as it is normally understood. The term 'Science' as used in this context recalls the Gnosis of the Early Church. Christian Science represents a peculiar form of Gnosticism, a religious pseudo-science which stresses the necessity of knowledge, and has, so far as its doctrines are concerned, strong affinities with the philosophical system known as Absolute Idealism. It might not unfairly be described as a popular presentation of this system in a Christian guise.

Christian Science was moulded by the remarkable personality of its founder, Mrs. Mary Baker Eddy (1821–1910). She was brought up in the Congregationalist household of a New England farmer. She had poor health and suffered from hysterical convulsions. She records that as a child she heard voices. In her youth she rebelled against the doctrine of predestination and came to oppose her orthodox father. In 1843 she married a contractor who died less than six months after the marriage. She now devoted herself to spiritualism, hypnotism and 'magnetism.' In the circles in which she moved there was a strong interest in the occult. Unitarianism was also much in vogue. Her second marriage in 1853 was to a dentist, but the union (which was unhappy) was dissolved twelve years later. She was ailing and, when medical treatment and a period in a sanatorium had no effect, she lost faith in medical science and became increasingly convinced of the existence of other paths to health.

It was at this period that she came into contact with a magnetist and hypnotist, Phineas Quimby. After taking a remedial course with him, she felt herself cured. Her enthusiasm for Quimby and his methods found expression both in verse and prose. Quimby had developed the theory that illness was founded on imagination and that the way to health was for the patient to cease to believe that he was ill. This doctrine later became the corner-stone of her own teaching. In the course of time a bitter quarrel broke out between the disciples of Quimby and Mrs. Eddy as to which of the two could claim priority in making this particular discovery. She herself maintained that her own theory and methods were radically different from those of Quimby.

Later in life she became convinced that she had made the discovery in 1866. On the way home from a Good Templar's meeting she fell in the street and sustained serious injury. The doctor held out no hope of recovery, but she asked for a Bible and to be left alone in the sick room. She read the story of one of the miracles in the Gospels and stood up cured. But a different picture of medical treatment and slow recovery of health is given by the physician in charge of her case.

She immediately began to teach the spiritual method of healing and held courses in the subject lasting three weeks. On those who attended she conferred the title of 'doctor,' but soon came into conflict with some of her pupils who broke with her and began to practise on their own account.

In 1875 she published her theories in a work called *Science and Health with Key to the Scriptures*, which was later revised in 1881 and 1891. Hundreds of editions have since been printed. In its final form it constitutes (together with the Bible) the canonical book of the movement.

Her followers first formed an association, but in 1879 registered themselves as a separate church under the name of 'The Church of Christ, Scientist.' In 1877 she married a devoted disciple, Asa Gilbert Eddy. When he died in 1882 she was convinced that this had been brought about by some of her pupils who had deserted her and that its cause was 'magnetism' or, as she expressed it elsewhere, 'arsenical poisoning mentally administered.'

Mrs. Eddy continued to publish new editions of 'Science and Health' and wrote newspaper articles, sermons and poems. She also founded an academy called 'The Massachusetts Metaphysical College.' She started several magazines, and (in 1908) a daily newspaper called *The Christian Science Monitor*, now one of the leading newspapers in the United States with an excellent news service. Mrs. Eddy undoubtedly possessed unusual gifts as an organizer.

Her followers regarded her with an admiration almost

approaching religious reverence which she made no great efforts to discourage. She compared her activity with the miracles of Jesus.

In 1895 a splendid church was built in Boston under the name of 'the First Church of Christ, Scientist.' It was intended to be the mother-church of a world-wide organization, and a flat named 'Mother's Room' was reserved in the building for Mrs. Eddy herself. One of her metaphysical works is dedicated to the two thousand Sunday School children who made a collection for the furnishing of the suite and another of her numerous works describes the dedication of the whole building.

Mrs. Eddy presided over her community with the title of 'Pastor Emeritus' until her death. A publishing house was associated with the church and a press bureau to deal with all public attacks made upon the movement. Lecturers who were sent on tour were required to submit their manuscripts to the head office of the movement for approval.

Christian Science reading-rooms in which approved literature is displayed have been set up in most large towns all over the world and adherents are expected to restrict themselves to authorized reading.

In 1895 Mrs. Eddy ruled that no more free sermons should be delivered at the services of her church. Since that time Sunday services have consisted of hymn-singing, music and Bible-reading accompanied by passages from 'Science and Health' according to a fixed plan followed throughout the world. Testimony meetings are held independently.

The number of followers at the time of her death was variously estimated. A Boston newspaper mentioned 320,000 registered members, a New York paper two million, while a third source put the figure at four million. It certainly amounted to several hundred thousand. Still further progress has been made since her death. The majority of her followers are in America.

The doctrine of Christian Science is a form of Absolute Idealism. The only thing that really exists is Spirit or, as Mrs. Eddy preferred to call it, Mind. In fact, God is the only form of existence. The doctrine of the Trinity is rejected as well as the application of the term 'Person' to God in any sense. God is the object of knowledge which is on a higher plane than faith.

The fundamental error made by man lies in his belief in the reality of matter and corporeality. Matter is merely non-existence. In this respect Christian Science approximates to Neoplatonism. Evil is an illusion which is due to the material or mortal mind. The gateway to release from sin, illness, pain and death is the realization that they are illusions. Prayer is a concentration of the mind with the object of overcoming these illusions. Forgiveness of sin is interpreted as release from the illusion of sin. The work of Jesus was to bring Christian knowledge to mankind. He is the greatest exponent of Christian Science of all time. Orthodox Christology is therefore rejected, and a sharp distinction drawn between Jesus the human person and the Christ principle which He exemplifies, and which rested upon Him. This resembles in some respects the Gnostic Christology of the Early Church. Christian Science certainly appeals to the Bible, but interprets it in an allegorical and artificial manner. 'Science and Health' is placed side by side with the Bible as the sole authentic commentary. The Christian sacraments are not observed in this religious community.

An official summary of the 'Tenets of Christian Science' to be signed by all who join this community comprises six points:

1. As adherents of Truth, we take the inspired Word of the Bible as our sufficient guide to eternal life.
2. We acknowledge and adore one supreme and infinite God. We acknowledge His Son, one Christ; the Holy Ghost or divine Comforter; and man in God's image and likeness.
3. We acknowledge God's forgiveness of sin in the destruction of sin and the spiritual understanding that casts out evil as unreal. But the belief in sin is punished so long as the belief lasts.
4. We acknowledge Jesus' atonement as the evidence of divine, efficacious Love, unfolding man's unity with God through Christ Jesus the Way-shower; and we acknowledge that man is saved through Christ, through Truth, Life and Love as demonstrated by the Galilean Prophet in healing the sick and overcoming sin and death.
5. We acknowledge that the crucifixion of Jesus and his resurrection served to uplift faith to understand eternal Life, even the allness of Soul, Spirit, and the nothingness of matter.
6. And we solemnly promise to watch and pray for that Mind to be in us which was also in Christ Jesus; to do unto others as we would have them do unto us; and to be merciful, just and pure.

CHAPTER III

JEHOVAH'S WITNESSES

WHILE the Adventists represent a form of Christianity which recalls the Jewish Christianity of the Early Church, their daughter sect, the movement known as 'Jehovah's Witnesses', lies decidedly outside the limits of Christendom as set out in this book. Originally known as the 'International Society for Bible Study' or 'the Watch Tower Bible and Tract Society,' they adopted the present name in 1931.

Their founder was Charles Taze Russell (1852–1916), an American businessman, born at Pittsburgh, Pennsylvania. He was a religiously-minded youth who became disquieted by the discord which existed between the Churches and reacted against the Congregationalism which had been the faith of his parents. Adventism shed some light upon his problems which were mainly of an apocalyptic nature. He claimed to have found the key to their solution in the fact that the Greek word Parousia in the Bible should be translated as 'Presence' rather than as 'Coming' or 'Return.' He then taught (probably from 1872 onwards) that our Lord would return as an invisible spirit in 1874, and supported this conclusion by numerical calculations based upon the Bible.

In 1877 he invited the various ministers of Pittsburgh and Alleghany to a meeting at which he put forward his views. These they repudiated as one man. From that time onwards he had no further use for the existing Churches and their ministers. Several strong statements to this effect are to be found in his writings. He nevertheless styled himself 'pastor' and 'professor,' though he was not ordained and had received no theological training.

In 1878 Russell started a magazine called *The Watch Tower and Herald of Christ's Presence*, which is still published in a number of different languages. His main work, *Food for thinking Christians* (1881), was re-issued five years later under the title *Millennial Dawn*. It also forms the first volume of a series of six entitled *Studies in the Scriptures* which appeared between the years 1886 and 1904. A seventh volume containing interpretations of the Book of Revelation and the Song of Songs appeared posthumously in 1917. Thirteen million copies of these studies are said to have been distributed.

In 1881 Russell founded 'The Watch Tower Bible and Tract Society,' which issued his publications. These were translated into many different languages and distributed by agents of the Society.

On Russell's death in 1916, Joseph Franklin Rutherford (1869–1942) succeeded to the leadership of the movement in his capacity of Chairman of 'the Watch Tower Board.' He was elected by 150,000 shareholders. He lived a secluded life, seldom appearing at meetings, but exercising his influence mainly through the printed word and to some extent through broadcasts on the wireless. As a writer he was even more prolific than Russell and there is no doubt that during the period of his leadership he wrote all the articles for the various magazines of the Watch Tower Society. In 1940 he declared that he had written ninety-nine books and pamphlets, which had been published in seventy-eight different languages with a total circulation of three hundred million copies.

Rutherford's death in 1942 seems to have come as a shock to many of the 'Witnesses,' who had expected him to live to see the Millennial Kingdom. His successor is Nathan H. Knorr (b. 1905), who now writes the books and pamphlets of the movement.

In his writings Russell had prophesied the coming of the Kingdom of God on earth in 1914. This was to be attended by peace, justice and blessing. As the year approached, however, his prophecies took on a more subdued tone. In the last volume of *Studies in the Scriptures* the date is put forward to 1918. Rutherford advanced the date still further to 1925. In that year the Patriarchs were to rise again and the Kingdom begin. When the year came to an end Rutherford wrote as follows: 'Everything is being fulfilled at this time and provides evidence that the Lord Jesus is present and that His Kingdom has arrived. Soon the Resurrection of the dead will take place. By soon we do not mean next year, but we believe that this will take place and count on it doing so before the century has passed.' This vague forecast rendered unnecessary any further revision during Rutherford's own lifetime.

Between 1920 and 1930 Rutherford launched an intensive campaign under the watchword 'Millions now living will never die.' He also started a new periodical, *The Golden Age*, edited in several languages. At one time the paper was said to have as many as 12,000 subscribers in Norway and Denmark alone. Since 1937 the American edition was called *Consolation*. In 1950 the name was altered into *Awake*.

Under Rutherford's leadership Russell's books fell into the background and were soon replaced by those of his successor. Except on a few points their views were in general agreement. Rutherford, for example, rejected Russell's theory that the course of world-history could be forecast from the dimensions of the Great Pyramid as well as from the Bible. Rutherford's main work is entitled *God's Harp* (1921), which depicts the theocracy or the establishment of the Kingdom of God, in which 'Jehovah's Witnesses' will rule side by side with our Lord, while all existing forms of authority, ecclesiastical as well as secular, will be overthrown at the great Apocalyptic battle of Armageddon.

The headquarters of the sect are in a nine-storied building at Brooklyn, which houses a printing press and offices. The two hundred employees live in Bethel House situated in the vicinity and take their meals communally. The movement also has a splendid house in California called *Beth Sarim* (the House of the Princes), in which rooms are fitted out in readiness for the return of David, Abraham, Isaac and Jacob. In the meantime they are occupied by the president and his colleagues. The community also possesses its own wireless station which broadcasts propaganda in several languages as well as recordings of Rutherford's speeches.

The most important medium of missionary activity is the printed word. According to current figures seven million copies of the two periodicals, *The Watch Tower* and *Consolation*, were printed in 1943. Their magazines and books are sold by most persistent agents at a very low price, and it is probable that many purchasers have little or no idea what they are buying.

The sect is organized on business lines. At its head is the

President and the Board of Directors. Under this Board are the various 'Religious Servants,' and at a lower level again a number of 'Zone Servants.' The local groups are called 'Companies' and meet in a 'Kingdom Hall.' At the head of each group is a 'Service Director' assisted by a 'Service Committee.' Each member of this hierarchy is expected to obey his superiors without question.

The active members of the sect are divided into two groups, called in America 'publishers' and 'pioneers.' The former continue their ordinary work and perform their religious duty of bearing witness in their spare time. In the normal way a 'publisher' has to bear witness for at least sixty hours a month either by standing at street corners selling *The Watch Tower* or going from house to house selling the publications of the Society. A return has to be made giving precise details of the hours spent and the copies sold. Contacts are followed up by a system of 'back calls.' The pioneers are full-time workers who have given up everything for the cause. They are maintained by the Society and receive a small wage. In 1943 there were 106,000 'publishers' and about 8,000 'pioneers.' Of these, 65,000 and 4,000 respectively were in the United States.

The total number of adherents in the wider sense of the term is difficult to estimate. Rutherford's figure of two million is certainly an exaggeration. In 1925 the number of those who took part in the annual celebration of the Holy Communion was 90,000. In subsequent years the numbers fell slightly and since 1927 it has been withheld.

The majority of the 'Witnesses' are in America. During the difficult years in Germany after the First World War, when poverty and unemployment were rife, the movement made some headway. The sect was banned there as early as 1923 because it was considered to be hostile to the State, though police measures failed to put a stop to its progress. It is reckoned that about 1930 it had 25,000 adherents. Under the Nazi régime the 'Witnesses' were arrested and about 6,000 of them met their deaths in the concentration camps. According to the national census of 1950 the movement had about 2,000 followers in Norway and perhaps three times as many in Sweden.

In many countries the 'Witnesses' have been imprisoned because of their refusal to perform military service. Yet their profession of pacifism contrasts strangely with the lurid pictures which they paint of the great apocalyptic battle of Armageddon. It is sometimes stated that they are prepared to take part in war if it is the will of Jehovah, but that all existing governments are the tools of Satan. The numerous court cases and imprisonments to which their attitude has led have given a certain moral strength to the movement by proving that the 'Witnesses' are prepared to face suffering and even death for their convictions.

Their approach to the Bible is Fundamentalist, and scientific criticism is viewed with abhorrence. The Bible is eagerly read by many of the 'Witnesses' who usually know a large number of texts by heart. All the teachings of the sect are 'proved' by references to the Biblical texts, though they claim that it cannot be understood apart from the interpretations of Rutherford, which are allegorical, unhistorical and often appear to be out of harmony with the spirit of Christianity. They maintain that they possess a complete doctrinal system capable of providing an answer to every question. Rutherford is considered a reliable Biblical exegete, and it has even been said that a complete knowledge of the Bible can be obtained from his writings.

God is known as Jehovah, a form of the divine name which is philologically incorrect. He is the Creator of Heaven and Earth as well as of Lucifer who rebelled against Him and was called Satan. For centuries Satan has ruled the world through its economic, political and religious organizations. All other religious communities are his instruments through which he leads the nations astray. 'Jehovah's Witnesses' are God's sole representatives on earth.

The doctrine of the Trinity is rejected. The Christology of the movement is a crude form of Arianism. Arius himself is regarded as a forerunner of Russell. In the preface to a collection of his sermons the following are named as his predecessors: Paul, John, Arius, Peter Waldo, Wyclif and Luther, but Russell ranks immediately after Paul and is greater than the other four. Christ is a creature who is sometimes identified with the Archangel Michael. He became Messiah only after His Baptism. The doctrine of His Bodily Resurrection is denied, and Russell even conjectured that His body was turned into gas. Little or nothing is said about the Holy Spirit.

The soul of man is not naturally immortal. Death is a final annihilation for those who do not recognize the theocracy or the millennial Kingdom. This is virtually identified with the organization of 'Jehovah's Witnesses.' The old order came to an end in 1914, when Christ was set on the Heavenly Throne by Jehovah and Satan was cast out of heaven. The battle of Armageddon is imminent, in which Satan and his followers will be destroyed by Christ and His angels. Our Lord is given the strange titles of 'the Avenger' or 'the Great Executioner.' A kingdom of happiness (in which 'Jehovah's Witnesses' will play a leading part) will be established upon the earth, and peace and justice will prevail.

The teaching of the movement leads to an extreme form of other-worldliness. It is useless to try to improve the condition of society, for the present world will inevitably be destroyed. Little significance is attached to works of charity for the same reason. All that matters for salvation is doctrine, and it is to its propagation that all the energies of the Witnesses are devoted. All hostility to the movement, real or alleged, only serves to convince them that they belong to the Elect.

Adult Baptism is practised but is merely considered as a token of obedience and profession of faith. It is not necessary for salvation and is not invested with any sacramental significance. At the beginning of the movement it was often carried out in Baptist churches, but the practice ceased when the Baptists insisted that the newly baptized should be registered as their members. It is usually now performed in a swimming pool either in the open air or indoors.

The Holy Communion is called 'Memorial Supper,' and is a purely commemorative meal to which no sacramental significance is attached. It is celebrated annually at Easter; at the beginning of the movement it was held as near as possible to the day and hour of the Last Supper. After much alternation between wine and unfermented grape juice, the former is now employed as being more biblical.

Hymns are no longer sung at their services which are now restricted to Bible reading, prayer and addresses.

The ethos of the 'Witnesses' is Puritan, characterized by integrity, a clean life, frugality, the spirit of sacrifice and normally total abstinence from alcohol and tobacco. But their aversion from politics and indifference to the fate of the world are entirely inconsistent with Puritanism and depend upon their pessimistic attitude to this present world. Marriage is not forbidden, but is sometimes discouraged on the ground that it is not advisable to bring children into the world, and that it is better to await the establishment of the millennial Kingdom. A religion so dominated by its Apocalyptic heritage leaves little room for the teachings of the New Testament taken as a whole.

CHAPTER IV

MORMONISM

1. ORIGIN AND HISTORY

ALTHOUGH the Mormon community calls itself 'The Church of Jesus Christ of Latter-Day Saints,' it is not so much a Christian sect as a religion based upon new revelations which has adopted certain Christian features. Its modifications of and additions to the Christian tradition virtually amount to the emergence of a new faith. The aim of Mormonism is not only to restore the original form of Christianity, but also through its own Scriptures to provide a new religion of Revelation. Certain features of its history recall Islam which also presupposes the Biblical world of ideas and supplements it through a series of new revelations which display a different spirit. Like Islam again, Mormonism at one stage of its history countenanced polygamy. But there are also important differences. Mormonism does not share the passionate insistence upon Monotheism which characterizes Islam and its adherents have always claimed to be Christians.

The peculiar character of the sect is derived from the strange personality of its founder, Joseph Smith (1805–44). Born at Sharon, Windsor County, Vermont, he came from a poor home. He was burdened by the heritage of a pathological constitution and received only the most superficial education.

These biographical details are important for an estimate of the man and his work. Many different verdicts have been passed upon him. His followers regarded him as a prophet and a martyr, whereas even during his lifetime his opponents frequently entertained the opinion that he was a swindler and a cheat. Critical research has turned to psychology to throw light upon his biography. It is now widely held that he acted in good faith, but that he was a visionary with little or no ability to distinguish between fantasy and reality. He interpreted his own wishes and dreams as revelations. His doctrines and oracles are a combination of reminiscences from the Bible and contemporary discussions on the origins of the primitive population of America with echoes of the revivalist campaigns of his childhood and his own wishful thinking.

According to Smith himself, the angel Moroni appeared to him in 1823 and informed him that he was called to re-establish the Church of Jesus Christ in the last days of the world. He was also informed of the existence and whereabouts of some gold plates upon which was engraved an account of the primitive population of America and of Christ's preaching there after His Resurrection. Four years later Smith dug up these gold plates. By their side lay a pair of spectacles with two precious stones set in silver as their lenses, which Smith recognized from their description in Exodus xxviii. 30 as the Urim and Thummin of the high priest's apparel. With the help of the spectacles he succeeded in deciphering the tablets which he claimed to have been written in Reformed Egyptian, a language unknown to the Egyptologists. It is known from other sources that during these years he dabbled in the occult, and that during these experiments he would stare for hours at certain kinds of stone.

For three years he worked on the translation. When this was completed, the angel Moroni removed the tablets. In 1830, Smith published a comprehensive work. Its long title opens with the words 'The Book of Mormon' and ends with the translator's name. In the first edition this is followed by the description 'author and proprietor,' which in later editions is altered to the words 'translated by.' The book has often been reprinted in revised editions with thousands of small changes, and a large number of translations have been made during the last hundred years.

As a preface to the official editions of the work there are two printed statements (with three and eight signatures respectively) made by witnesses who affirm that they saw the gold plates bearing the sacred text. The signatories of the first statement later broke with Smith, but still continued to assert categorically that they had seen the gold tablets. One of them caused the following inscription to be placed on his grave-stone: 'The Book of the Jews (The Old Testament) and the Book of the Nephites (the Book of Mormon) are one. The truth is eternal.'

The Book of Mormon claims to be a counterpart to the Old

Testament which Smith took as his model. In scope it covers about half of its original. The work is subdivided with titles like 'The first book of Nephi,' 'The second book of Nephi,' 'The book of Jacob,' 'The book of Enos.' In style it follows the English translation of the Bible, from which most of its contents are taken. In addition there are quotations from the Westminster Confession, a Methodist Book of Discipline, and even a passage from Shakespeare. The book is very monotonous; Mark Twain described it as 'chloroform in print.'

In the book of Mormon it is stated that America was originally inhabited by the Jaredites who came directly after the Fall of the Tower of Babel. It took them 344 days to cross the Ocean and reach the shore of the Promised Land. In the course of time they split up into the Lamanites from whom the Indians are descended, and the Nephites, or true believers to whom Christ revealed Himself after the Resurrection. These were later exterminated, but their holy scriptures were recorded by Mormon and his son Moroni, and buried in the ground until their discovery and subsequent publication by Joseph Smith.

On April 6th, 1830, Joseph Smith and his first followers organized themselves into a separate church in the State of New York. In the previous year Smith and a colleague had seen John the Baptist descend from heaven. They were ordained by him as priests of Aaron's line and commanded to baptize each other. Later Peter, James and John appeared to Smith and ordained him priest after the order of Melchizedek.

The congregation increased by leaps and bounds within a few years. Its temporary headquarters were established at Kirtland, Ohio, where Smith settled in 1831 and where his followers soon reached the number of 2,000.

Meanwhile, however, the Mormons had antagonized their neighbours and this animosity led to persecution and bloodshed in a settler area where brawls and murder were by no means infrequent. The Mormon colonies were destroyed in this way and a new settlement established further West met with a similar fate. In 1840 they moved once more across the Mississippi into Illinois where they founded the town of Nauvoo (the beautiful One). In his capacity as general of the Nauvoo legion Smith ruled like a dictator over the town. Under his direction a temple

was built and a Mormon University established. Missionaries
were sent to Europe. It was the duty of all converts to proceed
to Nauvoo and by 1844 there were close on 4,000 European
immigrants of this type.

In 1843 Smith introduced polygamy, but merely as a temporary measure and as a personal privilege for himself. This
innovation was authorized by an oracle addressed to his wife:
'And let my handmaid, Emma Smith, receive all those who have
been given unto my servant Joseph, and who are virtuous and
pure before me.'

Smith became more and more presumptuous, and in 1844 even
secured nomination as a candidate for the Presidential Elections,
sending out his missionaries to make election speeches. On
June 24th, 1844, the Governor of Illinois ordered his arrest
together with his brother Hiram. Three days later a band of
armed men forced their way into the prison and shot both
prisoners. The founder of the sect thus became a martyr.

The leadership of the movement now passed to the carpenter,
Brigham Young (1801–77), an energetic and despotic personality
and an excellent organizer. As the local population still continued to show hostility to the Mormons, he planned a new
Exodus. They were then living on the very frontier of the
civilized world, but across the great prairie there were stretches
of territory unpopulated except by nomadic tribes of Indians.
The country belonged to Mexico but her control was purely
nominal. In 1846 the new Israel left Nauvoo and began its
Exodus westwards. It is estimated that there were 15,000 people
in the wagon train with 3,000 wagons and much cattle. In the
following year, after great exertions and much hardship, they
reached the Great Salt Lake in what is now called Utah. Here
they began to build a town, and on the third day after their
arrival they laid the foundation stone of their temple. Their
colony was established on a theocratic basis.

While the Mormons were building a community in the desert
they sent missionaries to Europe. Thus, in 1849, the apostle,
Erastus Snow, travelled to Denmark to begin missionary work
in Scandinavia. After a few months' work he was able to perform
the first few baptisms, and as early as 1853 two hundred and

ninety-three Danish Mormons journeyed to Utah. The trip to the Promised Land took them six months.

After a war with Mexico, Utah was ceded to the United States and became a 'territory' governed by officials appointed by the Federal authorities. At first Brigham Young acted as Governor, but was soon replaced by an official sent from Washington.

Thanks to the unflagging industry and strict discipline of the Mormons the community grew apace both in numbers and wealth. In 1852, Young officially introduced polygamy and the possession of at least three wives became a necessary qualification for the higher ecclesiastical offices. His preaching gradually approximated to polytheism. Young ruled despotically and malcontents who attempted to flee the country were put to death. The notorious 'blood atonement' was introduced as a disciplinary measure. Any one guilty of sexual intercourse outside the permitted polygamy or of killing a Mormon had to give his life to atone for his sin. The perpetrators of such crimes were executed by having their throats cut over an empty grave so that the blood ran down into it. By this means they were able to secure redemption and join the Heavenly Host.

In the long run it was impossible for Utah to remain a purely Mormon State. When the gold rush started westwards into California and the Pacific Railway was laid down in 1869, the country was opened to other colonists. It was the end of their secluded existence and of the reign of terror.

Young died in 1877, leaving behind him seventeen wives and forty-nine children who inherited his large fortune. He was succeeded by John Taylor (1808–87), who was elected president. Polygamy was discontinued under his successor, Wilford Woodruff (1807–98). This was made a condition of the acceptance of Utah into the North American Union in 1896, The doctrine of 'blood atonement' was also repudiated by the president of the community.

The total Mormon population of the world is estimated at something over a million, of whom 900,000 are in America, mostly in Utah, where they constitute two-thirds of the population.

2. Organization, Doctrine and Ritual

Nearly all the male members of this community have the status of priests. Priesthood is of two kinds, Aaronic and Melchizedekian. The former ranks as the lower of the two, and consists of bishops, priests, deacons and teachers. All members of the higher priesthood have the right to preach and to conduct ordinations, and bear the title of 'elder.' Over them is a group called the 'seventy.' The name is derived from the seventy disciples of St. Luke x. 1-17, though in actual fact there are many times this number. Above them are the so-called 'high priests,' a further group of 'patriarchs' or 'evangelists,' a supreme council of twelve 'apostles,' and at the head 'the first president' assisted by two other presidents.

Co-ordinate doctrinal authorities are the Bible 'so far as it is correctly translated,' the Book of Mormon, the Book of Doctrine and Covenants (concerned with doctrine and church ordinances) and the Pearl of Great Price (a collection of oracles and imitations of Biblical texts).

Their theology starts from a crudely anthropomorphic picture of God. According to Brigham Young, 'the Father has a body of flesh and bones as tangible as man's' (Doctrine and Covenants 130, 22). He was a human being, but has advanced himself to become God. In the same way it is the task of human beings to become gods. This is not understood in a purely mystical way, but has polytheistic implications. Jesus is a Saviour and He will found a Zion on earth or, more specifically, in America.

The way of salvation involves faith, conversion, baptism and the imposition of hands. Faith is defined as 'belief in the fact that Jesus is the Saviour of the world and that Joseph Smith was a true prophet of God.' Conversion means the observance of God's commandments and of the ordinances of the Mormon sect. Valid baptism can only be performed by a Mormon priest, and he alone can confer the Holy Spirit by the laying on of hands.

Baptism can be performed with vicarious effect (1 Cor. xv. 29). A Mormon living at the present time can be rebaptized on behalf of a dead relative. This term is given the widest possible connotation, and the Mormons have set up genealogical bureaux in order to trace their relatives. In many countries they have begun

N

extensive micro-filming of church records to assist their investigations. Matrimony which has not been 'sealed' within their community can be 'sealed' vicariously by two living Mormons who go through the marriage ceremony on behalf of the deceased couple. This validates the marriage for eternity. It is said that in the main temple at Salt Lake City no less than twelve million vicarious ceremonies were performed on behalf of deceased persons between 1893 and 1927.

Only proven Mormons can take part in the temple ceremonies in Salt Lake City. They have been described by former members of the sect who have taken part in them. They are mystery rituals and bear a strong resemblance to the ceremonies of the Masonic Orders.

A tithe is exacted from all members of the Mormon community. Their young men are required to serve as missionaries for one or two years.

CONCLUSION

1. THE LIMITS OF CHRISTENDOM

WE have now surveyed the whole area of Christendom from its right wing composed of the Orthodox and Roman Catholic Churches to its extreme left wing, permeated by the principles of voluntary association, subjectivism and interiority. The position on the extreme left is occupied by the Society of Friends, who have no articles of faith, sacraments or ministry. We have also described and analysed certain sects which claim to be Christian, but which we have not been able to include within the limits of Christendom. These have been grouped together under the heading of 'Religious systems containing elements derived from Christianity.'

But where do the limits of Christendom really lie? Not even a Roman Catholic can identify it merely with his own Church. He also takes account of the fact that there are Christians outside the frontiers of the True Church. In modern Roman Catholicism it is not uncommon to hear both Orthodox and Protestants described as 'our brethren separated in the faith,' or as 'Christians separated from us' (*chrétiens dissidents* in the words of an authority like M. J. Congar). It is even more difficult for members of most other churches to restrict Christendom to their own communions. It is precisely those communities who hold most firmly to the principle of voluntary adhesion (such as the Congregationalists, the Baptists and the Quakers) which will be among the first to admit that there are Christians in other churches as well as in their own.

The limits which we assign to Christendom must therefore be wide. But how are they to be determined?

If we take the recognition and use of the Apostles' Creed as our test, both the Orthodox Church and a number of Protestant communions will fall outside the limits of Christendom, which would be absurd. If we select the Nicene Creed, Christendom will include the Orthodox, Roman Catholic, Anglican, Lutheran, and perhaps the Reformed Churches. Our instinct is rather to

355

take the Bible as the criterion. It is the common property of all Christians. But the Bible is also used, or more properly misused, by the sects which we have found it necessary to place outside the limits of Christendom.

From the standpoint of the Orthodox, Roman Catholic and Lutheran Churches, it would seem natural to regard the sacraments as characteristic of Christendom. Christendom represents the totality of baptized believers. But difficulties are caused here by the bodies which do not practise Baptism. Do the Quakers and unbaptized Salvationists belong to Christendom? From a Roman Catholic standpoint they may be included according to the express statement of an acknowledged authority like St. Thomas Aquinas. He distinguished three kinds of valid Baptism: baptism with water, baptism by martyrdom and baptism by the Holy Ghost. All three incorporate into Christendom, although it is the duty of the Church to adhere strictly to the practice of baptism by water. On these premises, however, it follows that the sacraments cannot be taken as forming the line of demarcation for Christendom in its widest sense.

There is really only one characteristic that must be present in any community which should be recognized as Christian: belief in Jesus Christ as the Son of God, as Lord and Saviour. Any faith which rests upon and is permeated by this belief must be said to lie within the limits of Christendom, while any faith which rejects or is inconsistent with the Divinity of Christ is beyond the pale. The doctrine of the Holy Trinity is organically related to the Divinity of Christ.

In 1948, on the occasion of the formation of the World Council of Churches, the conditions of membership were formulated in such a way as to extend its scope as widely as was consistent with the limits of Christendom. The basis of admission for its member churches was made the recognition of Jesus Christ as 'God and Saviour.'

It is in this way that the common faith of Christendom has been formulated in our own day. Many churches have not developed it further on more theological lines. But in those churches which have preserved the doctrinal heritage of the Early Church and therefore possess a fully integrated doctrine of the Person of Christ, this Christological confession reads as follows:

'I believe in one Lord, Jesus Christ, the only begotten Son of God, begotten of his Father before all worlds, God of God, Light of Light, Very God of very God, begotten, not made, Being of one substance with the Father, By whom all things were made; Who for us men and for our salvation came down from Heaven, And was incarnate by the Holy Ghost of the Virgin Mary, And was made man.'

2. FEATURES COMMON TO THE VARIOUS CHURCHES

When we consider the disunity prevailing within Christendom, its most striking characteristic is the variety and extent of divergence between the churches. It is difficult to pick out elements which are common to them all, or which can express their fellowship.

The Churches have no common Creed accepted by the whole of Christendom. This raises a difficulty which has often been felt in the history of the ecumenical movement and which led to the adoption by the World Council of Churches of the minimal profession of faith which has been mentioned above.

Neither the Apostles' Creed nor the Nicene Creed constitutes an ecumenical creed in the sense that it is recognized by all churches. It must, however, be said that the Nicene Creed is the most widely accepted of all existing Articles of Faith.

The question of a common creed for the whole of Christendom was raised at the ecumenical conference held at Lausanne in 1927, and the commission which worked upon the problem experienced to the full the difficulties to which it gave rise. After considerable discussion a statement was issued, part of which ran as follows: 'Notwithstanding the differences in doctrine among us, we are united in a common Christian Faith which is proclaimed in the Holy Scriptures and witnessed to and safeguarded in the Ecumenical Creed, commonly called the Nicene, and in the Apostles' Creed.' This formula also proved acceptable to churches which do not themselves regard these two Creeds of the Early Church as normative, but which are willing to recognize them as genuine expressions of the Christian faith.

But even if Christendom has no common Creed, it has at least a common doctrinal norm in the Bible. The Holy Scriptures have a place in the life of all churches. Considerable differences, however, emerge in the attitude adopted towards the Bible by the various churches. There is no completely uniform Canon of Scripture. The Orthodox and Roman Catholic Churches make no distinction between the Old Testament and the Apocrypha, whereas the Churches on the left wing reject the latter completely, and the Anglican and Lutheran Communions assign to it a lower status than that of the Canonical Scriptures. Deeper differences arise on the position occupied by the Bible in various churches, whether it is regarded as the sole authority, or interpreted in the light of tradition, and whether it is considered as the norm for doctrine alone, or as equally authoritative, for example, in the sphere of Church Order. Widely differing interpretations of Scripture are to be found in the Churches of Christendom.

Nor does Christendom display its unity in forms of constitution. Certain Churches have the Catholic ministry in its threefold form of bishop, presbyter and deacon, and further claim to possess the apostolic succession through continuity of episcopal consecration. In their eyes this represents the necessary condition for a ministry with real authority to administer the Sacraments. To this group belong the Orthodox and Roman Catholic Churches and, to some extent, the Anglican Communion. For these churches the possession of a proper constitution and ministry is an indispensable mark of the Church. The Lutheran Church is on principle indifferent to forms of constitution, but possesses a ministry and regards it as a necessary element in the life of the Church. On the left wing of Christendom, however, we find churches which, again on principle, have no ministry in either of these senses. Here no fundamental difference is made between minister and laymen. On purely practical grounds the congregation needs some officials, but, in effect, any member can administer the sacraments.

There are also wide divergences in divine worship. In the Eastern Churches, as in Roman Catholicism, the Holy Sacrament is the centre of the liturgical life of the Church, whereas preaching (though frequently practised) is not regarded as a necessary

feature. In other churches the preaching of the Word is considered as the substance of divine service, often even at the
expense of the Holy Sacrament, which is assigned a subordinate
significance. And there is one communion, the Society of
Friends, in whose public worship neither preaching nor sacrament
occurs. There is a wide difference between a Roman Catholic
Mass, a normal Reformed Church service and a Quaker meeting.
Indeed, so great is the difference that a cynical observer has
remarked that the only feature common to the services of all
churches is the collection.

The great dissimilarity between the churches becomes apparent
when the position occupied by the sacraments is considered.
Some churches acknowledge seven sacraments, others only two,
others again do not recognize any sacraments at all. But the
greatest divergence is not represented by disagreements on the
number of the sacraments. Much more fundamental is the
difference in the views held upon their nature and use. It is
possible to speak of sacramental and non-sacramental types of
Christianity. The former is found in its purest form in the
Eastern and Roman Catholic Churches, the latter is represented
by churches on the left wing of Christendom. The Holy Communion is celebrated in practically all Christian churches, but
there is a considerable difference between the presentation of the
Eucharistic Sacrifice at a Roman Catholic altar and the breaking
of bread in one of the Fundamentalist bodies. It is not only a
question of the outward forms, but even more of the doctrine
involved, the nature of the sacrament itself, the value set upon
it and the attitude taken towards it.

The greatest disunity is undoubtedly that which exists on the
subject of the Eucharist. In their eucharistic practice and doctrine
the churches are more sharply divided than at any other point.
The question of intercommunion is therefore the most delicate
of all ecumenical problems.

With regard to Holy Baptism the situation is somewhat
different. Baptism in the name of the Holy Trinity proves to be
a common practice among the churches to an extent which is
almost surprising. There is also a considerable uniformity of
procedure. In most churches it is performed by affusion and
accompanied by a baptismal formula in which the name of the

Holy Trinity appears. While there are great divergences in the doctrine of Baptism, there is a considerable measure of agreement to regard the sacrament as performed in all churches as mutually acceptable. Thus very few churches require converts from other churches to be rebaptized. This applies even to the Roman Catholic Church which, while reserving the right to conduct conditional Baptism in cases which appear to her to be doubtful, regards any Baptism as valid if it is of the right matter and form, irrespective of the character of the church in which it is performed. A different attitude is taken by the Baptists and other sects on the left wing, who restrict Baptism to adults who are avowed Christians, and refuse to recognize Christian fellowship in the baptismal sacrament with churches which adopt a different practice.

There are certain aspects of Christian devotional life which are to be found in all Christian communions. Concepts such as sin and grace, judgement, salvation, repentance, faith, and love of God and of neighbour are common to all, although the substance of the concept of faith (for example) may vary. Prayer is a practice common to all Christians, in which it is possible for members of all churches to have fellowship. The human heart is the same in all places and at all times, and all Christians turn to the same Lord in their prayers. This is a fact, although considerable differences exist in the devotional life. A Roman Catholic will differentiate between types of prayer and consider the meditative recitation of the Old Testament Psalter (for example) as prayer, and also give a place to mental prayer (or prayer without words), whereas those who belong to the Evangelical Churches would prefer to restrict the term to the turning of the heart to God expressed in words.

Some churches, particularly the Eastern and Roman Catholic Churches, prefer to use prescribed and formulated prayer, while the churches of the left wing normally prefer extempore prayers, in which the words are composed by the suppliant himself. One prayer, however, is common to the whole of Christendom—the Lord's Prayer. This has been correctly described as the one creed of all branches of Christendom. It is used in all churches with the exception of some of the extremer bodies on the left wing which are so apprehensive about fixed prayers and the mechanization

of the spiritual life which they believe to result from their use
that they do not use any set forms of prayers, not even the Lord's
Prayer.

We must not overlook the fact that there is fellowship between
the churches in the field of Christian ethics. There are, it is true,
considerable differences between the various ideals for Christian
living. We can distinguish between ascetic and non-ascetic types
of Christianity. There are churches which adopt a positive
attitude towards culture, and religious bodies which repudiate the
earthly benefits of the cultural life. But the impression remains
that in the sphere of ethics there exists an agreement which can
be easily perceived. The Christian love of neighbour is the highest
ethical norm for all Christians, and they all regard justice and
truth as unconditionally binding. One of the tasks confronting
all churches is to give effect to God's will in international relations,
in national and economic life, in education and in the administration of justice. There is no small degree of unity on the question
as to what is God's will in these spheres of human life. During
the last war attention was drawn by a speaker in the House of
Lords to the fact that Norwegian Lutheran bishops, a German
cardinal, Polish priests and Dutch Reformed pastors spoke on
these subjects as one man.

Agreement on the Christian ideals for the life of the individual
and of society is one of the strongest bonds of union in Christendom. This was the basis of the Life and Work Movement, one
of the two main streams of the ecumenical movement. Attempts
to bring the churches together in co-operation in tasks of a social
and ethical nature have had remarkable results.

But the outstanding feature common to all Christians is that
they have one and the same Lord. What kind of community
exists between a Roman Catholic who lives in a world of fixed
dogma, and whose life is permeated by sacramental piety and
regulated by precepts, and a Quaker who knows neither dogma
nor sacrament, and who recognizes no authority other than the
inner voice of the Holy Spirit? The bond between them is to be
found in the similarity of the attitudes which they adopt towards
the person of Jesus Christ. They both belong to one and the same
Lord. Here we have the strongest bond of union which holds all
Christians together. And from this it follows that they show a

similarity of outlook, however difficult this may be to conceive or define.

At the conclusion of the Faith and Order Conference held at Edinburgh in 1937 a statement on Christian Unity was read, which shows where the focus of unity really lies. 'We are one in faith in our Lord Jesus Christ, the incarnate Word of God. We are one in allegiance to Him as Head of the Church, and as King of kings and Lord of lords. We are one in acknowledging that this allegiance takes precedence of any other allegiance that may make claims upon us.'

'This unity does not consist in the agreement of our minds or the consent of our wills. It is founded in Jesus Christ Himself, Who lived, died and rose again to bring us to the Father, and Who through the Holy Spirit dwells in His Church. We are one because we are all the objects of the love and grace of God, and called by Him to bear witness in all the world to His glorious Gospel.'

3. THE DISUNION OF CHRISTENDOM: A THEOLOGICAL PROBLEM

The division of Christendom into numerous competing communions which not infrequently turn their weapons upon one another raises a serious problem for Christian thought. There should be one flock, just as there is one Lord, but there are many flocks which are widely separated and which differ greatly from one another. With regard to the non-Christian world, this disunity imports a serious weakness into every kind of missionary work. The disunited Church is weak. 'Make the mind of Thy Church one and strengthen it' runs one of the intercessions in the liturgy of the Norwegian Church. Nowadays forceful pronouncements on the sin inherent in disunity are voiced particularly by the younger churches. At the Faith and Order conference held at Lausanne in 1927 an Indian bishop said: 'In the West, a divided Church may be a source of weakness. In the non-Christian countries it is a sin, for it discourages thousands of people from joining the Church. Which of the many churches shall they join?'

The fact that the Church of Christ is not united constitutes a stumbling-block for faith. What is right and true when there is

so much dissension among the Christian Churches? Can any
Church claim to be the only right one? Must we end with
relativism?

The scandal of disunity can be mitigated, but not removed,
by the following consideration. The numerous different interpretations of Christianity are evidence alike of the universality of
the Gospel and the disparity which exists among mankind. For
the differences between the churches are to a large extent conditioned by differences in the historical development and national
characters of those who have received the Gospel. The author of
this book is a Lutheran, not because he has found through a
comparison of the various churches and their doctrines that the
Lutheran doctrine is the proper one, but because he was born
and brought up in a country in which practically the entire
population belongs to the Lutheran Church. He became a
Lutheran because this was the historical development experienced
by the Church of Norway. Doubtless we who have grown up
with the Lutheran tradition in our veins later discover, through
a study of Lutheranism in comparison with other creeds, valuable
elements in this heritage and can rejoice in it and feel grateful that
we belong to this Church. That should be the normal result of
theological study in our Church. But such a conscious adherence
to the Lutheran form of Christianity is conditioned by the fact
that we live in a Lutheran environment and have behind us a
church history moulded by the Lutheran Reformation. A
Methodist or a Roman Catholic who undertakes a similar study
will, in the normal way, come to set store by the distinctive
character of his own church.

Thus the differences existing within contemporary Christianity
spring largely from historical causes. We have inherited the
disunity prevalent among our forefathers. We carry our history
with us and have no alternative. At the same time we should
also gratefully acknowledge our history.

The psychology of the various nations has also helped to
determine the course of development. The special nature of the
Roman Catholic Church has been determined by the national
character of the Latin peoples. The English national character
has played a part in moulding the distinctive character of the

Church of England. The emergence of the Pentecostal congregations was made possible by the conditions of American society. The schism between the Eastern and Western Churches which grew progressively wider from the later part of Antiquity onwards, through the early Middle Ages to the rupture of 1054, is due not only to political friction between Constantinople and Rome, or to controversial questions such as the *Filioque*, but also to a difference in the development of Eastern and Western forms of piety, and in the accentuation given to dogma, canon law and ritual. And this difference was largely conditioned by national character.

When we consider the matter in this way we can say that the existence of numerous churches and the great differences which exist between them are evidence of the universality and richness of the Gospel on the one hand and of the diversity between people, nations and environment on the other. The disparity arises from the fact that the Gospel has been heard and interpreted by people of vastly different outlooks. The radiance of the Gospel has been diffused through the many-sided prism of humanity and therefore appears as a spectrum with many different tones.

On this view we may say that the manifold blessings of Christ are not exhausted by a single creed. The churches supplement one another and we can only obtain an idea of the fulness of Christ by considering the whole of Christendom together.

This consideration can undoubtedly mitigate the scandal of the disunion of Christendom. But it is not wholly satisfactory. Taken in isolation, it leads to sheer relativism. Are Roman Catholicism and Quakerism equally valuable forms of Christianity which are to be explained solely by reference to the positions which they occupy in the Christian spectrum? And is disunity due only to factors of national psychology and to historical circumstances, on which we can pronounce no objective judgement, but only understand and explain?

No theological appraisal of church history can overlook the question of truth. We cannot merely say that all are right. There is something which is rightly called heresy, falsity, perversion of the Gospel, the diminution of the divine message by abstraction or its perversion by additions. It is clear that both parties could not be equally right in the great questions of the Reformation period, which gave rise to so much disruption between the churches.

When ministers of different denominations were brought together to serve as chaplains to the British Army during the First World War, a Roman Catholic priest was told by one of his colleagues that they had the same Lord, but that every one worshipped Him in his own way. He replied: 'I understand: we have the same Lord. You worship Him in your way—and I in His way.'

In this comment lies the theological problem inherent in the schismatic state of Christendom. We all have the same Lord, and the differences which exist between our respective forms of worship, faith and constitution are conditioned by history. But it does not follow from this that everything is equally good. There is something which may be called 'His Way.' It does not, however, fall within the province of Comparative Symbolics to decide what is right on the basis of the Bible, Christian Tradition and sound dogmatic principles. Its own task is rather to analyse, describe and understand the churches which comprise Christendom. The normative problem belongs to the field of systematic theology.

APPENDIX

ECUMENICAL APPROACHES

In various periods of Church History we discover attempts to reunite the Churches, to establish co-operation between them or to promote contact between individual Christians or groups within the Churches.

Several attempts were made during the Middle Ages to overcome the schism between the Churches of East and West, the most important of which resulted in the Council of Ferrara-Florence in 1438–39 and led to a short-lived reunion between the two Churches.

During the Reformation period some unsuccessful attempts were made to reunite the Lutherans with Rome or to promote unity between the various Reforming Movements. The religious policy of the Emperor Charles V had as its aim the reconciliation of the German Lutherans with Rome. His efforts led to a series of conversations on religion, and a compromise imposed by force during the Leipzig Interim of 1549. But the rupture could not be healed. Neither did the attempts made in 1529 to unite the Lutherans and the Zwinglians or at a later date the Lutherans and the Reformed lead to any more positive result.

The most interesting example of ecumenical activity in the sixteenth century took place in Poland, where John à Lasco (1499–1560) was the chief advocate of a union between the Protestant Churches. A conference held at Sendomir in 1570 resulted in a confederacy of the Lutheran, Reformed and Moravian Churches, but it lasted only for some seventy years and was dissolved in 1645.

In the seventeenth century barriers which were felt to be insurmountable began to be set up between the different confessions. Theological controversy became the normal (though not the only) form of intercourse between the Churches. A more irenic tradition was represented by the sixteenth-century humanists such as Desiderius Erasmus (c. 1466–1536), Sebastian

366

Castellio (1515–63) and Jacob Acontius (d. 1566). The programme of Erasmus was unfolded in his work *De sarcienda ecclesiae concordia* (1533), while the *Strategemata Satanae* (1565) of Acontius came to exercise considerable influence on later generations. The principal thesis of the latter work was that, while the fundamental Christian doctrines were common to all Churches, they were induced by a strategem of the Devil to believe that those which were in dispute among them were in fact the most important.

This tradition was carried on by Georg Calixtus who developed the concept of the *consensus quinquesaecularis*, a common heritage passed down from the Church of the first five centuries which he advocated as the basis for mutual recognition between the Churches. During the seventeenth century the ecumenical ideal had an active ambassador in the person of the Scot, John Dury (1595–1680), who, through personal contact and travels, tried to unite Anglican, Lutheran and Reformed churchmen in the face of stiff opposition.

In the same century there were occasional contacts between the Church of England and the Orthodox Churches. If, however, High Church Anglicans had considerable sympathy with Orthodoxy, other Anglicans representing different traditions recognized their kinship with the Reformed Churches.

In the following century both Pietism and the Enlightenment in their respective ways prepared the ground for renewed approaches between the Churches. The age of the Enlightenment played its part in breaking down confessional barriers by giving prominence to the common elements of Christianity and the broad truths of natural religion at the expense of confessional differences. The common truths of Christianity were regarded as the fundamental doctrines. A scholar like Gottfried Leibniz (1646–1716), for example, negotiated with leading Roman Catholic theologians on conditions for reunion. Pietism, on the other hand, gave precedence to life over doctrine, and led to a considerable degree of fellowship between members of different confessions. Co-operation between the Churches could even be achieved in practical activities such as missionary work among the heathen. A typical example was the co-operation established in India through the efforts of Heinrich Wilhelm Ludolf

(1655–1712) between the Danish State Church Mission, the Halle Mission and the Society for the Promotion of Christian Knowledge.

New conditions for ecumenical co-operation emerged during the nineteenth and twentieth centuries. During this period a number of revival movements crossed national frontiers and the traditional lines of division between the Churches. In the Churches in which it has been accepted the historical study of the Bible has had the effect of weakening theological differences. Again research into the history of dogma helped to lay bare the historical background of inherited doctrinal differences. Intercourse between the nations, made possible by greatly improved means of communication, was becoming more widespread. A new internationalism emerged which found expression in a large number of international congresses and organizations of various kinds. Progress in this field can be measured by a comparison of the number of international congresses and meetings which took place at different periods. Between 1840 and 1860 twenty-eight meetings of this nature took place. Between 1900 and 1910 the number had risen to nearly eight hundred.

Yet during this period, in addition to these factors which favoured the emergence of the ecumenical movement, other tendencies can be noted which told in the opposite direction. The most important of these was the new confessionalism which emphasized the distinctive features of particular Churches, and gave rise to an attitude of reserve towards other confessions. This reaction from the non-confessional attitude prevalent during the age of the Enlightenment and of Pietism can be seen in the orthodox Neo-Lutheranism of Germany and Scandinavia about 1850 and the almost contemporary Oxford Movement in England. Another important factor was the marked nationalism of the nineteenth and twentieth centuries and the frequent antagonism between the nations, which only served to deepen the divisions between their respective Churches.

During this period three kinds of ecumenical approach and contact can be distinguished:

1. Personal encounters through voluntary inter-denominational organizations such as the Y.M.C.A.

2. Official approaches between the Churches with the aim of federal or organic union.

3. Practical co-operation between the Churches.

All three approaches have formed the basis for the modern ecumenical movement of the present century.

1. As we have seen, the revival movements of the nineteenth century often surmounted the barriers which separated the Churches, and produced a sense of fellowship between Christians belonging to different communions. These contacts also led to the establishment of a number of international and inter-denominational organizations.

Between 1840 and 1850 there was a widespread desire for the formation of a world federation of 'genuine Protestants,' which led to the formation of the Evangelical Alliance in London in 1846. It had an individual membership and represented a non-confessional, anti-liberal and (not least) an anti-Catholic outlook. Membership was based upon the acceptance of the Scriptures as the sole authority, the doctrine of the Trinity, the two Gospel Sacraments, the total depravity of man and Justification by Faith alone. The movement won considerable support in the English-speaking world, but the Lutheran Churches stood rather aloof. The Alliance held a number of World Congresses, of which the most recent took place in 1907, but since that date it has suffered a continuous decline.

The Y.M.C.A. (Young Men's Christian Association) was founded in London in 1844 as an English organization composed of Christian young men of different Churches. It had as its basis a religious fellowship worked out in practice in daily life rather than unity in doctrine. The experiment was copied in other countries, and in 1855 the World's Alliance of Young Men's Christian Associations was founded at the time of the World Exhibition held at Paris. It took as its doctrinal basis the acknow-ledgement of Jesus Christ *comme Sauveur et Dieu* ('as God and Saviour' in the English version). This 'Paris basis,' as it was called, is still maintained, and was destined to exert considerable influence on the ecumenical movement. The Y.M.C.A. has come to be of great significance for the consciousness of Christian unity.

A corresponding world-wide movement was the Y.W.C.A. (Young Women's Christian Association). The first national association was founded in London in 1855, but the World's Young Women's Christian Association was constituted as late as 1894.

Christian student associations had appeared in many universities between 1870 and 1890 as a result of revival movements. They too sought contact on an international basis, and during a conference of Christian Students at Vadstena in Sweden in 1895, the World's Student Christian Federation was formed. Its avowed aim was 'to lead students to become disciples of Jesus Christ as the only Saviour and God,' a formula clearly under the inspiration of the 'Paris basis' of the Y.M.C.A. In its early years the new movement fostered an entirely undenominational form of Christianity, but in most countries it became more closely associated with the Churches in course of time. While, however, the national federations tended to become more confessional in character, its international and interdenominational contacts were continued and maintained. The Student Christian Movement became the training ground of many of the men who were to assume leadership in the ecumenical movement from 1910 onwards.

In the course of time a cleavage occurred in Christian student circles, and some groups, partly of a more confessional character and partly of a conservative and pietistic outlook, reacted against the liberal tendencies of the Student Christian Movement. Independent organizations therefore grew up which formed an international organization of their own in 1947 under the title of the 'International Fellowship of Evangelical Students.'

All these organizations drew their support either exclusively or mainly from the Protestant world. With very few exceptions, Roman Catholics did not participate. On the other hand, the Y.M.C.A. and the Y.W.C.A. found some adherents in Orthodox countries, and a Russian branch of the Student Christian Movement was affiliated to the Federation in 1913, and still continues among Russians in exile from their own country.

Other world organizations of an ecumenical nature were formed with membership on an individual basis. Thus the Christian Endeavour Movement began in America in 1881 as a pietistic counterblast to the Y.M.C.A. Its aim was to bring young people together on the basis of wholehearted surrender to Christ, and a rule of prayer and Bible-reading. It has held a number of world conferences, but has made little headway during the past few decades.

The world congresses held by liberal Churchmen (of which the first was held in 1901) were of a different character. The initiative was taken by the American Unitarians, but other theologians took part, especially from Germany.

The movement known as the Oxford Group (renamed the Moral Rearmament Association after the Second World War), which began about 1920, is a non-denominational movement which has also helped to arouse a consciousness of Christian unity. Its connection with the Churches varies somewhat from country to country, and, in any case, it appeared too late to be considered one of the roots of the ecumenical movement.

2. Official approaches between the Churches have one of two aims. Their objective may either be federal unity, the combination for the purpose of co-operation of Churches which still preserve their independence as separate entities, and their distinctive constitution, doctrine and ways of worship, or organic unity with a reciprocal acceptance of clergy and communicants and, in some cases, a common system of Church government.

A further classification of such official approaches may be made under three heads:

(a) international unions on a confessional basis;
(b) the union of Churches within a single country, interconfessional, but national; and
(c) a union which is both interconfessional and international.

Since 1867 the Anglican Communion has had a bond of union in the *Lambeth Conferences* in which Anglican bishops from all over the world participate. They are held in Lambeth Palace, the London seat of the Archbishop of Canterbury, and are normally held every ten years. Since the member Churches retain their independence while possessing complete interchangeability of clergy and communicants, the resolutions of the

Conference are not by themselves binding upon all the constituent Churches. They, nevertheless, possess great moral authority throughout the whole Anglican Communion.

The Reformed Churches have a corresponding organ in the *World Alliance of the Reformed Churches holding the Presbyterian System* founded in 1875. Since 1881 the Methodists have had their *Ecumenical Methodist Conferences*. Similar international federations are the *International Congregational Council* dating from 1891 and the *Baptist World Alliance* founded in 1905. All these federations have held a number of World Conferences.

The Lutherans were the last of the Evangelical Churches to establish a world organization. From 1868 the German Lutherans had a federal organization in the *Allgemeine evangelisch-Lutherische Konferenz*, which became a world organization at its first meeting outside Germany at Lund in Sweden in 1901. It was reorganized as the *Lutheran World Federation* in 1947, with its headquarters at Geneva.

All these federations are expressions of federal unity between Churches with the same doctrinal basis.

The classical example of the establishment of organic unity on a confessional and national basis comes from the Church History of *Scotland* during the present century. From the middle of the nineteenth century three Presbyterian Churches had existed side by side in Scotland, the Church of Scotland (the national Church), the Free Church of Scotland dating from 1843, and the United Presbyterian Church, formed in 1847 by the union of two earlier Free Churches. The last two were combined in 1900 to form the United Free Church of Scotland, and in 1909 negotiations for reunion with the national Church began which reached their final completion in 1929.

In *England* the situation was different. Here 'Home Reunion' would involve a fusion between the Church of England and the Free Churches with a markedly different constitution, doctrine and way of worship. Interest was shown in the question from about 1870 onwards, but the difficulties proved formidable. An unofficial Free Church Council was formed in 1895, and reorganized in 1919 as the official Federal Council of Evangelical Free Churches, of which most of the English Free Churches are members. As its name implies, it represents a federal form of union. In 1942 the British Council of Churches was established to promote co-operation between the two national Churches of England and Scotland and a number of Free Churches at work in Great Britain. Even the Unitarians are represented, and a number of interdenominational associations such as the Y.M.C.A. and the Y.W.C.A. also send delegates.

As the result of political developments in *Germany* there came into being a number of independent *Landeskirchen*. The Prussian National Church, composed both of Lutherans and Reformed (the former in a substantial majority), was established by Royal Command in 1817. This example of organic union was followed by some other German States, but provoked a good deal of animosity in confessional quarters. Conferences at which all the Evangelical *Landeskirchen* were represented were held from 1848 onwards, and led in 1922 to the formation of *Der deutsche evangelische Kirchenbund*, which was reorganized after the Second World War as *Die evangelische Kirche in Deutschland*. Despite its name it represents a federal union in which the constituent Churches preserve their autonomy, and it is constantly impeded by a certain tension between its Lutheran and Reformed elements.

In the *United States* both types of approach have met with a certain measure of success. In 1939 the three largest Methodist Churches combined to form the Methodist Church, while the *Federal Union of the Churches of Christ in America*, established in 1908, was reorganized in 1950 under the name of the *National Council*. The Anglican and Lutheran Churches with their pronounced confessional consciousness did not join the National Council until a late stage of its development.

In *Canada* the Methodist, Presbyterian and Congregational Churches were brought together in 1925 in a form of organic union in the *United Church of Canada* which confesses general Protestant principles.

In virtue of its special character, the Anglican Communion has shown a particular interest in ecumenical approaches of an official and ecclesiastical character with the aim of establishing Intercommunion on the basis of a mutual recognition of Orders. In 1888 the Lambeth Conference formulated the conditions for the Reunion of the Churches under four heads which later came to be known as the *Lambeth Quadrilateral*:

  (*a*) The Holy Scriptures of the Old and New Testaments as 'containing all things necessary to salvation,' and as being the rule and ultimate standard of faith.

  (*b*) The Apostles' Creed, as the Baptismal Symbol; and the Nicene Creed, as the sufficient statement of the Christian Faith.

  (*c*) The two Sacraments ordained by Christ Himself—Baptism and the Supper of the Lord—ministered with unfailing use of Christ's woids of Institution, and of the elements ordained by Him.

  (*d*) The Historic Episcopate, locally adapted in the methods of its administration to the varying needs of the nations and peoples called of God into the Unity of His Church.

The term 'The Historic Episcopate' is interpreted by the Unity Committee of the Lambeth Conference of 1930 as synonymous with the continuity of episcopal consecrations within the Apostolic succession, but the Anglican Communion has never officially committed itself to any single explanation of its theological significance.

The Lambeth Conference of 1920 issued an *Appeal to All Christian People* on the basis of the Lambeth Quadrilateral in a slightly revised form. In this document the Anglican bishops 'acknowledge all those who believe in our Lord Jesus Christ, and have been baptized into the name of the Holy Trinity, as sharing with us membership in the universal Church of Christ which is His Body.' The ideal of unity is defined as 'the visible unity of the whole Church,' and involves 'an outward, visible and united society, holding one faith, having its own recognized officers, using God-given means of grace, and inspiring all its members to the world-wide service of the Kingdom of God.' In this 'reunited Catholic Church' all the spiritual resources of the Churches in separation would become the common property of the whole Church. 'Within this unity Christian Communions now separated from one another would retain much that has long been distinctive in their methods of worship and service.' But a common 'ministry acknowledged by every part of the Church as possessing not only the inward call of the Spirit, but also the commission of Christ and the authority of the whole body' was considered necessary. They went on to claim that the Episcopate was 'the one means of providing such a ministry.'

They had no desire to 'call in question for a moment the spiritual
reality of the ministries of those Communions which do not
possess the Episcopate' and they 'thankfully acknowledge that
these ministries have been manifestly blessed and owned by the
Holy Spirit as effective means of grace.' They also admit that
these Churches represent spiritual resources and elements of truth
which apart from their existence would have been obscured or
disregarded. But they claim that episcopacy is the best medium
for affirming the unity of the Church.

Anglican attempts to establish official contact with the Roman
Catholic Church received a decisive rebuff at the hands of
Leo XIII, who declared Anglican Orders invalid in the Papal
Bull *Apostolicae Curae* of 1896, and thereby rejected its claim to
Catholicity. Later contacts have been confined to unofficial
consultations such as the Malines Conference of 1921–25,
approaches of a private nature and occasional co-operation on
practical questions not involving matters of faith or doctrine.

Relations with the Orthodox Churches have had a happier
history. The Lambeth Conference of 1908 made the way clear
for members of these Churches to receive the Holy Communion
in Anglican churches. As, however, members of the Orthodox
Church are not permitted to communicate outside their own
Church, this measure was only of significance in providing
evidence of the Anglican attitude. No corresponding action was
taken on the Orthodox side. In 1922, however, the Ecumenical
Patriarchate of Constantinople recognized Anglican Ordinations
as valid, and similar action was taken by the Orthodox Churches
of Jerusalem, Alexandria and Cyprus, and by the Church of
Rumania. Such expressions of opinion on the part of individual
Patriarchates or national Churches do not, however, possess the
binding force of the decisions of an ecumenical council.

Among the Evangelical Churches, the Scandinavian national
Churches occupy a special position as episcopal Churches. The
first approaches were made to the Church of Sweden by the
Lambeth Conference, which in 1920 passed some resolutions on
the relations to this Church. The standing of its ministry was
recognized and it was recommended that members of this Church
should be admitted as communicants. It was also suggested that
Anglican bishops should accept any invitation from the Swedish

side to take part in an episcopal consecration. The Swedish Bishops' Conference in 1922 responded by adopting a similar attitude, although pointing out that the Church of Sweden practised full Intercommunion with all other Lutheran Churches, irrespective of their being episcopal Churches or not.

Negotiations with the Lutheran Church of Finland in 1934 resulted in a Report which was submitted to the Convocations of Canterbury and York in the following year. These recommended that members of the Church of Finland might be admitted to Communion in the Church of England provided that they were communicants cut off from their own Church. It was also recommended that a future invitation to take part in Finnish consecrations should be accepted. At a later stage, similar resolutions were passed on the Churches of Latvia and Esthonia after negotiations in 1938.

From the Anglican point of view the Churches of Denmark, Norway and Iceland presented a more difficult case as episcopal Churches outside the Apostolic Succession in the Anglican sense. Official negotiations with these Churches took place in Oslo in 1951, and the Report issued from these conversations was brought before the Convocations in 1954. The Convocations passed resolutions which recommended 'That baptized and communicant members of the Churches of Denmark, Norway and Iceland, when in England and cut off from the administration of their own Churches may be welcomed to receive Holy Communion in the Church of England.' On the same occasion, a resolution was passed 'That members of the Church of Sweden, qualified to receive the Sacrament in their own Church, should be admitted to Holy Communion in ours' (text of the Canterbury resolution). There is a slight difference in the wording, inasmuch as the principle of emergency is mentioned in the resolution dealing with the Churches of Denmark, Norway and Iceland.

Nothing is said in any of these resolutions about Anglicans receiving Communion in other Churches. Most Anglicans finding themselves in Sweden or Finland will certainly feel themselves free to accept the invitation of these Churches to receive the Sacrament at their altars, whereas Anglicans in the other Scandinavian countries may not feel thus free. Their attitude will in this case depend on their individual approach and does not represent any formal decision taken by the Church of England or other Churches of the Anglican Communion.

Since its organization in 1872, the Old Catholic Church has shown keen interest in ecumenical contacts. In 1874 and the following year it held two 'union congresses,' as they were called, in which Anglican and Orthodox Churchmen took part. As early as 1888, the Lambeth Conference admitted Old Catholics to the Holy Communion. Full Intercommunion was not, however, attained until 1932.

3. The policy of practical collaboration has resulted in a number of enterprises in which co-operation has taken place between individuals or groups within the Churches, or between the Churches themselves.

The pioneer of this policy was the Bible Society movement. In 1804 the *British and Foreign Bible Society* was founded. Here members of different Protestant Churches could co-operate in a common task. To avoid difficulties it was decided that the Society should only publish Bibles or Biblical texts without commentary. The problem of the Old Testament Canon was decided in 1826 in favour of the Reformed practice of omitting the Apocrypha.

The missionary revival at the beginning of the nineteenth century was largely non-denominational in character. Thus the London Missionary Society founded in 1795 was originally unconnected with any particular Church, though later its ties with the Congregationalist Churches were greatly strengthened. As Germany had no colonies, German Lutheran missionaries at first did service with English societies, but the new wave of confessionalism from about 1830 onwards led to a new emphasis upon the denominational character of missionary work.

In the mission field itself the problem of co-operation arose when missionaries of different Churches came to work in the same area. The minimum measure of co-operation consisted in avoiding the opening of new work in places where other Churches were already engaged, and in defining geographical boundaries between the fields of activity of different Churches. The first agreement of this character was reached in 1838.

A further stage was marked by conferences of a local or

regional character attended by representatives of various missions
and by co-operation in the translation of the Bible and the
establishment of schools and hospitals. Churches which were
closely akin to one another sometimes even combined in a
federal or organic union.

Co-operation in the mission field naturally led to similar
measures in the home country. Joint Councils of missionary
societies were established in particular countries, such as Germany
in 1885 and America in 1907. Important conferences were held
and magazines published on a joint basis. In America conferences
of this kind began in 1893.

In 1910 a world conference of missionary societies was held in
Edinburgh, which proved to be of the greatest significance, not
only for missionary work but also for ecumenical relations as a
whole. All evangelical missions of any importance as well as the
younger Churches were represented. It was, in fact, the first
Evangelical meeting of a really ecumenical nature which had
ever been held. From 1921 its standing committee was called the
International Missionary Council, and represented a permanent
organ for ecumenical consultation with regard to the missionary
activity of the Evangelical Churches. Similar world conferences
have been held at Jerusalem in 1928, at Tambaram in 1938, at
Whitby (Canada) in 1947, at Willingen (Germany) in 1952,
and in Ghana in 1958.

Another important factor in the development of the ecumenical movement lay in co-operation in humanitarian and social
work. The Red Cross was founded in 1863 under Christian
inspiration, but developed into a secular humanitarian organization. The Temperance Movement was originally connected
with the Evangelical Revival both in England and America, but
has undergone a similar change. Again, the movement for world
peace was to a great extent inspired by, and supported by, the
Churches. Plans for an International Christian Peace Conference
matured in 1914 at the same time as the outbreak of the First
World War.

4. The modern ecumenical movement was heralded by the
World Missionary Conference at Edinburgh in 1910 and the
ecumenical Peace Conference at Constance in 1914. The latter

deal with dogmatic questions nor frame canons, but only concern meeting set up a permanent organization known as the *World Alliance for Promoting International Friendship through the Churches.* In the period between the wars it ranked with the two movements of Faith and Order and Life and Work as one of the three main organs of ecumenical work, but in the course of time it became completely overshadowed and has virtually lost its significance since the Second World War.

The young American bishop, Charles Brent (1862–1929), who was present at the Edinburgh Conference, conceived the idea that, if it was possible for the Churches of Christendom to confer together on problems of missionary work, they should be able to discuss in a similar spirit the questions which confronted them at home, not only on matters in which they were united, but also on those in which their widest differences seemed to lie. He became a tireless advocate for the cause of a world conference of all churches which acknowledged Christ as Saviour and God for the discussion of matters of Faith and Order. He had in mind a conference of official representatives of the Churches, and his aim was in close harmony with the Lambeth Appeal of 1908.

The outbreak of the First World War was destined to make the establishment of ecumenical contacts extremely difficult. During this period the leading champion of the ecumenical idea was Nathan Söderblom who became Archbishop of Uppsala in Sweden in 1914. His position as Primate of a Lutheran Church in a neutral country, a Church whose special character places it midway between the right and left wings of Christendom, presented him with unique opportunities which he regarded as a duty to exploit to the full. These were reinforced by his remarkable personal gifts and his wholehearted devotion to the ecumenical cause which made him the genius of the movement.

During the war, Söderblom's efforts bore comparatively little fruit. There were no joint statements made by the Churches and no conferences apart from one held in 1917 between Churchmen from neutral countries. But owing to his tireless activity the foundations of later developments were laid. The idea of cooperation between all the Christian Churches in their common task gradually gained ground. The aim of Söderblom was an ecumenical conference corresponding to the Councils of the

Early Church with the important difference that it should neither itself with ethical problems and the application of the Christian message to social and economic questions. He spoke of a unifying ethical Creed which would inevitably emerge.

During the period after the First World War, ecumenical discussion turned on the two alternatives of Faith and Order, and Life and Work. Two different paths leading towards the attainment of unity in the Church could be followed. The two movements had different roots. The background of Faith and Order is to be found in the Lambeth Quadrilateral, the Anglican interest in organic union and the Edinburgh Conference, while the background to Life and Work lay in the Christian social movements, the Church's movement for peace and the attempt of the Liberal Protestant theology to find Christian unity in the sphere of practical ethics rather than in formulations of doctrine, as well as in the misery arising out of and following the war.

There were many difficulties to be overcome, longstanding antagonisms between the Churches, wide differences in Faith and Order, the fresh wounds of the war, the general lack of interest displayed by Church people as a whole and the refusal of many ecclesiastics to accept the ecumenical ideal.

The Life and Work Movement was the first to put into effect its plans for an ecumenical conference. This was held at Stockholm in August 1925 and was attended by six hundred delegates from the non-Roman Catholic Churches of Christendom. The Orthodox Churches were strongly represented together with the whole of the Protestant world. An invitation to participate was extended to the Roman Catholic Church, but was refused on the ground that the unity of the Church can only be realized through a reconciliation with Rome.

The subjects discussed at Stockholm covered four topics:

1. The Church and Economic and Industrial Problems (Property, Industry and Unemployment).
2. The Church and Moral and Social Problems (The Family and Home, Vocation, Crime and Leisure).
3. The Church and International Relations (Peace and War and Race).
4. The Church and Education.

Thus practical and ethical questions were the order of the day.

But faith and life cannot ultimately be separated, and the topic which Söderblom considered as the chief question in his book on the Conference was of a doctrinal character. On this matter there was a sharp difference of opinion. The extreme views were represented by some Americans and the German Lutherans. The former stood for a humanized and optimistic conception of the Kingdom of God upon earth; the Kingdom of God will come through Man's efforts when society is leavened by Christianity. The latter held a pessimistic view, and regarded the Kingdom of God in a purely eschatological light. The world in which we live is a sinful world, and it would be presumptuous to think that it can be transformed. The Kingdom of God will come when it is created by God at the end of time. There were, however, some intermediate points of view, and attempts were made to reconcile the intentions which lay behind these two extremes.

The climax of the Stockholm Conference was the celebration of the Holy Communion at which nearly all present partook of the Eucharist, Anglicans and Presbyterians, together with Lutherans.

The first World Conference of the Faith and Order Movement met at Lausanne in August 1927. Some four hundred delegates, representing a hundred different Churches, assembled there. The Orthodox were strongly represented while Roman Catholic participation had been forbidden by the Holy Office. The Chairman of the Conference was Bishop Brent.

The chief item on the agenda was 'The Call to Unity' and 'the Church's Message to the World.' The main differences of opinion on the question of Church Unity immediately became apparent. An Orthodox speaker maintained that a reunited Church must necessarily have a common dogmatic foundation as well as a common form of order. An Anglican claimed that unity in order was sufficient, and that this could be combined with considerable difference in the formulation of doctrine. The Lutherans stressed the need for unity in dogma, and regarded a common form of organization as of lesser importance. A representative of the Reformed Churches asserted that uniformity in faith and order was neither possible nor necessary, and that Christian unity should consist in the gathering of believers round the person of Jesus Christ.

Nevertheless, a surprising measure of agreement was achieved
in formulating the Church's Message to the World, and the
following Declaration was unanimously approved:

'The message of the Church to the world is, and must always
remain, the Gospel of Jesus Christ.

'The Gospel is the joyful message of redemption, both here
and hereafter, the gift of God to sinful man in Jesus Christ.

'The world was prepared for the coming of Christ through the
activities of God's Spirit in all humanity, but especially in His
Revelation as given in the Old Testament; and in the fulness of
time the eternal Word of God became incarnate, and was made
man, Jesus Christ, the Son of God, and the Son of Man, full of
grace and truth.

'Through His life and teaching, His call to repentance, His
proclamation of the coming of the Kingdom of God and of
judgement, His suffering and death, His resurrection and exaltation to the right hand of the Father, and by the mission of the
Holy Spirit, He has brought to us forgiveness of sins, and has
revealed the fulness of the living God, and His boundless love
toward us. By the appeal of that love, shown in its com-
pleteness on the Cross, He summons us to the new life of faith,
self-sacrifice, and devotion to His service and the service of men.

'Jesus Christ, as the crucified and the living One, as Saviour
and Lord, is also the centre of the world-wide Gospel of the
Apostles and the Church. Because He Himself is the Gospel, the
Gospel is the message of the Church to the world. It is more
than a philosophical theory; more than a theological system;
more than a programme for material betterment. The Gospel is
rather the gift of a new world from God to this old world of sin
and death; still more, it is the victory over sin and death, the
revelation of eternal life in Him who has knit together the whole
family in heaven and on earth in the communion of saints,
united in the fellowship of service, of prayer, and of praise.

'The Gospel is the prophetic call to sinful men to turn to God,
the joyful tidings of justification and of sanctification to those
who believe in Christ. It is the comfort of those who suffer; to
those who are bound, it is the assurance of the glorious liberty of
the sons of God. The Gospel brings peace and joy to the heart,
and produces in men self-denial, readiness for brotherly service,

and compassionate love. It offers the supreme goal for the aspirations of youth, strength to the toiler, rest to the weary, and the crown of life to the martyr.

'The Gospel is the sure source of power for social regeneration. It proclaims the only way by which humanity can escape from those class and race hatreds which devastate society at present into the enjoyment of national well-being and international friendship and peace. It is also a gracious invitation to the non-Christian world, East and West, to enter into the joy of the living Lord.

'Sympathizing with the anguish of our generation, with its longing for intellectual sincerity, social justice and spiritual inspiration, the Church in the eternal Gospel meets the needs and fulfils the God-given aspirations of the modern world. Consequently, as in the past so also in the present, the Gospel is the only way of salvation. Thus through His Church, the living Christ still says to men "Come unto Me. . . . He that followeth Me shall not walk in darkness but shall have the light of life." '

The Continuation Committee of the Stockholm Conference set up a study department which had its seat at Geneva from 1928 onwards. With this was also associated a centre for ecumenical activity, initially for the purpose of supplying information, conducting research and holding interdenominational conferences on a larger or smaller scale.

In 1930 this committee was reconstituted as the *Universal Christian Council for Life and Work*, a body of about one hundred members which was to meet every two years. Its most important meeting was held at Fanö in Denmark in 1934, at which, among other things, agreement was reached on the attitude to be adopted to the struggle over the Church which was being waged in Germany. It was also agreed to hold a new World Conference at Oxford in 1937. A research committee published several books, of which the most important were *Die Kirche und das Staatsproblem der Gegenwart* (1935) and *The Church and its Function in Society* (1937). The information service, an ecumenical seminary and a youth commission also became of great importance.

The Faith and Order Movement also had its own standing committee and promoted a number of conferences. Its theological commission proposed the 'Doctrine of Grace' as the next theme for ecumenical discussion and in 1932 published a work with this title. Later three commissions dealt with the following topics: 'The Ministry and Sacraments,' 'The Gospel and the Church' and 'Church Unity in Life and Worship.' In 1937 they produced three studies: *The Ministry and Sacraments, Die Kirche Jesu Christi und das Wort Gottes* and *A Decade of Objective Progress in Church Unity.*

The second World Conference on Life and Work was held at Oxford in July 1937 with 'Church, Community and State' as its principal topic. Between seven hundred and fifty and eight hundred attended, of whom about three hundred were delegates, one hundred were consultants, and the remainder visitors, youth representatives or officials (the latter in large numbers). It is noteworthy that on this occasion the Church of England invited every one to partake of the Holy Communion.

The second World Conference on Faith and Order was held at Edinburgh in August 1937, attended by about four hundred members from one hundred and twenty-three Churches and forty-three countries. It was divided into four sections: (1) The Grace of our Lord Jesus Christ; (2) The Church of Christ and the Word of God; (3) The Ministry and the Sacraments; and (4) The Church's Unity in Life and Worship. An extract from the statement on Church Unity issued by the Conference has already been quoted above (see page 362).

Experience of ecumenical work between 1930 and the outbreak of the Second World War showed that largely the same people had taken part in both types of conference, and that the two approaches were inseparable and convergent. Practical problems naturally led on to dogmatic questions, and matters of faith involved consequences in life. It was, therefore, natural that the experiment of treating them both separately should be followed by a union of the two lines. Both at the Oxford and Edinburgh Conferences it was resolved by an overwhelming majority to allow a fusion between the two movements, and to establish a World Council of Churches which was to continue and co-ordinate both lines of approach.

A draft Constitution for the World Council of Churches was provisionally approved at a small conference held at Utrecht in 1938, and the Council itself formed provisionally. Membership

was restricted to Churches and was not to be extended to individuals. Its doctrinal basis was defined as the 'acknowledgement of
our Lord Jesus Christ as God and Saviour.'

The World Council of Churches was officially inaugurated by
the next Ecumenical Conference which met at Amsterdam
between August 22nd and September 4th, 1948, after a delay
caused by the outbreak of war. The main topic of the Conference
was 'Man's Disorder and God's Design.' The ground was
prepared by some years of study on an international scale and by
the publication of four volumes dealing with different aspects of
the theme. The Conference was attended by representatives of
one hundred and forty-seven Churches from forty-four countries,
and on August 23rd the constitution of the World Council of
Churches was accepted by the Assembly.

The Council cannot be said to be an expression of the unity
of the whole of Christendom. The Roman Catholic Church
refuses to take part in the ecumenical movement. The Russian
Church is not a member, mainly for political reasons, and some
Protestant Churches have declined to join the Council on confessional grounds.

However, the formation of the Council provides the greater
part of non-Roman Catholic Christendom with a common
platform and an organ for collaboration between Churches
which for centuries have had no contact with each other. It has
also become upon occasion the means of expressing the common
mind of Christendom in the contemporary situation. Its establishment is evidence of the strong will to achieve unity which is so
marked a feature of the Church life of our time.

The World Council of Churches organized a third World
Conference on Faith and Order held at Lund in Sweden in 1952
and attended by about two hundred and fifty delegates. The
Armenian and Coptic Churches were represented as well as the
Mar Thoma Church of South India, and the young Churches of
Asia and Africa were much in evidence. The Churches in Eastern
Germany, Hungary and Czechoslovakia had been allowed by the
political authorities of their countries to send delegations. For
the first time in the history of the official conferences of the
Ecumenical Movement, Roman Catholic observers even partici-
pated in the discussion. No representatives of the Church of

O

Greece were present, but the Ecumenical Patriarchate of Constantinople sent a delegation. In preparation for the Conference three volumes of studies were published, on *Ways of Worship* (1951), *The Nature of the Church* (1952) and *Intercommunion* (1952). In these books, members of various Churches expound the tenets of the traditions to which they belong, but they also develop their own views. At the Lund Conference a serious attempt was made to pass beyond a mere study of the problems on the lines of comparative symbolics in which the positions of the various doctrinal traditions are stated and compared. The line of advance consists in a joint study of the problems themselves in the light of Biblical and Systematic Theology, to which the various doctrinal traditions may have important contributions to make.

The second plenary Assembly of the World Council of Churches was held at Evanston in the United States in August 1954. The Assembly was attended by five hundred delegates. The Churches of Asia were more strongly represented than at any previous meeting, the only absentees being the representatives of the Chinese Churches who were prevented from attending by political circumstances. The main theme of the Assembly was 'Christ—the Hope of the World,' and a report on this subject was commended to the Churches as a creative and provocative statement of the Christian hope in the present world. At the present time the World Council of Churches comprises one hundred and sixty-three Churches at work in forty-eight countries.

BIBLIOGRAPHY

THE number of books in languages other than English, French and German is restricted to a minimum. When a work occurs more than once its full title is in most cases given in the first section of the bibliography. Articles in encyclopaedias are listed when they are real monographs. Abbreviations: *ERE Encyclopaedia of Religion and Ethics*, *PRE Protestantische Realenzyklopädie*, 3rd ed.

Books covering the whole field or large parts of it

Recent books on 'Konfessionskunde': FERDINAND KATTENBUSCH, *Lehrbuch der vergleichenden Confessionskunde* (vol. i, Freiburg im Breisgau 1892: epoch-making; one volume only was published, dealing with Prolegomena and the Oriental Churches). E. F. KARL MÜLLER, *Symbolik* (Erlangen 1896; Reformed; deals with the four 'Hauptkirchen,' viz. the Orthodox, Roman Catholic, Lutheran and Reformed Churches, taking account almost exclusively of doctrinal issues). FRIEDRICH LOOFS, *Symbolik oder christliche Konfessionskunde* (vol. i, Tübingen 1902; the Creeds, the Oriental Churches, and Roman Catholicism; exact information and references to sources). WILLIAM A. CURTIS, *A History of Creeds and Confessions of Faith in Christendom and Beyond* (Edinburgh 1911). CHARLES A. BRIGGS, *Theological Symbolics* (Edinburgh 1914; doctrinal issues only, and confined to the Churches possessing confessional documents; valuable treatment of the history of dogma and theology). ALEXANDER STEWART, *Creeds and Churches* (London 1916; mainly interested in doctrine). WILHELM WALTHER, *Lehrbuch der Symbolik* (Leipzig 1924; deals with the four 'Hauptkirchen' only and pronounces judgements 'from Luther's standpoint'). KONRAD ALGERMISSEN, *Konfessionskunde* (Roman Catholic; in its first and second edition (Hanover 1930, 1939) an excellent handbook, with ample information and good bibliography; the third edition (Celle 1950) less valuable for the comparative study of Churches, as the book has been entirely re-written and turned into a handbook on Roman Catholic ecclesiology with some paragraphs inserted on the Churches; translations of the 1939 edition: *La Chiesa e le chiese*, Brescia 1942; *The Christian Denominations* (St. Louis 1945). HERMANN MULERT, *Konfessionskunde* (3rd ed. revised by E. SCHOTT, Berlin 1956; deals also with the left wing of Christendom: 'Konfessionskunde' in contradistinction to the old 'symbolics'). J. L. NEVE, *Churches and Sects of*

387

Christendom (3rd ed., Blair Nebraska 1952; Lutheran; the 'Konfessions kunde' viewpoint; historical information and statistical data, especially for the American Churches). WILHELM NIESEL, *Das Evangelium und die Kirchen* (Neukirchen 1953; Reformed, passing verdicts from a definite dogmatic point of view).

The great series *Ekklesia, eine Sammlung von Selbstdarstellungen der christlichen Kirchen*, ed. by FRIEDR. SIEGMUND-SCHULTZE (Gotha, later Leipzig, 1934–) deserves a place of its own. Each volume deals either with one Church or with the Churches of one country, which are described by members of the Church in question. Particular volumes will be mentioned in the appropriate places.

Sources: *The Creeds of Christendom, with a History and Critical Notes*, ed. by PHILIP SCHAFF (4th ed., 3 vols., New York 1905; confessional documents and dogmatic declarations from all the more significant Churches). *Corpus confessionum, Die Bekenntnisse der Christenheit*, ed. by C. FABRITIUS (Berlin 1931–; 3 vols. only have appeared; also includes Church ordinances, liturgies and official hymn-books). *Quellen zur Konfessionskunde*, ed. by K. D. SCHMIDT and W. SUCKER (Lüneburg 1954–).

Statistics: *World Christian Handbook*, ed. by KENNETH G. GRUBB and E. J. BINGLE (3rd ed., London 1959).

Books dealing with larger sections of the 'Konfessionskunde': Descriptions of the Church life of countries where many Churches are represented are useful for the comparative study of Churches. H. K. CARROLL, *The Religious Forces of the United States* (New York 1913). *Varieties of American Religion*, ed. by C. S. BRADEN (New York 1936). *Religious Bodies: 1936*, ed. by the United States' Bureau of Census (vol. i, ii, 1–2, Washington 1941; also contains descriptions of constitutional forms, doctrinal tenets and activities of all Churches and religious bodies in the U.S., written by representatives of the bodies themselves). W. L. SPERRY, *Religion in America* (Cambridge 1945). W. W. SWEET, *The American Churches* (London 1947). F. E. MAYER, *The Religious Bodies of America* 2nd ed. (Saint Louis 1956).

Bodies on the Left Wing of Christendom: P. SCHEURLEN, *Die Sekten der Gegenwart und neuere Weltanschauungsgebilde* (4th ed., Stuttgart 1930). ELMER T. CLARK, *The Small Sects in America* (New York 1949; valuable). J. BLACK, *New Forms of the Old Faith* (London and Edinburgh 1948). HORTON DAVIES, *Christian Deviations* (London 1954; critical). H. C. CHÉRY, *L'offensive des sectes* (Paris 1954).

Introductory Matter

The history and method of comparative symbolics: KATTENBUSCH (reviews the older German literature), E. F. K. MÜLLER, LOOFS, BRIGGS (valuable, with bibliography), MULERT.

'Church' and 'Sect': MAX WEBER, *Gesammelte Aufsätze zur Religions-soziologie*, vol. i (Tübingen 1920; epoch-making). ERNST TROELTSCH, *The Social Teaching of the Christian Churches* (Eng. trans., 2 vols., London 1931).

I. 1. *The Orthodox Church*

Reference should particularly be made to KATTENBUSCH, LOOFS and ALGERMISSEN.

W. GASS, *Symbolik der griechischen Kirche* (Berlin 1872; deals mainly with doctrine). B. J. KIDD, *The Churches of Eastern Christendom* (London 1927). S. ZANKOV, *The Eastern Orthodox Church* (Eng. transl., London 1929). A. FORTESCUE, *The Orthodox Eastern Church*, 2nd ed., (London 1929; Roman Catholic). S. BULGAKOV, *The Orthodox Church* (Eng. transl., London 1935). FR. HEILER, *Urkirche und Ostkirche* (Munich 1937; important). *Ekklesia*, vol. 45: *Die orthodoxe Kirche auf dem Balkan und in Vorderasien: Geschichte, Lehre und Verfassung* (Leipzig 1939; by a number of Greek scholars), vol. 46: *Die orthodoxen Patriarchate von Konstantinopel, Alexandrien, Antiochien, Jerusalem und das Erzbistum von Cypern* (Leipzig 1941). N. ZERNOV, *The Russians and their Church* (London 1945). R. M. FRENCH, *The Eastern Orthodox Church* (London 1951). R. JANIN, *Les églises orientales et les rites orientaux* (4th ed., Paris 1956; Roman Catholic).

Special features of the Eastern Church: A. VON HARNACK, *Der Geist der morgenländischen Kirche* (Berlin 1913, reprinted in *Aus der Friedens- und Kriegsarbeit*, Giessen 1916). F. GAVIN, *Some Aspects of Contemporary Greek Orthodox Thought* (Milwaukee 1923). N. VON BUBNOFF and H. EHRENBERG, *Östliches Christentum* (2 vols., Munich 1923–25; selections from Tchaadiev, Khomiakov Soloviev, Berdyaev, etc.). *Kirche, Staat und Mensch. Russisch-orthodoxe Studien* (Geneva 1937). V. LOSSKY, *The Mystical Theology of the Eastern Church* (London 1957). G. P. FEDOTOV, *A Treasury of Russian Spirituality* (London 1952).

Doctrinal documents: MANSI, *Sacrorum conciliorum nova et amplissima collectio* (vols. i-xii for the first seven Ecumenical Councils). ED. SCHWARTZ, *Acta conciliorum oecumenicorum* (1914–; the volumes which have appeared contain documents relating to the Councils of Ephesus

A.D. 431 and Chalcedon A.D. 451). T. H. BINDLEY and F. W. GREEN *The Oecumenical Documents of the Faith* (4th ed., London 1950, covering 325–451). E. J. KIMMEL and H. WEISSENBORN, *Libri symbolici ecclesiae orientalis* (2 vols., Jena 1843–50, with a Latin translation). PH. SCHAFF, *The Creeds of Christendom*, vol. ii.

Worship: The Liturgies of St. Basil and St. John Chrysostom in Greek are found in E. F. BRIGHTMAN, *Liturgies Eastern and Western*, vol. i (Oxford 1896). I. F. HAPGOOD, *Service Book of the Holy Orthodox Catholic Apostolic Church* (New York 1922; texts in translation). *A Manual of Eastern Orthodox Prayer* (London 1946). A. BAUMSTARK, *Die Messe im Morgenland* (Kempten 1906). A. SALAVILLE, *Liturgies orientales* (Paris 1932).

Monasticism: N. F. ROBINSON, *Monasticism in the Orthodox Churches* (London 1916).

Appendix: The Russian Sects

K. K. GRASS, *Die russischen Sekten* (2 vols., Leipzig 1907–14). F. C. CONYBEARE, *Russian Dissenters* (Cambridge, Mass. 1921). S. BOLSHAKOFF, *Russian Nonconformity* (Philadelphia 1950).

I. 2. Other Oriental Churches

ALGERMISSEN. FR. HEILER, *Urkirche und Ostkirche* (Munich 1937). A. FORTESCUE, *The Lesser Eastern Churches* (London 1913). F. MACLER, *Chrétientes orientales* (Paris 1923). R. JANIN, *Les églises orientales et les rites orientaux* (4th ed., Paris 1956). L. W. BROWN, *The Indian Christians of St. Thomas* (Cambridge 1956).

I. 3. The Roman Catholic Church

Reference should be made to ALGERMISSEN, and on the Protestant side E. F. K. MÜLLER, LOOFS (valuable), WALTHER, MULERT, NEVE. F. KATTENBUSCH, 'Römische Kirche,' *PRE* (1906). The great Roman Catholic encyclopaedias: *The Catholic Encyclopedia* (17 vols., New York 1907–22), *Dictionnaire de théologie catholique* (15 vols., Paris 1909–50), *Lexikon für Theologie und Kirche* (10 vols., Freiburg in Breisgau 1930–38); new edition 1957–), *Enciclopedia cattolica* (12 vols., Vatican City 1948–1954).

History: Standard works from a Roman Catholic point of view: *Histoire de l'Église depuis les origines jusqu'à nos jours*, ed. by A. FLICHE and V. MARTIN (Paris 1923–). F. MOURRET, *Histoire générale de l'Église* (2nd ed., 9 vols., Paris 1927–31; very readable). *Kirchengeschichte*, ed.

by J. P. Kirsch (Freiburg im Breisgau 1930–). F. X. Funk and K. Bihlmeyer, *Kirchengeschichte* (9th ed., 3 vols., Paderborn 1930–34). Sources: C. Mirbt, *Quellen zur Geschichte des Papsttums und des römischen Katholizismus* (4th ed., Tübingen 1924; sources from all centuries in the original languages, the selection slightly marked by a Protestant bias).

The special character of Roman Catholicism: J. A. Moehler, *Symbolik* (1832, 10th ed. 1921; classical work from the Roman Catholic side). K. von Hase, *Handbuch der protestantischen Polemik* (1862, 7th ed., 1900) (classical work from the other side). Fr. Heiler, *Der Katholizismus* (Munich 1923; standard work, combines criticism and sympathy). K. Adam, *The Spirit of Catholicism* (Eng. transl. London 1929; important reply to Heiler). E. Buonaiuti, *La chiesa Romana* (Milan 1933; excommunicated). K. Guggisberg, *Die römisch-katholische Kirche* (Zürich 1946; selection of texts in German transl., not free from Protestant bias). H. de Lubac, *Catholicisme* (5th ed., Paris 1952).

Papacy: E. Giles, *Documents illustrating Papal Authority A.D.* 96–454 (London 1952; English translations with brief comments). G. Krüger, *Das Papsttum* (2nd ed., Tübingen 1932; popular, Protestant). G. Castella, *Papstgeschichte* (3 vols., Zürich 1944–46; Roman Catholic). B. J. Kidd, *The Roman Primacy to A.D.* 461 (London 1936; Anglican). T. G. Jalland, *The Church and the Papacy* (London 1944; Anglican). E. Caspar, *Geschichte des Papsttums* (2 vols., Tübingen 1930–33; Protestant, an important scholarly work covering Antiquity and Early Middle Ages). J. Haller, *Das Papsttum* (5 vols., Stuttgart 1934–53). L. von Pastor, *The History of the Popes* (Eng. transl., 40 vols., London 1891–1953; standard work covering 1500–1800). J. Schmidlin, *Papstgeschichte der neuesten Zeit* (4 vols., Munich 1933–39, a continuation of von Pastor). L. von Ranke, *The History of the Popes* (Eng. trans., 2 vols., London 1851; classical, covering 1500–1800). G. Mollat, *La question romaine de Pie VI à Pie XI* (Paris 1932). R. Sencourt, *The Genius of the Vatican* (London 1935). Fr. Heiler, *Altkirchliche Autonomie und päpstlicher Zentralismus* (Munich 1941).

Official doctrinal documents: Mansi, *Sacrorum conciliorum nova et amplissima collectio* (53 vols., Leipzig 1901–27). J. Mainardi, *Bullarium magnum* (18 vols., Luxemburg and Rome 1733–68). C. Cocquelines, *Bullarium magnum* (28 vols., Rome 1739–62). A. Barbieri, *Bullarii Romani continuatio* (19 vols., Rome 1835–57, ends with 1838). *Acta*

Apostolicae Sedis (from 1909 onwards), the official bulletin of the Holy See, contains all decisions of the Curia. All the more important encyclicals are available in translations.

For the dogmatic decrees of the Council of Trent and the Vatican Council see P. SCHAFF, *The Creeds of Christendom*, vol. ii. A convenient selection of conciliary decrees and papal declarations will be found in H. DENZINGER, *Enchiridion symbolorum, definitionum et declarationum* (31st ed., Freiburg im Breisgau 1957; indispensable).

Expositions of Roman Catholic doctrine: M. J. SCHEEBEN, *Handbuch der katholischen Dogmatik* (4 vols., Freiburg im Breisgau 1873–1933). FR. DIEKAMP, *Katholische Dogmatik* (10th ed., 3 vols., Münster 1949–54). G. D. SMITH, *The Teaching of the Catholic Church* (2 vols., London 1948).

Church Order and Canon Law: *Corpus Iuris Canonici*, ed. by A. L. RICHTER and A. FRIEDBERG (2 vols., Leipzig 1879–81). *Codex Iuris Canonici*, issued in 1917 (many editions, the legislation in force). P. HINSCHIUS, *Das Kirchenrecht der Katholiken und Protestanten* (6 vols., Berlin 1870–97; important for the Middle Ages). O. J. REICHEL, *A complete Manual of Canon Law* (2 vols., London 1896). *Dictionnaire de droit canonique* (Paris 1935–). R. KÖSTLER, *Wörterbuch zum Codex Iuris Canonici* (Munich 1930).

Worship: H. LIETZMANN, *Ordo missae Romanus* (Bonn 1923; for a first orientation). P. BATIFFOL, *Leçons sur la messe* (Paris 1927; historical). A. FORTESCUE, *The Mass* (London 1917). L. EISENHOFER, *Handbuch der katholischen Liturgik* (2 vols., Freiburg im Breisgau 1932–33; standard work). J. A. JUNGMANN, *The Mass of the Roman Rite* (Eng. transl., 2 vols., New York 1951–55). P. OPPENHEIM, *Institutiones systematico-historicae in sacram liturgiam* (Torino 1939–). J. BRAUN, *Liturgisches Handlexikon* (2nd ed., Regensburg 1924).

Orders and congregations: M. HEIMBUCHER, *Die Orden und Kongregationen der katholischen Kirche* (3rd ed., 2 vols., Paderborn 1933–34).

Present-day hierarchy, activities, modern developments: *Annuario Pontificio* (Vatican City, yearly from 1850). *Mondo Cattolico* (Rome 1952; hierarchy, present status of orders and congregations, biographies). W. VON LOEWENICH, *Modern Catholicism* (Eng. transl., London, 1959; to which our chapter is greatly indebted; Protestant, well informed).

Appendix: The Uniate Churches of the East

R. JANIN, *Les églises orientales et les rites orientaux* (4th ed., Paris 1956). C. DE CLERCQ, *Les églises unies d'Orient* (Paris 1934). S. GASELEE in *Union of Christendom*, ed. by K. MACKENZIE (London 1938).

I. 4. The Old Catholics

E. K. ZELENKA, *Der Altkatholizismus* (5th ed., Freiburg 1924). *Ekklesia*, vol. 11: *Die altkatholische Kirche* (Gotha 1935; by a number of Old Catholic writers; important). C. B. Moss, *The Old Catholic Movement* (London 1949).

I. 5. The Catholic Apostolic Congregations (Irvingites)

E. MILLER, *History and Doctrines of Irvingism* (2 vols., London 1878). J. G. SIMPSON, 'Irving and the Catholic Apostolic Church,' *ERE* (1914; bibliography). P. E. SHAW, *The Catholic Apostolic Church* (New York 1946; bibliography).

I. 6. The Church of England and the Anglican Communion

H. H. HENSON *Anglicanism* (London 1921; Broad Church); *The Church of England* (Cambridge 1939). A. C. HEADLAM, *The Church of England* (2nd ed., London 1925). G. K. A. BELL, *A Brief Sketch of the Church of England* (London 1929). N. P. WILLIAMS and C. HARRIS, *Northern Catholicism* (London 1933; Anglo-Catholic). CECILIA M. ADY, *The English Church and How It Works* (London 1940). E. W. WATSON, *The Church of England* (Oxford 1944). C. GARBETT, *The Claims of the Church of England* (London 1947). A. T. P. WILLIAMS, *The Anglican Tradition in the Life of England* (London 1947). S. C. NEILL, *Anglicanism* (Pelican Book 1958). G. MAYFIELD, *The Church of England, Its members and its business* (Oxford 1958). G. F. S. GRAY, *The Anglican Communion* (London 1958).

History: *A History of the English Church*, ed. by W. HUNT and W. R. W. STEPHENS (8 vols., London 1899–1910). *A Dictionary of English Church History*, ed. by S. L. OLLARD, G. CROSSE, M. F. BOND (3rd ed., London 1948). S. C. CARPENTER, *Church and People 1789–1889* (London 1933). R. LLOYD, *The Church of England in the Twentieth Century* (2 vols., London 1947–50).

Statistics: *The Official Year Book of the Church of England* (yearly from 1883).

Church Order: F. MAKOWER, *The Constitutional History of the Church of England* (Eng. transl., London 1895). *The Apostolic Ministry*, ed. by K. E. KIRK (London 1946; Anglo-Catholic). *Episcopacy, Ancient and Modern*, ed. by C. JENKINS and K. D. MACKENZIE (London 1930; Anglo-Catholic). *The Historic Episcopate*, ed. by K. M. CAREY (London 1954). *Church and State. Report of the Archbishops' Commission* (2 vols., London 1935). *The Canon Law of the Church of England. Report of the Archbishops' Commission* (London 1947). C. GARBETT, *Church and State in England* (London 1950).

Doctrine: P. SCHAFF, *The Creeds of Christendom*, vol. iii (The 39 Articles). Commentaries: E. C. S. GIBSON, *The Thirty-nine Articles* (London 1898). B. J. KIDD, *The Thirty-nine Articles* (Oxford 1899). E. J. BICKNELL and H. J. CARPENTER, *A Theological Introduction to the 39 Articles* (London 1955). P. E. MORE and F. L. CROSS, *Anglicanism* (London 1935; documents from the seventeenth century). *The Lambeth Conferences 1867–1948* (London 1948). *The Lambeth Conference 1958. Doctrine in the Church of England. Report of the Archbishops' Commission* (London 1938).

Worship: F. PROCTER and W. H. FRERE, *A New History of the Book of Common Prayer* (London 1932). *Liturgy and Worship*, ed. by W. K. L. CLARKE and C. HARRIS (London 1933). A. G. HEBERT, *Liturgy and Society* (2nd ed., London 1936).

I. 7. *The Church of South India*

L. NEWBIGIN, *A South India Diary* (New York 1951); *The Household of God* (London 1953). A. E. J. RAWLINSON, *Church of South India* (London 1951). B. SUNDKLER, *Church of South India* (London 1954; standard work covering 1900–47, bibliography). M. WARD, *The Pilgrim Church* (London 1953; covering the period 1947–52).

I. 8. *The Lutheran Church*

Reference should be made to WALTHER, MULERT, NEVE, and E. F. K. MÜLLER (Reformed).

Ekklesia, vol. 5: *Die Kirche in Schweden* (Gotha 1935); vol. 6: *Die Kirche von Norwegen* (Gotha 1936); vol. 7: *Die Kirche in Danemark, die Kirche in Island* (Leipzig 1937); vol. 8: *Die Kirche in Finnland* (Leipzig 1938); vol. 9: *Die evangelischen Kirchen der Niederlande* (Gotha 1934); vol. 14: *Die evangelische Kirche in Österreich* (Gotha 1935); vol. 20: *Die Kirchen der Tschechoslowakei* (Leipzig 1937); vol. 21: *Die evangelischen Kirchen in Polen* (Leipzig 1938). *Kirchliches Jahrbuch 1945–1948*, ed. by

J. Beckmann (Gütersloh 1950). *Kirchliches Jahrbuch* (from 1949 yearly). *The Lutheran Churches of the World* 1952, ed. by A. R. Wentz (Geneva 1952). *Lutheran Churches of the World*, ed. by C. E. Lundquist (Minneapolis 1957).

Special features of Lutheranism: W. Elert, *Morphologie des Luthertums* (2 vols., Munich 1931–32; standard work on classical Lutheranism). H. Sasse, *Was heisst lutherisch?* (Munich 1934).

Confessional documents: *Die Bekenntnisschriften der evangelisch-lutherischen Kirche* (2nd ed., Göttingen 1952, with historical introductions and notes). G. Plitt, *Einleitung in die Augustana* (2 vols., Erlangen 1867–68). T. Kolde, *Die Augsburgische Konfession* (Gotha 1896; important for sources). Editions of the Augsburg Confession with notes by H. H. Wendt (1927) and L. Fendt (1930). E. Schlink, *Theologie der lutherischen Bekenntnisschriften* (Munich 1940). P. Tschackert, *Die Entstehung der lutherischen und der reformierten Kirchenlehre* (Göttingen 1910).

Worship: Y. Brilioth, *Eucharistic Faith and Practice* (London 1934). E. Yelverton, *The Swedish Rite* (London 1921). H. Holloway, *The Norwegian Rite* (London 1934). H. Asmussen, *Gottesdienstlehre* (3 vols., Munich 1936–37). G. Rietschel and P. Graff, *Lehrbuch der Liturgik* (2 vols., 2nd ed., Göttingen 1951–2). *Leiturgia*, ed. by K. F. Müller and W. Blankenburg (3 vols., Kassel 1954–56).

I. 9. The Moravians

G. Burkhardt, *Die Brüdergemeine* (2 vols., Gnadau 1905–12). H. Steinberg, *Die Brüderkirche in ihrem Werden und Sein* (Herrnhut 1921). O. Uttendörfer and W. E. Schmidt, *Die Brüder* (3rd ed., Gnadau 1922). *Corpus confessionum*, vol. x, 1 (Berlin 1936; church ordinances, catechisms, hymn-books). E. Langton, *History of the Moravian Church* (London 1956).

I. 10. The Reformed Church

Description, history, distribution: *Leben und ausgewählte Schriften der Väter und Begründer der reformierten Kirche* (10 vols., Elberfeld 1857–63; Zwingli, Calvin, Capito, Bucer, Bullinger, Olevianus, Ursinus, Oecolampadius, Vermigli, Beza, Knox). J. Dall, 'Presbyterianism,' *ERE* (1918). J. Moffatt, *The Presbyterian Churches* (London 1928). C. L. Warr, *The Presbyterian Tradition* (London 1933). G. D. Henderson, *Presbyterianism* (Aberdeen 1955). W. Hadorn, *Kirchengeschichte der reformierten Schweiz* (Zürich 1907). L. Knappert,

Geschiedenis der Hervormde Kerk (2 vols., Amsterdam 1911–12). H. J.
LANGMAN, *Kuyper en de Volkskerk* (Kampen 1950). I. RÉVÉSZ, S.
KOVATS, L. RAVASZ, *Hungarian Protestantism* (Budapest 1927). J. R.
FLEMING, *A History of the Church in Scotland* 1843–1874 (Edinburgh
1927); *A History of the Church in Scotland* 1875–1929 (Edinburgh 1933).
G. D. HENDERSON, *The Claims of the Church of Scotland* (London 1951).
R. E. THOMPSON, *A History of the Presbyterian Churches in the United
States* (3rd ed., New York 1907). A. C. ZENOS, *Presbyterianism in
America, Past, Present, and Prospective* (New York 1937). *Ekklesia*,
vol. 9: *Die evangelischen Kirchen der Niederlande* (Gotha 1934); vol. 10:
Die evangelischen Kirchen der Schweiz (Gotha 1935); vol. 20: *Die
Kirchen der Tschechoslowakei* (Leipzig 1937); vol. 21: *Die evangelischen
Kirchen in Polen* (Leipzig 1938).

Characteristic features: E. F. K. MÜLLER, WALTHER. W. MONOD,
Du protestantisme (Paris 1928; spiritualizing). A. DAKIN, *Calvinism*
(2nd ed., London 1941; doctrinal system, church order, ethos). A.
LECERF, *Études calvinistes* (Neuchâtel 1949). KARL BARTH, 'Das Schrift-
prinzip der reformierten Kirche,' *Zwischen den Zeiten* 1925. W. NIESEL,
Was heisst reformiert? (Munich 1934). MAX WEBER, *Gesammelte
Aufsätze zur Religionssoziologie*, vol. i (Tübingen 1920). E. TROELTSCH,
The Social Teaching of the Christian Churches (Eng. transl., 2 vols.,
London 1931).

Confessional documents: P. SCHAFF, *The Creeds of Christendom*,
vol. iii (the most complete collection). E. F. K. MÜLLER, *Die
Bekenntnisschriften der reformierten Kirche* (Leipzig 1903). W. NIESEL,
*Bekenntnisschriften und Kirchenordnungen der nach Gottes Wort reformierten
Kirche* (Munich 1938). Their history: SCHAFF, vol. i. A. STEWART,
Creeds and Churches (London 1916). J. PANNIER, *Les origines de la
Confession de foi et de la Discipline des Églises Réformées de France* (Paris
1936).

Doctrine: W. NIESEL, *The Theology of Calvin* (Eng. transl., London
1956). KARL BARTH, *The Knowledge of God and the Service of God
according to the Teaching of the Reformation* (London 1938). P. TSCHACK-
ERT, *Die Entstehung der lutherischen und der reformierten Kirchenlehre*
(Göttingen 1910).

Church Order and Legislation: J. L. AINSLIE, *The Doctrines of
Ministerial Order in the Reformed Churches of the 16th and 17th Centuries*
(Edinburgh 1940). J. A. HODGE, *What is Presbyterian Law?* (7th ed.,
Philadelphia 1894).

Worship: W. D. MAXWELL, *A History of Worship in the Church of Scotland* (London 1955).

Appendix i: The Waldensian Church

H. BÖHMER, 'Waldenser,' *PRE* (1908; bibliography). E. COMBA, *Storia dei Valdesi* (Torre Pellice 1930). A. A. HUGON, *Bibliografia Valdese* (Torre Pellice 1953).

Appendix ii: Puritanism as the Background of the Rise of New Religious Bodies

W. HALLER, *The Rise of Puritanism* (2nd ed., New York 1947). W. B. SELBIE, *Nonconformity, Its Origin and Progress* (London 1912). A. LANG, *Puritanismus und Pietismus* (Neukirchen 1941).

Social and political consequences: MAX WEBER, *Gesammelte Aufsätze*, vol. i (Tübingen 1920). E. TROELTSCH, *The Social Teaching of the Christian Churches* (Eng. transl., 2 vols., London 1931). R. H. TAWNEY, *Religion and the Rise of Capitalism* (London 1926). J. S. FLYNN, *The Influence of Puritanism on the Political and Religious Thought of the English* (London 1920). R. B. PERRY, *Puritanism and Democracy* (New York 1944). A. PEEL, *The Christian Basis of Democracy* (London 1943). G. P. GOOCH, *English Democratic Ideas in the Seventeenth Century* (2nd ed., Cambridge 1927).

I. 11. The Methodist Church

Origin and history: F. LOOFS, 'Methodismus,' *PRE* (1903; bibliography). W. J. TOWNSEND, H. B. WORKMAN, G. EAYRS, *A New History of Methodism* (2 vols., London 1909; standard work). M. EDWARDS, *After Wesley* (1791–1849) (2nd ed., London 1948); *Methodism and England* (1850–1932) (London 1943). E. J. DRINKHOUSE, *History of Methodist Reform* (2 vols., Baltimore 1899; the American schisms). J. M. BUCKLEY, *A History of the Methodists in the United States* (6th ed., New York 1907).

Characteristic features: J. S. SIMON and G. G. FINDLAY, 'Methodism,' *ERE* (1915). S. G. DIMOND, *The Psychology of the Methodist Revival* (London 1926). W. B. BRASH, *Methodism* (London 1928). H. BETT, *The Spirit of Methodism* (London 1937; important).

Doctrine and Church Order: *Doctrines and Discipline of the Methodist Church* 1956 (New York 1957). G. C. CELL, *The Re-discovery of*

398 CHRISTENDOM

John Wesley (New York 1935; a theological interpretation). W. E. SANGSTER, *The Path to Perfection* (London 1945). H. LINDSTRÖM, *Wesley and Sanctification* (Stockholm 1946).

I. 12. *The Congregationalist Churches*

Origin and History: F. LOOFS, 'Kongregationalisten,' *PRE* (1901; bibliography). F. J. POWICKE, 'Brownism,' and W. WALKER, 'Congregationalism,' *ERE* (1909, 1911; bibliography). C. BURRAGE, *The Early English Dissenters* (2 vols., Cambridge 1912). R. W. DALE, *History of English Congregationalism* (London 1907). W. B. SELBIE, *Congregationalism* (London 1927). G. F. NUTTALL, *Visible Saints. The Congregational Way* 1640–1660 (Oxford 1957). W. WALKER, *A History of the Congregational Churches in the United States* (6th ed., New York 1907). H. M. DEXTER, *Congregationalism as Seen in its Literature* (New York 1880).

Characteristic features, doctrine: W. WALKER, *The Creeds and Platforms of Congregationalism* (New York 1893); *The Validity of Congregational Ordination* (Hartford, Conn. 1898). R. W. DALE, *A Manual of Congregational Principles* (London 1884). C. J. CADOUX, *Catholicism and Christianity: A Vindication of Progressive Protestantism* (London 1928); *Essays Congregational and Catholic*, ed. by A. PEEL (London 1931). B. L. MANNING, *Essays in Orthodox Dissent* (London 1953).

I. 13. *The Baptist Churches*

History: R. J. SMITHSON, *The Anabaptists. Their Contribution to Our Protestant Heritage* (London 1935). W. T. WHITLEY, *A History of British Baptists* (2nd ed., London 1932). A. C. UNDERWOOD, *A History of the English Baptists* (London 1947; important). A. H. NEWMAN, *History of the Baptist Churches in the United States* (6th ed., New York 1915). *Seventh Day Baptists in Europe and America* (2 vols., Plainfield 1910). J. H. RUSHBROOKE, *The Baptist Movement in the Continent of Europe* (London 1923).

Distinctive character, doctrine, Church order: W. J. MCGLOTHLIN, *Baptist Confessions of Faith* (Philadelphia 1911; collection of official statements). SCHAFF, *The Creeds of Christendom*, vol. iii. Acts of the Baptist World Congresses (especially important: Stockholm 1923, Toronto 1928, Berlin 1934, Atlanta 1939). C. WILLIAMS and W. T. WHITLEY, *A Baptist Catechism* (London, no date). C. WILLIAMS, *Principles and Practices of the Baptists* (London 1903). H. WHEELER ROBINSON, *Baptist Principles* (London 1926); *The Life and Faith of the*

Baptists (London 1927). E. A. PAYNE, *The Fellowship of Believers: Baptist Thought and Practice Yesterday and To-day* (London 1952).

I. 14. *The Disciples of Christ*

H. L. WILLETT, 'Disciples of Christ,' *ERE* (1911). W. W. JENNINGS, *Origin and Early History of the Disciples of Christ* (Cincinnati 1919). W. E. GARRISON and A. T. DE GROOT, *The Disciples of Christ* (St. Louis 1948).

I. 15. *The Pentecostalists*

E. MOSIMAN, *Das Zungenreden geschichtlich und psychologisch untersucht* (Tübingen 1911). H. J. STOLEE, *Pentecostalism* (Minneapolis 1937; critical). D. GEE, *The Pentecostal Movement* (London 1949; Pentecostalist). N. BLOCH-HOELL, *Pinsebevegelsen* (Oslo 1956; standard work, bibliography).

I. 16. *The Salvation Army*

Biographies and memoirs: H. BEGBIE, *Life of William Booth* (2 vols., 2nd ed., London 1926). ST. J. ERVINE, *God's Soldier, General William Booth* (2 vols., London 1934). J. STRAHAN, *The Marechale* (15th ed., London 1930). BRAMWELL BOOTH, *Echoes and Memories* (2nd ed., London 1928); *These Fifty Years* (London 1929).

History: R. SANDALL, *The History of the Salvation Army* (3 vols., London 1947–55).

Distinctive character, practice: L. PETRI, *Frälsningsarmén* (Lund 1921; historical parallels).

I. 17. *The Plymouth Brethren (Darbyites)*

F. LOOFS, 'Darby,' *PRE* (1898; bibliography). J. McCULLOCH, 'Brethren (Plymouth),' *ERE* (1909; bibliography). W. B. NEATBY, *A History of the Plymouth Brethren* (London 1902). E. T. CLARK, *The Small Sects in America* (2nd ed., New York 1949).

I. 18. *The New Church, The Church of the New Jerusalem* *(Swedenborgians)*

S. TOKSVIG, *Emanuel Swedenborg* (New Haven 1948).

I. 19. *The Adventists*

F. LOOFS, 'Adventisten,' *PRE* (1896; bibliography). M. ELLSWORTH OLSEN, *A History of the Origin and Progress of the Seventh Day Adventists*

(2nd ed., Takoma Park 1926; Adventist). E. T. CLARK, *The Small Sects in America* (2nd ed., New York 1949; critical). L. R. E. FROOM, *The Prophetic Faith of Our Fathers* (4 vols., Washington 1946–54; standard work on the Millenarist interpretation of Holy Scripture in Church History and on the rise and development of Adventism).

I. 20. *The Society of Friends (Quakers)*

History: R. BUDDENSIEG, 'Quäker,' *PRE* (1905; bibliography). W. C. BRAITHWAITE, 'Friends, Society of,' *ERE* (1913; bibliography). T. E. HARVEY, *The Rise of the Quakers* (London 1905). W. C. BRAITHWAITE, *The Beginnings of Quakerism* (2nd ed., Cambridge 1955); *The Second Period of Quakerism* (London 1919). R. M. JONES, *The Later Periods of Quakerism* (2 vols., London 1921). E. RUSSELL, *The History of Quakerism* (New York 1943; bibliography).

Distinctive character, practice: *Christian Life, Faith and Thought in the Society of Friends* (London 1921). *Christian Practice* (London 1926). *Church Government* (London 1931). E. GRUBB, *What is Quakerism?* (3rd ed., London 1929). R. M. JONES, *The Faith and Practice of the Quakers* (7th ed., London 1949).

II. 1. *Unitarianism*

History: O. ZÖCKLER, 'Socin und der Socinianismus' and 'Unitarismus,' *PRE* (1906, 1908; bibliography). J. E. CARPENTER, 'Unitarianism,' *ERE* (1921). E. M. WILBUR, *A History of Unitarianism* (3rd ed., Cambridge, Mass. 1947; standard work); *A History of Unitarianism in Transylvania, England and America* (Cambridge, Mass. 1952).

Doctrine and distinctive character: W. C. BOWIE, *What do Unitarians believe and teach?* (London 1906). *A Free Religious Faith. A Report presented to the General Assembly of Unitarian and Free Christian Churches* (London 1945). J. MARTINEAU, *Study of Religion* (2 vols., Oxford 1888; a representative expression of Unitarianism).

II. 2. *Christian Science*

History: MARY BAKER EDDY's books *Science and Health*, 1875, and later editions), *Retrospection and Introspection* (1891), *Pulpit and Press* (1898), and *The First Church of Christ, Scientist* (1913). A. E. STETSON, *Sermons which Spiritually Interpret the Scriptures and Other Writings on Christian Science* (New York 1926; a collaborator, and later a rival, of Mrs. Eddy). S. WILBUR, *Life of Mary Baker Eddy* (St. Louis 1908; the official biography). G. MILMINE, *The Life of Mary Baker Eddy* (New York 1909; hostile). E. F. DAKIN, *Mrs. Eddy. The Biography of a Virginal Mind* (New York 1929; critical). L. P. POWELL, *Mary Baker Eddy* (New York 1930; authorized). A. JOHNSON, 'Eddy, Mary Baker,' *Dictionary of American Biography* (1931; critical). E. M. RAMSAY, *Christian Science and Its Discoverer* (Boston 1935; authorized).

Characteristic features: K. HOLL, *Der Szientismus* (Berlin 1918, reprint in his *Gesammelte Aufsätze zur Kirchengeschichte*, vol. iii). H. A. L. FISHER, *Our New Religion* (London 1929; critical).

II. 3. *Jehovah's Witnesses*

Primary sources: C. T. RUSSELL, *Studies in the Scriptures* (7 vols., New York 1886–1917). RUTHERFORD's writings (Bibliography in H. H. STROUP's book, see below).

Biography: E. S. BATES, 'Russell, Charles Taze,' *Dictionary of American Biography* (1935; critical).

Characteristic features: H. H. STROUP, *The Jehovah's Witnesses* (New York 1945; critical, well documented). R. PIKE, *Jehovah's Witnesses* (London 1954).

II. 4. *Mormonism*

Primary Sources: *The Book of Mormon* (1830). *Doctrine and Covenants* (1835); *The Pearl of Great Price* (1851).

History: *History of the Church of Latter-Day Saints*, ed. by B. H. ROBERTS (6 vols., Salt Lake City 1902–12; official). J. H. EVANS, *One Hundred Years of Mormonism* (Salt Lake City 1905). EDUARD MEYER, *Ursprung und Geschichte der Mormonen* (Halle 1912; sources and parallels, critical). J. F. SMITH, *Essentials in Church History* (13th ed., Salt Lake City 1953; a Mormon manual). W. A. LINN, *The Story of the Mormons* (New York 1923; critical). B. DE VOTO, 'Smith, Joseph,' and 'Young, Brigham,' *Dictionary of American Biography* (1935, 1936; critical, bibliography).

Doctrine: J. E. TALMAGE, *A Study of the Articles of Faith* (32nd ed., Salt Lake City 1955; Mormon dogmatics).

Supplement: Ecumenical Approaches

Bibliography: H. R. T. BRANDRETH, *Unity and Reunion* (London 1945).

Prehistory of the Ecumenical Movements: N. SMYTH and W. WALKER, *Approaches towards Church Unity* (New Haven 1919). N.

P

KARLSTRÖM, *Kristna samförståndssträvanden under världskriget* 1914–1918 (Stockholm 1947; to which our chapter is greatly indebted).

The Ecumenical Movement: L. HODGSON, *The Ecumenical Movement* (Sewanee 1951; covering the period 1910–50). *A History of the Ecumenical Movement* ed. by R. ROUSE and S. C. NEILL (London 1954; standard work).

The Ecumenical Conferences: *The Universal Christian Conference, Stockholm* 1925, ed. by G. K. A. BELL (London 1926). *World Conference on Faith and Order, Lausanne* 1927, ed. by H. N. BATE (London 1927). *Church, Community and State* (8 vols., London 1937; published in connection with the Oxford Conference 1937, vol. 8 containing the official Report). *Second World Conference on Faith and Order,* ed. by L. HODGSON (London 1938). *Man's Disorder and God's Design* (5 vols., published in connection with the Amsterdam Conference, 1948; vol. 5 containing the official Report, London 1949). *Lund, 1952: An Account of the Third World Conference on Faith and Order* (ed. by E. H. ROBERTSON (London 1952). *The Evanston Report: The Second Assembly of the World Council of Churches,* 1954, ed. by W. A. VISSER 'T HOOFT (London 1955).

Other texts: *Documents on Christian Unity,* ed. by G. K. A. BELL (4 vols., London 1930–58; comprises the period 1920–57). *Texte zur Geschichte der ökumenischen Bewegung,* ed. by K. BÖHME (Berlin 1948; a small collection of official statements).

Status and evaluations: *The Reunion of Christendom,* ed. by J. MARCHANT (London 1929). H. P. VAN DUSEN, *World Christianity: Yesterday, To-day, To-morrow* (New York 1947). K. S. LATOURETTE, *The Emergence of a World Christian Community* (New Haven 1949). L. A. ZANDER, *Vision and Action* (London 1952; Orthodox).

Other discussions of ecumenical problems: A. C. HEADLAM, *The Doctrine of the Church and Christian Reunion* (London 1923). *Union of Christendom,* ed. by K. MACKENZIE (London 1938; contributions from members of many Churches on the subject of organic union).

Roman Catholic evaluations: MAX PRIBILLA, *Um christliche Einheit. Stockholm-Lausanne-Rom* (Freiburg im Breisgau 1929). M. J. CONGAR, *Divided Christendom* (Eng. transl., London 1939). G. THILS, *Histoire doctrinale du mouvement oecuménique* (Louvain 1955). E. DUFF, *The Social Thought of the World Council of Churches* (London 1956).

Periodicals: *The Ecumenical Review* (Geneva 1948–), published by the World Council of Churches. *Irénikon* (Chèvetogne (1926–), published by Belgian Benedictines. *Istina* (1954–), published by French Dominicans.

INDEX OF PERSONS

Major, G., 211
Marheineke, P., 3
Maritain, J., 116
Martineau, J., 334
Mary (Queen), 142, 156
Mauriac, F., 105
Maurice, F. D., 283
Melanchthon, P., 190, 193, 203–4, 207–8, 211, 250, 314, 332
Methodius, St., 15, 29
Micklem, N., 286
Miller, W., 316–18
Milton, J., 262
Mogila, P., 18
Monod, F., 243
Mumford, C. (*see* Booth, Catherine)
Myconius, O., 250

Napoleon (Emperor), 243, 262, 307
Naylor, J., 324
Neiiendam, M., 305
Nestorius, 41
Newman, J. H., 48
Nikon, 36
Nitschmann, D., 236
Nordström, N. J., 296

Oecolampadius, 250
Olevianus, C., 250
Olga (Grand Duchess), 12
Oncken, J. G., 292
Origen, 24, 93
Osiander, A., 211
Owen, J., 281–2, 286–7

Parker, T., 335
Pascal, B., 314
Patrick, S., 143
Paul, St., 16, 57, 198, 312, 345
Paul, J., 303
Payne, E. A., 296
Pelagius, 19, 21
Penn, W., 324
Perronet, V., 268
Peter, St., 16, 350
Peter the Great (Czar), 13, 17–18, 37
Pethrus, L., 303
Pitt, W. (the elder), 144
Pius IV (Pope), 111
Pius VI (Pope), 103
Pius VII (Pope), 111
Pius IX (Pope), 111, 122, 127
Pius X (Pope), 48, 51, 70, 108–9, 113
Pius XI (Pope), 78, 104, 120
Pius XII (Pope), 106–7, 110–12, 115, 120, 122–4
Planck, G. J., 2
Polycarp, St., 94–5

Priestley, J., 334

Quimby, P., 337–8

Ramsey, A. M., 172
Reinkens, J. H., 128
Roberts, E., 300–1
Robinson, J., 281
Rupp, G., 231
Russell, C. T., 341–2, 345
Rutherford, J. F., 342–5

Sayers, D., 173
Schleiermacher, F., 103, 228, 240
Schott, A., 114
Schwenkfeld, C., 211
Seeberg, R., 229
Selivanov, 38
Sergius, 14
Serveto, M., 331–2
Seymour, W. J., 301
Simeon, C., 147
Simons, M., 290
Smale, J., 301
Smith, Emma, 351
Smith, Hiram, 351
Smith, J., 348–51, 353
Smith, U., 318
Smyth, J., 290–1, 294
Snow, E., 351–2
Söderblom, N., 231, 379–81
Soloviev, V., 23
Soubirous, B., 122
Sozzini, F., 332–3
Sozzini, L., 332
Spangenberg, A. G., 237–8
Spener, P. J., 224
Spurgeon, C. H., 292
Stange, C., 231
Stanley, H. M., 308
Stead, W. T., 308
Swedberg, J., 313
Swedenborg, E., 313–15
Sykes, N., 7

Taylor, J., 352
Tertullian, 68, 93
Thiersch, H., 134
Thils, G., 119
Thomas, St., 41
Thomas Aquinas, St., 51–3, 67, 101, 105–6, 356
Thomasius, C., 228
Thornton, L., 172
Tichon, 13
Torrey, R. A., 300
Troeltsch, E., 229
Twain, M., 350

INDEX OF PLACES

INDEX OF SUBJECTS

Creeds, as standards of doctrine, 18, 129, 144, 149, 176–8, 191, 202, 204, 285–6, 327, 334, 355, 357
in public worship, 25, 32–3, 50, 63, 86, 88, 91, 114, 136, 150, 160–2, 216, 233, 278
Crown Rights of the Redeemer, 244–5, 295
Culture, attitude to, 361
positive, 45, 147, 173–4, 197–8
negative, 346 (*see also* Asceticism, Puritanism)

Deacon, 25, 27–8, 33, 76, 114, 136, 166–7, 240, 258–9, 287
Dead, Prayers for, 17, 23, 33, 93, 151, 155
Dean (Provost), 167
Declaration, Savoy, 283, 287–8
Deification, doctrine of, 20–2
Deism, 334
Democracy (in Church Government), 265, 282–3, 285–6, 295
Diaspora activity (Moravian), 238
Didache, 68
Disciples of Christ, 298–9
Discipline of Secrecy, 48
Divorce, 78
Dominican Order, 50, 80, 86, 92, 100–3, 109, 112
Donatism, 62, 199
Drama Religious, 174

Easter, 30, 34, 81, 85, 87, 90–1, 114, 136, 148, 239
Anthem, 159
Candle, 85
École Biblique, 109
Ecstatic phenomena, 38, 131, 136, 300–2, 304
Ecumenical approaches, 366–78
attitude, 119–20, 135, 165, 171–2, 299
Councils, 16, 18, 24, 34, 153–4, 276, 375, 379–80
Movement, 120–2, 129, 177, 283, 285, 326, 361, 378–86
Education, religious, 104, 169, 210, 218, 229–30, 284
Elder, 136, 235, 237, 258–9, 281, 287, 299, 304, 325, 327, 353
Election, doctrine of (*see* Predestination)
Ember Days, 81
English Ladies, 102
Enlightenment, 2, 103, 210, 227–8, 232, 325, 334, 367–8
Enthusiasm, 187–8, 209, 266, 321–2

Entrance, Great, 32
Last, 33
Little, 31
Epiclesis, 26–7, 33, 87, 155
Epiphany, Feast of the, 30, 90
Epistle, 32, 86–8, 114, 161, 166, 232
Episcopate, Historic, 22, 76, 127–8, 144, 148–9, 153–4, 165–6, 176, 179–81, 254, 374–5
Epitome articulorum, 210
Eschatology, 23–4, 92–3, 230, 319, 346 (*see also* Judgement and Second Coming)
Establishment of Religion, 13–14, 139–41, 148, 154, 157–8, 167–70, 216–19, 222–3, 241–2, 244–5, 267, 276, 280–2, 284, 294–5
Ethical teaching, Agreement in, 361
Eucharist (Holy Communion, Mass), 17, 26–7, 30–4, 46–7, 54, 60, 64–71, 84–90, 113–16, 125, 133–7, 147, 149, 153–6, 161–5, 189, 192, 199–200, 204, 206, 208, 211, 231–3, 237, 239–40, 249–50, 257–8, 260–1, 264, 269, 277, 279, 288, 296–7, 299, 310, 312, 315, 320, 328, 332–3, 340, 346, 358–9
consecration, formula of, 26–7, 33, 46, 66, 87, 89, 155, 164, 199, 240
doctrine of, 26–7, 64–71, 135–6, 153, 156, 163, 189, 200, 204, 213–14, 249–50, 257–8, 277, 288, 296, 332–3
elements, nature of, 27, 65, 84–5, 125, 200, 279, 346
liturgy of, 17–18, 30–4, 84–90, 133–4, 155–6, 161–5, 192, 215, 231–3, 239–40, 260, 279, 312
Eucharistic Sacrifice, 17, 27, 46, 50, 61, 64, 67–70, 75, 88–9, 93, 135–6, 146, 153, 189, 206, 215, 359
Evangelical, 144–5, 184–5, 327
counsels, 82
party in Church of England, 139, 145–7, 154, 157, 165, 170, 176
Evangelical Alliance, 369
Evangelical Church (Germany), 186, 373
Evangelist, 136, 353
Evensong, 91, 150, 159–61, 166
Ex cathedra, 49–51
Ex opere operato, operantis, 62, 78, 199, 205
Existentialism, 230
Exorcism, 25, 63, 78
Experimental religion, 274–5

Faith, doctrine of, 16, 46, 49, 52, 56–7, 59, 130, 148, 194, 201, 205, 212, 251, 275, 296, 309, 353, 360 (*see also* Justification)
Faith and Order Movement, 165, 177, 179, 362, 378–86 (*see also* Lausanne, Edinburgh)